T5-CRR-567

Current Concepts in Library Management

Current Concepts in Library Management

Martha Boaz

Editor

Libraries Unlimited, Inc., Littleton, Colorado
1979

FERNALD LIBRARY
COLBY-SAWYER COLLEGE
NEW LONDON, N.H. 03257

Z
678
C88

Copyright ©1979 Libraries Unlimited, Inc.
All Rights Reserved

No part of this publication may be reproduced, stored in a retrieval
system, or transmitted, in any form or by any means, electronic,
mechanical, photocopying, recording, or otherwise, without the
prior written permission of the publisher.

Printed in the United States of America

Copyright © 1979 Ellsworth Mason for
"Managing the Planning of Library Buildings"

LIBRARIES UNLIMITED, INC.
P.O. Box 263
Littleton, Colorado 80160

Library of Congress Cataloging in Publication Data

Main entry under title:

Current concepts in library management.

Includes index.
1. Library administration. I. Boaz, Martha
Terosse, 1913-
Z678.C88   025.1   79-20734
ISBN 0-87287-204-1

87321

This book is bound with James River (Scott) Graphitek®–C Type II nonwoven
material. Graphitek–C meets and exceeds National Association of State Textbook
Administrators' Type II nonwoven material specifications Class A through E.

TABLE OF CONTENTS

INTRODUCTION

Current Concepts in Library Management addresses the practical aspects of administering various types of libraries and information centers. Intended as a *primer* in the field, it attempts to assist library school students to become familiar with the purposes, principles, and techniques of administration and to provide them with an understanding of the objectives, functions, and organization of libraries. It also gives useful, practical, and sensible counsel to both new and experienced administrators.

The contents include a general discussion of management principles as well as the application of administration policies in various types of library environments: public, college and university, school, media, technical, and library education. Although these libraries have many similarities, they differ in their legal bases, their clients, and in their materials and services. In addition, some unique features and related areas that are of importance in the development of some of these fields are covered. These deal with management decisions in the application of computers to library tasks, the planning of library buildings, the development of fund-raising and support activities, and the administrator's commitment to the profession and the community. Additional sections (in the appendixes) emphasize the importance and the need for research in the field of library and information science, the role of library education, and the wisdom of planning for the future. These are all components of good management in the library profession.

Several authors, by invitation from the editor, have contributed chapters to this book. Styles of writing vary from one author to another. Each has an excellent educational background and each has had practical experience in the area about which he* writes. Because of limitations of space, no attempt has been made to cover the many and varied concepts of management. The emphasis here has been on its practical application in real situations in which administrators and staff work together toward common goals. The overall concept is that managerial processes do not exist as an end in themselves. Rather, management leadership, authority, objectives, and plans all focus on the organization's program of services to the public.

---

*For purposes of simplicity, the pronoun "he" is used in a generic sense throughout this book.

DESCRIPTION OF CONTENTS
AND NOTES ON CONTRIBUTORS

"The Library Administrator's Commitment to the Profession and the Community: Planning for Individual and Staff Development," by Martha Boaz (Dean Emeritus of the School of Library Science, University of Southern California), is concerned with the characteristics, responsibilities, and opportunities of professional people (with particular attention to the public library field). Martha Boaz holds the B.S. degree from Madison College, B.S. in L.S. from George Peabody College, and M.A. and Ph.D. degrees from the University of Michigan. She has had practical experience in libraries in Virginia, Kentucky, and California and was Professor as well as Dean at Southern California for many years. She has been active in the work of state and national professional library associations and is currently a Research Associate in the Center for the Study of the American Experience, University of Southern California.

"Current Concepts in Management," by Neely Gardner (Professor of Public Administration, School of Public Administration, University of Southern California), provides a generalized approach to the principles of organization and administration. Gardner defines mechanistic and organismic systems of management; he discusses the objectives of management, qualities of leadership, managing by objectives, various linkages, and evaluation. His major academic interests are in the fields of management and training and development. He has served as Deputy Director of California Department of Water Resources, State Training Officer with the California State Personnel Board, Personnel Training Consultant with the California State Personnel Board, Supervisor and Coordinator with the California State Department of Agriculture, and member of the Los Angeles Employee Relations Commission. He was also a consultant to the Iranian Local Government Training Program, the United Nations, the United Arab Republic, Arkansas, California, Florida, Hawaii, Nevada, Vermont, U.S. AID, East Pakistan Water and Power Development Authority, Republic of Singapore, University of Minnesota, University of California at Los Angeles, Aerojet General, and Southern Regional Conference.

"Managing the Public Library," by Peggy A. Sullivan (Assistant Commissioner for Extension Services, Chicago Public Library), begins with an explanation of the legal basis of public libraries, goes on to organizational models and then describes the library as a complex organization, pointing out the importance of communication as a management tool. Also included are sections in managerial styles and the library program. Peggy Sullivan has been in her current position since mid-1977. Her previous experience includes teaching in several graduate library education programs, directing the Knapp School Libraries Project for the American Library Association, and working as a children's librarian, supervisor, specialist, and project director in public and school libraries as well as at the American Library Association headquarters. She has written a number of articles in the fields of children's literature, school media programs, library administration, and library education, as well as children's books. Her monographs include historical studies, project reports, and a book on library careers. She is president-elect of the American Library Association, and an active member of the Chicago Library Club, the Illinois Library Association, and Special Libraries Association.

"Managing the College and University Library," by Duane E. Webster (Director of the Office of University Management Studies, Association of Research Libraries), in the author's words, "reviews the key issues associated with recent efforts to strengthen the management of academic libraries, with an emphasis on describing some of the major concepts and trends influencing library managers today." Webster deals with the pressures for change, presents a conceptual model for change, and explains the necessity for goals and objectives of the organization; he discusses the major determinants of organizations and points out the need for effective application of technological advances to the execution of library tasks. Duane Webster has held previous positions in public, academic, and special libraries. He has authored a number of studies published by the Association of Research Libraries, as well as articles in such journals as *Journal of Academic Librarianship* and *College and Research Libraries.* In addition, he has conducted a number of seminars and training sessions dealing with various aspects of library management.

"Managing the School Media Library," by Chase Dane (Supervisor and Director of Libraries, Santa Monica Unified School District), covers the administrative aspects of a state school system. He writes about the functions, role, and management of the school library and the development of the media center concept. Other topics covered are personnel, finances and budget, collections and services, cooperation with other libraries, standards, buildings and equipment, professional associations, and evaluation. Chase Dane has been in his present position since 1959. He has taught in the library schools of the University of Southern California and the University of California at Los Angeles, and has been editor of the official journal of the California Association of School Librarians seven times. His special interest is in school libraries and comparative librarianship.

"Managing the Technical Library," by Jerry Cao (Assistant Professor, School of Library Science, University of Southern California) defines the work of the technical library and its director. He discusses the place of the library in the parent organization. He also delineates the library's functions and objectives as administered by the library manager and discusses budgeting, staffing, services, space requirements, and evaluation. Jerry Cao holds a B.A. degree from Loma Linda University and the M.S. in L.S. and Ph.D. degrees from the University of Southern California. He was an HEA Title II-B Fellow while he was in the doctoral program. He has held library positions in the catalog departments of the University of Southern California and the University of Iowa. He was also Head of the Government Documents Department of the University of Iowa. When he served as Senior Librarian at the TRW Systems Group in California for several years, his responsibilities included all aspects of bibliographical control: monographs, serials, technical reports, and microform formats. An online catalog for technical reports was initiated during his tenure, and he was one of the persons primarily responsible for record content, thesaurus building, and input and access. His teaching specialties are in technical libraries, government publications, and cataloging and classification.

"Managing the Library School," by Martha Boaz, discusses the legal basis of the university and the library school, the administration of the school and the authority of the dean and other administrative officers, the goals and objectives of the program, the curriculum, the faculty, students, financial resources and business affairs, evaluation, and future trends.

"Managing the Planning of Library Buildings," by Ellsworth Mason (former Director of Colorado College, Hofstra University, and University of Colorado Libraries), stresses the importance of the librarian being at the center of the planning process for a library building. He lists four distinct stages of the planning: 1) the local decision and learning phase, 2) the programming phase, 3) the design development phase, and 4) the construction phase. Ellsworth Mason holds B.A., M.A., and Ph.D. degrees from Yale University and an honorary L.H.D. from Hofstra University. Following eighteen years as a library director, he is Head of the Special Collections Department and Professor at the University of Colorado. He has published two books, four monographs, and more than eighty articles in the fields of librarianship, English and comparative literature, Western history, and book collecting. In twenty years of library building planning, he has consulted on 121 buildings for elementary, secondary, high and preparatory schools, community colleges, four-year colleges, research universities, and private research libraries in the United States, Canada, Puerto Rico, and Colombia. He has received three architectural awards. His book, *Mason on Library Buildings*, will be published by Scarecrow Press in the near future.

"Managing the Planning of Facilities for Library and Information Science Education Programs," by Martha Boaz, deals with planning for a specific facility, namely the library school building. Points covered include: general principles for planning a building, location, financial matters, writing the building program, environment for learning, furniture and equipment, specific details in the building, planning for expansion, and "after the move into the building."

"The Application of Computers to Library Tasks," by Hillis L. Griffin (Director of the Technical Information Services Department and Library Director, Argonne National Laboratory), deals with the administrative factors involved in the use of library automation in libraries and information centers. Because the effective control of the quality, flow, and use of information has become an increasingly pressing problem, the time has come to manage these activities on a planned basis to be sure that they contribute to the goals of the organization. Griffin stresses the need for each library to examine its goals and objectives and to investigate whether computerized services might free staff and space for more appropriate work. He gives suggestions for developing and evaluating computers and computer programs. Hillis L. Griffin is a graduate of the School of Librarianship of the University of Washington. Since 1958, he has been active in developing and implementing applications of computers to library operations and services. He has taught courses on this topic for many years at the Graduate School of Library Science of Rosary College and has taught similar courses at the University of Illinois, the University of Washington, and the University of Wisconsin. He has also presented seminars in this country and abroad.

"Extra-Institutional Funding: Management and Strategy for Survival," by Martha Boaz, anticipates economic problems for educational institutions, libraries, and information centers and gives guidelines to fund-raising and development staff for identifying prospective donors. These include 1) foundations, 2) government agencies, and 3) private donors. Suggestions are given about steps to be followed in the "Plan for attack," contents of a formal proposal, and follow-up procedures.

Appendixes, by Martha Boaz, include the following:

I: "The Need for Research in a Young Profession" gives introductory background about the development of research in the United States and discusses the need for research in the library and information science profession.

II: "Research as a Basis for the Recognition of Librarianship as a Profession" attempts to ascertain the attitudes, opinions, and beliefs of several hundred faculty members about the status of research in selected professional fields.

III: "The Role of Library Education for National and International Needs" discusses general trends in the library and information science field, and the impact of technology on the profession. There are also some suggestions for change in library education.

IV: "Looking Ahead—Managing the Future" is concerned with the critical issues and challenges that the library and information science profession will have to handle in the future. The main thrust of the material is the need to plan for change and to prepare to manage the future, not to be managed by it. The topics covered include: reasons for planning ahead, forecasting patterns, some predicted developments, and recommendations for planning for change.

—Martha Boaz

THE LIBRARY ADMINISTRATOR'S COMMITMENT
TO THE PROFESSION AND THE COMMUNITY:
Planning for Individual and Staff Development

by Martha Boaz

PROFESSIONALISM

Personal and Professional Philosophy

From the first day of library school, the library administrator made a commitment to professionalism in general and to the library profession, in particular. He was made aware that in the library profession, as in other fields, certain basic abstract principles that provide a theoretical orientation to the profession are taken for granted. These theories are subject to change from within the profession and/or from society and with the passage of time. Along with the basic theories are practical techniques for the application of principles, which are also subject to modification as theories and principles change. The library administrator has a special responsibility to continually review the tenets and principles on which the profession is based. Some of these philosophical concepts are discussed in the paragraphs that follow, with special attention given to the public library field.

Characteristics of a Professional Person

The professional librarian is concerned with the status and prestige of the profession. He works for the recruitment of competent professionals and for their subsequent education, registration, and licensing. He is also concerned with a community approach to common interests, goals and activities for all professional librarians. The library administrator should remember and review with staff the characteristics of a profession that Abraham Flexner enumerated in 1915: 1) a profession is *intellectual* in nature and based on a *substantial body of knowledge* that can be transmitted from one generation to another; 2) at the same time, *a profession is practical* in that the body of knowledge can be put to a practical benefit for others; 3) a profession also involves *techniques and skills* that can be used to solve relevant problems; 4) a profession has *organized associations* of practitioners; and 5) a profession is service oriented, with the ideal of service as against mere money making.[1]

The ideal of service, one of the prime requisites of a professional person, is based on the needs of the patron, not the self-interest of the practitioner. This is usually accompanied by what might be termed a sense of mission on the part of the professional; this person believes that he has a unique service to perform in a situation where emphasis is placed upon the professional's response to client needs and upon the high standards of professional performance in relation to professional norms.

Professional values are in opposition to the money-making objectives of business and serve the profession in some of its goals, such as influence on political and social issues and on legislation favorable to budgets or programs of the profession. The truly professional librarian believes in his job and thinks it is important. He believes that books, printed and audio-visual materials—all forms of communication and informa-'tion—are indispensable to civilization and to an enlightened society. He thinks that the library is a valuable and positive influence for improving the quality of life.

The library profession may well examine its activities in a grouping such as that given by C. Turner and M. N. Hodge under the following headings; they note those specific activities relating directly to occupation:

1) the development of substantive theory;
2) the development of practical techniques;
3) the transmission of substantive theory;
4) the transmission of practical techniques;
5) the provision of materials and equipment;
6) the regulation of working conditions;
7) the regulation of market conditions;
8) the identification of practitioners and the recognition of qualifications for practice;
9) the promotion of standards of practice;
10) the promotion of internal relations between members;
11) the promotion of public recognition.[2]

The matter of attitude is important for the professional librarian. As someone has said, professionals *profess*. They are concerned with the universal aspects of knowledge, with the organization and communication of knowledge, with curiosity about the particular and the universal, with loyalty and commitment to the employer, the institution, and the profession.

Importance of Knowledge

Knowledge, the growth and procreation of knowledge, and the application of it have become more and more important, as have the institutions that create, use, and transmit it. Knowledge is power. It provides opportunity for progress. As one writer has said, "Scientists and scholars are no longer merely 'on tap', they are 'on top'. They must be listened to by policy makers."[3] And, "the learned are no longer poor. On the contrary, they are true 'capitalists' in the knowledge society."[4] Knowledge is the basis of modern society. It provides access to progress, it governs modern economy, and it is the guiding light for social action. Thus a library, with its stores of knowledge and its vast array of communication channels through its various media, is an important, major tool and a central force in the society of today and of the future.

The library is commonly thought of as a social agent in a constantly changing social environment. Eric Moon quotes a British spokesman who demands a reaffirma-tion of faith in the public library, saying that it is

a bank of indestructible knowledge, saving the money of the rate payer
and taxpayer alike. For no modern country, at least not an industrial
democracy, can afford the wastage caused by general ignorance, by
intolerance, by the lack of understanding of vital social and economic
forces, by the lack of reasoning power, by a superfluity of unskilled labor
and by the ill-health of its citizens. When a country stops learning—it is
already dead![5]

It is agreed, as the foregoing statements point out, that libraries are important
social institutions with almost unlimited possibilities for social, educational, and economic developments. They should press for participation in planning these developments
and for financial and moral support in their accomplishment.

Objectives of the Public Library

Robert Leigh has stated that the general objective of public library development is service to the community as a general center of reliable information. It also
has a responsibility to provide opportunity and encouragement for people of all ages
to educate themselves continuously.

The beginning and continuing function of libraries has been to help the individual to self-education wherever that person is and in whatever condition. The educational function is also extended to groups and to agencies, and it may be that, if the
individual can only be reached, as Grace Stevenson has pointed out, by means of an
"organized group to which he belongs, or through an unorganized, social grouping
of which he is, not necessarily by choice, a member, then it is through this avenue
that the approach must be made. This is not in conflict with the library's time-honored
responsibility to the individual. It is only finding ways to extend that responsibility
to individuals other than those whose use of the library is self-motivated."[6]

While only about twenty-five percent of the public uses a public library (as the
quoted statistics say), the public library is of benefit to the entire community, for,
although the person who uses the library is the major beneficiary, the community is
also helped. This statement is based on the theory that the actual user of the library
is better educated, better informed and, as a result, a better citizen in the community.

The librarian as a professional person participates in two institutions: the profession and the institution within which that person works. With an assigned position
and particular responsibilities in the special organization, the individual librarian becomes a part of an environment in which professional and organizational lives are
interfused and interpretation of one's own role is based on work satisfaction and its
value to society. He is involved in group professionalization that has responsibility
for effective professional service, which ensures that organizational decision making
is carried out within a formal structure characterized by its expertise and by skills that
are exclusively those of the library profession.

Some of the weakness in the public library may be attributed to both the education and practice of the professional. Frederick C. Mosher discusses these deficiences
as typical of professions in general. Mosher's points are listed in summary form below:
1) there is insufficient stress upon and concern about human and social values,
although all professions proclaim their dedication to a useful and beneficial service to
society. Actually, there has been little reexamination of these assumptions in relation
to a rapidly changing society; 2) there is a need for more professionals who have a

realistic understanding of social, economic, and political elements and problems with particular relationship to their own work; 3) there is a need for humility, for tolerance of other ideas, and for communication with others on shared problems; 4) there is a need to work in uncertain situations and on problems for which there are no clear cut definite solutions; 5) there is a need for understanding of organizations and how they work, especially in the setting of government and American politics and in getting things done with and through other people; 6) there is a need for greater incentive for creativity, experimentation, innovation, and initiative; 7) there should be a much higher degree of mobility—within agencies, between agencies, between governments, and in and out of government; 8) there should be greater opportunity for advancement for the able young, for the underprivileged, and for women. In government, this means opportunitities for professionalizing the non-professionals.[7]

ADMINISTRATORS AND STAFF

A library administrator should be satisfied with only the most able staff. This includes department heads, professionals, and clerical employees. The head administrator is responsible for planning, delegating, and clarifying responsibility and authority for the staff. The head administrator and all other administrative personnel should encourage and develop initiative and ability on the part of every member of the library staff. The purpose of this is two-fold: 1) to develop the most efficient and effective methods possible for delivery of the library's informational services, and, 2) to develop the highest capabilities of each employee for both service to the library and personal satisfaction and self-fulfillment.

Library supervisors should combine a clear honest appraisal of each staff member with a genuine interest in and appreciation of each person and promotion when it has been earned. Fairness and honesty in dealing with people; clear, efficient instructions; courtesy and appreciation for equals, subordinates, and superiors—these are essential traits of a good administrator.

The library needs people who have expertise in librarianship, who have depth-knowledge about information resources and information needs and requirements. With this, they need technical knowledge about the acquisition, organization, retrieval, and service principles in providing library services. The librarian also has a very human role in supplying information to clients, for, in addition to providing materials, the librarian may direct, counsel, advise, and assist library users in many ways. Thus, the librarian needs qualities of concern, enthusiasm, interest, intellectual curiosity, warmth, pleasure in working with people, enjoyment in work, and genuine interest in service to clients.

The library administrator has an obligation to fully utilize the knowledge and expertise of staff members. Too many librarians are doing work that does not require advanced professional educational background. Instead, they are doing chores that are professionally shallow or clerical in nature. A professional's interest, enthusiasm, and participation should be encouraged and included in organizational responsibilities. The library profession is somewhat conservative and still guards its exclusive rights to perform certain services, failing to recognize a greater responsibility for more demanding intellectual work. This is exemplified by the resistance of many professional librarians to the employment of library technicians for the more clerical tasks of librarianship. Fluidity and a departure from narrow rigid ideas of excluding paraprofessional workers should prevail. In a democratic society, people believe that all work has inherent value regardless of what it is and that each person can make a real contribution to the organization in which he works.

QUALITIES EXPECTED OF THE ADMINISTRATOR

The administrator is responsible for planning and coordinating the various services and specialties of a library so that the functional operations are efficient and effective. The administrator receives and reacts to reports and requests, and also initiates plans, delegates responsibilities, and plans new developments.

Role Relations

The library administrator has a difficult role. He owes the staff respect for their competencies. Whether the library administrator owes subordinates the formal duty of consultation and participation in management is different under different circumstances and settings. In technical matters, he must consult the authority in the field. On matters of general principle, the policy may vary widely. Logan Wilson points out that in getting decisions made and work done, the equation of "democratic" with "good" is subject to challenge.[8]

Creative Administration

In working inside and outside the library, the library administrator should be informed and up to date in his knowledge of various types of administrative management and should use a style that is suited to his ability, background, education and the type of institution in which he is located. In one instance, it might be wise or it might be required that he follow a bureaucratic form; in another situation, he might well include the entire staff in participatory administration or might combine various administrative styles. Whatever the form, it is mainly important that the administrator be concerned with administration as a matter of orderly, planned change rather than orderly continuation of traditional patterns. The emphasis should be on design and re-design of problems instead of on one unchangeable model.

The library administrator should be well informed and know the latest trends and techniques in budgeting, in systems analysis procedures, and in all library operations that will provide efficient, effective and, if possible, economical services. It is not likely that the library administrator will be an expert in all or even in many business or technical aspects of library work, but he should ensure that the staff is equipped to do whatever is required.

In order to achieve objectives, says Douglas McGregor, the library administrator must develop "an organization capable of meeting external demands and pressure in such a manner that it will compete successfully. The belief is that if members of the organization are identified with this goal, they can cope with reality. . . ."[9] McGregor explains further:

> In order to cope with reality, the organization must know what reality is. This requires open communication, mutual trust, mutual support, and the management of conflict by working it through. The basic requirement is not mere acceptance of goals and standards, but commitment.[10]

The matter of commitment is a very important element of being professional. McGregor says, "The principle is that human beings will direct their efforts, exercise self-control and responsibility, use their creativity in the service of goals to which they are committed."[11]

The library administrator has the responsibility of trying to unite the staff members to work for the common goals of the institution; at the same time, he must be aware of the interests and talents of each individual and of the personal development of each staff member. He has the problem of enforcing institutional policies and of providing individual flexibility. Often the administrator is compelled to make unpopular decisions and to exercise authority for the overall welfare of the institution. An administrator must have the strength and the conscience to make such decisions in order that the institutional and individual objectives may balance each other. Efficient and effective management are usually geared to the needs of the situation.

Today's managers rely more on the human resources available to them than have managers at any time in the history of complex industrial organizations. Douglas Basil says that "the education and sophistication of even the most menial employees in an affluent society require the manager to have an ever more highly developed set of leadership skills. These skills can be developed only through an understanding of human behavior in organizations."[12] Basil's major thesis is that "neither the leader nor the followers control the destiny of the organization. Rather, it is the interaction of the leader with each of his followers, with groups of followers, and with the economic and social situation which will determine the effectiveness of the leadership supplied to the organization."[13]

Participative Management

Today's organizations must deal with the dynamics of today's environments and this, according to organization theorists, means the decentralization of management, or participative management (PM). Participative management is the process of involving subordinates in the decision-making process and is based on the theory of shared authority. Administrators delegate certain jobs to subordinates but hold these subordinates accountable for the wise exercise of the delegated authority. The subordinates accept responsibility for carrying out their duties as efficiently as possible and are willing to be held accountable for their performance. Advocates of participative management insist that managers also still have to make decisions and exercise authority, as this form of administration is not an excuse for inaction.

Some of the more traditional ways in which PM can be implemented in an organization, according to William P. Anthony are: "popular training methods such as Management by Objectives, leadership and motivation, human relations or interpersonal skills training, and general management training and development . . . others are brainstorming, open-door communications, linking-pin structure, a supportive climate, suggestion systems, and proper use of task forces and committees."[14] All of these can aid in implementing PM.

During the last two decades, government agencies have developed three surrogate profit measures that may be used in participative management. These are cost benefit analysis, Management by Objectives (MBO), and Program Planning Budgeting Systems (PPBS). These are defined by William P. Anthony: 1) "Cost benefit analysis attempts to place dollars on benefits produced . . . and to compare these with costs of services . . . "; 2) "Management by Objectives (MBO) can act as a profit incentive and measure by providing governmental managers with clear-cut objectives and standards to use as the bases to focus program effort and as the basis of program or agency evaluation . . . "; and 3) "Program Planning Budgeting Systems (PPBS) is a modified form of MBO usually using zero-based budgeting."[15] Under the latter system, each agency specifies its measurable output objectives and builds a budget from the ground up (zero base) to show how much it will cost to build each objective.

Managers and administrators must assess the problems and benefits of participative management in their organizations and then decide its usefulness in each particular situation. Two dominant concerns of managers are productivity and job satisfaction. Two job design strategies are involved here, and according to one research study, "what is needed is an integration of goal setting techniques and job enrichment techniques with goals facilitating higher productivity and job enrichment promoting job satisfaction and improving the quality of working life for employees."[16] There are, of course, many variables that enter into an overall model for job design, but there will be continued research in the field.

Stress

Today, the matter of stress and work pressure in organizations is receiving considerable attention; this applies to both managerial and staff positions and is caused by organization size, degree of bureaucratization, unionization, specialization and technology. Gary Cooper and Judi Marshall, in a recent book, suggest that more research be done on the topic of stress, for "the individual's self-awareness, motivations and aspirations (and how these change) are important determinants of his approach to and expectations of work. . . . Researchers must, therefore, look more closely at work attitudes, especially in the area of stress where they play such an important mediating role."[17] In such a study, both individual job satisfaction and company performance interest should be represented.

Professional-client Relationships

The professional-client relationship is the most important responsibility of the librarian, who provides professional judgment and guidance to the client. The librarian may find facts in published sources, in book or non-book or other myriad forms, or he may obtain the information through a long distance call or through other alternate informational and communication media.

Professionalism

Paul Wasserman claims that librarianship tends to be responsible only to itself, that "the structure of its work, its commitments, and its loyalties are identified institutionally and professionally, rather than with the human beings who are the focus of its work. . . . The range of contribution, the sophistication of effort, and the ethical responsibility to client versus employer are all exceedingly variable."[18] Wasserman urges a dedication to professionalism that "transcends rhetoric and equates genuinely with clients."[19]

The library does not exist for the sake of the library staff, although the library provides opportunity for each staff member to pursue personal objectives. Its main responsibility is to the community, and the members of the staff should accept their positions knowing this—that they are colleagues in an organization where the individuals do not "run the show." Instead, by their standards and performance, they work toward the goals of the library, which is judged by the results of the total institutional work force in achieving its objectives. The final test is performance. Peter Drucker extends this thought when he says that "organizations do not exist for their own sake. They are means: each society's organ for the discharge of one social task. Survival is not an adequate goal for an organization as it is for a biological species."[20] Then he comes back to the point that the first decision that an institution must make is what it wants to do, what its objectives are.

It is important that objectives be clearly stated; otherwise energy, time and resources are wasted—the more specific the objectives, the more likely will be the success in attaining them. Decisions will involve judgments about what programs to cease, the priorities on which to concentrate, and setting up alternatives to the goals that are established. Objectives should be realistic and based upon the library's resources. These objectives should be re-examined frequently and, if necessary, changed. The library as an institution must be capable of change and willing to initiate and to devote energy to change.

Importance of Planning

High-level goal statements have been made by almost every public library, or they have adopted goals such as the following one made by the American Library Association as long ago as 1956: [the goal is] "Public Library Service that will help every American discharge his obligation as an informed citizen and achieve full self-development."[21] This is a worthy goal, one that all libraries should strive to attain; but as Philip Ennis points out, such statements reveal failures: "either a failure to allocate energies according to a priority ranking of goals, or a retreat from high-level statements into administrative objectives of efficiency or expansion."[22] Ennis stresses the need for libraries to set goals first; otherwise they dissipate their energies by trying to do everything.

Planning is an important aspect of library development. This process should include a plan or plans as well as a planning process, for, with the constant change in technology and in society, all plans are tentative. William Alonso has put it this way:

> What is needed is a continuing planning, which produces every year a plan for the next few years, and every few years a plan for the next two or three decades, so that the next steps and distant goals are known at all times. With this concept, plans have become the companions of policy. . . .[23]

After goals and objectives have been set, a program should be developed, standards adopted, and policies and procedures for carrying out the program established. Specific plans should also be made for testing and evaluating the program at definite intervals of time.

THE IMPORTANCE OF BELONGING
TO PROFESSIONAL ORGANIZATIONS

Why Professional Associations?

The library administrator has a responsibility to belong to professional associations and to encourage staff to participate in professional association work. Why do persons within a profession join together in a formal group association? Obviously, they have similar interests and aims, and truly satisfactory professional life cannot be achieved in isolation. After they have finished a period of formal educational training, librarians, as do other professionals, feel a need for talking with other persons who are engaged in the same type of work, and their knowledge is influenced and reinforced by meeting at regular intervals within this associational framework. Members are made aware of their own individual responsibilities and their part in the total social contribution of the profession. A. Carr-Saunders and P. A. Wilson point out this dual role:

> All occupations are dependent on the individual contributions of those persons who pursue the occupation. But the effectiveness of an occupation is not gauged by individual efforts alone; the total efforts of occupational members working together with some degree of cooperation must also be considered. The public image of an occupation, then, is in part individual and in part collective.[24]

Professional associations had their beginnings in the guilds that existed in Europe several centuries ago. Since that time, one reason for promoting any professional association has been to raise its status and respectability and to protect its rights and interests. Professional associations have become vital to the process, growth and development of a professionalization. According to Corrine Lathrop Gilb, a formalized professional association puts the stamp of legitimacy on meetings and conferences that assemble to permit the practitioners opportunity to discuss and present papers on matters of intellectual and professional interest as well as to make plans and take unified action on matters of common concern.[25]

Within the library profession, the community approach to the profession itself is important. W. J. Goode outlines the following as characteristic of a professional community:

> (1) Its members are bound by a sense of identity. (2) Once in it, few leave it, so that it is a terminal or continuing status for the most part. (3) Its members share values in common. (4) Its role definitions *vis à vis* both members and non-members are agreed upon and are the same for all members. (5) Within the area of communal action there is a common language, which is understood only partially by outsiders. (6) The community has power over its members. (7) Its limits are reasonably clear, though they are not physical or geographical but social. (8) Though it does not produce the next generation biologically, it does so socially through its control over the selection of professional trainees, and through its training processes it sends these recruits through an adult socialization process.[26]

The United Front

Perhaps the main rationale for formal professional organization, says Wilbert E. Moore, is in "dealing with various interests and publics outside the professional group. as distinct from maintaining communications within a self-contained community ... ,"[27] for only "by incorporating all or most practitioners in a common organization is there any chance of exercising both internal controls over competence and performance and external influence over legislatures, training centers, and other relevant components of the professional environment."[28] Peter Havard-Williams, professor of library studies at Loughborough University (England), speaks of the importance of the unity of a national library association: "in these days of pressure groups— ... *one* association ... can speak for the whole profession, when pressures from other quarters (e.g. from political party interests) might easily rout professional opinion if it were beset by internal conflict."[29]

Influence of Professional Association on Public Policy

A national library association, made up of members representing different types of libraries and with varied interests (some of them opposing each other) can still unite for universal national causes and present a united cohesive body in support of issues of interest to the membership as a whole.

Divisions and Specialties

Recognizing the value of unity, one should also stress the importance of diversity. Divisions or groups organized by type of library such as public, college and university, special, and public school represent special interests in certain types of institutions. Other groups are organized by type of activity, such as reference or cataloging. Then there are specialized types of libraries such as law, medicine, architecture, business, and many others.

Characteristics of Professional Associations

Professional associations operate with varying degrees of success. Some of the characteristics, aims, and activities of professional associations that apply to library organizations include the following: 1) professional associations set their own standards and their own codes of conduct; 2) professional associations provide channels of communication among the members and through lectures, formal papers, symposia, panel discussions, committees; and through other methods, they present information on standards, new developments and programs, ethics, and other ideas of value to professionals and their clients; 3) they stimulate study and analysis of problems and continued education, which may be informal or formal in nature; 4) they initiate discussion, research, and publication; 5) professional associations sponsor programs that present new technical information; 6) professional associations may exert great power in their ability to accredit schools and to control the training of professionals; 7) the attainment of appropriate salary levels is a goal of a professional association (members of well established professions usually receive a comparatively high level of remuneration and it is up to the members to press for both status and salary, as they usually go hand in hand); 8) professional associations sponsor one or several periodical publications, which serve as channels for professional exchange; 9) professional associations may assist in winning public confidence for the profession by group action; 10) professional associations may influence legislation and gain financial and moral support for programs; they may conduct public relations campaigns and promote high standards of library service.

Some professional associations are well organized and support political lobbies that are very effective in legislation at national, state and local levels. The work of library associations in influencing legislation favorable to libraries has been very beneficial to the library profession. Maintaining cordial relationships with various administrative agencies is very important to libraries, also.

There are many library problems that cannot be solved by individual work and that require collective action. For example, in internal management affairs, many personal management problems can be solved more readily after exchange of information and discussion of similar situations that have involved fair dealings with employees. In dealing with external affairs, the organized profession can carry on a good public relations program and, when necessary, can operate as a pressure group in establishing public policy.

Library Associations and the Individual

A library association can help the individual member become acquainted with the library profession and its organization, with its scope and its potential. It can also promote a feeling of responsibility on the part of its members, especially the younger members, for the promotion and development of librarianship and library service. Formal programs provide opportunities for younger people to gain experience in public speaking, organizational procedures, and human relations. The educational benefits are often as valuable as several years of formal classes.

Types of Professional Activities

There are various types of professional associations within any one profession. In the United States, the American Library Association is considered to be the national association by most librarians, and librarians working in all types of libraries belong to this association. There is also the Special Libraries Association, which is a national association whose membership consists, on the whole, of librarians working in special or technical institutions. Still another national association is the American Society for Information Science. A large professional association such as the American Library Association is also a framework or umbrella for topics of concern to the total membership and, at the same time, it is a kind of umbrella for more narrow specialized interests.

In the many types of library associations, everyone can find a type of division or activity specialization of interest. For example, within the ALA, there are five type-of-library divisions, including the American Association of State Librarians, American Association of School Librarians, Association of College and Research Libraries, Association of Hospital and Institution Libraries, and the Public Library Association. There are eight type-of-activity divisions. These include the Library

Administration Division, Adult Services Division, American Library Trustee Association, Children's Services Division, Reference Services Division, Resources and Technical Services Division, Young Adult Services Division, and Information Science and Automation Division.

State, regional, and territorial associations were organized after the ALA was established. These included ones such as the New York State Library Association, the Mountain-Plains Library Association, the Pacific Northwest Library Association, and the Southeastern Library Association.

Some of the organizations affiliated with ALA are the Association of Research Libraries, American Association of Law Libraries, Medical Library Association, Music Library Association, Association of American Library Schools, Theatre Library Association, and others. There are other national library associations such as the already named Special Libraries Association, the Council of National Library Associations, and the Bibliographical Society of America.

Influence and Contributions of ALA

The American Library Association has been effective and instrumental in many of its programs. First, it has accomplished a great deal in its legislative and federal relations work. The Washington Office of ALA has been watchful and alert to every opportunity for legislation favorable to libraries and their financial support. Federal aid to libraries has been a direct result of ALA's persistent and continuing legislative efforts. Second, through its Intellectual Freedom Committee, ALA has been a stronghold for intellectual freedom. It has resisted censorship and claimed the right to read of every citizen. Third, through its social responsibilities organization, ALA has fought racial and other forms of discrimination. Fourth, in its international activities and in working with members of Congress, leaders in ALA have assisted in the establishment of information libraries around the world. Fifth, in its various divisions, ALA has established sets of standards for libraries, their administration, building, budgeting, organization, personnel, service, and other matters affecting library services. These standards have been incentives for better libraries and better services. And, sixth, through its publications office and its journal publications, ALA has provided a literature that has been effective for and influential on libraries and librarians.

Some members of the library profession will not join a professional association. Admittedly, there is a price to pay in dues, in the time to attend professional meetings, in working on committees, or in taking part in studies or other activities. A few people claim that they are unwilling to pay dues because they say they get nothing from belonging to an association. But, paraphrasing a statement of former president John Kennedy, the dedicated professional person does not ask what he will get from the association but what he can give to it. The library administrator has an obligation to the profession to belong and to participate in library association work; he also has an obligation to try to get staff to join library associations and be involved in such work.

THE LIBRARY AND THE COMMUNITY

The library administrator should emphasize the importance of community involvement. This may be a public, school, university, or special library community. The library has an obligation to work with individual and community problems and to provide services for community development. The librarian and his staff can cooperate with or initiate plans for working with other community agencies and by so doing, can complement the work of other organizations, gain patrons for the library, increase its use, and improve its opportunities for securing larger financial appropriations. The library can thus become a partner with other professional agencies in dealing with community problems and in relating to larger issues of social involvement. The theory of the "Model Cities" approach is that of coordinated and cooperative attack by all agencies.

Librarians and library boards may find advantages in seeking to work more closely with other city departments in getting funds; in cooperation, several departments may secure more support than can be achieved separately. Ralph Conant gives an example of this when, in 1961-1962,

> the St. Louis Public Library collaborated with the Zoo and the Art Museum in a campaign to increase the tax levies supporting the three institutions. This campaign involved securing state legislative authorization and city council and voter approval. The last two stages were carried on in conjunction with school tax and bond issues and a dozen other city bond proposals, including one for branch library construction. Several of the issues aroused far more interest and commitment from civic notables than the library proposal alone could have done. There seems little doubt that, to some extent the latter rode the coattails of the bigger proposals.[30]

The constituency of the public library is one of infinite variety. It ranges from pre-schoolers to senior citizens, from the affluent to the poor and underprivileged, from the educated to the illiterate, from individuals to organized groups and institutions, from the foreign-speaking ethnic groups and non-readers to highly educated and sophisticated readers. The library also could be the focal point, the nucleus for local action involving political, religious, educational and social issues. The community image of the library and its strength are important in its impact on the community.

Community Planning

Community planning for coordinating library services with those of other relevant bodies should involve teachers and school administrators, planners, government officials, sociologists, and representatives of all types of libraries. Dynamic leadership is needed to develop and foster inter-agency work, to establish goals, to measure progress, and to chart new directions.

Community Groups and Agencies

Groups and agencies that might logically work with the library are academic institutions such as public schools and colleges and universities, the local mental health association, the League of Women Voters, the YMCA, drug abuse clinics, groups working with minority and disadvantaged persons, and many others. These organized agencies have specific clienteles and ways of communicating with them.

Learning the needs of the unorganized and the non-users of libraries is more difficult and requires the involvement of the personnel of libraries and of other service agencies in person-to-person relationships. Ruth Gregory has discovered allies for insights into the needs of the unorganized:

> These allies include: (1) the responsible and articulate leaders of socioeconomic groups; (2) the workers in Head Start, adult literacy projects and other anti-poverty programs; (3) the specialists in varying disciplines who work together through reciprocal referrals; (4) the leaders in adult and young adult continuing education activities of churches, schools and other community agencies; (5) neighborhood coordinators; (6) credit and consumer cooperatives; (7) union councils; (8) government field representatives; (9) area committees of human resources; (10) lay advisory committees for mental health and special education movements; (11) senior citizens organizations; (12) visiting nurses and rural extension agents; and (13) university extension instructors and advisors.[31]

Gregory also lists aids used by many agencies that have been effective in the recognition of the needs of organized groups:

> These include: (1) community studies; (2) discussion groups and town meetings; (3) clearing-house files of data on organizations, their objectives and programs; (4) affiliation with coordinating councils; (5) cooperation with and use of area communication media; newspapers, TV, and radio stations; (6) program planning institutes and leadership training courses; (7) staff participation in a diversity of organizations; (8) assignment of staff as institutional and group resource people; and (9) involvement in adult education programming.[32]

The people other than librarians who may be associated in the delivery of library services are: 1) co-workers, outside of the professional group, who are involved because of their part in the labor force; 2) other professional associations that may be complementary in their work; 3) educational institutions; 4) government agencies having administrative or legislative responsibilities related to the library organization, or, having complementary service interests; 5) other individuals, groups, associations, or organizations with knowledge and interests that may be helpful to the library. These concepts point to the library as a center of community involvement and reiterate the necessity for the library profession to fulfill its role in identifying and serving the needs of individuals and groups at all levels.

The public library may have many alternate programs. These may be attempted simultaneously, or priorities may be set for accomplishing the objectives of one or more particular programs before moving on to other projects. These might, at one time, concentrate on service to the educationally and culturally deprived, on the black or Spanish-speaking segments of the population. At another time, the emphasis could be on service to the business community, or, at still another time, on cultural programs involving music, art, literature, and intellectual pursuits. The idea is to establish objectives, select priorities, and then work toward carrying out the particular program(s). When these are underway, or have been evaluated, completed, or extended, steps can be taken to undertake new and additional objectives. But to go back to the original premise, as has been well stated by Edward C. Banfield, "What the library needs, is, first, a purpose that is both in accord with the realities of present-day city life and implied by some general principles, and, second, a program that is imaginatively designed to carry its purpose into effect."[33] This assumes, of course, that the library expects to accomplish its goals and contradicts Banfield's statement that public organizations often "exist as much to symbolize something as to accomplish something."[34]

It is easy to speak of services to minority, disadvantaged, or culturally and educationally deprived groups. To attract these people to libraries is another matter. In trying to reach them, only library staff members should be involved who understand or who will become informed about the culture and life styles of these people. This is not easy, for, as Lowell Martin says, "libraries readily become institution-oriented rather than people-oriented."[35] He goes on to say that the "integrity of existing collections and the continuation of established staffing patterns are often the underlying determinant of service decisions."[36] The hard fact is that librarians should be going to the users of libraries, to local leaders, working in organizations, learning about the needs and interests of people, reaching into the ghettos and out to the sophisticated cosmopolitan neighborhoods. The librarian, after learning the needs of the community, can then plan a program of service for it. These services will be geared to user-oriented and community-oriented programs. Highly diversified library programs should be designed for local neighborhoods, and these should change as neighborhoods change.

Service to special groups should be delivered: to preschoolers, young adults, business men, parents, community leaders, technicians and professionals, senior citizens, ghetto residents, and cosmopolitan suburbanites. The library staff should represent a diversity of personnel to fulfill the diversity of tasks, ranging from clerks to professionals, and with specializations to provide special services. The public library should be a part of a network of libraries with a service program coordinated with public schools, colleges and universities, and special libraries.

Channels of Communication

Channels exist for reaching every community corner. There are bookmobiles; branch libraries; lending programs for school systems; special services to business and industry; interlibrary loans; telephone, teletype, and telefacsimile services; and daily delivery services. The means, methods, and technology exist for communicating with communities, states, and nations and for providing information to them in a very brief time.

The importance of communication cannot be overemphasized. Channels of communication should be established on a regular, continuing basis between professionals, between other people or agencies involved in the planning and provision of services, and with clients or patrons.

The Librarian: A "Joiner"

The library administrator may feel obliged to become a "joiner" and hold membership in service clubs and in civic and fraternal organizations in order to publicize the library, to create interest in it, and to gain support for it. Since it is almost impossible for the head librarian to belong to all of a community's organizations, he will probably try to involve department heads and other members of the staff in such activities; in this way, there is more participation and greater contribution. The benefits should come not only to the individual library staff members but also to the organizations.

Typical organizations to which male librarians belong are service clubs such as Lions, Rotary, Kiwanis, Chamber of Commerce, and the Parent Teachers Association, to name a few. Women librarians may belong to the Women's Division of the Chamber of Commerce, to the Parent Teachers Association, the League of Women Voters, the Business and Professional Women's Club, the American Association of University Women, and others. Both men and women may work with the Red Cross, or in Community Chest drives or in Urban League work; or they may join clubs of people interested in poetry, or gardening, science, history, or a variety of interests. At the meetings of these groups, the librarians become friends with people who may be very important in community and political actions affecting the library.

Heavy involvement in civic and service organizations often leaves librarians with little time for other interests or for their families. Often, they must be away from home for night or weekend meetings and must sacrifice family time for professional service. But this is a choice that a professional person makes, and the most successful professionals usually have been those who have given greatly of their time, interest, energy, and hard work. The true professional is work-oriented in the highest possible degree. This ideology extends beyond the work situation to become a life style and exemplifies the service ideal of the professional, which is one of the major characteristics of any profession.

After studying the community, the librarian and staff plan a program of service. The program should be put in writing and the necessary library materials, physical facilities, and staff assembled for the implementation of the service program. If the library is to be an effective agency, it must have resources with which to work, for regardless of aims and ideals, anyone who wishes to have programs and give service must have the financial assets with which to execute the objectives, otherwise the aims are academic only and without results.

Granting that the library has a commitment and a social responsibility to the community it serves, it should not only improve the traditional services already being given, but it should also change as social needs and community values change and as technology progresses. There may be opportunities for assistance and leadership in education, in working with the poor in the urban ghetto, with the needs of the business community, with housing problems, with civil rights issues, with health care and with an over-all awareness of those public needs for which libraries are socially responsible. The library is an institution that, through its services, can improve the quality of life.

Public Relations—Publicity

Good public relations should prevail inside and outside of the library. Every staff member has a part in a public relations program. This extends from the lowest position in the library to that of the top administrator.

The most personable and outgoing members of a staff should be posted at public desks and at points of public contact, for it is at these places that the library is first judged by its patrons. Such positions may not necessarily be professional; on the contrary, they may be paraprofessional or clerical. The important matter is to win friends for the library at the point of entry.

The Public Servant

As Kate Coplan expresses it, "Perhaps one of the most meaningful phrases in the English language is *public servant*. Recognizing the importance of reading as part of intelligent living in today's complicated world, and dedicated to developing a love of books and learning, librarians wear the badge proudly."[3 7] Through well-planned, skillfully executed public relations programs, the library can win friends and support for its services. Energetic, enthusiastic, resourceful librarians can make contacts, develop good public relations, and create a favorable atmosphere for the library.

The librarian has a responsibility to keep the public informed about the library, its programs, and its services. A strong public relations campaign should be pursued vigorously through regular and varied media to inform the community of the library's materials, services and programs. The library also can play an important role in dispelling community lethargy and inertia. This can be done inside the library and in the community by encouraging librarians and library users to work for individual and community improvement through the use of the information resources of the library.

A good public relations program does not come about by accident. It usually results from careful planning, which begins with surveying the community to learn what its needs are, then designing a program to provide the desired services and then, through publicity and personal contacts, informing the public of the available services. A good public relations program defines and describes the library's objectives and services and invites people to use these services.

Publicity about library services should be directed to non-users as well as to users of libraries. The theory is to reach *all* of the people, not a small percentage only, but the publicity should not be vague and general. Rather, it should be directed to certain groups or individuals. The publicity should be repeated frequently and actively in all media and through all channels of communication.

Public Relations Devices and Techniques

Various devices and techniques can be used to give information about and to implement the library's program. One of the most effective of these is the press, which probably reaches more people than any other single channel of communication; for, although television and radio have large audiences, they have specific and limited programming schedules. Once a program has been given, it is over, except in a few cases where there are reruns; whereas the newspaper can be picked up at random, re-read, and stored for future use.

Other media serving the library are television and radio. Spot announcements are often available as free public service donations from radio and television stations, and these are effective on day and night programs. These can be prepared in advance and forwarded on a regular basis to TV and radio stations. Various staff members can be assigned to write these "spots," which may vary in length from ten seconds to a minute to longer periods of time. Without doubt, radio, television, and cable satellites will become increasingly important media for publicizing libraries.

The newspaper can provide coverage for literacy news in various forms, says Kate Coplan. These may be in: 1) straight news, 2) feature stories, 3) weekly listings, 4) staff stories, 5) incidental publicity, 6) accounts of exhibitions, 7) neighborhood news in weeklies, 8) comments of columnists, 9) editorials and letters to the editor, and, 10) special promotion.[38]

Special promotional energy and work are required when bond issues for financial support are being proposed or when referendums are involved. Every kind of publicity should be used and extensive promotion enlisted through civic, educational, cultural, religious, business, labor, and service organizations. A speaker's bureau should be set up, and posters and fliers distributed and displayed everywhere. Notices should be put in newspapers, in church bulletins, and in leaflets distributed at markets and grocery stores.

Booklists, throughout the year, on various topics and for special programs such as those for National Library Week or other particular days or events, are effective methods for telling the library's story. Displays and visual aids are invaluable methods for highlighting ideas and communicating information about the library and its materials and services. Librarians should seize every opportunity to stimulate community interest and enlist patron participation in the library's support and development and in the publicizing of its services. These efforts should not be sporadic, but planned and continuous. Otherwise, an occasional project has no long-range benefits and is expensive and wasteful.

It is important to remember, also, that the library is judged by the performance of its entire staff—professional and non-professional, from the maintenance crew to the head librarian. Each comes in contact with other people, each represents the library to somebody in the community.

Personal contacts, publicity about the library and its work, about the work of individual staff members, or about the help given to the library by friends and residents of the community—all of these are helpful. Items of both personal and institutional publicity have merit, create good relations, and act as morale boosters.

POLITICS—PARTISAN STANDS—PERSONAL BELIEFS

The Professional Image

The respect paid to a professional is balanced by duties and restraints imposed in work with colleagues, administrators, clients, and the general public. Behavior reflects personal and professional standards. The professional person is expected to work in the public interest, to keep up-to-date and informed in the field, and to maintain a continued commitment to the profession and to its service.

The Political Arena

The political arena is a sensitive area for a professional person. In some civil service institutions, this is particularly true, and the public librarian may be in a complex situation that requires personal value judgments and decisions. There is the question of how free public servants can be to engage in political activities. These are the dilemmas: 1) on the one hand, there is the guarantee in the First Amendment of the rights of public servants to freedom of speech, press, assembly, and petition; 2) on the other hand, there are the rights of the public to have policy carried out without prejudice due to political or religious affiliation, race, national origin, or for any other reason. The Hatch Act Commission was appointed in 1966 to investigate any federal laws that "limit or discourage the participation of Federal and State officers and employees in political activity with a view to determining the effect of such laws, the need for their revisions or elimination, and an appraisal of the extent to which undesirable results might accrue from their repeal."[39] As a member of the Hatch Act Commission, Charles O. Jones has summarized some of the Commission's conclusions in its report: "The prohibitions would be only those that Congress finds necessary to protect employees against actions that would threaten the integrity, efficiency and impartiality of the public service."[40]

There was no consensus for allowing public servants to speak publicly for candidates or to become candidates themselves for certain local offices, but these were included as permissible in the Commission's recommendations. There was, however, a tendency on the part of the Commission to prohibit employees to serve as officers in political parties. The thought was that public servants in official party positions would compromise the public service in the eyes of the public.

Traditionally, like most other public institutions, the library has generally not participated in and has been neutral in partisan politics. Librarians and teachers have usually been careful to maintain professional neutrality on public issues involving partisan politics or any other issue that might be in conflict with their professional responsibilities or that might impair the work of the institution. It is important for the librarian to separate personal beliefs, whether political or religious or racial or in any other way likely to seem biased, from professional work. It may be that personal alignments are in conflict with professional commitment; in which case, if he remains in the professional assignment, he should adhere to the requirements of the profession or the institution in which he is working. Otherwise he should sever the connection with an organization in which he cannot work according to its policies and beliefs. This is not to say that the librarian cannot question, challenge, or attempt to change his setting, but he does have an obligation to cooperate with "the system" if he stays in it and has been unable to change it.

The employment situation and the institution must be maintained in relationship to the total responsibility of the profession to society. T. H. Marshall, commenting on the relationship between the client and public relations, says that "the relationship of trust implies a deep obligation to the client. But an organized profession rightly regards itself as a body placed in charge of an art or science and responsible for directing its use in the interests of society. These two obligations can be reconciled without difficulty if the true interests of society and of the individual are harmonious."[41]

Everett C. Hughes says: "The professional is expected to think objectively and inquiringly about matters which may be, for laymen, subject to orthodoxy and sentiment which limit intellectual exploration. Further, a person, in his professional capacity, may be expected and required to think objectively about matters which he himself would find it painful to approach in that way when they affected him personally."[42]

Hughes says that the professional also asks to be trusted, using the motto *credat emptor*. "Thus is the professional relation distinguished from that of those markets in which the rule of *caveat emptor* exists, although the latter is far from a universal rule, even in the exchange of goods. The client is to trust the professional...."[43]

Intellectual Freedom and Censorship

The matter of book selection in libraries is often subject to challenge by outside censors. Most public libraries operate on the principle of selecting "the best books, for the largest number, at the least cost," the theory being that budget and space restrictions prevent buying everything. Accordingly the book collection reflects the best judgment of the staff in selecting books on their merits alone, books that the library can afford and that represent the needs and interests of the community. But censorship of certain titles often becomes a public problem as citizens or vigilante groups ask for certain controversial titles to be removed. These controversial titles usually involve sex, race, religion or politico-economic issues. In other cases, a person or a group may demand that a particular title be put into the library. Hence, the politics of book selection can be a very real problem. Librarians should anticipate and be prepared to face this issue squarely, courageously, and with decisive plans about what course of action to take. It is wise to alert library boards to possible censorship problems and to ask the boards to establish written statements about principles of book selection and policies for the handling and maintenance of collections. The American Library Association, through its Intellectual Freedom Committee, has sought to resist all forms of prejudice, and librarians, in general, have fought for the principles of intellectual freedom.

Need for High Standards

Librarians have not been bold in their defense of high standards for libraries and programs of excellence in library services. They should be vocal, even militant, in seeking and demanding support for libraries that meets not merely minimum standards but represents standards of excellence.

Need for Better Support for Libraries

The public library enjoys approval as a respected institution, for, although many people—about three-fourths of the population—do not use it, they think that the library should be maintained. Yet it suffers from limited financial support. This is understandable in light of Oliver Garceau's statement, "Although the library has no natural enemies, it suffers concurrently from the fact that it has no natural political allies."[44] Garceau comments on the political system in the United States in which government action follows pressure from producer groups; and the library, serving only a minority of consumers, is not a significant force. He thinks that the alliances that have developed, in some instances, between libraries and big business research are of great importance.

Garceau acknowledges the library faith and the idealism that he has observed among librarians, but he says that the practicalities of life must be recognized:

> Day-to-day local politics are immediately governed, not by such abstractions, but by the pulling and hauling of local interests. The librarians and their profession may need an occasional rededication to their mission, and they should constantly assess their activities in the terms of their true function. But they must also realize that they do not live by poetry alone. In local politics the potential of libraries, like that of other public services, is measured chiefly in terms of consumer service. If the newer services of the library can increase the number of library consumers or the value received by them, by so much the library gains in political power.[45]

Following Garceau's suggestion, which seems valid, librarians should find ways to work more effectively in relating their work and community activities with political reality. They should realize, too, that they must constantly reassess their plans in a rapidly changing social and increasingly competitive political arena.

Strategies for pressuring or developing library programs should be readily available. Ralph Nader, at the 1973 Midwinter meeting of the American Library Association, urged librarians to do battle for libraries and their "human programs," which were being cut off from federal funds. Telling of the role libraries had played in his own development, Nader called on librarians to speak out for libraries, making the public and legislators aware of their value. He declared that librarians should get acquainted with members of Congress, that they should send packages of information about the library crisis to local, regional, and national editorial staff in the electronic and print media.[46]

The library profession, like other professions, requires the skill of persuasion and library practitioners, particularly administrators, should have insight into the values, beliefs, needs and interest of men and organizations.

Philip Selznick says that the executive becomes a statesman in making the transition from administrative management to institutional leadership.[47] This leads to the question of what constitutes institutionalism; Selznick thinks that the more fully developed its social structure, the more will an organization become valued for itself, not as a tool but as an institutional fulfillment of group integrity and aspiration.[48]

Competition for Scarce Resources

The public library has a commitment to the community to try to secure funds for quality library service. Every institution in a community is in competition with every other one for public funds. The budget allocation for the library, in large measure, indicates its place in the community power structure and often indicates, also, the interest of the people in support of the library and the sensitivity of voters in support of library bond issues.

A librarian who is politically astute will make every effort to work with city officials and cultivate other people who have access to persons who make budget decisions. This may involve the mayor, the city manager, or whoever appoints the library board. In turn, members of the board are likely to have connections with civic leaders who can assist the library in obtaining money for its program.

87321

FERNALD LIBRARY
COLBY-SAWYER COLLEGE
NEW LONDON, N.H. 03257

The enlightened librarian and staff members will also try to gain access to groups such as organized labor or political parties and to business, educational, and social agencies. Lines of communication and close personal relations with individuals, groups, or agencies will help the library to get its share of community resource allocations.

Need for Political Acumen

Librarians need to develop political acumen. The head librarian, in particular, should have special training for this type of work, along with extensive background in administrative understanding and skills. Library schools are developing courses that give this background. Librarians at middle-management or top-level positions who have not had such courses should arrange to take them in evening classes or in some other type of continuing education program.

The library administrator may be in a role to be a political strategist in working with members of the library board. The board can support and back him in efforts to improve the library and extend its services. Upon occasion, board members may actively campaign for specific causes, make public speeches, work with their clubs and other organizations, push door bells, and make telephone calls for the library.

In addition to the library board, another group that can be of great help to a library is the "Friends of the Library" organization. This group can be a very effective source of assistance—as it includes leaders and intellectuals and others— for a variety of activities, including building up fine book collections, or putting on a drive for a new building or new branches, or working for a host of other matters.

TEMPORARINESS AND NEED FOR CHANGE

One of the questions of concern to the library administrator is the nature of the future society that the library will serve and the implications for the library as a public service institution. The only sure thing about this society is that it is and will be temporary. The adjective was used in a book, *The Temporary Society*, by Warren G. Bennis and Philip E. Stater.[49] The authors point out that this society is temporary, that it will be transformed into another society in a short span of years, and that institutions and organizations will change as will individual roles and associations within them. The major point made is the trend toward temporariness and the significance of this for American public service in the future.

Librarians have a duty to their profession, to the institution in which they work, and to the society they serve. In the future, as Walter Stone points out, there will probably be

> new institutions which are no longer concerned with supplying specific
> media but rather with providing access to recorded knowledge and com-
> munication services generally: recorded knowledge that may be distributed
> on demand by light beam pulses or via micro-wave technology drawn from data
> banks stored in electronic memories or new microforms and which may be
> searched out, retrieved, transmitted and/or reproduced as required. . . .
>
> The charge which now must be put to those concerned is that of assur-
> ing continuing and easy access to recorded knowledge regardless of its rate
> of growth, present mountainous proportions, and growing variety of
> forms.[50]

Active vs. Passive Role of the Library

A debate today revolves around two issues: 1) the traditional concept of the library as a reservoir of books and as an institution that should be governed by the educational and cultural goals of the librarian; this type of institution attracts middle-class, better educated people in the population, who are already motivated to use libraries; 2) the second theory views the library as an educational institution with a responsibility to be a change agent; this is the user-oriented concept and considers the library to be basically responsible for supplying the needs, demands and interests of its users. It seems reasonable to expect the library, as a public service institution, to fulfill both of these missions. "The more used the better" could well serve as an administrative motto, for a library that is not extensively used is a waste of public resources.

It has been said earlier that the role of the library should probably change, from the passive one of waiting for people to come to the library to the aggressive act of librarians taking the library to the people. The public library can well afford to perform its traditional role and, at the same time, take on new functions and adapt to changing times; otherwise it may go out of business and be unable to perform at all.

No opportunity should be lost or overlooked for extending library services to every user and every potential user who might be contacted. The most certain method for getting better financial and business support for libraries is through satisfied library users. One of the most effective ways for securing political and legislative help is through excellent service to government officials who use the library.

Discovering Needs of Users and Non-users

Identifying user needs and their satisfaction is a complex process that requires careful research techniques, if any valid, quantifiable, objective findings are to be obtained. Henry Voos thinks that users' satisfaction is not a structural criterion, it is behavioral. Voos says, "It involves not the logic and rationality of hardware, but the psychologic and irrationality of people. It is very difficult to measure by observing and interviewing users, but it cannot be measured at all by observing only the system."[51] In further discussing psychological research on the information needs and the information-seeking behavior of the intended users of any system, Voos notes: "The difficulty of studying these variables is compounded by the fact that users' expressed desires for information and their habits of search are conditioned in part by their previous experiences with information systems,"[52] and "measurement of information needs is a measure of attitude rather than a measure of use."[53]

The recommendations of research specialists such as Voos should be studied and followed by the library administrator. Surveys and studies should be authorized in order to secure information that would not only give better service to regular users of libraries but would also bring in new clients.

Research Needed

Research is designed to produce new theories for improved operational techniques. The library profession should encourage research into its work activities and encourage the development of critical attitudes toward existing theories and practices in the profession. Thus will be developed a high degree of professionalism and an awareness of the changing nature of professional goals, of the limitations imposed by new technology, and of the new appraisals of social trends. A profession does not stand still; it is itself "in process" and shifts, extends, or changes into new cultural roles that are yet to emerge but that bring about institutional and personal change.

It has been said that the test of a profession is its belief in the value of the service it renders to society and the concurrant belief that withdrawal of this service would be very harmful to society. Research related to this concept might produce interesting findings.

Factors That Affect Libraries

Many factors affect libraries. These include the complexity of the modern city; the social and economic systems; the change in size and structure of cities; the location of work, shopping, home, and recreation areas; the racial, economic, and age factors of the residents and their tastes and interests; geographic fragmentation; the redistribution of population, business, and industry—all of these economic, social, and psychological forces affect libraries and require varied informational services. The pattern of the future may be one of megalopolises—that is, a group of metropolitan areas standing shoulder to shoulder, but in interacting, functioning groups.

Library administrators will be required to work with city planners and other agencies to establish their responsibilities and service. What will their responsibilities involve? What will their clients need? What will be their goals?

Innovation Needed

The library administrator should be aware of what the library *is not doing* and probably *should be doing* and should instigate activity, for it is not likely that the users of libraries will take the initiative in suggesting new library programs or services. William R. Monat (director of the Institute of Public Administration at Pennsylvania State University) following a study that he made in five Pennsylvania cities, noted that

> only during interviews with library administrators and the most deeply committed and knowledgeable board members, did we encounter any proposals or ideas concerning an enlarged agenda and new and untried library services. . . . In practically every area of public policy, the most prolific and consistent sources of innovation are the professional administrator, the specialist, and the deeply committed involved layman. The consumer is least likely to initiate change.[54]

Monat proposes that the community library be an active information center and not merely a repository of books, that the library administrator must provide dynamic leadership in making the library a center with vital new purposes, designed to serve a broad range of interests and diverse local institutions. He further says that the library administrator "must be willing to enter the maelstrom of community decision-making and to recognize that he is best equipped by training and purpose to define the goals, develop the role, and protect the interests of the community library. He must have the professional self-confidence to do more than respond to demands; he must be willing to take risks by telling the community what his professional judgment tells him that the community needs."[55] In this approach, it behooves the administrator to take a practical stand, for as James Guyot points out, when the economy becomes more stringent, it is likely that administrators and managers will become less philosophical and more pragmatic. And as one wit has said, they will move from the idealistic concept that the "unexamined life is not worth living to the applied doctrine that the unexamined program is not worth funding."[56]

Innovation and resourceful approaches to community needs require commitment on the part of librarians, a willingness to experiment, and the courage to risk failure. As noted earlier, this implies study and research into the characteristics, needs, desires, and requirements of both users and *non-users* of libraries, for libraries are very valuable terminal centers. Their real worth has yet to be discovered. The library profession, as other professions, strives to be international and global in its concepts, yet it is often only parochial in its influence. The ever-beckoning challenge of the future will point to new patterns of universal exchange of knowledge. The library administrator should be a leader in this movement.

NOTES

[1] Abraham Flexner, "Is Social Work a Profession?," in *Proceedings of the National Conference of Charities and Corrections* (Chicago: 1915), pp. 576-90.

[2] C. Turner and M. N. Hodge, "Occupations and Professions," in J. A. Jackson, ed., *Professions and Professionalization* (London: Cambridge University Press, 1970), p. 37.

[3] Peter Drucker, *The Age of Discontinuity* (New York: Harper and Row, c1969), p. 372.

[4] Ibid., p. 373.

[5] Eric Moon, ed., "Right Kind of Critic," *Library Issues: The Sixties* (New York: R. R. Bowker Company, 1970), p. 284.

[6] Grace T. Stevenson, "Introduction: Group Services in Public Libraries," *Library Trends* XVII (July 1968), p. 4.

[7] Frederick C. Mosher, "The Public Service in the Temporary Society," *Public Administration Review* XXIX (January-February 1969), pp. 47-62.

[8] Logan Wilson, "Disjunctive Processes in Academic Milieu," in Edward A. Tiryakian, ed., *Sociological Theory, Values, and Socio-cultural Change* . . . (New York: Free Press, 1963), p. 293.

[9] Douglas McGregor, *The Professional Manager* (New York: McGraw-Hill, c1967), p. 127.

[10] Ibid.

[11] Ibid.

[12] Douglas Basil, *Leadership Skills for Executive Action* (New York: American Management Association, 1971), p. v.

[13] Ibid.

[14] William P. Anthony, *Participative Management* (Reading, Massachusetts: Addison-Wesley Publishing Co., c1978), p. 71.

[15] Ibid., pp. 110-12.

[16] Denis D. Umstot, Terence R. Mitchell, and Cecil H. Bell, "Goal Setting and Job Enrichment: An Integrated Approach to Job Design," *Academy of Management Review* III (October 1978), p. 868.

[17] Gary L. Cooper and Judi Marshall, *Understanding Executive Stress* (New York: Petrocelli Book, c1977), p. 204.

[18] Paul Wasserman, *The New Librarianship, A Challenge for Change* (New York: R. R. Bowker Company, c1972), p. 259.

[19] Ibid., p. 261.

[20] Drucker, pp. 189-90.

[21] American Library Association, Co-ordinating Committee on Revision of Public Library Standards, *Public Library Service: A Guide to Evaluation with Minimum Standards* (Chicago: American Library Association, 1956).

[22] Philip H. Ennis, "The Library Consumer," in Ralph W. Conant, ed., *The Public Library and the City* (Cambridge: The MIT Press, c1965), p. 31.

[23] William Alonso, "Cities and City Planners," *Daedalus* XCII (Fall 1963), p. 826.

[24] A. M. Carr-Saunders and P. A. Wilson, "The Historical Development of Professional Associations," in Howard M. Vollmer and Donald L. Mills, eds., *Professionalization* (Englewood Cliffs, New Jersey: Prentice-Hall, Inc., c1966), p. 159.

[25] Corrine Lathrop Gilb, *Hidden Hierarchies: The Professions and Government* (New York: Harper and Row, 1966), pp. 28-33.

[26] W. J. Goode, "Community within a Community: The Professions," *American Sociological Review* XXII (April 1957), p. 194.

[27] Wilbert E. Moore, *The Professions: Roles and Rules* (New York: Russell Sage Foundation, c1970), p. 160.

[28] Ibid.

[29] Peter Havard-Williams, "The Role of a Professional Association," *Library Association Record* LXXIV (October 1972), p. 189.

[30] Ralph W. Conant, ed., *The Public Library and the City* (Cambridge: The MIT Press, c1969), pp. 150-51.

[31] Ruth W. Gregory, "The Search for Information about Community Needs," *Library Trends* XVII (July 1968), p. 16.

[32] Ibid., p. 15.

[33] Edward C. Banfield, "Needed: A Public Purpose," in Ralph W. Conant, ed., *The Public Library and the City* (Cambridge: The MIT Press, c1965), p. 102.

[34] Ibid., p. 113.

[35] Lowell Martin, *Library Response to Urban Change* (Chicago: American Library Association, 1969), p. 22.

[36] Ibid.

[37] Kate Coplan, "Some Thoughts on Library Public Relations," in Kate Coplan and Edwin Castagna, eds., *The Library Reaches Out* (New York: Oceana Publications, 1965), p. 342.

[38] Ibid., pp. 348-52.

[39] Public Law 89-617, 89th Congress, 2nd Session, October 3, 1966.

[40] Charles O. Jones, "Reevaluating the Hatch Act, A Report on the Commission on Political Activity of Government Personnel," *Public Administration Review* XXIX (May/June 1969), pp. 249-54.

[41] T. H. Marshall, "The Recent History of Professionalism in Relation to Social Structure and Social Policy," *The Canadian Journal of Economics and Political Science* V (1939), pp. 329-30.

[42] Everett C. Hughes, "Professions," *Daedalus* XCII (Fall 1963), p. 656.

[43] Ibid., p. 657.

[44] Oliver Garceau, *The Public Library in the Political Process* New York: Columbia University Press, 1949), p. 135.

[45] Ibid., p. 147.

[46] Ralph Nader, "A Strategy for Librarians," *American Libraries* IV (May 1973), pp. 275-78.

[47] Philip Selznick, *Leadership in Administration* (New York: Harper and Row, 1957).

[48] Ibid.

[49] Warren G. Bennis and Philip E. Stater, *The Temporary Society* (New York: Harper and Row, 1968).

[50] C. Walter Stone, "The Library Function Redefined," *Library Trends* XVI (October 1967), pp. 182, 185.

[51] Henry Voos, *Information Needs in Urban Areas; A Summary of Research in Methodology* (New Burnswick, New Jersey: Rutgers University Press, 1969), p. 39.

[52] Ibid.

[53] Ibid., p. 44.

[54] William R. Monat, "The Community Library; Its Search for a Vital Purpose," *ALA Bulletin* LXI (December 1967), p. 1308.

[55] Ibid., p. 1310.

[56] James F. Guyot, "Management Training and Post-Industrial Apologetics," *California Management Review* XX (Summer 1978), p. 84.

CURRENT CONCEPTS IN MANAGEMENT

by Neely Gardner

Cooperative effort to achieve the better life can only occur by organized effort. Managing this effort becomes more complicated as levels of education are elevated and visions of personal freedom increase. Organizations cannot exist apart from the world, and managers can only manage well when they study the world in which they operate. In earlier management literature, much attention was directed to the well-being of the organization itself. That of course is essential, for to exist, organizations must achieve their purpose and prosper. The quality and quantity of this achievement presumably relate to the effectiveness with which an enterprise is managed.

Nurturing the organization is only one part of the management task. Vital organizations contribute to the quality of life in the social milieu in which they operate, and organizations are also responsible for the well-being of employees who work within their structure. So we might better understand the above "three faces of management" if we comprehend the nature of organizational structures as they relate to the environment and to an organization's employees.

Managers have been most inventive in discovering ways to order their activities. Organizational forms bear many labels, but the two major ones are "mechanistic" and "organismic." In general, hierarchical organizations structured on the bureaucratic model are called mechanistic. Very few "pure" types of organismic agencies exist, but matrix and project organizations tend toward the organismic. Since the industrial revolution, by far the most common way or organizing has been along hierarchical or bureaucratic lines. In recent years, the term bureaucracy has become pejorative. In this chapter, however, we use the term as Max Weber used it, when he defined a bureaucracy: "a bureaucratic organization in which people operate in fixed jurisdictional areas in a way described by rules and regulations. People are assigned fixed duties. Authority to command is distributed in a stable way and is limited by rules. Positions are filled with persons seen as having the general qualifications. Offices are graded in hierarchical levels and there is supervision of the lower offices by the higher. Employees occupy but do not own offices."[1]

Whatever the mode of departmentation, hierarchical organizations require a chain of command. Chains of command suggest that attention be given to the scalar system and to the span of control. (Scalar refers to each level's subordination and responsibility to the person in the level above to whom they report.[2] Span of control relates to the number of subordinates reporting to each person in the scalar system.) As management theory has evolved, it is clear that many seminal thinkers have given support to a strong chain of command concept in which: "The more clear the line of authority from the top manager to every subordinate position the more effective will be the responsible decision making and organization communication."[3]

V. A. Graicunas was one of the early management specialists to point out the limits that should be observed as to the number of subordinates reporting to one superior. It was his belief that in the higher levels of an organization, the number of persons reporting to one superior should be even smaller than that at lower levels of supervision. In his essay, "Relationship in Organization," Graicunas demonstrated how inter-relationships and thus complication increase with the addition of each subordinate. He concludes that four or five subordinates is about the right number.[4] Without taking away from the importance of Graicunas's work, it should be mentioned that with the development of more sophisticated communications systems, and with the emergence of organizations with greater numbers of professionals, many managers pay little heed to the concept of span of control. In fact, the trend seems to be toward creation of flattened organizations, ones having fewer levels in the hierarchy.

Hierarchical or bureaucratic organizations may be arranged or departmented in several ways.[5] Some options include departmentation by:

1. numbers (armies are divided into regiments, battalions and companies, each having a fixed complement of persons)
2. time (shifts)
3. functions (the type of work done, such as manufacturing, engineering, sales)
4. territory (districts)
5. product (automobiles, steel, health care)
6. line and staff (operations, personnel, budgeting, etc.).

Much criticism is levied at hierarchical and mechanistic organizations.[6] Most of the criticism suggests that the bureaucratic organization tends to make for:

1. slow decisions
2. inflexibility
3. isolation and insulation from the public
4. maintaining the organization at the expense of the client
5. creating balkanized work limits
6. alienation of employees.

Although the larger volume of new management literature assails hierarchical structures, there are those who maintain that bureaucracy is dependable and, what is more, is here to stay.[7]

As one would suspect, there also is a middle group who say that "it all depends" on the situation. Joanne Woodward is one of these. Without addressing the morality of organizational structures, Woodward engaged in a comprehensive research project in which she examined the relationship between organizational structures and technology. She found in her survey sample that:

1. firms with greater technical complexity had more levels of authority.
2. companies that engaged in process production employed over three times as many managers as mass and batch production organizations.
3. the supervisory span of control was greater in mass manufacturing organizations.
4. the span of control for top management increased as technology increased.
5. organizations with higher technology had less labor costs.
6. the ratio of administrative and technical personnel to production workers increased as technology became more complex.

7.   the complexity of the product determined the proportion of professional staff.
8.   written communications increased in process-oriented firms.
9.   pressure on production line employees was more severe than in process production settings.
10. pressure was less severe when people worked in small groups.

Woodward makes the case that the organizational structure tends to follow technology and that the most successful firms are those that take the middle of the road of the technology group of which they are a part.[8] A later study by Burns and Stalker determined that stable organizations operated successfully as mechanistic structures, while more organismic systems were adapted to less stable conditions.[9]

Organismic is the general term used to describe organizational structures that move away from the hierarchical or mechanistic. An organismic structure is organic in nature, is fluid and changing and relates to its dynamic environment. As Burns sees it, mechanistic systems tell employees what to do, how they must do it, what not to do, what is not expected of them, and what is none of their business. Individuals operating in organismic systems are expected to commit themselves to the success of the organization's undertaking as a whole and to be fully implicated in any required activity that emerges. Boundaries disappear in organismic systems.

MECHANISTIC AND ORGANISMIC SYSTEMS OF MANAGEMENT

A mechanistic management system is appropriate to stable conditions. It is characterized by:

1.   the specialized differentiation of functional tasks into which the problems and tasks facing the concern as a whole are broken down.
2.   the abstract nature of each individual task, which is pursued with techniques and purposes more or less distinct from those of the concern as a whole.
3.   the reconciliation, for each level in the hierarchy, of these distinct performances by the immediate superiors.
4.   the precise definition of rights and obligations and technical methods attached to each functional role.
5.   the translation of rights, obligations, and methods into the responsibilities of a functional position.
6.   hierarchic structure of control, authority, and communication.
7.   a reinforcement of the hierarchic structure by the location of knowledge of actualities exclusively at the top of the hierarchy.
8.   a tendency for vertical interaction among members of the concern to be between superior and subordinate.
9.   a tendency for operations and working behavior to be governed by superiors.
10. insistence on loyalty to the concern and obedience to superiors as a condition of membership.
11. a greater importance and prestige attaching to internal (local) than to general (cosmopolitan) knowledge, experience, and skill.

The organismic form is appropriate to changing conditions, which give rise constantly to fresh problems and unforeseen requirements for action that cannot be broken down or distributed automatically arising from the functional roles defined within a hierarchic structure. It is characterized by:

1. the contributive nature of special knowledge and experience to the common task of the concern.
2. the realistic nature of the individual task, which is seen as set by the total situation of the concern.
3. the adjustment and continual redefinition of individual tasks through interaction with others.
4. the shedding of responsibility as a limited field of rights, obligations, and methods (problems may not be posted upwards, downwards or sideways).
5. the spread of commitment to the organization beyond any technical definition.
6. a network structure of control, authority, and communication.
7. omniscience no longer imputed to the head of the concern; knowledge may be located anywhere in the network, this location becoming the centre of authority.
8. a lateral rather than a vertical direction of communication through the organization.
9. a content of communication, which consists of information and advice rather than instructions and decisions.
10. commitment to the concern's tasks and to the 'technological ethos' of material progress and expansion is more highly valued than loyalty.
11. importance and prestige attach to affiliations and expertise valid in the industrial and technical and commercial milieux external to the firm.[10]

There are several variations on the organismic theme. Two such variations are found in project and matrix organization. Project organizations are geared to achieving specific goals in a set amount of time. Project organization came into prominence in the aerospace and sophisticated weapons systems programs. Under project management, purpose, progress, and responsibility are clear. Theoretically, once project goals are achieved, the project disbands. In fact, however, successful project groups tend to perpetuate themselves by finding new projects on which to work.

Matrix organizations are a combination of functional and project activities. In the aerospace world, we often find such functions as engineering, finance, procurement, manufacturing and industrial relations giving support in the form of people, material, and services to several discrete projects (see Figure 1, page 44).

In some cases, employees from functional organizations are "seconded" (loaned) to the project and work for the duration of the project under direction of the project manager. In some matrix organizations, employees continue to work in the functional units that do the necessary tasks under "contract" with the project. In those instances, the project manager has control of the money, but the actual project staff may consist of the project manager and two or three highly technical subordinates.

A not unusual organization is the combination of hierarchical and project approaches. Under this arrangement, projects are placed within a bureau or division, with project managers reporting to persons in the regular hierarchy. This arrangement places a strain on the system, largely because the project manager has responsibility for the output, has the knowledge of the product, and deals with the client. Thus,

Figure 1

	Project Sky Lab	Project Venus	Project Sky Wanderer	Project Weather Satellite	Project Search
Engineering— Employees & Services	x	x	x	x	x
Manufacturing— Employees & Services	x	x	x	x	x
Procurement— Services	x	x	x	x	x
Finance— Services	x	x	x	x	x
Industrial Relations— Services	x	x	x	x	x

the bureau or division chief is redundant to the transaction. In a number of organizations, researchers have observed that division and section heads are generally bypassed by top management who find it necessary to communicate directly with the project manager.[11]

Project and matrix management has been most extensively used in organizations involved in advanced technology—aerospace and research organizations being illustrative of the type of user. It is usual for persons in continuing service functions to take the position that project management has no utility to them. However, a growing number of instances illustrate how project organization can be effective in service-type units such as personnel, training, and even budgeting. The key factor seems to be the willingness to formulate clear and pragmatic operating objectives.

OBJECTIVES OF MANAGEMENT

Students of management are accustomed to finding management defined, management redefined, ad infinitum. Earlier writers such as Fayol tended to be rather bold in spelling out the nature of the manager's job. Fayol, for example, says the manager should: plan, organize, command, and control.[12] Gulick enlarged on this list, declaring that management consists of planning, organizing, staffing, directing, coordinating, reporting, and budgeting.[13] Chester Barnard thought of coordination and maintenance of communications, the scheme of organization, the personnel system, and an informal executive organization as being major functions. From this perspective, the executive also secures essential services by bringing people into the organization and, once in, eliciting their services. Also of major importance is the formulation of purpose and objectives. Barnard believed that the last function should be widely distributed among employees and stimulated and coordinated by the executive.[14]

THE MANAGEMENT SYSTEM

Managerial activities bridge operating structures designed for production, maintenance, environmental support, and adaptation. Complexity of organization has caused the management function to be complex. In the view of Katz and Kahn, this complexity suggests three basic management functions and four types of dynamics created by the sub-structures of the organization. The three functions are:

1. the coordination of sub-structures,
2. the resolution of conflicts, and
3. the coordination of external requirements.[15]

Four types of managerial dynamics emerge from interaction with the organizational sub-structure; these are often in conflict, thus requiring resolution. These are:

1. forces within the structures that deal with proficiency
2. conflict dynamics
3. working for stabilization
4. pushing for environmental manipulation.[16]

At any given time, some functions and some dynamics will take precedence over others. In the long term, however, all functions and the dynamics attached thereto require attention.

All too often, little thought is given to the environment in which organizations operate. If a major *raison d'être* of an organization is to contribute to the well-being of clients and to enhance the general quality of life, then much managerial attention could be directed to the environment. Sensing external needs through marketing studies and user surveys is not uncommon. Going beyond these focused considerations to the emerging situation in the larger society is far less common, but, for all that, it is a responsibility that managers should address. Internally, there are core instrumental activities in organizations that are integral to the management process. These are training, budgeting, organization and management activities, and personnel.

Training is perhaps the most overlooked but most effective management strategy. For one thing, training is an important way for managers to communicate on vertical and horizontal levels. Training based on participative methods clearly contributes to employee understanding of processes, policies, and objectives. If management is listening during these interactions, it will pick up ideas for improvement, learn of reasons for resistance, and be able to make appropriate adjustments before serious errors are made. When undertaking new tasks, employees almost always examine these as they may fit their concepts of their present jobs and their perceptions of how the new activity contributes to their own well-being. Training is one of the better ways of providing employees with the knowledge required for quality performance; and if training is executed in keeping with the adult learning model, employees will have a chance to integrate and accept their new knowledge. They will also have an opportunity to interpret and add to knowledge of the subject under scrutiny. Of course, accepting and understanding will not lead to changed performance unless employees develop the skill to carry out what they know. Therefore, assisting employees to develop new skills is a function of training.

Action or operational training is often not seen as training, because it is intimately connected with the introduction of new policies, procedures, systems, organizational forms, or technology, all of which require adjustment and change. This type of training differs from formal, more traditional classroom training. There is a vast difference between introducing and helping people understand, accept, influence, and know how to use MBO (Management by Objectives), for example, and teaching classroom students about MBO. The first approach involves learning by doing, the second, learning concepts and processes in the abstract. Finally, participative action training is one of the few ways to change the norms of an organization, and without normative change, most technology transfer fails to meet its promise.

Budgeting strategies are better known and used more often than are training strategies. Even though the power of the purse is used more, it is not necessarily used better. One very valid criticism of public budgeting is that it impedes change and improvement and thus assures preservation of the status quo. New programs typically fare poorly in the budget process, while many less worthy and obsolete activities are allowed to continue year after year with little critical examination.

Budgets also tend to occupy an inordinate portion of the manager's time. Budget making has become over-elaborate to the extent that questions are being raised about the cost effectiveness of many public budgetary processes. Public budgeting, since its United States advent in 1922, has followed an accountant's model, with emphasis being placed on economy rather than effectiveness and productivity. Typical object-of-expenditure budgets have only remote connection with the program activity of an organization.

Managers may find themselves constrained by larger systems. Still, they must work at allocating for (or obtaining allocations that relate to) future plans and programs. They must be prepared to phase out older programs that have long since served their purpose and to put the money thus saved into new and more vital areas. Insofar as managers can influence the larger system, they should use budgets to enhance agency plans. It is also important to use funds to reward solid performance.

O&M (organization and methods) relates to those activities intended to improve organizational structure, procedures, or technology. As technology has become more and more complicated a new generation of the O&M discipline has emerged under the name of "systems analysis." There can be no doubt about the value of systems analysis as it relates to introduction and use of technical and mechanical systems. Both O&M and systems analysis tend to take the empirical/rational approach, which works very well until the mechanical system infringes on people. At this point, training and systems strategies should be brought together. People in systems tend to react more favorably to normative/re-educative efforts than to empirical/rational approaches.

How an enterprise is organized has a significant influence on how well its objectives are attained. Managers would do well to become conversant with organization theories, particularly those that help a manager focus on output. O&M specialists should be of assistance in this area.

Personnel is the fourth major intrastructural system in which the manager should have expertise. Most public jurisdictions now operate under civil service systems, and enough has been said of the rigidity of many of these systems and about the inhibiting effect that central personnel agencies have on operating organizations. The fact is that the "reformist" model system, which is dominant in the United States, shows little propensity for folding or re-reforming simply because of the anguished cries of line managers. What is beginning to change personnel systems is a growing union presence. Insofar as collective bargaining is concerned, most public jurisdictions now operate within the general procedures that evolved under the National Labor Relations Board. As a result, there is an indication that hiring and compensation processes will change quite drastically. It could well be that as in Great Britain, France, and Israel, union action will create even greater rigidity than exists presently. The present union system relies almost exclusively on adversary approaches. Solving differences in the adversary way is costly of time, morale, and money. Today's managers would do well to become familiar with the field of collective bargaining. At the same time, they might help their organizations, the morale within those organizations, and the productivity of employees if they would develop the capability of working with employees in a problem-solving way to prevent issues from arising that create labor strife.

Management can take steps to offset some of the debilitating influences of personnel systems. When developing work assignments, managers may be guided by some of the psychological requirements of employees. Employees have the need

- for the work to be reasonably demanding

- to be able to learn on the job and to go on learning (but not too much or too little)

- for social support and recognition in the work place

- for the individual to relate what is done at work to the social processes of life and

- to feel that the job leads to some sort of desirable future.[17]

The overall management system should be studiously geared to external and internal environmental requirements, should meet the changes that occur independently in the external environment, and should be sensitive to changes induced by the institution itself. It is clear that effective performance of the management function emerges from the appropriate exercise of leadership and authority carried out in the enrivonmental context.

LEADERSHIP

Those who are managers have the opportunity to operate in a leadership role. Legitimacy that attaches to the managerial position creates an expectation that the person in that role will wield influence. But authority and power of position do not automatically create a leader. Some managers are leaders, while other managers lead hardly at all. To be a leader, one must understand the unique forces that motivate different individuals at different times, be able to inspire those persons, and have the ability to develop an organizational climate in which individuals can become motivated.[18] Leadership is defined by Katz and Kahn as "the influential increment over and above mechanical compliance with the routine directives of the organization."[19] This influence is used in addressing questions of organizational structure; or when structural change is undertaken to engage in the "piecing out"; or by participating in the interpolation of existing structures; or employing existing organizational devices with the frequency and intensity appropriate to the situation.[20]

To be successful in support, interaction facilitation, goal emphasis, and work facilitation requires the exercise of influence. For the leader, however, just any old influence is not sufficient. The influence of leaders stems from the legitimacy of their positions, from the charismatic qualities that they may possess, and from any expertise or referrent power that they have accumulated. Power usually is vested in a person with expertise. The expertise may be political, social, administrative or technical, but if it is clearly recognized by followers, then the expert person has power and influence among those followers. Referent influence comes generally from an individual's network of relationships within an organization. These relationships usually transcend the chain of command and other formal structures. There are persons in almost every organization who hold no formal managerial position but who are actually leaders, because they are able to assist or impede collective effort through personal influence. Such persons tend to be respected by their colleagues.

We may look at leadership as having four additional dimensions:

1. support—activities that increase the individual's sense of personal worth and importance.
2. inter-action facilitation—which creates and maintains a network of inter-personal relations in a work group.
3. goal emphasis—involving the creation, changing, clarifying, and achieving member acceptance of group goals.
4. work facilitation—behavior that serves to provide methods, facilities, and technology for goal achievement.[21]

Managers who are also leaders necessarily have the trust and support of many persons of influence in the informal organization. Referent support is kept alive by communication and consultation. Persons in the referent group obviously gain psychological rewards as a result of the relationship, even if this is no more tangible than the excitement of backing a winner. Each person in the referent network obviously gains a degree of influence. Sometimes, persons in authority positions are leaders. Often, persons attain positions of authority because of their leadership qualities. Leadership may accompany authority and vice versa, but the nature of the two are different.

Authority

One cannot separate the managerial function from the structure of authority. Organizations cannot survive unless they have ways of obtaining role performance, replacing lost members coordinating the work between people and units, and responding to changes in the environment.[22]

Organizational authority is conveyed to occupants of positions through rules, regulations, procedures, and norms. In other words, the influence of the office holder is made legitimate because it is "legal." A subordinate's compliance with authoritative instructions and requests is generally understood when an individual accepts employment. The relationship is part of the psychological contract that one has with the organization. Authority of superiors is further reinforced with whatever power the organization has given them to reward and punish. Authority conferred on a supervisor or manager by organizational rules or regulation is termed rational-legal. Rational-legal authority gives the manager or supervisor the right to govern. The actual power those persons possess regulates the degree to which they wield that authority. Two persons holding positions of equal authority will have, in many instances, a difference in the amount of power they may exercise.

Styles of management vary from authoritarian to participative. While authoritarianism still exists, many research studies indicate the greater desirability of participative approaches, particularly in professional organizations.[23] Management proficiency depends upon the successful exercise of leadership and wise use of authority. Managerial energy then can be directed toward accomplishing a multiplicity of organizational jobs, not the least of which is planning.

Planning

Managerial planning consists of making advance decisions regarding what is to be done, who will do it, how it will be done, and when. A plan represents the manager's vision of the future. Organizations need to make plans concerning their work force, physical facilities, policies, operating processes, and budgets.

Plans come in a variety of sizes and shapes. In the last few years, for example, there has been a steady increase in long-range planning by public organizations, particularly at county and city levels. These jurisdictions have developed so-called master plans. In many cases, these have been regional plans largely relating to physical features of communities. Plans need not be this grand, however. City and county assessors are planners in the sense that the determinations of these officials have tremendous influence, generally much greater than that of planning departments; for by their actions, they will determine how communities will (or will not) grow, the use to which land will be put, and how various departments within the jurisdiction will prosper. Likewise, actions taken in the budget condition the future activities that may be undertaken taken by the organization. Plans may concern a long or short time period, for large schemes or small operations. Every manager from top administrator to first line supervisor is obligated to be a planner.

Long-term planning is speculative and more often than not, imprecise. Five- and ten-year plans are useful in that they provide an idealized picture of some desirable future toward which to work. As a consequence of their imprecision, long-range plans need to be updated often, perhaps even annually. Five- and ten-year plans provide a framework for short-range operational planning.

For the functional manager, operational plans with a more confined horizon seem most useful. Even in the present uncertain world, it is possible to plan two or three years in advance with considerable realism. Managers can approach the planning process with greater facility if they are acquainted with the essential steps of planning.

Awareness of possible problems and opportunities is the actual take-off point for planning. Such awareness requires a familiarity with the social, political, and economic situation in the community and a "state of the art" knowledge of the technologies that might be employed by or affect the organization. In the pre-planning phase, the manager will do well to cultivate an awareness of the desires of clients, the nature of competing demands on resources, and the strengths and weaknesses of the organization.[24]

Next come the formulation of goals and objectives that specify the procedures, budgets, and programs necessary to accomplish anticipated results.[25]

Once objectives are clarified, the time has arrived to consider alternate means of achieving them. This leads to making a decision favoring the most desirable alternative. At this point, decision makers need to be in agreement as to the nature of the premises on which their plans will be based. Premises are planning assumptions. At the heart of making premises is forecasting. It is the belief in the integrity of such forecasts that conditions the choice between alternatives.[26]

Overall organizational plans should be supported by sub-plans related to hiring and training staff, developing work methods, assuring that needed facilities are available, obtaining the needed equipment and supplies, and developing a budget that is compatible with the plan.

One could say that the following is a hierarchy of planning:

- mission or purpose
- objectives
- policies and procedures
- programs
- budgets

As important as the total planning process may be, by far the greatest pay-off to the department or work unit is derived from well-formulated objectives by which the manager can manage.

MANAGING BY OBJECTIVES

Perhaps the single most important role of the manager is that of helping the organization to articulate, clarify, and implement its objectives. Objectives give an organization a sense of purpose. If people do not know where they are going, they are doomed to wander hither and thither without destination. Worse, they will never know if they have arrived and work will lose meaning. Objectives represent the end to which management activities are directed and give the needed sense of direction.

The general mission of public organizations is usually noted in the statutes. But neither laws nor other statements of general purpose can serve as operating objectives. Operating objectives must be specific. In our wonderful, flexible, imprecise way, we use the terms goals and objectives almost interchangeably.[27] The objectives by which one may manage, however, must be more concrete. An operating objective calls for explicitly stated expected results, results that, when reached, are observable and recordable. While these results must be observable and recordable, it is not required that they actually be measureable or countable, although if that is possible, so much the better.

Objectives stated in terms of expected results make it possible to judge whether or not the actual outcome meets expectations. In addition, the understanding of such statements makes it possible for employees working toward the achievement of objectives to prepare a schedule of events that leads to achievement. These "events" become subobjectives. Reaching targets and being able to note achievements satisfies some rather fundamental human needs. A person's life is spent in a succession of goal-achieving activities. In an organization, people's objectives emerge from the ways in which those individuals derive satisfaction from what they give to and receive from their work. It is important to understand and build upon these personal objectives.

There is a hierarchy of objectives represented by individual objectives, unit objectives and organization objectives.[28] Other sub-units will also have objectives. The art with which this hierarchy is managed will have much to do with the effectiveness of the organization. It is clear that individuals have different needs just as work units have a variety of differing functions. Objectives in the different units, therefore, should be compatible, but not necessarily uniform. This suggests that any pragmatic approach to managing by objectives will utilize individual and group objectives as building blocks on which to rest over-all organizational objectives.

There are also long-range and short-range objectives. Both are necessary. Short-range objectives permit employees to answer the question, "How are we doing?" Reaching immediate objective provides immediate gratification and sense of purpose. Long-range objectives require more vision. Long-range objectives require that gratification be deferred. Organizations achieve long-range purpose through an orderly process of reaching sub-goals. Indeed, the nature of long-range achievement will be altered and modified by the quality and timeliness with which more immediate check-points are reached and the quality of work that was involved in reaching them.

Managing by objectives often fails. Failure is due to overlooking the necessity of involving employees in the formulation of desired results. When employees participate in a meaningful way in formulating objectives, two major results are present:

1. employees develop an understanding of the objectives, and
2. they tend to become committed to the objectives that they have helped formulate.

An underlying value that attaches to MBO is that people will exercise self-direction and self-control in the service of objectives to which they are committed.

Another problem experienced in some MBO programs is related to its superimposition on the organization without integrating it into reporting, budgeting, and accounting systems. Reports should give monthly progress. Budget dollars should be attached to achievement of objectives, and the accounting system should equate expenditures with production. The basic concept of managing by objectives may be summarized as follows:

1. Objectives (explicitly expressed expected results) are diverse and multi-dimensional.
2. In order to be most useful, objectives need to be understood and sub-scribed to by the persons designated to achieve them.
3. Objectives developed by persons who are to achieve them are likely to be more acceptable and have greater utility than those developed for them by management.
4. Organizations must take cognisance of goals and objectives of the individual so that *integration* of those goals and objectives supplants *differentiation* of goals and objectives.
5. Statements of goals and objectives are of little use unless they enable the organization to determine whether or not the desired result has been achieved in the time specified. When objectives are so conceived they may be considered operating objectives.
6. Operating objectives are inadequate if they do not permit a schedule of events which communicates progress toward achievement of results.
7. Objectives should meet the needs of individuals and organizations for both immediate and deferred gratification.
8. Individual responsibility for the achievement of objectives should be a matter of specific understanding.
9. Progress toward objectives should, at a minimum, be included as a basic part of the organizational reporting system and, most desirably, should be reflected in budgeting and accounting systems.

10. Once objectives have been accomplished resources should be oriented toward achievement of other organization and individual objectives, which should in turn strive for ethical, psychological, educational and material improvements for individual, organization and society.[29]

PROGRAMS AND SERVICES

Managerial processes do not exist as an end in themselves. A manager who structures; leadership and authority; plans and objectives—all these exist to help the organization provide programs and services to the public. As organizations age, they are prone to an insularism that detracts from the quality of programs and services. One important remedy for this is to obtain constant feed-back on organizational programs from the environment. Otherwise, goal displacement tends to occur.

Goal displacement describes a situation in which work units replace original goals with other, more self-protective goals. For example, a personnel department may spend great effort in perfecting and enforcing rules and regulations while losing sight of their original purpose, which was to provide competent workers for operating departments, to see that selection is made on merit, and to encourage the development and growth of employees. Accounting departments may begin to exist for the sake of the accounting system alone, rather than for the enhancement of programs and services. Staff units are not the only culprits. Sometimes operating units also isolate themselves from the public. They do this by developing multitudes of impersonal rules to protect their system from the client.

Crozier describes a "vicious circle" that inhibits organizations from learning. These are:

1. development of impersonal rules;
2. centralization of decision;
3. strata isolation and concomitant group pressure on the individual;
4. the development of parallel power.[30]

Impersonal rules reduce the discretion of both superior and subordinate. While they are thus deprived of initiative, they are free from personal interference. Employees are also excused from responsibility for acts taken in accord with rules and regulations.

Centralization of decision comes about in order to preserve a climate of impersonality. Decisions not covered by the rules tend to fall on superiors who are distant from the point of action. This centralization tendency eliminates discretionary power and creates greater rigidity.

Isolation of strata occurs when discretion is removed from middle managers. As a result, supervisors and employees, through impersonality and centralization in each level of the organization, become isolated. Isolation occurs because communication becomes more and more limited. People within a unit are bound by a wall of rules. Within these boundaries, peer group pressure becomes stronger because the peer group is the predominant vehicle for dealing with the organization.[31] Groups also develop rituals to reinforce the notion that their functions are among the most important in the organization. Such rituals help to enforce group solidarity.

Parallel power develops because human ingenuity has not enabled organizations to invent a system in which impersonal rules and centralized decisions will cover every possible predictable situation. When gaps exist, parallel power relationships develop. To illustrate, in today's uncertain world, we see a proliferation of staff units. Strata of experts emerge to carry out tasks that cannot be described in any detail.

Impersonal rules, centralization, strata isolation and parallel power all contribute to a vicious circle that results in displacement of goals. When this occurs, there are increasing problems with clients, poor communications with the environment, isolation from the rest of the organization, and lower productivity. The result is that the organization grows more tense. The organization then creates even more restrictive regulations, which are again processed by the vicious circle. Under these circumstances, organizations become more and more rigid.[32] Unfortunately, organizations caught up in the vicious circle are often unable to break out unless confronted by crisis.

Antidotes to the vicious circle are greater interaction with clients in order to obtain feedback, accompanied by managerial systems within the organization that guarantee that feedback will be taken seriously. Client surveys might be conducted on a regular schedule. Those employees having direct client contact may be empowered to act on a situational basis, rather than "according to the book." Having clear objectives with equally clear acceptance of responsibility for meeting those objectives is a clear way out of the vicious circle.

Programs and services offered to the public should certainly reflect the needs of the public served. What the public needs can only be determined in cooperation with the public itself, which suggests that managers should work assiduously at finding out what the public is saying. By far the most effective means of linking with clients is through employees who are in direct contact with clients. An organization that has evolved a norm wherein employees care for each other and for the clients they serve has a prime vehicle for two-way communication.

CLIENTS

Determining "who is the public?" is not a simple matter for public agencies. Usually there are several publics, some of whom may have similar interests and some of whom may appear to have interests that are in conflict. Mediating such conflicts is a task for administrative as well as political arms of government.

Public managers have an ethical obligation not only to serve direct clients or publics, but to act in behalf of the larger public as well. Relating to the multiplicity of publics requires a systematic sensing of the environment. There are a number of ways to go about sensing, but some of the ideas developed in institution-building theories provide an effective framework for action.

Institution-building studies tend to examine internal organizational dynamics as these relate to both the focused and diffused environments. One way in which institution-building theorists have approached these environments is by becoming familiar with linkages. Milton Esman describes four types:

- enabling linkages
- functional linkages
- normative linkages
- diffused linkages[33]

Enabling Linkages

Public organizations depend upon other organizations for authority and resources. Relationships with enablers make it possible to obtain support for organizational survival. Enabling linkages for a normal public agency would be constituted of such persons or agencies as its legislative body, its board; a civil service commission; the president, governor, mayor, city manager, or other supra-departmental executive; the budget officer; accounting officer, and auditor. Those same entities that provide authority and resources for operations also have similar relations with other agencies that have competing needs.

Functional Linkages

In the functional sense, there are linkages with organizations that are complementary in that they supply each other with inputs and/or use each other's outputs. Schools, libraries, and recreation departments might have such linkages as departments of social service, mental hospitals, and juvenile institutions. Functional linkages also exist between real or potential competitors. Departments of social service compete for support and funds with police, fire, and sanitary departments. Organizations make innovations and introduce change through the assistance of their functional linkages.

Normative Linkages

Normative linkages are socio-cultural. A community that places high value on education will be supportive of educational facilities. Some communities support cultural activities such as symphonies, ballet, and art galleries because citizens value things artistic. Norms, rules, and regulations that are supported by the public can facilitate or be obstacles to institutional accomplishment and well-being.

Diffused Linkages

Diffused linkages carry us one step further away from recognized organizations and identifiable sources of norms, rules, and regulations. Although there appears to be a fine line between normative and diffused linkages, the latter linkages are with the general public, and they include relationships between the institution and public opinion. Organizational leaders pursue this linkage by working through news media in an effort to communicate and by following with care the daily march of events that might influence the organization's future. Not the least of these indicators are the polls that reflect the general mood of citizens at election time.

It is the sense of institution-building theory that organizations prosper when the linkage groups value the "doctrine" of the organization. Doctrine refers to missions, values, and beliefs of the institution. It is largely around doctrine that the organization transacts its business with society. The outcome of transactions consists not only of physical inputs and outputs but also of social interaction. "The purposes of transactions have been identified as (1) gaining support and overcoming resistance, (2) exchanging resources, (3) structuring the environment, and (4) transferring norms and values.[34]

The arena of linkages seems to contract as the unit moves down the hierarchical scale. Even so, some elements requiring sensing are present at all levels, but the definitions of enabling and functional linkages are partially interdepartmental rather than interorganizational.

EVALUATION

Organizations do a much better job of evaluating special functions and programs than they do in evaluating over-all activities. After all, it is very difficult to assess the effectiveness of a department of social works or employment or even a library. When pressed into making evaluations, such organizations frequently fall back on statistical approaches, which more often than not relate to means or activities rather than to ends or outputs. In the case of some statistical approaches, the information may be less than worthless. Worse, it may be misleading. For instance, in adopting centralized services such as reproduction units, computer centers, or stenographic and motor pools, it is often easy to demonstrate increased performance at less cost. What is not evaluated is the time lost and the problems created for persons who must use the services. In non-construction and non-profit organizations, it is probably inappropriate to rely on the typical statistical evaluations except in a minor way. The problem here is somewhat the same as that faced in research on human behavior. There are so many variables, and so many circumstances that infringe on the situation that measurement in the arithmetic sense is not possible.

Evaluation is more feasible when it relates to objectives. If operating objectives are sufficiently explicit, managers should be able to determine when they have been achieved. What is needed is evidence that will convince a reasonable person that what was supposed to happen, in fact, did happen. When managing by objectives, one not only evaluates results, but is also able to assess the progress being made at any point in time. After a management by objectives approach has been established fully, it is possible to provide criteria by which accomplishment will be judged.

It is important to develop an understanding of the purpose of evaluation. Far too often, the evaluation process is used to determine "who is to blame" rather than to discover the nature of the problem and how it might be solved. It is for this reason that many resist evaluation. Evaluation should concentrate on improvement rather than punishment. If evidence can be collected and fed back in automatic and non-punitive ways, the organization or unit is less likely to resist or to be defensive about initiating self-improvement and self-correction. Perhaps the most effective evaluation systems are those in which actual performance is examined in relation to predicted performance. When a difference exists between prediction and performance, this is the area of difference on which to concentrate.

Evaluation studies are occasionally conducted for the purpose of deciding on resource needs. If this is the primary reason for evaluation, then the agency must muster evidence on how much is being done and how well. It is of further help to relate the quantity and quality of work to resources. In project-type organizations, it is possible to collect such evidence because of the more precise definition of work objectives. In the typical service organization (structured functionally), evidence pertaining to quality and quantity of performance is more difficult to secure.

Always in evaluation, it is important to ask the question, "compared to what?" A study of effectiveness can only give one a reading on what is occuring presently. If evaluation is to measure progress, it should have a "before" as well as an "after."

Some assessment is needed at a point of beginning to provide a base against which to judge progression or regression. Common methods for evaluation include:

- citizen surveys
- employee attitude surveys
- cost benefit studies
- productivity studies
- case studies
- audits
  —fiscal
  —management

Some activities that are labeled evaluations are not evaluations in the strict sense of the term but are investigations. Generally, investigations grow out of a sense that something is wrong. As necessary as investigations may be to assist in discovering misdeeds, such investigations leave agencies scarred. Recovery time is slow.

A higher use of evaluation is to provide feedback that leads to improvement. Managers are responsible for several areas that are worthy of regular evaluation. These fall at the employee, organization and citizen levels.

The employee level may be evaluated in terms of:

- individual freedom
- meaningful activity
- participation
- recognition of worth
- safe and amenable working conditions
- needed skill and knowledge
- growth opportunities
- security

Organizations should be examined for:

- employee acceptance of legitimacy of the organization's mission
- achieving objectives
- supportive clients
- adequate linkages
- leadership
- doctrine
- communications
- program
- internal structure

Citizen evaluation should address:

● client satisfaction

● timely delivery of goods and services that are useful and economical

● compliance with societal norms

● presence of choice as to whether services are used and wanted.[35]

Evaluation processes round out the management cycle. Effective evaluation provides the feedback necessary to organizational renewal. With each evaluation, management can change organizational direction, correct flaws in operations, and make needed amendments to programs and services.

It is only through evaluation and feedback that organizational learning occurs. Through learning, organizations become and remain dynamic. In the learning organization, there is excitement for the employee, satisfaction for the manager, and benefit for the public.

NOTES

[1] Max Weber, *On Charisma and Institution Building* (Chicago: The University of Chicago Press, 1968), pp. 66-77.

[2] L. Urwick, "The Functions of Administration," in *Papers on the Science of Administration*, ed. by Luther Gulick and L. Urwick (New York: Institute of Public Administration, 1937), p. 123.

[3] Harold Koontz and Cyril O'Donnel, *Essentials of Management* (New York: McGraw-Hill Book Company, 1978), p. 241.

[4] L. Urwick, *op. cit.*, p. 185.

[5] Koontz and O'Donnel, pp. 198-217.

[6] See such works as Chris Argyris, *Integrating the Individual and the Organization* (New York: John Wiley and Sons, 1964); Warren G. Bennis and Philip E. Slater, *The Temporary Society* (New York: Harper and Row, 1964); and Donald Schon, *Beyond the Stable State* (New York: W. W. Norton and Company, Inc., 1964).

[7] See Herbert Kaufman, "The Direction of Organization Evolution," in *Public Administration Review* (July/August 1973), p. 300; and Charles Perrow, *Organization Analysis: A Sociological View* (Belmont, CA: Brooks/Cole Publishing Company, 1970), pp. 50-89.

[8] Joanne Woodward, "Management and Technology," in *Organization Theory*, ed. by D. S. Pugh (Middlesex, England: Penguin Education, 1971), pp. 56-69.

[9] Tom Burns and G. M. Stalker, *The Management of Innovation* (London: Tavistock Publications, 1961).

[10] Tom Burns, "Industry in a New Age," *New Society* (January 31, 1963), pp. 17-20.

[11] The author has observed this by-passing phenomenon in at least three diverse organizations where projects are placed within units in the hierarchy.

[12] Henri Fayol, "The Administrative Theory in the State," in *Papers on the Science of Administration* (New York: Institute of Public Administration, 1937), p. 63.

[13] Luther Gulick, "Notes on the Theory of Organization," in *Papers on the Science of Administration* (New York: Institute of Public Administration, 1937), p. 13.

[14] Chester Barnard, *The Functions of the Executive* (Cambridge, MA: Harvard University Press, 1938), pp. 215-34.

[15] Daniel Katz and Robert L. Kahn, *The Social Psychology of Organizations* (New York: John Wiley and Sons, Inc., 1966), p. 94.

[16] Ibid., p. 96.

[17] Fred E. Emery and E. L. Trist, "The Causal Texture of Organizational Environments," in *Human Relations* 18 (1965), pp. 21-32.

[18] Koontz and O'Donnel, p. 440.

[19] Katz and Kahn, p. 302.

[20] Ibid., pp. 302-303.

[21] D. G. Bowers and Stanley E. Seashore, "Changing the Structure and Functioning of an Organization" (Ann Arbor, Michigan: Survey Research Center, 1963). (Multilith).

[22] Katz and Kahn, p. 203.

[23] See especially Rensis Likert, *New Patterns in Management* (New York: McGraw-Hill, 1961); Chris Argyrus, *Personality and Organization* (New York: Harper and Brothers, 1957); and Douglas McGregor, *The Human Side of Enterprise* (New York: McGraw-Hill, 1960).

[24] Koontz and O'Donnel, pp. 70-71.

[25] Ibid.

[26] Ibid., p. 72.

[27] Most common dictionaries define "objective" as something aimed or striven for, "goal" as an object or end one strives to achieve, "purpose" as something one intended to do or obtain.

[28] Koontz and O'Donnel, p. 95.

[29] Neely Gardner, *Group Leadership* (Washington, DC: National Training and Development Service Press, 1974), pp. 83-84.

[30] Michel Crozier, *The Bureaucratic Phenomenon* (Chicago: University of Chicago Press, 1963), p. 189.

[31] Ibid., pp. 193-95.

[32] Ibid., p. 194.

[33] Milton J. Esman, "Institutional Organizational Literature," in *Institution Building Source Book*, ed. by Melvin G. Blase (Beverly Hills, CA: Sage Publications, 1973), pp. (1)/4-(1)/11.

[34] Ibid. (1)/6.

[35] Adapted from Neely Gardner, "Action Training and Research—Something Old and Something New," *Public Administration Review* (March/April 1974).

MANAGING THE PUBLIC LIBRARY

by Peggy A. Sullivan

The administration of public libraries is conducted by the group that has final responsibility for legal and fiscal commitments and for determining policy. Usually, this is a board constituted specifically for this purpose, with its members elected or appointed. However, a board that has major responsibility in other areas, such as for public education or for administration of another governmental unit such as a city or county, may also be the administrative body for the public library. In the period since World War II, as more public libraries have been federated into systems, the practice of having administration by a board representing the several library units in the system has been followed. The critical point is that policies are set by the administrative body, whatever its name or other responsibilities.

In common parlance, however, the salaried personnel who may have such titles as director, chief librarian, or administrator are often called—and may describe themselves as—administrators. Since they implement policy rather than establish it, however, they are managers. They also have the responsibility for providing the information, background, analysis, and probably opinions as well, on which the administrative body can base its decisions. The manager with major responsibility (whom we can, for clarity, designate as director) usually has other staff members to share some of the responsibility for management and leadership; this person also usually serves as a nonvoting participant in meetings and actions of the administrative body. Again, for clarity, this group may be described as a board, with the understanding that its name may vary in different instances.

Typical decisions of the board concern the development of a philosophy of service to the library's public; contracts with architects, auditors, or library consultants; interaction with the state library agency, and approval of budgets. Usually the presiding officer and one or more representatives of the board have the task of representing the library to the governmental authority that may have final responsibility for its administration, and also to the public. Groups of the public may address the board to request improvements or extensions of service, and votes on bond issues or taxing requirements are other occasions when the board needs to represent the library, its accomplishments, and its needs to the public.

Library boards have traditionally been free of the controversies that have swept through boards of education, but as libraries have become more powerful as major providers of educational and cultural resources and as their budgets have become larger components of the public fund, their boards have begun to include not only noncritical supporters, but also representatives who question the direction and value of the library's contributions and purposes.

The director of the library, in contrast with board members who usually serve without payment but who may receive reimbursement of expenses or some perquisites such as travel, is almost always a full-time salaried employee. There are small libraries in residential areas where a part-time or volunteer librarian may seem to suffice, but recognition of the need for good quality of library service, the growing complexity of library management, and necessary interaction with other library units are constantly diminishing the number of such appointments.

The managerial responsibilities of the director typically include the recruitment, appointment, deployment, and evaluation of personnel; approval of expenditures; direction of all aspects of public relations; decisions concerning hours and patterns of service; development of staff in educational and travel opportunities, and development of collections. The size of the library is the major determinant of the number and kinds of personnel who may assist in these responsibilities. The director also maintains all communications with the board and with major external sources of funding and/or information and is the library's usual representative to the public.

The library board often has the power to levy taxes, but limitations on the amount or kind of taxing authority may be set by local governments or state legislatures. The board derives its authority from these agencies and eventually, of course, from the public to which it is responsible. The geographic limits of a library's service area may be fixed by action of the board, but public elections may be required to allow such action. There are many variations in the provisions for use of a library, with property owners, residents, students, and workers within those geographic limits usually constituting the library's designated public, but with contractual arrangements often in effect with neighboring public or other kinds of libraries for the provision of full or partial service. It is rare for access to a library's physical facility to be limited, and such services as internal use of materials, attendance at public programs, and reference assistance are customarily provided fairly generously. Lending and/or reserving of materials for loan, use of inter-library lending, and reservation of meeting rooms are the services most likely to be limited to the library's designated audience or service area.

Formal authority for library development lies with the board, with such constraints or allowances as its relationship to other governmental units may require. In practice, much of that authority may be delegated to one or more officers of the board and to the library's director. The ability to delegate authority and the necessity to retain responsibility are the major reasons that effective communication and trust are important. Even when the library may not have a direct line of responsibility to other services of government, its relationship to them must be maintained by these same factors of communication and trust. Acquisition and use of property, maintenance of safety, and access to transportation routes are obvious concerns of the library, and they require rapport with other governmental departments, as do other requirements of the library.

As noted, the board of the library may delegate authority to officers and to the director. The chain of command within the library usually requires representation on an organizational chart and may be determined by the director. Even the smallest units of the library should have established chains of command based on the same principles as the library's overall scheme. The line of responsibility should be clear so that staff and public can be informed who is responsible in the absence of the designated manager, and levels of responsibility should be clearly associated with positions rather than personalities. The biggest problems are likely to be caused by senior staff members who, by default or design, take responsibility and authority that belong logically to more recently appointed members of the staff whose positions include the responsibility and authority, but who may lack the experience and/or the confidence to exercise both most effectively.

Other problems may arise from the practice of having positions that are primarily consultative or advisory in nature. Such positions as those of age-level specialists, who are responsible for an aspect of service but who typically have no line authority or supervisory responsibility, are examples of these. Such problems can be diminished or avoided by clear indications of lines of authority and responsibility and by appropriate dissemination of such explanatory materials as organizational charts and job descriptions.

Tradition and habit affect attitudes toward the administrative structure, probably more than they should. When the head of general reference in a central library, for example, has seniority, interest, and competence in the area of administration, that individual may be second in command; but it may be unwise, even disastrous, to perpetuate this practice if the head of reference is succeeded by someone less able to assume this responsibility, especially if some other head of a unit or department is able to assume such responsibility. Clear job descriptions are an asset in such instances, since they should indicate tasks definitely and permanently assigned to the position, as well as those assigned to the individual, with the understanding that the latter—and any requirements or perquisites associated with them—always can be reassigned to some other position.

Span of control is usually measured by the number of persons whose work a supervisor directly oversees. A prevalent rule of thumb recommends that the number not exceed fifteen, but many characteristics can affect the appropriateness of the number. Among these are: geographic locations of work assignments, patterns of responsibility at various levels, nature of work, level of persons supervised, and financial control exercised by them. To consider these in order, it may be noted that direct supervision of fifteen heads of branch libraries whose job locations may be spread over many square miles is likely to be more complex than supervision of fifteen persons in technical services, all working within one large area. Patterns of responsibility at various levels mean that in some parts of the library, small groups or clusters of supervisors may be created, establishing a hierarchy and making it possible, for example, for one person to supervise five people, each of whom might supervise five more, and each of those to supervise three, so that 105 people could be eventually responsible to one supervisor without any individual's having an unwieldy span of control.

The nature of various positions and the impact that this can have on span of control can be exemplified when a library director may have two or three office staff members reporting directly to him, as well as a director of personnel and a director of public relations (two positions traditionally requiring direct access to the director) and perhaps two or three persons with major supervisory responsibilities for different aspects of library service. The director may function with the first category of personnel rather like an office manager, with the personnel and public relations directors like an advisor and senior decision-maker, and with the supervisors more like a chairperson or team leader. The different skills required in such instances make the inclusion of a maximum of eight persons in such a span of control reasonable.

When the administrative structure has several persons with diverse responsibilities reporting to one supervisor, there may be more need to limit the number to fewer than the traditional fifteen, if the supervisor is to work effectively to assist them in developing diverse programs and to unify their efforts for the best results for the library. Similarly, when several individuals have major fiscal responsibilities, e.g., for purchasing materials and supplies, contracting for maintenance and repair of facilities, or allocating salaries, a more limited span of control may be advisable for the individual supervising their work.

The enemies of efficient span of control are the willingness of individuals to accept new responsibilities and the desire of many people to report to a supervisor at as high a level `as possible. Several years ago, when a consultant reviewed the work assignments and structure of a medium-sized public library, she discovered more than twenty persons, out of a staff of fewer than fifty, reporting to the library's director. In the course of three decades, the director had systematically expanded programs and services, thus requiring more staff; and in order to get them off to good starts, she had supervised them personally. But she had been less systematic in establishing a chain of command, and the staff members concerned had accepted some of the difficulties in communication in exchange for the privilege of direct supervision by the library's director. Such a situation is probably extreme, but the constant growth of program responsibilities and restatement of the library's goals require constant review of supervisory responsibilities and recognition of the need for flexibility in the establishment of reasonable spans of control.

BACKGROUND THEORIES AND APPROACHES TO ADMINISTRATION

The fact that most managers and directors of public libraries have advanced from other specialties within the library profession is probably the major reason that little emphasis is placed on theory in the administration of public libraries. There was some impact from library administrators whose military experience during and after World War II had provided them with background and experience in some of the skills associated with administration, but that impact appears not to be a lasting one. A persistent problem in the education of librarians is that many of them enter the field because they have tastes and career goals almost antithetical to interests in supervision or administration. The fact that some prevalent characteristics of librarians (such as a sense of order) are the same as those important for persons in responsible positions does help librarians who do achieve work assignments where they have administrative responsibility.

A good outcome of the present-day emphasis on continuing education is that many library staff members are studying management and developing skills long associated with business, such as marketing, supervision, and program budgeting. Also relevant are the numerous in-service opportunities offered by individual libraries, library systems, library and management associations, and short-term courses aimed at librarians by universities. There are shortcomings in all of these, of course. One-day workshops or two-week seminars are usually aimed at the initiate in administration, and the individual who wishes to perfect administrative skills usually does so by studying in another field, such as business. As educational programs in business administration develop curricula in management of non-profit organizations, they become even more useful for public library managers.

There are problems in management or administration courses in library education programs. One stems from the aforementioned attitude of students, which often is, "It will be years (or never!) before I'm a supervisor or administrator. So why do I need this?" Basic or required courses in this area are difficult to design if they are to appeal and be useful to librarians in various kinds and sizes of libraries. In courses relating to specific kinds of libraries, administrative skills are more likely to be introduced with regard to development and management of budget and organization and supervision of employees. Except for the most clearly autonomous libraries, such as privately funded research libraries, the pattern is for most libraries to be part of some other system, so that many techniques of management are necessarily based on the requirements of the larger system. As an example, the reporting of statistics in a public library is most readily done to satisfy the requirements of the governing authority and in a format to make them most comprehensible when reviewed along with other educational or social agencies within that authority.

Problems relating to students in library education have been mentioned. Of equal or greater significance is the problem of recruiting faculty members with appropriate skills in teaching public library management. The advanced degrees customarily required for faculty members in graduate library education programs are in short supply among practitioners in public libraries, and there is little incentive for them to acquire them. So the teaching of such courses tends to be divided among librarians who teach on a part-time basis, the retired or semi-retired librarians who accept full-time teaching assignments, and the faculty members who combine little or limited public library experience with competence in management and teaching. This mix of faculty tends to produce a yeasty, practice-oriented approach to public library administration, but it does not provide well for the development of theory, for the encouragement of research on which theory can be based, or even for the adaptation of theory from other fields and specialties.

All of this is a long-winded way of saying that scientific theory has had little impact on the management of public libraries. Even when such systems as program budgeting are introduced to public libraries, they are promoted with appeals to common sense, efficiency, or economy. This is not always bad for public library management, but it does tend to make it a somewhat unsophisticated field and to make its practitioners somewhat insecure in their roles. All of these negative characteristics do have some positive results, however.

Managers who achieve positions of responsibility and prominence in public libraries tend to develop management styles of their own, and, with no formal pattern of internships, would-be administrators often learn from their seniors, either in a fairly formal way as staff assistants or deputies or by careful observation. Personal style is important, and when combined with experience in two or more public libraries, common sense, general competence, and openness to experience and learning, it can be enough to make an administrator not only competent but inspiring to others.

For a practical art or skill, management is fraught with immeasurable intangibles. The ability to make decisions, for example, is often recognized as an important managerial competence, but it is virtually impossible to assess except in practice. The individual who specifies the need to acquire every bit of information before deciding on a course of action may produce effects as disastrous as the one who delays for less important reasons. And the ability to lead or motivate others as a manager is one that may not be possible for a manager to transpose from direct limited supervision to a broader audience when moving to a position of greater authority. Even drive or ambition, usually required of persons who would be managers, may be possessed in inappropriate abundance, or may not be logically related to one's present competence, or may be resented or misunderstood by others lacking those same characteristics.

In librarianship, there are several specialties where some of the characteristics of good managers are almost negatively related to the work of persons in that specialization. Cataloging, for example, requires concentration on the specific in a way that may limit the competent cataloger from becoming a manager with the vision to see tasks as parts of a whole plan and to lay out reasonable standards of production for others to achieve appropriate goals. Librarians whose experience is largely or entirely in public service, on the other hand, may be unable to make the transition to making decisions about public service when they are deprived of regular, direct communication with the public.

The generalist may seem to be the person best fitted for public library management, and, because of the variety of sizes and kinds of public libraries and the common lack of competition for positions of responsibility, it is possible for one's whole library career to be spent in managerial positions or directorships. Personal and managerial style takes on increased significance in these instances. These individuals may seem to be the antitheses of the legendary well-meaning but bumbling bookmen of an earlier day, but they also usually lack the genius for innovation and the ability to conceptualize library goals and achieve them, which characterizes many administrators who have the advantages of rich practical library experience.

It should be clear that there is no one path, nor even just a few paths, to competent public library management. Characteristics of good managers may be translatable from one specialty within a field to another, but the need to be able to recognize, to define for others, to attempt to achieve, and to measure success in achieving the purposes and goals of public libraries is one distinctive characteristic that the public library administrator must possess.

The activities of a manager include direction, review, and evaluation of the work of others, decision-making, articulation of programs and goals, presentation of reports, determination of budget and other priorities, setting of structural and communication patterns within the library, implementation of policy, and representation of the library. As noted, these are similar in kind to the activities of other kinds of managers, but knowledge of public librarianship pervades all of the individual activities. Typically, a library's staff members look to the director as a role model, and expect that person to be knowledgeable and active as a leader in the library profession as well. This kind of activity—including writing, consulting, speaking, and service in library associations—is significant for an administrator in two major respects. Such activity has value for the library in extending its reputation and influence, which can have positive effect on recruitment, local support, and morale. And the second major benefit is that such activities provide the manager with an opportunity to work with peers and others outside of one's own area of direction. The testing of ideas, exchanging of problems and solutions, and learning how other similar libraries or institutions are administered are experiences that the manager needs to have for personal growth, which in turn further benefits the library and the profession.

Public library management requires knowledge of librarianship, its historical development, its diversity, and its place in the whole social setting, rather than simple knowledge of the status quo. Ability to learn from the experiences of others and to see relationships among various responsibilities can compensate for experience in the many different functions of librarianship, but recognition of their various relationships to the library's overall goals is essential.

Although it is fashionable to laugh at the stereotypical bookman-turned-manager, it is true that something is lacking in the library administrator who has never been touched by the passion to read and the enthusiasm to share the experience of reading with others. The initial passion may have been tempered by diffusion to other media, for all of the library's collections should hold interest for their manager, and the pressures of responsibilities may also have limited that person's time available to spend as a reader; but a library administrator who does not read in several genres for personal pleasure is one who probably performs the tasks of management without informing them with personal spirit.

ORGANIZATIONAL MODELS

Order and categorization are essential concepts of librarianship, so bureaucratic structures of management would seem to be logical extensions of those concepts. No library is too small to have such a structure, which may be recognized in the fact that, even in a two-person staff, one person must have the major responsibility. It should also be recognized that any formal plan for assigning tasks and responsibilities has a kind of shadow structure, sometimes parallelling it, sometimes supporting it, and sometimes contending with it. This shadow structure is composed of the personal relationships of the members of the staff, the proverbial grapevine of informal but library-related communications, and the other patterns of relationship that may be related to professional organizations or unions. The administrator who ignores these is naive, and although the one who uses them does so at some risk, there can be benefits to organization and morale in having access to them.

Most public libraries operate within bureaucracies, as well as containing bureaucracies. The manager, for example, may be, by virtue of having that position in the library, the head of a city or county department or a member of an administrative group directing the governmental unit of which the library is one component. In this assignment, the responsibility is not only to represent the library and to champion its interests, but also to relay and, when necessary, to interpret and to defend the decisions and policies of the larger organization. Because the library is often one of the smaller components of such an organization, directors who acquire the prestige and moral force to be recognized as spokesmen for the larger organization often benefit their libraries by enhancing their roles also.

An organizational chart outlining chains of command and communication is the most frequent statement of the library's internal structure. A similar one may show the library's relationship to other public agencies within the same sphere of government.

Recognition of the professional and administrative skills of engineers, accountants, personnel specialists, legal counsels, and others is important to a library's organization. It should be clear that the professional staff of a library is not limited to the librarians but includes a variety of professionals, some of whom may be retained on a consultant or part-time basis. Public relations specialists, for example, may be hired at times when new programs are being introduced, and legal counsel may be retained for times when they are needed. Personnel specialists and finance officers or comptrollers may be a part of the full-time staff. Having specialists in various fields can make it difficult to plan an equitable pay scale, because compensation needs to be related to the amounts specialists can command in other fields. Librarians often resent the intrusion of specialists into what they consider their field, especially at comparable or higher rates of pay. The individuals from other fields may, on the other hand, feel that they are making sacrifices to work in the public sector in libraries, although there may be compensations in such forms as reduced tensions and increased job satisfaction.

Professional personnel need to be aware of their places in a bureaucracy and of some of the constraints a bureaucracy places on them. Just as various jobs are closely related among themselves, the individuals performing those jobs need to know how and where they interrelate with others.

Participatory management is discussed more than it is practiced in public libraries. Initially, it is a very appealing concept, promising staff participation in management decisions. In practice, however, it can be cumbersome and disappointing. Individuals who clamor for it may find it embarrassing to have to defend an unpopular decision that they helped to make; and they may be surprised, if not appalled, to discover that their colleagues present views as much different from their own as those of the administration, and that these require exploration, review, and compromise. In such practices as team interviewing of candidates for employment, participation can take time and may result in the loss of promising recruits who are able to find employment more readily elsewhere, disappointment on the part of the team at having to accept compromise candidates, and/or confusion on the part of the interviewee about the chain of command and the responsibility owed to the person to whom the new employee may later report.

Participatory management usually results in a kind of controlled democracy, with final decisions made by the responsible manager, but with many people participating in the process. The result can be better understanding between manager and staff and development of staff competencies in such areas as human relations, decision-making, and responsibility. The practice of participatory management is not much different from that of open administration, and individuals may find the latter preferable when they consider the cost-effectiveness and the allocations of their own time in both kinds of administration. Readiness for participatory management requires the development of attitudes, skills, and information resources of the staff. It is not uncommon for initiates to participatory management to find that one of the first things they must discover or prepare is an agenda for action and decision.

Committee work within the library's structure can combine some of the best values of participatory management with responsible traditional management. Acting as information-gatherers, codifiers, and/or advisors, staff members can offer their recommendations to management and still maintain an independence that permits them to observe, evaluate, and comment on the eventual decisions.

It is usually far more difficult for staff to function effectively in relaying communications and rationales for decisions from top management to the rest of the staff than it is for them to represent staff views to management. This is true in participative management as well and is another of the problems in practice. Those who envision participative management as a means of sending and receiving full information to the administration and of having all views of the staff represented in decisions are doomed to disappointment. This kind of management is only as good as the lines of communication.

Collegial management, customarily practiced in public libraries in combination with other patterns, is most easily identified with organization by team or cabinet at the managerial level. While responsibility and authority are shared, still one person remains responsible for major decisions. When participants in the collegial group have positions of similar scope and responsibility as well as mutual respect, and when openness of communication and tolerance of divergent views are encouraged, collegial management is probably at its most effective. It, too, can be well combined with other organizational models, and it also can be practiced within individual units of the library. A subject department or a regional branch library, for example, may have a group of individuals with various subject or service specialties who may function in this way with the person in charge. It is usually not practical for all members of the staff at all levels of responsibility to be formed into such a group.

Ironically, it is often the new or the insecure manager who encourages more active participation by others in the management process. But strength and skill are, if anything, more necessary in these styles of management than in styles more autocratic in nature. To stimulate discussion, criticism, or controversy and then to be unable to channel it or respond thoughtfully to it is to create a merciless monster.

Also, it is easier to introduce guides for more open management after having established one's position than it is to regain authority once it has been dissipated.

Management models built on mutual respect and open communication are the ones that result not only in intelligent decisions and implementations but also in satisfaction on the part of the staff. The development of a better understanding of the risks and rewards of management is an asset not only to the library but to individual staff members who experience it.

THE LIBRARY AS A COMPLEX ORGANIZATION

The public library is always associated with a unit of government, a board, a system, a state library, or an administrator, and it has lines of responsibility with each of these. Within the library also, the lines of responsibility should be clear. Some functions may be advisory or exemplary, with individuals recommending actions or decisions to others or providing them with a model to emulate. Other functions may be directional, with a supervisor assigning specific tasks, setting schedules for work, and evaluating the work of others. These are customarily considered line responsibilities, and those where advice or example is offered are staff responsibilities.

The external functions that have their effect on the library, as noted, include the advisory assistance typically available from state library consultants or members of a library system's staff. These individuals may have no direct authority, but their power lies in the giving or withholding of support. This support is usually financial. A state library agency may, for example, limit the flow of federal or state funds to a public library on the basis of mismanagement. It may in effect require a reordering of priorities when a library has set goals at variance with those recommended by the state agency or system.

Yet state library consultants may serve as advisors to the library without having any direct authority, and they may be teachers, role models, confidantes, and sounding boards for the local public library's personnel. Such experience also gives added value to their opinions of individual directors or other personnel. Those opinions, when favorable, can be of great importance to an individual in terms of personal development, job opportunities, and general professional reputation. Thus, the state library or system personnel may wield considerably more influence than might at first appear.

On the other hand, the board or the governmental executive to which the library is responsible usually has the power to hire and fire as well as the range between of directing specific tasks, requiring certain standards of performance, and evaluating that performance. This power may be shared between a board and an executive, and many of the responsibilities associated with it may seldom be exercised. For example, library directors with considerable longevity may not be formally evaluated by the persons to whom they are responsible, but the fact that the power is still there certainly affects their behavior and is the ultimate evidence of their responsibility to the public.

The corollary to these external relationships is the assignment of line and staff positions within the library. Examples of the former are all supervisory positions, such as heads of branches, directors of central libraries and chief custodians. These individuals are customarily responsible for assigning tasks to personnel within their area of work, for evaluating their performance, and for judging and making recommendations concerning their tenure, promotions, transfers, etc. All of the direct supervisory responsibilities for personnel are theirs, although many of these may be shared. For example, in large libraries, supervisors of smaller units may not participate in selecting personnel for their units, and in many instances, the opinions or reviews of others may be a part of performance evaluation.

Staff positions, by contrast, are ones where individuals may have no direct supervisory responsibility (although in most instances, each such person supervises one or more persons, such as secretaries, assistants, etc.). The major thrust of their work is advisory. Specialists in services to various age groups may, for example, offer assistance to personnel in their respective specializations by providing in-service educational programs and by observing and commenting on work performance.

In practice, the differences between line and staff positions may often be blurred. Personal styles on the job may make many of the recommendations of a person in a staff position sound like directives, and they may participate directly or indirectly in the recruitment and evaluation of personnel; but they do so by working with the individual's supervisor. One major reason for dividing responsibilities by this staff-line rubric is to make it possible for individual staff members to receive help in improving their work without having to reveal their inadequacies or insecurities to the person who will eventually evaluate them. Other reasons include the fact that, being relieved of supervisory responsibilities, persons in staff positions can devote their competencies and time to planning and development of programs of service. It is not as easy, and probably not as desirable, for line supervisors to be free of program responsibilities, but their work requires opportunity to learn new techniques of supervision and to become competent in many aspects of service, such as maintenance of facilities for which they are responsible, which may not have been a part of their experience.

A continuing problem is the assignment of equitable status—including salary, perquisites, promotional opportunities, and freedom—to line and staff positions. The head of a branch may chafe, for example, at the necessity to adhere and to require others to adhere to strict time schedules necessary for public service, while the specialist in selection of materials may be equally concerned about meeting a variety of deadlines or working out a plan for reviewing materials, feeling all the while that these responsibilities limit the freedom that may be the most apparent characteristic of the job.

Typically, there are fewer staff positions than line positions, and good communications among both kinds of position that are in the same area of service are essential. Ideally, persons in staff positions may benefit and have better understanding of the difficulties of implementing their recommendations if they have had line experience. Some individuals are clearly more competent and more interested in one kind of responsibility than the other, but judicious management requires careful balancing of opportunities for individuals to have both kinds of experience.

Most organizational patterns in public libraries mix several forms of organization. Given the fact that the form of organization may be based on function, subject, clientele, geography, and format, it is clear that one library—for example, the Chicago Public Library, which has a Finance Office, a Business Science and Technology Division, a Children's Services Specialist, a Southwest District, and an Audiovisual Center—can have each form of organization represented. Problems with such mixes arise when there is inequitable allocation of resources among them or an attempt to fit incomparable elements into a fixed pattern. The important judgment is the decision about which kinds of services or functions are best divided in which ways. And the reason that flexibility of organizational patterns is important is to allow ways to reorganize or to modify patterns when use, novelty, physical facility, or other variables suggest the need for a change.

When a service or function is new, its relationship to other parts of the organization is difficult to ascertain. The initiation of data processing, for example, often occurs before the full implications and uses of the service are recognized. It may be associated with the financial or business functions of the library, and its place in the organizational pattern may be set accordingly. When the application of data processing to personnel records, inventory of collections, or circulation procedures is considered and implemented, though, the full benefit of the service may not be achievable without a shift of its place in the organizational pattern.

Similarly, when nonprint media were first introduced to public library collections, it was customary for a department or service area to be designated with the responsibility for selecting, maintaining, and recommending their use. However, this limited their integration into other parts of the library's collection and tended to stress the differences rather than the similarities that exist between these and more traditional media. A flexibly responsive organizational pattern can limit the problems resulting from such initial decisions.

Physical facilities are probably the most prevalent factor that conditions a form of organization. When a new central library is built, for example, it may include cataloging, acquisitions, bindery, and similar functional services. Similarly, where collections of materials are concerned, organization by subject is basically reasonable, but almost immediately, two problems arise: the cataloger who works in one or more specified subject areas may have, or may perceive, different relationships with the cataloging department and with the public service subject departments, and there may also be problems in integrating collection development activities among smaller units, such as branches of the library, and the subject areas.

Clientele as a determinant of organizational form may be divided several ways. Most common is division by age group, with children, young adults, adults, and senior adults being the usual categories. These divisions are more prevalent in terms of patterns of service, with personnel and programs designated to serve one of these groups, although collections may also be physically divided or designated as being of main interest to those groups. Recognition of the special needs of other population groups usually leads to some response in terms of organizational form. Thus, in a long historical span, some of the groups singled out in this way are immigrants, the poor, the Spanish-speaking, the blind, parents, the deaf, business personnel, the physically handicapped, shut-ins, institutional residents, students, hospital patients, and probably many others. As can be seen here, too, there is no one kind of category. Ethnic background, physical condition, location, and requests for special services are only a few of the identifiers for various groups.

There is a pattern often repeated in which a group identifies itself as wanting a specified kind of library service. The message may be conveyed in several different ways and to several different levels of the library's system of communication. Initial response may be informal, but as more parts of the library become aware of the request (as acquisitions or interlibrary requests for example, reflect the new request), there may be an effort to assess the library's present collections and competencies (number of Spanish-speaking staff members, for example) to respond. Although improvement of such service and integration of it into the library's full program of service may be the eventual goal, there may be a period of time when coordination of such service is a separate part of the library's pattern of organization. Consistent review and assessment of such designated areas of service are essential for several reasons: to ensure provision of good service and to note its special characteristics, to provide for the integration of special services when this can be accomplished, and to see that the service is coordinated with other parts of the library's program.

Geography as a form of organization can have several meanings, from the efficient allocation of space within one facility (e.g., having supplies and storage areas located near shipping facilities, with the several areas supervised by the same person) to division of supervisory responsibility for far-flung agencies of public service. The latter is more commonly recognized as a reason for consideration of geography in the pattern of organization. Proximity and availability are important for supervisors, so it makes sense to have supervisory responsibilities divided so that districts or regions are assigned to supervisors. Sometimes, this may be done with several branch libraries clustered with a larger regional library. In other instances, the supervisor may work from an office or library in the area but without having the responsibility for one of the libraries. Specialists in some services, e.g., outreach or children's, may be assigned by area or district, also providing staff assistance just as the supervisor provides line direction. Sometimes, division of a whole service area may be on a simple geographical basis, with boundaries dividing the areas fairly evenly and usually combining various publics in each area. Sometimes the division is made on the basis of similarity of publics, so that a supervisor who is skilled and experienced, for example, in providing service to the urban poor has leadership responsibility for branch libraries that serve that public primarily. Because service to shut-ins, institutional residents, and others usually cuts across all geographic boundaries, coordination of all aspects of service is a significant responsibility. The balance between providing general library services and offering services for specified population groups can be difficult to maintain, but coordination of work assignments and an open system of communication are important components of such balance.

Government documents, rare books, and nonprint media are three examples of formats or kinds of material that may be organized for use in a way that affects the pattern or organization. When formats cut across several subject areas and audience groups, as these do, and when special staff are needed to provide access and information so that most effective use can be made of them, it seems logical to consider housing them in separate areas and treating them as separate services. There is a trade-off between the advantages of providing for their more efficient use and of ensuring that the public will have access to them in conjunction with the use of other resources. In this respect, unified catalogs of all parts of the library's collection, communication among personnel and encouragement to refer to such collections, and thoughtful promotion to the public about these collections are important for their best use.

COMMUNICATION AS A MANAGEMENT TOOL

The two most difficult things for a novice manager to learn about communication are that what one says is important and that what one says is not important. An offhand comment about a color preference or a style for letters may start ripples of change resulting in torrents of reaction, while a carefully, logically prepared directive on how a new service is to be offered may be cheerfully disregarded as irrelevant or sulkily received without much comment or concern about its implementation.

Internal communication sets the style of the manager. Meetings, conversations, and written materials are all parts of this. Individual style should be encouraged, but some consistency among managers is also desirable. For example, if positions are available and advertised in different parts of the library, it is reasonable for them to be in similar formats not only so that they can be read and compared, but also so that a record of job descriptions can be compiled and used.

While communication is usually seen as being vertical—i.e., linking individuals at various levels in the library—horizontal communication among peers has considerable importance. In a large library, this may be the hardest to achieve. When newcomers, for example, want to get acquainted with others also new to the library staff, they may not even know how to go about finding their names. In these and similar instances, library-related groups such as the staff association may be helpful. So may be thoughtful administrators who assist such communication. Horizontal communication can be a good way to defuse many difficult situations when a telephone call or a visit to determine facts or to observe a service or program can avert or diminish problems that otherwise might affect other people. If one subject division, for example, receives several complaints from its users about the poor service of another division, the best response may be the simplest: to relay the comments, without evaluation or further comment, to the other division and/or to visit it and to learn what factors—shortage of personnel, loss of some equipment, or difficulty with telephone service, to name only three—may have caused the complaints. If all else fails, one division head may feel that it is necessary to report serious problems in another division to a supervisor, but the result can be resentment, backbiting, and further deterioration of service and communications.

It is easy to assume that too little or no communication is the common problem, but in reality, there can be problems just as great if there is so much communication that significant or urgent matters (not necessarily the same!) are buried with the less critical. Many communications turn out to be explanations, expansions, or corrections or earlier ones. Careful preparation of communications in the first place should ideally include having one of the audience to which it is addressed receive and respond to it to check for clarity and tone. When that is not feasible, review of the content by the originator may accomplish the same purpose, if some time is allowed to elapse after the first writing.

Effective communication also entails using the means most appropriate to disseminate information. The astute manager knows how to use the grapevine as well as the dictating machine, and when to schedule a meeting instead of issuing a memorandum. Meetings, for example, are useful when one wants to get a range of reaction, wants to present information and get reactions promptly, and/or wants to have participants hear the views of others; but written memoranda are good for one-way communication or for laying out procedures that need to be clear and available for a number of people to follow.

Written communication can have added impact if some codification of it exists. Staff manuals in which directives are compiled and organized for easy reference are indicators of a well-managed library. Before a procedure or recommendation is added, it may be tested for clarity and utility as a memorandum. The addition of new items or substitution of revised items in a staff manual should be a regular process, so that a manual is not static; but too frequent revisions can mean that decisions are not made with consideration of their long-term impact or that some items are not drafted clearly in the first place.

Usually significant for good morale is a staff newsletter. These are sometimes informally prepared, sometimes sponsored by the staff association or a similar group. If prepared by volunteers, the newsletter can scarcely be an official communication, but there is an argument for having such a publication be a lively and informative part of administrative communications. Announcements of personnel actions such as transfers and promotions probably should be a regular part of the newsletter. Other features may include reports of conferences from the point of view of staff members attending, comments on service from the public, or information about forthcoming events or new programs of the library. Few people write well when they wish to be informal, and careful editing of such a newsletter includes the responsibilities to improve writing as necessary and to provide coverage on some equitable basis, so that the same people or parts of the library are not always highlighted. These are good reasons for this editing to be a part of administration, with appropriate support, but at least when it is not, the administration must allow it freedom and scope.

Information that staff members need to do their jobs—outlines of procedures, forms for reports, recommendations on how to work with the public, etc.—should be available for handy reference at all locations where it is likely to be needed. This may require the preparation of numerous copies and the maintenance of a supply, but the effort pays off in good communication, which in turn pays off in good morale and good service.

It is always difficult to determine what information should be distributed to staff in advance of or in conjunction with public announcements. Decisions affecting individuals, e.g., resignations or transfers, should be announced with some consideration of their wishes in terms of timing, but when a choice must be made between the preferences of an individual and the welfare of the institution, the latter has clear precedence. For example, when an administrator is planning to retire, the individual may prefer to give minimum notice and to leave with little fanfare, but if the position is important enough, there must be time to advertise for and to recruit an appropriate successor.

There is nothing intimate or confidential in a library's employing more than, say, five people, but most staff members will make an effort to treat as confidential what is presented to them in that way. Staff morale can be enhanced when information is given to the staff before it is generally released, but timing is important. The news value of information about a major grant can be greatly diminished if it is common knowledge among staff before it is announced publicly, but even simultaneous receipt of the information via the library's own channels can inform the staff and make them feel like participants in the action rather than observers only.

Reliable delivery systems within the library are essential. These may require truck deliveries to branch libraries, systematic telephone communication, and messengers to carry materials within buildings or fairly short distances outside. It is also essential for the delivery system to be seen as a channel of two-way communication, with information coming to the administrative offices being handled as expeditiously as the information given out from those offices.

Oral communication—including individual or group conferences, meetings, the grapevine, and telephone conversations or conferences—is an important part of the communication process. Direct immediate replies, group responses, and enhancement by body language or tone of voice are among the advantages or oral communication. Among the disadvantages are the lack of a record of decisions and the difficulty of easy review or recording of events. Coordination of written records with effective oral communication can enhance both kinds of communication. It is increasingly common for individuals to be willing to comment in conversation on what they would not write. Information about personnel references, evaluations of service, or recommendations about future directions may be more easily obtained in conversation than in writing, and there are good reasons for using these channels of communication.

The management of meetings, where oral communication is central but where written agendas and highlights or minutes support the record of action, is an important administrative skill. Repetition of discussions, inequitable time for various participants, and overemphasis on one-way communication are among the problems to be avoided. One of the best effects of well-managed meetings is that others learn by example how to conduct such meetings themselves. The benefits to the library, and potentially to society, can be immeasurable.

Although the grapevine of communication has been mentioned from time to time, it is seldom treated seriously enough by administrators. It is the informal means of communication that links various levels and areas of the library. Its rapidity is legendary; its reliability is usually fairly good, and, since its content includes opinions, predictions, and hypotheses as well as facts, that reliability can be high when more of the predictions come true than not. It can be risky for an administrator to use the grapevine for issuing communications, but it is useful to know what the grapevine is reporting, not only because this is one way of knowing what staff members are hearing and saying, but also for two other reasons. The grapevine reveals the informal links among the staff, so that family and social relationships and sources of influence among the staff can be seen. The administrator may also occasionally need to correct an exaggerated story that appears on the grapevine, or at least be aware of it in communicating with staff or the media.

The media of external communications for the library are also diverse. It is essential to have a formal plan of public relations, with a staff responsible for preparing informational releases, fielding inquiries from the media, assisting other staff in recognizing what is newsworthy and publishable, and getting the best coverage from such media as newspapers, television, and radio. While a media representative may wish to feature children as users of the library, the library's own specialist in public relations has the responsibility of seeing that other publics of the library are also highlighted from time to time. The specialist is also the person who may need to prod library staff members to make the most of their efforts by publicizing them or allowing the specialist to publicize them—as effectively as possible. A library page who wins a musical competition or a librarian who spends a vacation on a climbing expedition in Nepal should be featured as part of the library's public relations program. Too often, media representatives respond to the public library's public relations efforts by saying, in effect, "Yes, it's very nice, and you do good work, but it's not news." The knowledgeable library publicist can help to stimulate news stories as well as to write them.

In the area of external public relations, lines of communication are especially important. Individuals seeking back-up information for wire service stories about censorship cases elsewhere should know that at least one library staff member can assist them. It is not always easy to provide necessary information on some of the library's problems and to present the most favorable possible image of the library, but a public relations staff should be able to achieve that more often than not. The staff need not be large, nor need it be devoted exclusively to this function in smaller libraries. However, it should be designated for this purpose even on a part-time basis, and its purposes, functions, and lines of communication and responsibility should be clearly understood both within and outside the library.

Libraries often have areas designated for exhibits and displays and for public programs associated with them. There may be a variety of reasons for such displays: to feature the accomplishments of members of the library's community, to attract newcomers to the library, to call attention to some part of the library's collection or service, or to enhance the attractiveness of the library. At different times, staff members may be faced with having to choose from several possible exhibits or having to scrounge for prospective exhibits. Selection of appropriate exhibits is an important aspect of public relations, and guidelines or a policy statement may be necessary. The librarian who casually rejects an offer of a collection of beer cans for display may find that action hard to defend if the next display used is a collection of stamps. Is the latter more library-related than the former? And are library exhibits not intended to attract new publics? The newsworthiness or personality of the exhibitor may be a factor in determining the value to the library of having such an exhibit. The knitting of a pro wrestler or the photography of a congressman's wife may have value far out of proportion to the objective evaluation of their abilities.

When displays or exhibits are selected, most of the task still remains. Mounting them effectively, publicizing them, providing security for them, and maintaining them (e.g., straightening the pictures displayed in a meeting room) are all parts of the effort. Preparation of reading lists related to the exhibits is often a much-appreciated contribution of the library and, when done well, their usefulness can be extended far beyond the location and time-span of the exhibit itself.

Public programs, such as receptions for the artists or craftsmen exhibiting or talks by critics, may stem directly from the exhibit, but thoughtful planning may extend to more serendipitous possibilities. Photographs of a community may be a good backdrop for a series of talks and films on community life or home maintenance, just as African students may be good speakers with a local resident's display of artifacts from that continent.

The amount of time and effort required to make the most of an exhibit should be assessed as carefully as possible before one is undertaken. The length of time for an exhibit should also be stated clearly for the sake of the exhibitor, the public, and the library; and "down-time," the period of time between exhibits, should be kept to a minimum. A long-range plan for what is to be displayed should provide for appropriate seasonal exhibits as well as balance and variety among those used.

For an institution committed to obtaining and disseminating the publications of others, the public library is conspicuously poor at producing and disseminating its own publications. Annual reports, book lists, flyers announcing special programs or services, directories of personnel, evaluations and reports of projects are examples of materials regularly prepared by members of the library staff but of interest to the public. The ideal would probably be to have one staff member or office designated to collect and distribute such materials after the initial supply has been disseminated. Often, the individuals who prepared the reports or other materials wish to handle the publication as well, but there usually needs to be more attention paid to three points: continuing to have items available in response to requests, designating and reaching a larger audience than the one initially envisioned, and maintaining the library's historical record.

More ambitious publications—such as histories of the library, catalogs of special collections or exhibits, or biographies of early directors—are sometimes undertaken by libraries. When a wide audience and an extended publishing life are possible for them, another publisher should probably be sought. Unless the library wishes to make a major commitment of funds and staff on a long-term basis, even with production details handled elsewhere, its continuing involvement in publishing is questionable.

It is a truism that any library's real public relations program is everybody's job. The atmosphere of a library's public service areas, the tone of voice of a desk assistant, the provision of information by an administrator's secretary are a part of that program. They need not ooze sweetness and light, but they should be pervaded with a sense of purpose and of respect for the library's community—and that includes its potential as well as its present public, the youthful non-reader as well as the library-minded civic leader, and the new U.S. resident with limited skills in English as well as the senior citizen who considers the library as a daytime home.

Informal, consistent, two-way communications with the community are most effective. Government agencies, institutions such as churches and schools, community organizations, and local newspapers may be ways of reaching out to the community; but visits to local businesses, maintenance of a mailing list for individuals who want to know what is going on at the library, and courteous service to those who use the library are other elements of good public service that are also good public relations. The two-way emphasis is important. The library that maintains a community bulletin board may have easier access to neighborhood stores to post announcements of library events.

Ideally, every aspect of library service should be available throughout the library, regardless of the size or location of the agency. It should be natural for desk assistants to suggest reserving or requesting from elsewhere in the library a title or information on a topic about which a library user inquires. Information about such services as those for the blind or shut-ins should be available, not just in the parts of the library where they are provided, but also in every area where inquiries might be directed. It should go without saying that public relations requires internal communication to be as effective as external communication. The staff member who notices a heavy demand for certain materials and finds that it is stimulated by contest questions serves the library as well as its users by alerting other staff to the demand. Follow-up action may include encouragement of photocopying to prevent loss or damage, reserving of some items, and/or extensive searching for other sources of the information.

One of the most ticklish problems of public relations is how to publicize the library's needs and problems. Should the impact of overdue and lost materials on the library's resources be stressed so that people are aware of the importance of responsible borrowing? Or does negative response ("Well, if they keep things out, I will too!") outweigh the advantage? Similarly, if the library needs more money but is competing for public funds with police and fire personnel, how does it state its case most persuasively? Good public relations personnel differ among themselves as to the answers to these and other questions, but they should know that the decisions on what to publicize and how best to do so involve the administration and other staff of the library, the governing unit, such groups as the "Friends of the Library," the media, and the community at large. The day-in/day-out effort of maintaining good public relations pays off when problems can be shared and solved, just as achievements can be shared and appreciated.

MANAGERIAL STYLES

The style actually used by most successful managers is eclectic, drawing upon the several major types and depending on the situation, the personnel involved, and the goal. To confuse the matter further, declarations and self-analyses about styles are seldom accurate. The manager who says, "I never make a decision without arriving at it with my team," may sound as though he's working on a collegial basis, but if what the team sees is only a finished version of his proposal as it goes before the board for review, they may more accurately consider him autocratic in style. For that matter, there are elements of each of the major styles within any one style, and when combined with capriciousness, varying senses of time, and different kinds of communication, each style may appear to be in some aspects different from what it is.

There are few true autocrats in public administration, but dominant personalities and articulate leaders may appear to work in an autocratic way. Often, they have one or two close associates, not necessarily their deputies or individuals in high level positions, who are their advisers, sounding-boards for their ideas. The person who tends to be an autocrat probably has the greatest difficulty in manipulating communications because she or he is torn between plunging through all levels of personnel or administrative structure to get or to give the desired information and between observing the sense of order and rank that is usually a strong characteristic of the autocrat. True to the initial syllable of the word, autocrat, the manager who is one uses all of the first person pronouns frequently. It is always "my library," "my staff," "my new charging system," "my annual report," regardless of the originators of the work or even of the manager's tenure with the library. Although austerity and aloofness are often associated with the autocratic style, personal charm can disguise much of the emphasis on self in the manager's style. A self-effacing manner, epitomized in the administrator who, on the point of retirement, shuffles about and takes a step backward saying, in effect, "Aw, I didn't do so much," without referring in any way to the broader picture and many other doers present, may go with the autocratic style to disguise it further.

There are times when a library needs to be organized or reorganized or to exert more leadership and drive than it has in the past. And an autocratic administrator may be most effective in such times, being willing to accept the risks of making changes and to do so without waiting for cumbersome machinery of administration to function. But long-lasting accomplishment usually requires a different style simply because the initiative of others within the system is likely to be stifled during the tenure of an autocratic administrator; and a library can not survive to very good effect without the development of other staff members and the mix of ideas and efforts that they can help to produce.

The supportive administrator is customarily working best with a board or other agency setting the job framework. This person's style is low-key and directed toward others, both in responsibility and in implementation of decisions and ideas. Precedent will determine many decisions, and the style may be extremely popular with a staff that enjoys the security of encouragement and that does not require the stimulus of leadership from the top manager. Logic and predictability are likely to characterize this manager's actions, although, as noted, the eclecticism of most management styles in practice means that the supportive manager, also, will occasionally break out of a pattern in order to accomplish a specific goal.

The facts that most public libraries have grown in size in the recent past and that there is in society more emphasis on participation by a variety of individuals in decisions have resulted in a generally more team-oriented approach to administration, with a collegial manager working with other responsible staff members in the style of an ideal dean and faculty. As has been said of faculties, the team assembled by such an administrator needs to be well-balanced, but that does not require individually well-balanced people. Quite the opposite. Diversity and innovation can be encouraged as long as an open, collegial atmosphere exists. Responding to the individuals fairly, the collegial manager may encourage competition among them and, when channelled appropriately, this competition can strengthen and refresh the library.

The stir of competition among staff members not only tends to develop their individual competencies, but when necessary decisions are still made by the collegial administrator with consideration for the diverse elements within the system, there can still be unity and direction in the library's overall management. The collegial manager is more than a chairman or a team captain; this person functions as a participant in the open atmosphere for which she or he is responsible, and, if effective, many of the ideas or proposals that come from others will be recognizable as ones that the manager initiated or encouraged to develop. In the long run, satisfactions may well come from the development of other individuals who may compete for leadership, just as frustrations are likely to be caused by the openness of atmosphere and the exchange of ideas that have been allowed to develop.

In a way, the custodial administrator is a mix of the supportive and the collegial. In this view, management is a trust placed upon one person who is likely to be more concerned with preserving that trust than with creating a reputation or insuring a future new job. This type of manager too, is most effective when associated with a stimulating and stimulated staff to assist in making and implementing decisions; but this person is not likely to attract or to encourage that kind of staff. There are times when libraries benefit from such custodial managers, usually epitomized in the interim administrators appointed after a more highly visible or imaginative manager has been in charge. Literally, the custodial manager would seek to maintain the status quo, but the problem is that it is extremely difficult to determine how much action is required to maintain that status quo and whether the status quo can be maintained. The mistake most often made by the custodial administrator, and often made by others as well, is to believe that lack of action or decision-making can allow a library to continue to function as it has in the past. In fact, what is likely to happen is that it will founder or at least fall behind in response to its community. Inertia as a motivating force does not generate itself, although it can sustain a library for a period of time. When the custodial manager is able to use that time to plan for the future, to evaluate the past, and to persuade others of the need for action, this may be most effective; and since this manager, like others, is probably eclectic in style, those plans may be accomplished.

Managerial styles are more varied than this brief statement can describe, and in practice, when they are often combined, they become even more varied. The skillful manager not only knows how and when to use the styles best for a specific purpose, but also how to encourage others to develop complementary styles and assist in the achievement of the best for the library. As is true in most enterprises, the real measure of the accomplishments of the person at the top is the extent to which colleagues have developed, ones who are able not only to succeed but to surpass their leader in some respects, at least.

THE LIBRARY PROGRAM

Although the term, program, is used in many ways with reference to the library, it has an encompassing meaning as the total of all of the actions and plans that affect the objectives of the library. Building programs, programmed budgets, public programs, and others are only some of the aspects of the overall program. The function of planning is itself an aspect of the program that it helps to achieve. It is simply a fact that a library has a program, whether the manager or others advert to it or not. What they can provide is the dynamism and the care to make the program viable and good.

Planning techniques are pretty much the same in many enterprises. Implementation of them requires a constant sense of reality and imagination. Realistic planners need occasionally to free themselves of tradition and of concern with the necessary limitation of resources in order to "blue-sky" what they hope to accomplish; but they also need to be able to readjust their thinking and their plans in realistic terms of time, finances, and other resources when that is the appropriate next step. Especially in this last quarter of the twentieth century, a time of general conservatism and retrenchment following a strong expansionist period, planning is important. It is necessary to plan for limitation of resources just as much as for their development, but it is not likely to be as personally or professionally satisfying.

Planning techniques include the identification of the area or situation to be planned. It is necessary to see that area or situation in context without being distracted by peripheral details. A series of questions may suggest the format for planning and might include these: does something need to be done? if so, what? who can help to decide? what resources, including time, will be required? how can these be best deployed or utilized? how can a solution or recommendation be attained? is it possible to develop a flexible plan that may be implemented in whole or in part, or over some period of time? if possible, is it desirable? what other parts of the system are likely to be affected by this plan?

An essential technique in planning is the ability to state and to structure questions so that they will lead to a logical conclusion. And, while a sense of orderly progression is important, the good planner also needs to be able to move at different paces and to adjust intermediate objectives in order to achieve what is appropriate or possible at a given time. Let us say, for example, that a library is planning for the more equitable deployment of service over a fairly large geographic area, and priorities have been established for where new library locations are required. In a middle-priority area, a site and the money to develop it become available. Good planning suggests that these should be utilized, even if they delay some higher-priority development, but the overall plan and the recommended priorities are not discarded. The problem with many excellent planners is that they can not adjust to the practicalities of time, other resources, and pressures when those affect their lovingly developed plans. That means, of course, that they are not really excellent planners, although they may have the reputation for being such.

Some constraints on planning are self-inflicted. The manager who allocates time for planning a program and who does not recognize the need to adjust that allocation is placing a constraint that may doom the plan that emerges. There also needs to be room for conflict or at least differences in point of view in the development of a plan. One advantage of having these expressed in the course of planning is that they may help the planners to anticipate what negative reactions they may encounter when the plan is presented to others. Consensus may not be possible in every aspect of the plan, but participation should be such that the planners have some loyalty to the overall effort and can even defend aspects with which they may not have agreed initially or about which they have their own reservations.

Some element of confidentiality is essential to most planning. Details need to be defined and the ways of handling them settled. Alternative approaches need to be explored. The impact of the plan needs to be considered, and the means of announcing it in its final form must be determined. Interim reports on the content and the general progress of planning are important, not only for the morale of the planners, but also as a means of insuring that the staff and the community as a whole will be prepared and interested in the forthcoming plan.

Interestingly enough, plans developed within libraries and for libraries often fall short in a most unlikely respect: failure to review the collective experience of other libraries either through the literature or through communication with people who may have participated in similar plans or dealt with similar problems. Part of the difficulty probably lies in the conviction that one library's experience is so unlike any other's that a review of history may not be productive. This conviction is strengthened by the hunch that it may be as time-consuming and costly to look into records as it is to stir around in one's own planning sphere. Add to that the likelihood that the former activity may not be nearly as much fun or as stimulating as the latter, and the reasons why initial research is often minimal or poor are clear enough. Yet people who may not have much else to offer to the planning effort may be tremendously effective in searching out information about similar efforts or in helping to determine that there is little that is similar. Their talents should be utilized, just as those of the imaginative thinker should be utilized in planning. This search is a part of the technique of seeing the area of planning in context, and it should not be omitted.

While it is important to maintain some confidentiality in planning, it is also important to have some range of people involved. This range would usually include persons other than staff members of the library, and when plans concern other agencies or organizations, it is essential for them to be involved as early as possible in the planning. One of the most difficult kinds of organizations with which to deal is the local community group. Hidden hierarchies are powerful in such groups, and currently elected officers may not be the real driving force of such organizations. While it is desirable to approach such groups in as straightforward a manner as possible by communicating with the titular leaders, it is a good idea to keep in mind that another layer of leadership may be discovered, and that it, too, will need to be informed if not involved in the planning. Similarly, there are often more than one community group to speak for an area, and the library can ill afford to "play favorites" among them. Since the library itself should be neutral territory, the best plan may be to issue as open an invitation as possible for all interested groups to participate in a planning session there.

There are lulls and flurries in every planning operation, and to the extent possible, personnel who are engaged in planning need to be aware of this in the beginning, and to realize that there may be times when plans are being reviewed by others so the only thing to do is to wait, just as there may be times when the need for revised estimates or new ideas or information requires several people to drop everything else to provide for that need. Morale and commitment on the part of planners must be high to overcome the problems that would otherwise be associated with such time patterns.

Often a good approach to the initiation of planning is to describe the project or action to be accomplished to as many individuals as might be likely to be involved eventually, and then, openly, to designate some persons from that group and some others to become the organized planning group. The first group may be asked to communicate ideas and suggestions to the second group, and it may be required to report progress on some regular basis. This permits a flow of information, but it also permits the planning group to work without a lot of checks. As the group's work cuts across the work of others, more individuals may be invited to participate more formally in its activities. In a large library, it may be easy to envisage this kind of operation, but it is equally desirable in a small library, where each group may be proportionally smaller but where the same needs exist to provide information and freedom.

Short-range operational planning is usually done fairly well in libraries. There is a monthly and an annual rhythm to reporting and to the need for decisions on budgets, bids, establishment of new positions, termination of projects, etc., that makes it fairly easy to plan for a year at a time. This is true at all levels. Public programs and exhibits need to be planned in advance, and seasonal planning works fairly well.

Almost unconsciously, staff members develop skills in this, assessing available resources, determining community interests and needs, evaluating staff members and collections and facilities, and allocating the necessary time and budget for the activity. Yet in two areas, problems customarily arise: a failure to recognize that staff time itself is customarily the most expensive resource to dedicate to an activity and lack of recognition of the need to coordinate planning with all who might need to be at least informed if not involved.

The problem of time allocation is important, because individuals typically think of their own time as being within their power to allocate, and they may be unaware or uncaring about the need to assist in other areas. The head of a community library, for example, may see that the library's participation in the local art fair is important and may be planning toward that end until brought up short by news that the children's librarian will be attending a puppet workshop over the art fair weekend and that the proverbial mainstay assistant is being married on the same Saturday. While all the vicissitudes of illness, accident, etc., can not be anticipated, a good manager needs to be able to plan with some assurance that staff support will be sufficient and, ideally, that other staff members can be encouraged to share that manager's interests and enthusiasms for the commitment made on behalf of the library.

The coordination of planning is related to this point, but it may involve more than internal resources. While it is clear that planning for a new facility will almost immediately require coordination with outside groups, it may be less clear that even activities that will be conducted within the library should be brought to the attention of others while in the planning phase. And this should be done as a point of information and coordination, not just when financial or moral support is sought. Both oral and written communications are important. Informal reporting of forthcoming activities at meetings of community groups may help to achieve some coordination, but written announcements of developing plans should also be distributed.

Long-range planning—interpreted here as being longer than one year—occurs much less effectively. For this reason, public libraries are often in the position of responding to outside pressures rather than creating pressures and plans of their own. The difficult point here is also the coordination of timing. As the area served by a library grows and changes, it is important for its personnel to be aware of planning needs for services in terms of collections, staff, and physical facilities. Regular review of earlier management decisions is important, and so is the acquisition of information about the community and the plans of other public agencies. Too often, the library manager reads about a plan for a new shopping mall or subdivision in the newspaper and notes that one idea is to have some public services, such as libraries, included. An important aspect of long-range planning may be the provision of information to other units of the governing authority about what the library's major priorities are.

Long-range planning also requires accurate, current information about the library's present resources and plans. Commitments to present programs may need to be reconsidered before a major shift of focus is contemplated, and there also needs to be concern that necessary support is not removed from day-to-day operations in order to achieve some far-off goal, unless it is a goal so overwhelming that the day-to-day operations can be required to suffer in this way. For example, when a plan for establishment of several major regional libraries is underway, it may be necessary to deploy some personnel planning time for that effort, but it is unconscionable to let regular maintenance of existing facilities fall behind while concentrating on new ones.

Too often, discussion of what libraries will be like—or should be like—in the year 2000 is scheduled away from one's own library, so that managers discuss the future among themselves and return to share with their staffs and communities only their immediate concerns. More "blue-skying" on the part of staff is good, but this is not real long-range planning. That effort would also benefit from wider participation and concern. It would also have the effect of making plans for the future develop from needs of the present, which would make staff more responsive to their implementation. Interestingly enough, people who are defensive about the need for change in the immediate future are often most aggressive in recommending drastic changes on a long-range basis because they see those as more remote, less threatening. If really free in terms of personal security and openness of discussion, many people have valuable comments to make concerning the library's long-range goals and plans.

A review of how libraries' futures have been projected and proposed reveals that technology has developed at least as rapidly as predicted, but its implementation, and especially its implementation on a broad and equitable basis, has lagged far behind that rate of development. And the library's capability in developing personnel with more sophisticated knowledge about technology and its usefulness to others is also more limited than the dreamers anticipated. Overlooked, all too often, were the ethical concerns about responsibility for collection development or programming. Also overlooked was the need to develop greater individual commitment on the part of those engaged in planning libraries to be more aware of all of the parts of life around them, which, in turn, have much to do with necessary library planning.

Long-range planning is really not for the dreamers and predicters. It needs to be based on realities and information, not just ideas for the future. It needs to be attuned to fiscal and political realities as well as to bibliothecal and community potentials. Like most aspects of administration, it requires a top manager with a sense of purpose and imagination who is secure enough to be surrounded with similar and complementary staff members and advisers.

SUGGESTED READINGS

Asheim, Lester. "Library Education and Manpower." *ALA Bulletin* LXII (October 1968), 1096-1118.

Berelson, Bernard. *The Library's Public.* New York: Columbia University, 1959.

Bloss, Meredith. "Standard for Public Library Service—Quo Vadis?" *Library Journal* CI (June 1, 1976), 1259-62.

De Prospo, E., and others. *Performance Measures for Public Libraries.* Chicago: American Library Association, 1973.

Drucker, Peter. *Management: Tasks, Responsibilities, Practices.* New York: Harper and Row, 1974.

Edwards, R. M. "The Management of Libraries and the Professional Functions of Libraries." *Library Quarterly* LXV (April 1975), 150-60.

Etzioni, A. *Modern Organizations.* Englewood Cliffs, New Jersey: Prentice-Hall, 1964.

Evans, G. Edward. *Management Techniques for Librarians.* New York: Academic Press, 1976.

French, W. *The Personnel Management Process*. 3rd ed. Boston: Houghton Mifflin, 1974.

Garceau, Oliver. *The Public Library in the Political Process*. New York: Columbia University Press, 1949.

Ladenson, Alex. "Is the Library an Educational Institution?" *Wilson Library Bulletin* LI (March 1977), 576-81.

"LJ Mini-Symposium: The Branch Library in the City . . . Options for the Future." *Library Journal* CII (January 15, 1977), 161-73.

Martin, Allie Beth. *A Strategy for Public Library Change: Proposed Public Library Goals–Feasibility Study*. Chicago: American Library Association, 1972.

Monroe, Margaret. "A Conceptual Framework for the Public Library as a Community Learning Center for Independent Study." *Library Quarterly* LXVI (January 1976), 54-61.

National Commission on Libraries and Information Science. *Toward a National Program for Library and Information Services*. Washington, DC: Government Printing Office, 1975.

Public Library Association. *Minimum Standards for Public Library Systems*. Chicago: American Library Association, 1966.

Shields, G. R. *Budgeting for Accountability in Libraries*. Metuchen, New Jersey: Scarecrow, 1974.

Stevens, C. H. "Governance of Library Networks." *Library Trends* XXVI (Fall 1977), 219-39.

Trezza, A. F. "The Role of Local and State Government." *Library Trends* XXIII (October 1974), 229-38.

Young, Virginia. "Library Governance by Citizen Boards." *Library Trends* XXVI (Fall 1977), 287-97.

MANAGING THE COLLEGE AND UNIVERSITY LIBRARY

by Duane E. Webster

INTRODUCTION

During the last decade, the management function in academic and research libraries has gained a great deal of attention. In part, this is due to the growing size and complexity of these libraries, which creates new needs for accountability and coordination. It is also due in part to demands for improved service, which come at a time when the budgets of these libraries have stabilized and costs have skyrocketed. Such pressures have led academic libraries to rethink managerial philosophies and roles. This paper reviews the key issues associated with recent efforts to strengthen the management of academic libraries, with an emphasis on describing some of the major concepts and trends influencing library managers today.

The single most important challenge facing the academic library manager is securing constructive change and improvement in library performance. Any organization must grow and develop in order to successfully accommodate a changing environment, and libraries are no exception. If libraries are to succeed as active partners in the instructional and research programs of universities, they must be sensitive to changing conditions both within their internal structure and in the external environment. This requires an improved ability to perceive changing circumstances and to use that information in an internal decision-making process that allows for a flexible, timely response. Furthermore, the library must move toward a more assertive role within the community it serves, influencing university plans, programs, and priorities rather than simply coping with events as they occur.

PRESSURES FOR CHANGE

Economic, societal, technological, and institutional changes exert strong pressures for libraries to alter the way in which they deal with their client groups, their governing bodies, and their internal operations. The most obvious pressure for change is financial. The recent high rate of inflation, the need for more equitable library salaries, and the dramatic increase in costs of library materials—combined with relatively stable budget allocations—have moved academic libraries from the period of growth and expansion that characterized the 1960s to a period of stabilization, with the prospect of irreversible deterioration of library capabilities. However, the financial troubles that beset libraries have some positive implications. Libraries have been forced to re-examine and redefine their roles in higher education, research, and public service, and to develop new systems and procedures for fulfilling those roles. Furthermore, these financial pressures have forced more careful consideration of fundamental innovations in collection development, resource sharing, and use of technology. Library managers accustomed to budgetary growth must now plan library development under conditions of severely limited resources.

Another perceptible pressure for change involves libraries' client groups, which have more diversified interests than ever before and have increased the intensity of their demands. Library users today are more sophisticated, possess higher expectations, and want more assistance in using library resources. As a result, libraries' service requirements have tended to increase in both dimension and areas of specialization, while net available resources have declined. Consequently, a new emphasis on biblio- graphic instruction and expanded services can be seen developing in libraries. A further response to user service pressures has been adoption of technological developments that enable libraries to restrain costs and improve services—especially in areas such as cataloging, processing, and circulating material. In addition, significant service improve- ments are emerging in such areas as bibliographic access to on-line data bases.

The character of academic institutions is also experiencing alterations that exert great influence on libraries. Increasing costs and limited funding have prompted acade- mic fiscal conservatism that looks to target areas for cost savings, demands new and better-articulated budget requests, and calls upon the library administration to take an active role in fund raising. Furthermore, competition among academic departments for limited funds has siphoned off traditional faculty support for the library budget. Declining student population forces academic institutions to compete for enrollments. This development calls for all parts of an institution to look at how they might help strengthen the competitive posture of the college or university. In many instances, the library is the most visible educational resource and can contribute to the univer- sity's attractiveness. And maybe most important, there is a basic reshaping of higher education programs. Professional and career-oriented courses of study are increasingly popular, as students seek a challenging education that leads to achievement. New interdisciplinary course work places special strains on library support, and more and more professors are looking at innovative ways of teaching.

The size, complexity, program emphasis, and decision-making style of the parent academic organization shape the management approach and operating philosophy employed in any academic library. It is abundantly clear that the library manager must find a way to tune into the distinctive organizational context of higher educa- tion, both in order to secure necessary support for library services as well as to influ- ence and shape university planning and program decisions. In addition to these environ- mental forces, a series of historical, situational, and resource characteristics exert con- siderable pressure on library managers. These forces are related to the distinct nature of an institution's collections, its bibliographic structures, and the staff, which consti- tute the principal resources of the library.

Academic library collections provide support for the research and educational programs of the parent institution. Therefore, the development of these collections requires librarians to develop close working relationships with the teaching and research faculty as well as with university planners. Academic collections frequently stress coverage by unique titles and aim at program comprehensiveness rather than user access and convenience. The amount of world publishing has grown exponentially during the last decade, and libraries have attempted to maintain collection strengths by radically increasing the size of their collections. This has led to multi-million dollar budgets, large staffs, new buildings, and increased organizational complexity. The managerial process, in turn, has had to become more sophisticated, more technical, and less directly personal in order to direct this rapid growth. While managers at one time focused on amassing collections, facilities, and staff, it now appears that managerial attention is more directed toward the effective utilization of these resources.

The bibliographic structures designed and maintained by academic libraries also reflect the needs and interests of the parent institution. These structures are often prepared as scholarly tools, with elaborate attention paid to the quality and extent of the bibliographic access. The result is critical but costly, requiring elaborate and time-consuming attention. As time progresses, the tool becomes even more costly. Certainly, changes are required to allow libraries to continue providing this service.

The staff of academic libraries also comprise a distinct managerial challenge. The interests, values, and orientation of staff members again reflect the character of the academic institution of which they are a part. Many staff possess extraordinary credentials in terms of advanced degrees, language specialties, and research skills. The choice to work in an academic setting is influenced less by economic considerations and more by environmental and situational factors. Yet there are changes occurring in staffs' expectations and demands regarding their role in library organizations. Staff members are demanding increased organizational attention to their professional and personal needs and are seeking job responsibilities so that they can contribute more meaningfully to organizational goals. This has forced management to move toward more open organizations with wider staff involvement in decision making. While this trend offers opportunities for creative, positive change, it also creates tensions and frustrations for library managers accustomed to more traditional modes of authority, responsibility, and decision-making. Library managers, like managers in other enterprises, find traditional management styles and leadership assumptions increasingly less effective.

The existence of these pressures for change is apparent. Yet universities and their library components appear unable to define new roles and performance expectations for these libraries. Staff protests, faculty complaints, and abrupt changes in directorships are symptomatic of the failure of academic institutions to deal successfully with the fundamental issues of change.

A CONCEPTUAL MODEL FOR CHANGE

There is a view in some academic circles that changing the library director is the best way to resolve the "library problem" and to secure required improvement in library performance. In the past, executive leadership has often served as the primary impetus for building excellent library collections and service programs. However, the more we learn about the dynamics of organization and the pressures facing libraries, the more disillusioned we become with simplistic answers and quick solutions. As noted earlier, the director is frequently dealing with issues beyond his or her control and is not getting needed support from either the university or the staff. Library and university managers have had limited experience with planning change and almost no opportunity for acquiring the skills needed for involving staff in change processes. Thus, the issue of change in libraries deserves a broader examination within a conceptual framework that relates inputs and outputs to library programs and managerial processes. The systems view of organizations offers such a framework.

A contemporary approach to understanding the complex relationship between the academic library and its environment is to portray the library as an open system made up of a variety of sub-systems interacting both with each other and with the environment. The systems view of organizations defines libraries in terms of 1) the inputs (i.e., resources) required to operate them, 2) the managerial processes employed in utilizing these resources to meet desired objectives, and 3) the expected outputs from these several processes and activities. These various components and sub-systems all exist within an environment and must maintain a dynamic relationship with that environment. As external pressures increase, library managers are forced to make design adjustments in the areas over which they have control in order to respond more effectively to demands for improved performance.

Academic library input generally includes four basic resources: facilities, collections, personnel, and annual financial allocations. The unique aspects are the library facilities themselves and the collections. Invariably, the facilities and collections have enormous impact on the way the library operates, the nature of its organizational structure, and the type of performance it is able to achieve. Understanding and characterizing the impact of such facilities and collections is a critical part of understanding any library system.

The managerial processes by which these resources are employed to meet desired objectives will be discussed in detail in the following section. Essentially, four interacting variables make up management processes in library organizations. The first is definition of organizational objectives. Every library operates and provides services with certain purposes in mind; for example, libraries build bibliographic structures to provide efficient access to the libraries' collections. Another variable is organizational structure. Every organization has a broad, more or less permanent framework that arranges the workflow and allocates resources and people in some sort of sequence and hierarchy. The third variable is the human element. Organizations get work done through people. The way in which these people are employed and how they work together is a critical question in the study of organizations. Human abilities can be categorized as knowledge, skills, and attitudes that are brought together for the accomplishment of organizational purposes. A fourth variable is technology—the technical tools and problem solving interventions like work measurement, automation procedures, and so forth that are used to improve the efficiency of the organization. Automated circulation systems, the Anglo-American Cataloging rules (AACR and AACR 2), and the Ohio College Library Catalog (OCLC) are examples of technologies used by libraries. Most organizations attempt to incorporate technological advances and provide tools that enable people to perform tasks more efficiently.

The management processes that take place within a library allow the inputs/ resources to be brought together in a way that desired outputs are achieved. The performance of the library is the final element of the systems view of library organizations. The outputs of a library generally are viewed as the activity level of its several units, the use of its service and facilities, the satisfaction of information needs of its constituents, and its support of university programs. Considerable attention is currently being devoted to developing more concrete measures of library performance. Concepts such as availability, accessibility, and utility are being employed to assess the effectiveness of collection development efforts. The attention on performance assessment is deserved because of the need to demonstrate accountability and the effective management of limited resources.

In summary, a systems view of library organization portrays the essential components of library operations as a dynamic process of resource input, management processes, and performance. The parts themselves are of less significance than are the varied and multiple relationships among them. Changing any one of them will clearly affect all of the others. This approach to library organization allows careful examination of optional managerial responses to environmental pressures.

The following sections address the key issues related to the management processes and their relationships to organizational change, including goals and objectives, human resources, organizational structure, and technology.

GOALS AND OBJECTIVES

Traditionally, the standard library functions provide the core around which structure, people, and technology are deployed. Various organizational studies have defined library functions as including: acquisition of library materials, processing of materials, development and maintenance of bibliographic structures, access to library collections and information, instruction in the use of library materials, and overall management and coordination of library resources.[1,2] Understanding and effectively directing these activities continues to be an important concern of library managers. The emphasis, however, is shifting from organizing and controlling activities to a concept of managing for predetermined results. Instead of reacting to situations or problems with an ad hoc decision, there is an emerging orientation toward defining what is being accomplished and developing the capabilities needed to work toward desired future objectives. The requirement for library managers, then, is to define what the library has to do in order to obtain the continued support, financial and otherwise, of the university. This might be viewed as a process of defining goals, objectives, or priorities.

Many libraries have recognized the importance of developing a formal, carefully considered system of goals and objectives, one that emphasizes results and toward which all library programs, procedures, and operations may relate. The advantages of an objectives-oriented management process are numerous. Goals and objectives statements provide staff members with a basis for understanding and accepting the library's purposes and functions; they formalize assumptions; and they promote mutuality of intent. A system of goals and objectives also can assist with allocation of resources, setting of priorities, measurement of library performance, and promotion of library activities to users and the university community.

Establishing written objectives for planning is vital for any organization that wishes to make rational, informed choices from among various courses of action. These courses of action may be oriented toward short-term objectives capable of complete accomplishment or they may be directed toward approaching an ideal condition, possibly unattainable in the absolute sense. To be meaningful, however, objectives must be stated realistically and must take into consideration the various factors that will play a role in their realization, such as time, human resources, and financial resources.

For many libraries, the assignment of formulating or revamping a comprehensive goals and objectives system is an onerous chore. Unclear or ambiguous views of library purpose, unranked priorities, real differences of opinion, and skepticism among staff members as to the utility of goals and objectives statements have proven to be obstacles to the development process. In order to diminish these difficulties, many libraries are now following a systematic procedure in developing goals and objectives statements.

Basically, two strategies are used in developing objectives: first, the development of broad overall system side objectives, which are then translated into unit and individual goals; and second, the specification of present activities, which leads to the development of unit and individual goals. A model process developed by the Association of Research Libraries (ARL) Office of Management Studies begins with obtaining support and a firm commitment from the library's top management.[3] The orientation in this process is toward creating statements that reflect an accurate assessment of the parent institution's missions, goals, and objectives; environmental factors; and clientele needs—both current and projected. The model suggests recruiting the general staff to help formulate individual departments' goals and objectives, and developing mechanisms for periodic review, evaluation, and revision of the statements. Final steps involve informing staff and university officials of the new goals and objectives statements and then using them in the library's operations. Essential elements in this approach to the formulation of goals and objectives statements include: greater precision in describing both unit and individual goals and objectives; greater concern with determining those goals that are quantifiable and with determining ways to measure level of achievement; broad staff involvement in the goal-setting process; recognition of the need to coordinate goals and objectives from disparate departments and units; and inclusion of justification statements rationalizing individual goals and objectives.

An example of the second approach to the development of library objectives was employed by the McGill University Libraries with assistance from the ARL Office of Management Studies.[4] This approach emphasizes unit review of present activities as a step toward conceptualizing objectives. In this format, staff are involved in a training and developmental effort aimed at clarifying current activities and obtaining agreement and commitment to future directions.

Regardless of the method used, it is widely viewed that organizational purpose should determine library functions and the way in which work is organized, performed, and evaluated. The management process is viewed as a resource for getting people to work to achieve definitive results instead of performing routine activities that have a historical precedent but may not make any useful contribution to library success today. This orientation toward purpose allows a movement away from reactionary or crisis management, and it also suggests a different approach to the management of human resources.

HUMAN RESOURCES

The managerial emphasis on achieving results requires an organizational setting wherein talented people can work together to accomplish library objectives. Generally speaking, this is a movement away from a system of tight control and authority over the work of staff to a system of individual commitment to organizational goals and self-direction. This movement focuses attention on issues of motivation, individual development, performance appraisal, supervisory style, and staff development.

In the area of motivation, considerable study of people working in organizations suggests that individual needs are much more complicated than traditional carrot/stick or reward/punishment philosophies recognize.[5, 6] While financial incentives are basic, current management thinking provides for motivational factors in addition to monetary incentives. The fundamental idea is that the work itself is a basic motivational force. Meaningful work that clearly contributes to library goals can go a long way toward securing high level performance from its staff members. Staff want to be able to advance personally and professionally. Finally, individual contributions should be encouraged and recognized. This view of motivation calls for supervisory styles that emphasize coaching and development of staff rather than close checking and control.

The rise of the faculty status movement in academic libraries is one obvious example of staff searching for structures that allow an expanded role for individual contributions. But more important and widespread are the changes resulting from management's attitudes and its awareness that staff have much to contribute to the design of libraries' objectives, policies, and procedures. There is evidence in recent library studies that staff and administrators can collaborate rather than compete in win/lose struggles to resolve each other's commitments to the organization.[7, 8]

This process of shared commitment and responsibility has created situations where individual growth can proceed within a context of organizational growth, one in which the skills and understanding of individual library staff members can be more fully utilized, providing greater fulfillment to the individual while enhancing the performance of the library. The growth of the individual is no longer restricted to increased technical awareness but includes an increased understanding of the opportunities and constraints facing libraries and the array of forces leading to managerial decisions. Fuller involvement can and frequently does lead library staffs to an expanding awareness of the library's problems, and to solutions.

Innovative approaches to performance appraisal are particularly illustrative of the changing climate in libraries. Peer review processes, based on dual considerations of individual professional growth and individual contribution to organizational performance, provide one such approach. Another is the rise of goals-based performance review programs that move away from traditional review of individuals' personal characteristics to review of individuals' actual job accomplishments. Of particular significance is the rise of review processes that focus on problem-solving and planning, rather than on merely identifying past successes and failures. Many of these processes include, and even emphasize, elements of career counseling and staff development. What appears to be happening is a restructuring and reordering of libraries' reward systems, so that remedies are more important than punishments, the future is more important than the past, and the provision of opportunity for individuals to grow is as important as the administration of salaries and wages.

The preceding changes can occur only to the extent that library managers and supervisors see them as helping to achieve results. The increase of faculty governance structures within libraries, the apparent stronger roles of committees and task forces, and the increased recognition that management alone cannot solve the library's problems have led to renewed consideration of the proper role of managers. While individual leadership styles continue to vary, managers are increasingly turning to their staffs for advice, counsel, and feedback on major decisions. This shift from the more autocratic traditional leadership model is responsive to both staff and management needs, and it creates a requirement for a new set of leadership characteristics and skills, including negotiating among diverse interests, communicating effectively within the organization, and tolerating some diffusion of power.[9] While there may not be a single best leadership style that fits everybody in all situations, it is clear that library managers are experimenting with alternative approaches that lead to increased staff commitment and higher morale. Such changes may be more obvious when they occur at the top, but there is substantial evidence that the same shifts are occurring at the department and work unit level. Front-line supervisors also recognize the value of mutual trust and supportive relationships for getting the job done.

Another area of human resources receiving increased attention is staff development. While libraries have traditionally supported personal professional growth through tuition assistance plans and support for conference attendance, there has been some movement toward operating on-site development and training programs that provide skills and knowledge specifically required by the organization. These programs range from formal training in catalog filing to instruction in management skills such as communication, supervision, and employee counseling. In many cases, training programs have been developed and operated with the recognition that the development of library staff is an important task in improving organizational performance during periods of financial decline, particularly in labor intensive organizations.

One approach to filling libraries' needs for special skills and expertise is the recruitment and utilization of non-librarian technical and managerial specialists. In larger libraries, this has included specialists in personnel, budgeting, planning, facilities, and automated systems. The number and range of these positions have increased in recent years, particularly in libraries that have grown substantially in dimension and complexity. This trend indicates a realization that a range of non-library skills is needed, and that in many cases, these skills are not available among professional library staffs.

The movement in human resource management is toward making greater use of the various staff resources in determining the desired results of both unit and overall library performance and the manner in which these results will be achieved. People are employed in an organizational situation where their role and contribution is valued, recognized, and well used. Opportunity for growth and accomplishment is provided, while the goals and objectives of the library are recognized as the reason for existence. A principal means for relating individual needs and aspirations to library goals and objectives is the organizational structure for distributing authority, resources, and responsibility.

ORGANIZATIONAL STRUCTURE

The people of the library staff are generally deployed within an organizational framework that establishes and delineates functions, reporting relationships, staff size and span of control for administrators, distribution of financial resources, and decision-making methods. One way to present this structure is through an organization chart. The charts used by libraries generally describe the reporting relationships among the various units within the library. The major determinents of organizations—such as physical facilities, finances, university requirements, historical background, communication patterns, and the presence of key advisory groups—are less frequently described.

We have learned from the study of library organizations and their historical development that organizational structures that have simply evolved without specific planning may be unable to meet current needs. We have learned that organizational design and structure require systematic study and fresh thinking. Clearly, the organization's structure should follow a strategic pattern of development. Any work on structure must start with objectives in terms of a clear understanding of the reason for a particular library and the distinctive contribution that the library expects to make in the future. Sound organizational structure needs both a hierarchical structure of authority, decision-making, and accountability as well as flexibility to organize temporary groups or individuals for work on projects or problems of temporary concern.

Two fundamental organizational questions confront every library manager. First, how should the work and resources be divided (i.e., the structure of the organization) and second, once this division is secured, what are the best ways for coordinating these efforts in an effective fashion?

There are at least three basic ways to approach academic library structures: functional distribution of responsibilities; organization by product, process, or project;

or distribution of responsibilities based on geographic or subject area. In practice, most libraries use a combination of forms, since each structure is good for some things but no one structure is good for all things.

In the functional organization, for instance, there is division of labor, budgets, and work responsibilities, all on the basis of special competence. The functional organization emphasizes grouping of activities related to a particular central activity such as reader services, technical services, reference cataloging, or acquisitions. The principal advantage of a functional organization is that the emphasis is on performance of a particular activity. Thus, it is possible to get in-depth competence focused on that function, and to bring together an array of specialists who can work with each other and can, in fact, specialize in that particular functional area. This results in rather stable, predictable execution of that function. The drawbacks to this form of organization are that it promotes interdepartmental conflict; that few members of the unit will have a good overall picture of the library organization, resulting in major decisions being pushed to the top of the organization; and that it is difficult to shift or to accommodate new directions and projects. A serious consequence of these factors is that it is difficult to introduce changes within a functional form of organization.

A second organizational form centers on a particular process or product. In libraries there is an increasing incidence of special organizational forms that focus on the delivery of services, such as access services, or on the completion of specific products, such as catalog cards, processed books, or instructional assistance. There are also examples of temporary organizational forms being created to complete projects, such as planning on closing the catalog, conducting a management study, or reviewing and analyzing the library's collections. In this form of organization, people do multiple tasks and integrate their skills around a particular output. In this mode, coordination with different parts of the organization is essential, and a fair amount of power and influence can go to those who are able to produce or deliver a product or service effectively. The strengths of this approach are that it promotes teamwork, encourages coordination around a particular output, and allows people the opportunity to develop a variety of skills, including interpersonal skills. The principal advantage, however, is the emphasis on completion of a particular service to users or of a particular product that is visible and valuable. A drawback to this form of organization is that in-depth subject competence is not encouraged, and thus it is harder to attract specialists. In addition, internal priorities in the functional areas sometimes conflict with the product or project. And in certain instances, involvement of staff in organizational studies can be time consuming and expensive. Organizational focus on completing a product or delivering a service also requires conceptual and interpersonal skills that frequently are not readily available in library organizations. And finally, this form of organization requires multiple working and reporting relationships, which are an unfamiliar pattern of operation.

A third form of organizational structure in libraries is a geographic or subject branch form. In these settings, service facilities are established to meet on a decentralized basis the particular needs of a college, of a professional school, or of a distinct group of faculty within the university. In this type of organizational form, the services offered may range from a very minimal type of available book collection service to a complete range of bibliographic references, curriculum planning, and in-depth professional assistance. An advantage of this form of organization is that it provides personal and rather individualized service to faculty, which results in a strong relationship between library and faculty. A disadvantage is the expense of operation and the duplication of resources that might be available elsewhere on campus. This costly duplication of effort is frequently compounded by poor use of highly skilled professional staff, who are forced to manage clerical and routine duties in addition to their own service responsibilities.

It is clear that organizational design depends upon the nature of the work and the capabilities of the staff. In those situations where the work is product-oriented, such as in technical services, the best approach is to organize around the work flow in a fashion that allows development of quantitative measures of productivity. In situations where collections and bibliographic tools are the cornerstone of services, then these collections and tools must be organized and staffed in a way that allows easy, convenient user access, which suggests geographic groupings. Where collection development and instructional services require dynamic professional attention, a structure should allow maximum flexibility and individual initiative independent of facilities and technical restraints.

Organizational structure and strategy is a critical tool that a library manager can employ to enhance performance. While there is no perfect design, the organizational structure has an extensive impact on both people and the organization's performance. Equally important in making full use of resources and securing changed performance is effective application of technological advances to the execution of library tasks.

TECHNOLOGY

Simultaneously with the increased influence of behavioral science on management, libraries have seen substantive technological developments that have considerable potential for restraining operating costs and extending service capabilities.

Automation through computerization is currently being used to accomplish a variety of necessary tasks in libraries. Surveys by the ARL Systems and Procedures Exchange Center identified the major targets for automation as the acquisition, cataloging, and circulation functions in academic libraries.[10, 11, 12]

The procedures required to acquire materials—including searching, selection, input of order information, fund accounting, receiving, and processing—are highly labor-intensive when handled manually. In addition, academic libraries are coping with growing amounts of published information, continuing user demands and acquisitions workloads, and more complex bibliographic and management information needs. Since the early 1960s, many academic libraries have turned to automation to deal with at least some of these challenges. Most libraries report that automation has helped to standardize processes and has resulted in more efficient use of staff, but few libraries report reduced costs for processing as a result of automated acquisitions.

Libraries have been developing and utilizing automated cataloging systems since the mid-1960s. Although some early development was directed toward local systems, the emergence during the late sixties and early seventies of national or regional on-line networks has proved of most significance to academic and research libraries. While some benefits have been production-oriented, such as rapid production of catalog cards, the shared on-line systems also have led to economies in original cataloging by providing shared catalog records to all users of a particular system.

The largest shared cataloging system is the Ohio College Library Center (OCLC), with over 800 participating libraries. Other systems include: BALLOTS, developed at Stanford University and used by over eighty libraries; the system developed and used by the New York Public Library; the UTLAS system available to Canadian libraries from the University of Toronto; the Washington Library Network (WLN); and the Library Data Management System developed at the University of Chicago.

Circulation systems are also a frequent target for automation. In fact, nearly all libraries without circulation systems cite lack of funding as the reason for not automating. The decision to automate is based upon the need to handle routine tasks more efficiently and to release staff to handle direct public services, as well as to reduce costs per item processed. For the most part, circulation systems are able to effect these changes in libraries. Reduced costs are attributed mainly to the ability to handle increased workloads by existing staff rather than to any reduction of staff size.

In addition to these major functions that are being automated, there has been considerable advancement in enhancing bibliographic access services in academic libraries. Not only do automated catalogs represent an advancement in managing the technical service people and tasks, but the potential of improved access for users to the library holdings is also possible. Furthermore, on-line access to data bases and literature search services such as ERIC, MEDLINE, Lockheed Information Service, and the Systems Development Corporation provide new dimensions of library service that have yet to be fully exploited by the library's clients. While the promises and potentials of automation are high, it seems that automation has not had as much impact upon library procedures and performance as was predicted in the 1960s. Only a few libraries report having truly integrated multi-functional systems, and there is little evidence that automation has resulted in large-scale redefinition of library tasks.

In general, however, academic libraries reportedly have benefitted from the use of automated systems. Some of these benefits have been economic, but the most important have been performance-based. It is also clear that these systems are relatively young and that libraries' experience with them will lead to additional developments, both in the systems and in the organization and programs of the libraries themselves. Automated internal systems also provide the first step in the development of a national library network. They allow dialogues among libraries to occur efficiently and inexpensively, and they indicate the potential for greater utilization of the nation's library resources.

In recent years, considerable progress has been made in developing improved automated systems and technologies for libraries. Libraries, however, have experienced some difficulties in introducing these technologies and frequently do not fully exploit the added capabilities. But the need for cautious advancement in this area is clear. The speed of technological change makes it difficult to assess the utility and permanence of many of these systems. In addition, it is impossible to gauge the full impact of a new technology on library service operation or clients. Given such constraints, libraries must carefully study new developments and follow rational systematic procedures for introducing these changes.

CONCLUSION

Organizations tend to foster the continuation of the status quo, but internal and external pressures produce change in all organizations. External or environmental pressures include inflation, reduced public support, technological developments, and increased client needs. Internal pressures include changing staff values and attitudes and the tension that develops within organizations operating with stable or declining budgets. To the degree that these forces are operating, it is not a matter of whether an organization will change, but rather, how it will change and whether it will control and influence change or simply react to it as it occurs.

The approaches to change that have developed in libraries represent attempts to place the organization in a proactive rather than reactive stance. These approaches frequently include attempts to gain further understanding of environmental factors, but usually they lead to internal changes designed to deal more effectively with largely unchangeable external factors.

In the future, these management issues will continue to challenge the ingenuity and creativity of academic librarians. Attention needs to be paid to the methods used for selecting, developing, and promoting the talent needed for effective library management. Clearly, not all librarians are suited for managerial responsibility, yet organizational structures and reward systems force them into career patterns that can be unrewarding to them and to their libraries. The leadership roles of library managers need further refinement to allow a proper focus on creating climates where the full potential of a talented staff can be directed toward accomplishment of clearcut library goals. The training of these library managers should emphasize development of a self-awareness of their managerial strengths and weaknesses, as well as an enriched repertoire of skills, techniques, and concepts. Their leadership responsibilities in libraries will emphasize new roles in interpersonal relationships and communication.

This movement toward coordination of a complex enterprise of highly professional and dedicated staff calls for improved methods that can help these managers in introducing change, solving problems, and making decisions. Some efforts in these areas are underway. One approach has been the development of organizational self-study programs in which library staff identify strengths and weaknesses among the library's management systems and procedures and recommend changes. While this process in the past has occurred in an ad hoc fashion, with committees or individual administrators dealing with specific areas of interest, there are several recent examples of comprehensive, structured self-study programs involving large numbers of staff. One such program, the Association of Research Libraries' Management Review and Analysis Program (MRAP), has been applied to 22 ARL member libraries.[14] The Council on Library Resources-funded Academic Library Development Program at the University of North Carolina at Charlotte is another example.[15] In other instances, individual libraries have designed and operated their own self-studies without outside assistance. The programs have been experimental in nature and have recognized the organizational benefits of developing among staff a greater awareness of organizational constraints and a stronger commitment to alleviating the impact of those constraints on organizational performance.

It is easy to criticize the variety of management systems and innovations developed over the years in libraries and other organizations. Unfortunately, many ineffective theories and techniques have been marketed to libraries desperately looking for good, quick solutions to tough complex issues. Despite this, academic libraries must continue to invest in new efforts and experiment with new ways of looking at issues and operating these institutions. Only through aggressive, effective leadership of these organizations will academic libraries maintain a central role in higher education.

NOTES

[1] Morris Hamburg and others, *Library Planning and Decision-Making Systems* (Cambridge: MIT Press, 1974).

[2] Booz, Allen and Hamilton, Inc., *Organization and Staffing of the Libraries of Columbia University: A Case Study* (Washington, DC: Association of Research Libraries, 1973).

[3] Jeffrey J. Gardner and Duane E. Webster, *The Formulation and Use of Goals and Objectives Statements in Academic and Reserach Libraries* (Washington, DC: Association of Research Libraries, Office of Management Studies, 1974).

[4] *Staff Performance Evaluation Program at the McGill University Libraries* (Washington, DC: Association of Research Libraries, Office of Management Studies, 1976).

[5] Harry Levinson, *The Great Jackass Fallacy* (Boston: Harvard University Graduate School of Business Administration, 1973).

[6] Harry Levinson, *Psychological Man* (Cambridge, MA: The Levinson Institute, 1976).

[7] Duane Webster, "The Management Review and Analysis Program," *College and Research Libraries* 35 (March 1974), pp. 114-25.

[8] Association of Research Libraries, Office of Management Studies, *List of Management Review and Analysis Program Reports* (Washington, DC: Author, 1978).

[9] Harlan Cleveland, *The Future Executive: A Guide for Tomorrow's Managers* (New York: Harper and Row, 1972).

[10] Association of Research Libraries, Office of Management Studies, "Automated Circulation Systems in ARL Libraries," *SPEC Flyer 43* (Washington, DC: Author, April 1978).

[11] Association of Research Libraries, Office of Management Studies, "Automated Acquisitions in ARL Libraries," *SPEC Flyer 44* (Washington, DC: Author, May 1978).

[12] Association of Research Libraries, Office of Management Studies, "Automated Cataloging in ARL Libraries," *SPEC Flyer 47* (Washington, DC: Author, August-September 1978).

[13] Association of Research Libraries, Office of Management Studies, *Annual Report, 1977* (Washington, DC: Author, 1978).

[14] Association of Research Libraries, Office of Management Studies, *List of Management Review and Analysis Reports* (Washington, DC: Author).

[15] P. Grady Morein and others, "The Academic Library Development Program," *College and Research Libraries* 38 (January 1977): pp. 37-45.

MANAGING THE SCHOOL MEDIA LIBRARY

by Chase Dane

EDUCATIONAL SYSTEMS AND THE SCHOOL LIBRARY

We tend to forget that the American educational system is different from that in most other countries. Ours is a state system rather than a national system. This goes back to the Founding Fathers, who omitted education from the Constitution at their convention in Philadelphia. Anything not prohibited by the Constitution or not covered by it was left to the states. So, since 1787, education has been the right of the states rather than of the federal government. This has shaped the entire development of education in the United States.

The differences between a state and a national system of education are profound. Under a state system, as in the United States, education is largely a local affair. Boards of education are elected by the local community and are responsible for running the schools. Local boards hire a superintendent, who in turn hires administrators and teachers. There are state boards of education, and they do establish policies and guidelines for the districts in the states, but most of the educational program is left to the local communities.

Under a *national system* of education, the minister of education establishes the policy for the whole country. There is a national curriculum, teachers are hired by the central government and assigned to local schools, and taxes to support education are levied nationally. The result is a uniform system of education that is basically the same throughout the country. As a result, changes come slowly, but when they do come, they have an impact on all schools in the land. Schools are not truly community schools and do not always reflect community needs and desires. Authority is removed from the local community, and the schools tend to resist change.

With a *state system*, we establish the concept of the neighborhood school. The school is responsive to the needs of the community, which results in great diversity and, often, in rapid change. When a school board fails to change with the community, its members are voted out at the next election. The community does not have to wait for the national government to swing into action. A state system is less ponderous, and it is able to change direction in a brief time.

So, in the United States, the schools belong to the people. They become whatever the people want them to be. The school library is a part of the school, and its aims must be the same as the aims of the school. If a community desires a return to basics—a re-emphasis on reading, writing, and computation—the school library, along with the school, must do what it can to achieve this. If the community wants more vocational education, the school library will reflect this—in its collection, its program, its services. The school library and the special library are alike in that they both must serve the larger organization of which they are a part. The school library cannot have aims of its own. It exists to help the school achieve its goals.

This accounts for many of the characteristics that distinguish the school library from other types of libraries. It explains why the school library's collection of materials is primarily curriculum oriented. A good school library does have a broad collection of materials, but most of its materials will be related in some way to the courses of study offered by the school. The level of materials will coincide with the grades where a subject is taught—United States history in the fifth and eighth grades, biology in the tenth grade, civics and government in the eleventh grade. When students come to the library, they often come with their class, and the librarian must work with a group of patrons who are all approximately the same age. This is seldom true of other types of libraries. And not only are all the patrons the same age, but they may all be looking for the same information at the same time. It is as though the public library at ten o'clock in the morning were filled only with fifty-year-old patrons all seeking information on economics.

FUNCTIONS OF THE SCHOOL LIBRARY

The functions of the school determine the functions of the school's library. To discover what the school library is supposed to do, we must know what the school is trying to do, and this changes from time to time. Lists of what schools should do appear frequently—in newspapers, in professional journals, and in textbooks. A recent list stated categorically that schools have five main functions: 1) to introduce children into the society of which they will become working members as adults; 2) to sort people out for different future roles by grading, testing, evaluating them while they are in school; 3) to give students knowledge and training in the skills they will need to succeed in life; 4) to encourage creativity and self-reliance in students and to develop their communications skills; 5) to take care of students—keep them healthy, out of trouble, and off the streets. Any number of similar lists of functions of the school could be made; but taking this one set of functions as an example, what do they mean for the school library?

In order to introduce children into the society of which they will eventually become working members, the school library must have a good collection of career education materials. At the elementary school level, these materials will be largely exploratory in nature. Today, there are excellent materials available on career clusters—health services, construction work, service trades, manufacturing industries, food production, and merchandising. In keeping with today's media center concept of the school library, these materials will be both print and non-print. The school library will offer career materials in many formats—books, pamphlets, 16mm motion pictures, sound filmstrips, cassette tape recordings, microfiche, and study prints. All are designed to help students explore the world of work.

At the secondary school level, these materials will offer more how-to-do it help. The library will contain materials with information on the training necessary for a particular job, on how to conduct a successful job interview, and on the rewards and compensation to be obtained for the work. All of these materials must be updated constantly. The school library differs from some other types of libraries in that it is not primarily interested in preserving materials for historical research. The school library collection of materials needs to be current, attractive, and relatively small in comparison with the collections of many other types of libraries. The emphasis is on use and value now—not tomorrow or ten years from now.

Sorting students out for the different roles that they will play in the future is mostly done in the classroom. Teachers test, grade, and evaluate their students. The school librarian does this sometimes but never as much as the classroom teacher.

However, the librarian often supplies students with the materials that will prepare them for tests and examinations, unless these are based solely on the textbook. Modern education plays down the importance of the textbook, and a good teacher encourages the use of many sources of information. The school library or media center is the logical place to keep these materials, which are usually too expensive to be housed in the classroom, except on a short temporary loan. In the library, they are available to all students, and the cost can be spread out among all the students who use the materials.

The school library helps brighter or slower as well as average students, not by testing them but by providing them with materials suitable to their needs and abilities. The school media center contains simple as well as advanced materials on the same subject, for use by students of different abilities. The school library assists students after they have been sorted out by testing, rather than by participating in the actual testing. True, the media center does participate directly in testing and sorting when the librarian gives quizzes at the end of a library skills lesson, but this is a minor role.

ROLE OF THE SCHOOL LIBRARY

The library's main role comes when the school seeks to meet the third function—to give students knowledge and training in the skills they will need to succeed in life. One of these skills relates to the student's need to continue education after school. Many, perhaps most, of the jobs that will occupy students after they become adults do not yet exist. If they are to become successful adults, they must know how to use a library and its many sources of information after their formal schooling is over. This is why lessons in library skills usually form an important part of the media center's program. Reading will also be an essential part of this training for successful adult life. And the library contains the kind of reading material that they will need to prepare for this future. The library's media collection covers the basic knowledge students will need after they leave school, and the librarian will show them how they can use this collection to meet their needs now and in the future.

The library or media center also helps the school in meeting its fourth function—to encourage students to be creative and self-reliant. The student who has learned how to use the library to find information has already become self-reliant. This person does not have to depend on a teacher or parent to supply the wanted information. The student knows what can be found in the library and how to find it. The librarian's lessons in how to use the card catalog or how to use simple reference tools like the encyclopedia and almanac and atlas have shown the way.

The media center aids the student in being creative by showing, through books and films and filmstrips, what others have done in art and science and history. Creativity begins with something old and expands it into something new. The media center is filled with the ideas of writers, artists, musicians, and thinkers. By encountering these ideas, the student develops personal ideas and begins to create new ideas. Communication skills become sharper by seeing how others write or think or photograph, and the student learns that communication can be achieved in a variety of ways. When asked to prepare a report on the causes of the Civil War, the informed student knows that this can be done by using slides, by showing a filmstrip, by writing a report, or by preparing a series of drawings. Information is gathered in the media center, and it can be communicated in many different ways. The student thus becomes skillful in selecting the way that will be most effective personally.

The final function, to take care of students, to baby-sit them, is often forced on the librarian by the principal . . . not by the school or community. When the wood-shop teacher is ill, and there is no substitute industrial arts teacher available, the principal sends the absent teacher's classes to the library. This is not the wisest use of the media center, but it is one way of involving the center in a function of the school. Some principals also send individual students to the library when they cannot meet with their regular class. A typing student who has broken a wrist ends up in the library because there is nothing to do in the typing room, or a student who has fractured a leg is sent to the library, unable to play soccer with the physical education class.

A better use of the library occurs when students look forward to their use of it, or decide to stay in school because of what it can do for them. Many students do find a home in the library. They don't mind school if they can spend part of their time in the library. In this way, the library or media center contributes more directly to the function of taking care of students. It provides interesting things for them to do during the school day—things completely different from their classroom assignments. This is enough to show how the aims of the school library can be tied into the aims and functions of the school. No matter what the functions of the school are, the school library must aid the school in carrying them out.

SCHOOL LIBRARY MANAGEMENT

There are two aspects of school library management. At the district level, there is the administration of the central office library for teachers and of the libraries in the schools. At the building level, there is the administration of the library program for one school. These two sides of school library management require different skills and techniques.

District Librarian

The district librarian is responsible for supervising and coordinating the library programs in the schools. This calls for leadership by persuasion rather than by rules and regulations. The district librarian has the support of policy statements adopted by the Board of Education, of course, but these alone will never get the job done. The real work is achieved by working closely with the librarians in the schools.

The successful district librarian constantly supports the building librarians. The librarians in each school must always feel free to call on the district librarian for help. It may involve nothing more than asking which business office form to use in requisitioning materials for a federal project, or it may be a much more serious problem involving a conflict between the librarian and teachers or between the librarian and the principal. In either case, the building librarian must be free from fear in approaching the district librarian. It has been said that a supervisor is someone who either gets ulcers or causes them in others. This is a mistake that the successful district librarian does not make.

Only a series of positive experiences will prove to building librarians that their district librarian is always ready to help them. If their calls for help are answered promptly and with kindness and understanding, they will not hesitate to ask for more help. In this way, the district librarian achieves an influence that cannot be accomplished in any other manner. Sensitive school librarians often realize that they are making heavy demands on the district librarian. They may remark, "We cry on your shoulder—but whose shoulder do you weep on?" The answer, of course, is no one's— as Harry Truman noted, the buck stops here. This is why the district librarian receives more pay than a building librarian. It is one of the responsibilities assumed upon taking the job.

Role of the District Librarian

Besides being ready to help building librarians at any time, with problems large or small, the district librarian has to plan for all of them. It is the district librarian who sets up a schedule for inservice meetings and workshops. This should be done with the cooperation and suggestions of the school librarians, but the final responsibility rests upon the district librarian. He or she plans the meetings, invites outside speakers, and sets the date and time, and sends out the notices for the meetings. Individual school librarians can provide valuable assistance, but they will leave the ultimate execution to the district librarian, as they should.

When there is a threat to reduce or eliminate the number of librarians in the schools, the district librarian must rally the troops to fight that threat. Building librarians should look to their district librarian for help in such a situation. The threat may come from the superintendent or the board of education. In that case, the district librarian will already have worked out a plan for mounting a counterattack. He or she knows that it is only a matter of time until the administration looks around for ways to cut the budget, and service personnel—librarians, counselors, nurses—are always the first target of such cuts.

Several things can be done when this happens. The district librarian will have three or four plans that can be put into action immediately. One may be to gather the teachers who use the library and are aware of its value to them and to the school's educational program. Over the years, they have indicated their willingness to support their librarian in a time of need. Now they are asked to come forth and explain to the board of education what a reduction in library services would mean. Their good will cannot be developed at the time it is needed. It has to be cultivated over a long period of time. The district librarian, with the building librarians, has done this before the need arises. Another plan may be to send to members of the board of education copies of the school librarians' monthly reports. The district librarian has built up a file of these reports for just such an emergency. Members of the board of education are probably not aware of the many things a school librarian does; they do not realize the variety of tasks they perform each day. A sample selection of the monthly reports received from the librarians will show the board that there is more to a library program than merely checking out books or keeping the catalog cards neatly filed. Whatever plan is adopted to meet this threat must be worked out by the district librarian, who alone knows the needs of all the schools and what is happening in them.

To be informed of the library programs in all schools requires a constant effort. The district librarian cannot be bound to a desk in the central office. An important part of the work is to visit the schools daily. This is most effective when done on schedule, as a schedule forces the district librarian to get out into the schools and to observe what is going on. It is all too easy to be overwhelmed by desk work. There is always a letter to answer, a questionnaire to fill out, a telephone call to return. These can provide an excellent excuse for never leaving one's desk. But it is more important to go to the schools, to talk to teachers and librarians and principals.

Besides building up a good relationship between the district librarian and school personnel, these visits may eliminate some desk work. When the building librarians know that the district librarian will be out to see them soon, they are content to wait to ask a question that does not need an immediate answer. By visiting the schools frequently, the district librarian becomes aware of potential problems before they reach a crisis, and it is much easier to deal with a problem in its early stages than after it becomes a disaster.

The Educational Products Information Exchange Institute has as its motto: "Your decisions are only as good as your information." This is equally true of the work of the district librarian. Sound information is the basis of wise decisions, and this information can best be gathered during visits to the schools. The district librarian needs to be a good listener. Listening carefully is still one of the best ways to acquire information. It has been said that a wise district librarian keeps eyes and ears open and mouth shut. Besides listening to gather information, the district librarian listens in order to help the building librarians. There are times when little can be done about a problem, but verbalizing it helps relieve the tension. The librarians in the schools need to know that they can unburden themselves to the district librarian and find an understanding listener. Just talking about a problem may be a partial solution to it.

By visiting the schools, the district librarian learns that there are many ways to do the same thing. In one elementary school, library circulation cards may be filed by author and then title. In another school, the cards are filed by date due and then by author. In a third school, the cards are filed by teacher. Each method has its advantages and disadvantages. The district librarian observes these, and when a building librarian encounters circulation problems, is able to suggest several ways of solving them. In this way, the district librarian carries ideas from one school to another, ideas that might not occur to the building librarians. They work in isolation, with few opportunities to learn from each other.

The district librarian is the cohesive force that holds the programs in the schools together. Without this leadership, there would be no district library program. There would be only a multiplicity of school programs, often working at odds with each other. The district librarian molds the schools' programs together into a unified district program.

If there is a special library program during summer school, the district librarian is responsible for organizing and supervising it. The program may involve serving two or three small schools with one librarian. In that case, the district librarian will help select librarians and assign them to their schools. If there is a shortage of credentialed librarians who want to work during the summer, the librarian will need to train teachers to take their place. Using teachers has the advantage of making them more understanding of library problems during the regular school year.

Relation of District Librarian to Other Administrators

The district librarian is a staff rather than a line member of the management team, a person who has to accomplish things by persuasion, not by decree. This calls for tact and diplomacy. An outside observer might conclude that the district librarian works for the building librarians rather than the other way around. This is true, and is as it should be in a school library situation. The district librarian is an administrator, but one whose chief value lies in helping librarians in the schools do their jobs.

In many cases, the district librarian is responsible to the assistant superintendent of education or instruction. This makes sense, since the librarian supports the curriculum and supplies materials that are a vital part of it. This person stands ready to advise central office personnel, principals, teachers, and librarians on matters relating to the media center program, and also serves as a liaison officer between the business office and the librarians in the schools, between curriculum supervisors and librarians, and between the staff in the district and the media center staff in other districts when this becomes necessary.

The district librarian attends meetings and conferences outside of the district on behalf of the librarians. Thus, they are represented in professional associations when they are not able to attend themselves. Within the district, the librarian prepares, with the help of committees, approved lists of materials for use in the schools . . . maps, periodicals, books, audiovisual equipment, and textbooks.

Building Librarian

Management of the school library by the building librarian calls for different skills. The outstanding characteristic of the school library, the thing that sets it aside from most other types of libraries, is that it is normally a one-person library. There is no other professional staff to assist with materials selection, cataloging, circulation, reference work, or the preparation of special bibliographies. All of these, and much more, have to be done by one librarian. School libraries are always understaffed, and there is never time or personnel to do all the things that need to be done.

As a result, school librarians constantly think of first things first. Management of the school library is largely a matter of managing one's time and energies. This leads to cutting corners at every turn and to simplifying everything. School librarians avoid original cataloging whenever possible, not because they dislike it, but because there isn't time to do it. School librarians take advantage of commercial processing whenever it is available. School librarians are happiest when materials can be purchased ready to put into circulation, so many publishers and jobbers have developed commercial processing to meet their needs.

The management of a school library centers on establishing priorities. There are many things that the school librarian would like to do but knows cannot be done. There simply isn't time. So what things come first?

Service to students and teachers has the highest priority. Anything that contributes to this is also important. In an elementary school, library service to students consists of helping them find the materials they need, telling them stories, helping them locate information, and teaching them how to use the resources of the library or media center. In a school with 500 to 700 students or more, the librarian has to work fast to do all this. The school day is short, and every minute is precious. To accomplish everything in such a brief time, the librarian must plan carefully and well in advance. There is little margin for error.

Work Routine of the Building Librarian

The school librarian needs to take more work home than many other types of librarians. The day is filled with meeting classes, helping teachers, and assisting individual students. Tasks like book selection, preparing lessons, compiling bibliographies, and ordering materials have to be done after school is over for the day—or in some cases, before it begins. This puts a premium on good management. The school librarian needs to be aware of deadlines, and to have them in mind constantly.

In school districts, certain things can be ordered only once a year. This is often true of orders for library supplies or library furniture. If the school librarian runs out of catalog cards or book pockets before the next annual order for library supplies, there may be no alternative to doing without them until the next requisition date. So the librarian keeps a running record of supplies needed, to be ready when the annual order date arrives. If the librarian has no paid clerical help, the typing of the order may have to be done at home or after school hours.

There is seldom time during the day for book selection or reading reviews. This must be done at home or on weekends. The same is true of selecting a story to read or planning for a special program. The school librarian's day is shorter than that of many other librarians but also more intense. Because it is so intense, the school librarian has longer and more frequent vacations. But these are often used to plan the work that will carry the librarian through the year.

Service to teachers ranges from gathering material for them to use with a unit on American history to helping them select a textbook for a group of slow learners. This service calls for a wide-ranging knowledge of materials. Experience is the most valuable aid that a school librarian has. Over the years, each one builds up a background of know-how to get through the crowded day. Experience is important in any profession, but it is especially important in the work of a school librarian.

There is no end to the service that the librarian can provide for teachers, but there is a limit to the number of things that can be done for them and still leave time to help students. One of the school librarian's most important management skills is knowing when and how to say, "No." Is a request for help from a teacher more important than a request from a student? That is, does a teacher's need for assistance come before that of a student? Recently, someone observed that there are no solutions to our problems, only choices. The school librarian is faced with choices every day—but no solutions to problems—and thus must decide whether it is more important this moment to help the teacher or a student. Some librarians favor the teacher, because the teacher will be there next year while the student may be gone. Others favor the student because that person's life may be influenced by aid received at the moment. It is not an easy choice, and today's choice may be quite different from tomorrow's.

Today the management of the school library is complicated by the presence of a wide range of instructional materials. Gone is the day when the school librarian needed to worry only about books, periodicals, and a few pamphlets. Today's media center specialist must cope with a variety of new materials—16mm motion pictures, 35mm filmstrips, cassette and disc recordings, overhead transparencies, realia, models, video tapes, and 8mm film loops. Managing so many different materials calls for new skills and knowledge.

The modern school librarian has to know how to select and evaluate these materials, and how to store and circulate them. Again, there are no final solutions, only choices. Should the materials be integrated on the shelves in the media center, or should materials in the same format be shelved together? Those who argue in favor of integrated shelving claim that this forces the student to concentrate on the needed information and to ignore the package in which it comes. The student, or teacher, who is seeking information about butterflies will find everything in the media center on this topic together on the shelves . . . books, films, filmstrips, recordings, mounted specimens, study prints, film loops, and overhead transparencies. Those who are opposed to integrated shelving say that it wastes space, that the same thing can be achieved through an integrated card catalog, and that the machines needed to project or play back the materials should be close to them. Both methods have good and bad points, but a choice must be made between them.

It is not too difficult to circulate a book or periodical. Circulating a film or microfiche can be more of a problem. And circulating a filmstrip projector or cassette tape recorder can be a real problem. Some school librarians have decided not to circulate non-print materials or the equipment that goes with them. This limits the use of these materials to the media center. But it reduces losses and damage to them. Other librarians have chosen to circulate the materials—filmstrips and cassettes—but not the equipment, and still others have elected to circulate everything. They argue that not all students have time to use the materials in the media center. If they cannot check them out, they are denied access to these essential information media.

Training Helpers

The school librarian, because he or she is the sole paid staff of the media center, spends considerable time training helpers. This requires management skills to train student assistants and volunteer parent workers. Student assistants will not willingly work in the library if the work is dull or uninteresting, so the librarian must be able to motivate as well as train students to do the tasks that will keep the center going. Variety is an important factor here. The librarian must avoid assigning a student to the same job for too long. The easy thing is to start each student on a particular job and then leave each one doing that task. But this is the surest way to end up with no student help. The librarian needs to be alert to signs of boredom. Before the student begins to lose interest in the task being done, the librarian should have the next work assignment planned.

The same is true of tasks for parent volunteers. Adults are a little more tolerant of boredom, but they too will soon stop volunteering if the work is not appealing. Here also, variety in assignments is important. The parent who looks forward to each new task will keep coming back for more. The work for volunteers also needs to be work that can wait if the volunteer does not show up on the day promised. This kind of work may not be the labor that will help the librarian most. Pressing work can't wait until someone shows up to do it, but the librarian has to work around this as well as possible.

MEDIA CENTER CONCEPT

In the 1960s and 1970s, the media center concept took over the school libraries of the nation. This was not a new idea, as multimedia school libraries had existed for decades. But the technological and communications developments of the 1960s and 1970s made it possible for school libraries to have more media than ever before. Improved and less expensive overhead projectors came on the market, and along with them, whole libraries of commercially prepared transparencies. The super 8 film loop was introduced during this time, and for a while, seemed to threaten the use of 16mm motion pictures in schools. The cassette tape recorder was invented, and educators quickly realized its value in the classroom. Color study prints became common; before this time, they had been too expensive for most schools to afford. The price of video tape recorders and cameras was drastically reduced, and the equipment became compact and simple enough to be used in schools. Educational film companies began to make their motion pictures available on videotape as well as on acetate.

Then came video cassettes, which were even easier to use. At the beginning of this period, most educational films were produced in black and white only. By the end of the period, almost all educational films were in color. Cable television became common in schools, and some districts could even afford computer terminals. Schools that had never made much use of microfilm adopted microfiche with enthusiasm. Producers began to publish microfiche material suitable for use in elementary school media centers. Sound filmstrips largely replaced captioned filmstrips during this time, except for special uses with deaf students. Automatic sound filmstrip projectors came on the market, and most of the customers were schools. Publishers issued study prints with sound (an accompanying tape recording) and study prints with acetate overlays. They offered books with the text on an accompanying cassette in a handy plastic bag. These are only a few of the developments which have taken place during this time. Many of them were made primarily with a school use in mind, and the school media center welcomed them.

The *idea behind the media center concept* is that students learn in different ways from a variety of materials. Reading is only one of these ways, and for some students, it may not be the best way. One student may learn better from listening to a recording, and another may find that watching a motion picture is more effective. And even a student who likes to read may discover that some things are learned better from studying pictures or working with a three-dimensional model. The media center concept is based on these differences.

The school library takes advantage of another quality of multimedia. Perhaps because they see and listen before they learn to read, some students can absorb more sophisticated material when it is presented pictorially or aurally. If they had to take in the same information through print, they would function at a much lower level. Thus a high school student who would have trouble reading a biology textbook can digest the same information easily when it is presented in a motion picture, or a photograph, or a recording. The problems of the slow reader are well known, but we seldom worry about the handicap of the slow listener or slow watcher. Audiovisual materials are not a barrier to the student with normal intelligence, but print often is. When something must be learned, this becomes important. It is doubly important when the learning must take place in a short time.

When students come to school, they already have the skill to understand spoken language and to interpret much of what they see in the world around them. It is only in school that they have to learn to understand the written language, and some never learn this lesson well. Yet they remain the responsibility of the school, and one of the functions of the school is to teach them. Faced with this problem, schools have found that audiovisual materials succeed where print fails. And the school library or media center is the logical place in the school to house all instructional materials, both print and non-print. Materials, especially audiovisual materials, are expensive and costly to duplicate. If housed in the classroom, they are available to a limited number of students, but if they are stored in the media center, they are accessible to all students in the school.

For these reasons, then, the media center concept has become an important part of the school library. A media center, with its wide range of materials, helps the school to achieve its aims. Through a media center, the school is better able to carry out its functions.

Media and Information

The school media center contains information in as many different formats as it can afford. Today's media center will have study carrels equipped with rear screen projection for motion pictures, automatic sound slide and sound filmstrip projectors, cassette tape recorders, record players, microfilm and microfiche readers and printers, computer terminals, and small television monitors. The center may have production facilities for making videotapes, for developing slides and film, for producing transparencies, and for recording speeches and lectures. Of course, it also contains print materials—books, periodicals, maps, pamphlets—but these are no longer the main ingredient of the library collection. They are only a part of its armory in the arsenal for learning.

No longer does a student have to travel a single road to learning—the highway of the printed page. If this route is not pleasing or comfortable, the road to learning is not blocked; there are other choices—and they all lead to the same end. Whatever the student needs to know, there is a way to get there—through pictures, the spoken word, models, motion pictures, print—singly or in combination.

Selection Criteria

The school librarian must be familiar with the criteria for selecting all kinds of instructional materials. It is no longer enough to know typefaces, type sizes, bindings, illustrations, footnotes, and bibliographies. The media specialist has to be equally at home in judging films, filmstrips, recordings, transparencies, and realia. Fortunately, many of the same criteria can be used in evaluating all materials. Is the work appealing to pupils? Is the content accurate and up to date? Is it free from bias and prejudice? Does it meet the needs of the curriculum?

These questions must be answered whether the material is a book or a film or a recording, but evaluating such a wide range of materials calls for considerable skill and knowledge. Luckily, many of these skills can be acquired by examining a great quantity of materials. The librarian who sees a lot of films or listens to a great many recordings soon learns to tell the good from the bad.

Personnel

As noted earlier, one characteristic of the school library is that it is understaffed. The staff of most school libraries consists of only one person—the librarian. That one person must do everything. The school librarian is the media center's cataloger, reference librarian, chief administrator, head of technical processing, book or materials selector, head of circulation, business manager, department head, public relations officer, director of public services, and occasionally custodian. There is no time to specialize, and everything has to be done on the run. National and state standards for school libraries recommend an adequate staff, one with clerks, technicians, graphic artists, and electronics experts. But in real life, these are seldom available, and the school librarian has to learn to do everything alone.

The *training of school librarians*, aside from courses in library science, is much like the training required of teachers. In some states, school librarians must have two credentials, one in education and one in library science. The school librarian needs to be familiar with the curriculum, with the problems of classroom discipline, with school administration, with child growth and development, and with the peculiar needs of schools. The school librarian who has had classroom teaching experience has a definite advantage over the librarian who has no teaching experience.

When there are two librarians, one is usually designated head librarian and becomes responsible for dividing duties, arranging schedules, signing requisitions, preparing annual reports, and conferring with the principal on problems related to the library. In situations where there are two librarians, one usually takes charge of the audiovisual materials while the other takes care of books and periodicals. This may lead to the segregation of materials in the library, or it may result in a struggle for power between the two librarians.

Use of Volunteer Workers

Because the school library is understaffed with regular paid help, it makes use of volunteer help whenever possible. PTA volunteers often perform valuable service in the school library. They can reshelve books and other materials, clip and mount pictures for the picture file, mend books, type ditto masters for library skills lessons, pull catalog cards for discarded books, and prepare bulletin board displays. With this help, the librarian is free to do other things—work with students in the selection of materials, offer reference service, tell stories, prepare bibliographies, and aid teachers.

Volunteer help is often a mixed blessing. Mothers may not be able to come at the time promised because of an emergency at home. They may have typing skills but no ability to arrange a bulletin board. They grow tired of doing over and over the few tasks they are capable of performing well. They become bored and drop out of the program. Nevertheless, they can be a great help and many librarians feel that they could not survive without them.

Volunteers must be trained carefully. It is wise to have a manual or handbook for them. A manual for library volunteers will make it possible for the librarian to give all volunteers the same basic training. A manual will assure that library procedures carried out by the volunteers are consistent. It will save the librarian time. Much of the beginning instruction can be provided by the manual, leaving the librarian free to do other things.

Student Assistants

Along with volunteers, the school librarian depends on student assistants for help. Their value cannot be overestimated. Many of the routine housekeeping chores necessary to keep a library running smoothly can be done by students, but the librarian needs to guard against the temptation to exploit them. But when this happens, the students themselves usually solve the problem—by forgetting to come to the library to help.

The school librarian needs to decide early whether he or she wants student assistants because they can be of help or because the librarian can help them. There is a basic difference between the two viewpoints. The librarian who wants student helpers only because of the assistance they can give him will ignore the needs of the students. Such a person will assign them repetitive tasks that lead to boredom, will demand more than they are willing to give, will forget that if the work is not fun for them, they will soon stop doing it. On the other hand, if the librarian decides to have student assistants because she or he can help them, can contribute to their education and development, this person will think of interesting and exciting things for them to do in the library. Such a person will work hard to see that they are not bored by routine tasks, will create as much variety in their work assignments as possible, and will be mindful of what they are getting out of their experience, and how it adds to their education.

The *proper use of student assistants* requires careful planning. The librarian should have a program that will meet the needs of the students as well as the needs of the library. There should be a plan for recruiting and selecting students who want to work in the library. The librarian needs to develop a training program so that students will become skillful workers in various areas of the library. Student helpers can perform a variety of tasks in the library. In an elementary school, they like to check out books: stamp the due date on the circulation card and arrange the cards alphabetically by author or numerically by call number. Sitting at the circulation desk, in the throne of power, delights almost all of them. Students can reshelve books, but it is not their favorite task; they can help check in textbooks and stamp them; and they can make bookmarks. Upper-grade students can read stories to primary-grade students; they can deliver textbooks to classrooms; and they can stamp and check in new periodicals.

Secondary School Student Assistants

In the secondary school, students are capable of performing a much greater variety of tasks. The secondary school media center often has a large collection of periodicals, perhaps as many as 300 or 400. Student helpers perform a valuable service in checking in new periodicals and in circulating them to other students. Yet, student assistants may not be welcomed at the circulation desk in the secondary school library, as they are prone to favor their friends, and valuable materials sometimes disappear from the collection. Lost and stolen books become a serious problem at this level. In the second half of the 1970s, this problem grew so serious that many school libraries installed a security system to reduce their losses. Detection systems are expensive to install and operate, but they pay for themselves in a year or two.

Many secondary school library assistants can type and assist the librarian in preparing overdue book lists, bibliographies, and order lists for new books. Credit may be given to students who take library service as a regular course. These students can be trained to do more complicated tasks: they can pull catalog cards for discarded books, they can check materials being considered for purchase to see if they are in print, and they can show other students how to use the audiovisual equipment in the library. They can make overhead transparencies for the librarian and teachers, and they can duplicate materials for independent study in the classroom. When credit is given for work done in the library, more can be demanded of the students working there, and a higher quality of work is expected.

One of the values of student assistants is that they introduce other students to the resources of the media center. Students learn from each other, and the student who works in the library helps friends to find their way around the stacks and through the card catalog. In the long run, this service may be more valuable to the school than the work they actually do in the library. Ultimately, many students benefit from the work of a few who directly help the librarian.

Rewarding Student Assistants

There are various ways of rewarding the students who help the librarian. It may be possible to pay them a minimum wage. They often have the first chance to check out new materials. Some librarians are able to get sample copies of new materials, which they give to students after the materials have served their intended purpose. The librarian may be able to arrange an author tea for student helpers, giving them a chance to talk and listen to someone who has written books, or may be able to take them on a tour of a printing plant, or provide a field trip to a special library. It is important to reward the students in some way for the help they have given the librarian.

FINANCES AND THE BUDGET

Schools normally receive their monies from local taxes, and a school's fiscal year begins July 1 and ends June 30. The budget is based on the local tax rate and on the average daily attendance of students enrolled in the school. An increase in enrollment or daily attendance, or an increase in the tax rate, means more money for the school. A decrease in enrollment or in the tax rate results in less money for the school— for teachers' salaries, for maintenance of the school plant, and for the library or media center. Work on the school's budget usually begins six to eight months before the July 1 on which it goes into effect.

Since a school's income is largely determined by its average daily attendance (ADA) and assuming that the tax rate does not change greatly, the library's budget is computed in terms of dollars and cents per ADA. The allotment for the library, not counting salaries, may vary from a few cents to a few dollars per ADA. This provides the library with a lump sum, which then has to be divided or pro-rated among the services of the library's program. If the library receives $8.00 per unit of ADA, the librarian or principal of the school must then decide how this money is to be divided among books, periodicals, non-book materials, library supplies, and binding. Once the money has been divided into these accounts, it is often difficult to re-allocate it after the budget has been adopted by the board of education. Transfers can be made, but they usually require board approval, and business managers or superintendents are reluctant to take such requests to the board. It is an admission that the original budget planning was not done as carefully as it should have been.

Spending Money

When all of the money budgeted in an account is not spent by the end of the fiscal year, it usually reverts to the general fund and is divided among all the accounts in the school or district the following year. Unlike a business, a school or media center tries to spend all of its money before the end of the fiscal year. If the library saves money one year, it does not get that money plus new money the next year. Instead, the saving is passed on to other departments, and the library starts the new fiscal year with its regular budget allocation.

The need to spend the library's money before the end of June each year becomes an important part of the librarian's financial planning. Most of the book money should be spent by the end of December. Then in February or March, when the librarian learns of money not counted on (because of discounts, books out of print, and cancelled orders), there is time to re-order before the business office closes its books in mid-June. A list of desired materials must be kept on hand, then, to be used as soon as it is known that there is money left in the book account. Materials must be received and paid for before June 30; if materials are ordered in April, received in June, and not paid for until July—they will be charged against the next year's budget. Instead of spending this year's leftover money, the librarian would end up spending some of next year's money. Toward the end of the fiscal year, timing becomes critical.

Some things that the school librarian needs may be obtainable only on an annual order. Periodical subscriptions are usually made just once a year. Some business offices refuse to accept off-schedule orders for magazines, so the librarian needs to plan carefully for the coming year. This is also true of library supplies, which are customarily ordered only once a year. It saves the library money, because there is a discount on quantity orders, but it is not always convenient. If the librarian runs out of book pockets or mending tape in the middle of the year, the library may have to do without them until the next annual order. Through experience and proper planning, the librarian learns to avoid these awkward situations.

Business Office Procedures

Since the school library has to work through the district business office, and since purchasing procedures are complicated, there is a delay in obtaining whatever is needed. After the librarian types a requisition for a set of an encyclopedia, for example, the requisition goes to the principal for a signature. The principal sends it to the district librarian, if there is one, who signs and forwards it to the purchasing agent in the business office. The buyer in the business office verifies the information on the requisition and then checks with the fiscal department to make certain that there is money in the account for the books. After this, a purchase order authorizing the vendor to supply the books is prepared. A list of this purchase order number with others for the same period is submitted to the board of education for approval. Following the board's approval, the purchase order is mailed to the vendor. After all this, the vendor has procedures to follow, so it is no wonder that there is usually a long time between placing an order and receiving the merchandise.

Need to Foresee Problems

The school librarian learns to expect these delays—and to plan ahead for them—but the librarian also learns to expect the unexpected. Toward the end of the school year, the principal may discover unspent money in several accounts. These monies may be transferred into the library's book account, and the librarian has one or two weeks to spend it. The experienced librarian has been waiting for just such a windfall, and all year has been making a list of books—or films, or filmstrips, or recordings—to have ready when extra money suddenly becomes available. Now the librarian only needs to take the order slips and type a list of the desired materials. They previously have been evaluated and selected, so the money is not wasted on materials that may never be wanted or used.

Preparation and alertness are the keys to the successful financial management of the media center. The librarian constantly keeps in mind the deadlines and due dates for all orders, and prepares for them in advance; knows when an account is exhausted, and when funds should be transferred into it from another account. The librarian studies the bi-weekly or monthly computer printouts of the center's accounts in order to know immediately when a wrong purchase order has been charged to an account.

It is often recommended that the librarian have a petty cash fund with which to buy small but immediately needed items. This may not be possible. The business office or district policy may not allow a petty cash fund for a department—only for the principal of the school. When the principal has a fund, the librarian may be allowed to make small purchases and reimburse the fund when presenting the invoice for the items or the sales receipt. One solution to this problem is the open order. The librarian turns in a requisition for a specified amount of money, not to exceed "X" amount with any one vendor for future purchases. The librarian can then go to the vendor whenever necessary and obtain the needed things until the not-to-exceed amount has been reached. The vendor then submits an itemized listing of the materials given to the librarian and is paid by the business office. Some librarians solve the problem by asking the PTA for a cash donation to the library to be used in buying small items. An accounting is made to the PTA to show how the money has been spent and for what materials. If the media center charges for overdue materials, the money received in fines can sometimes be used to buy materials needed in a hurry. In some cases, the money collected in fines has to be turned over monthly to the business office, which then credits it to the library's account.

The librarian's financial management of the media center tends to revolve around ways of working within limitations set by others. He or she may have little say in the amount of money set aside for the operation of the center and cannot do things in a simple, straightforward manner. The district's business office procedures must be followed, but within these rules and regulations, there are opportunities for some flexibility, and the librarian learns to take advantage of them.

LIBRARY SERVICES

The school library collection is functional and up to date. There is no need for a large collection and, in most cases, there is no need to preserve materials. The exception will be school records and history, and local history, when it is a part of the curriculum. The school library is not a research center in the way that college and university libraries and special libraries often are. Students and teachers are seldom interested in old materials, unless they are classics. The school media collection needs to be a working collection, a collection of materials that are used frequently and that contain current information.

Size of School Media Collection

In an elementary school media center, 10,000 volumes, considering books only, will probably be an adequate collection. In a secondary school, 20,000 volumes will be needed. In each case, most of the volumes should be recent works, published within the last ten years. To a sixteen-year-old student, something published or produced ten years ago is pretty old. It can't be relevant, as it came out when that student was in the first grade, a whole lifetime ago. To an eight-year-old child, in the second or third grade, something published ten years ago appeared before that child was born. Anything that old can't be true about today's world.

Since there is an optimum size to a school library collection, weeding becomes a perennial problem. As fast as new materials come in, once the right size of the collection has been reached, old material must leave. For one thing, there will be no space to add more and more materials. The shelving space of a school library is usually fixed, and there is no chance to enlarge it. In a way, this is good, for it forces the library to discard old material as fast as it adds new material, which keeps the collection alive.

One of the most important services of the school library is reading guidance. The patrons of most other types of libraries can read, or they don't come to the library. The school library, on the other hand, has many patrons who can't read, or who can barely read—or who don't want to read. The school librarian must help all of them, must help them find material at their level, material that will interest them, material that will assist them in their studies. The school librarian cannot be a passive observer of students' reading needs and interests. The librarian must be an active participant in their search for material that is suitable for them.

This calls for a knowledge of each student's reading ability that the librarian cannot hope to have. In a school of 700 or 800 students, the librarian will be fortunate to know the reading abilities of half the students, and needs the help of the classroom teacher. By working together, the librarian and teacher can find the right book for each child. This is why it is important for the teacher to accompany the class to the library, as this person knows the reading abilities of the students. The librarian knows which books in the collection will match that ability.

Teaching the Use of the School Library

The school librarian also offers instruction in how to use the library's resources. Parents and teachers often feel that teaching library skills is the most important part of the library program, since students who learn how to use the school library efficiently can go on to other types of libraries. After they learn how to use the school library, they will be at home in their public library, they will not be lost in a college library, and they will get the most out of their business library. The elementary school librarian devotes a great deal of time to teaching library skills—how to use the card catalog, when to go to an almanac instead of an encyclopedia, how to use a periodical index to find the most recent information on a topic.

To many students, learning how to use the card catalog is not the most exciting lesson in the world. So the librarian makes use of a variety of teaching aids—oversize catalog cards, games, puzzles, contests, motion pictures, filmstrips, overhead transparencies, quizzes, treasure hunts. The school librarian needs to repeat these lessons over and over. Practice does make perfect; and the librarian has to find ways of teaching the same lesson many times without ever seeming to do it twice. Drill is an essential part of mastering any skill, and in this respect, learning library skills is no different from hitting a golf ball or playing the piano. Repetition, without boredom, is the secret to success.

Service to Teachers

Much of the school librarian's success depends on working with teachers. It is as important as working with students. There are many things the librarian can do for teachers: prepare special bibliographies for them; purchase materials to go with the units they are teaching; call their attention to the resources of the collection that will be useful to them. Perhaps the librarian helps them most by helping their students. By finding a student a compatible book, the librarian creates an interest in reading for the student—an interest not gained from the assigned textbooks in the classroom. And by reading this book, and others recommended by the librarian, the student improves personal reading skills. Today the watchword in education is accountability, and the teacher whose students become good readers is adjudged a good teacher. The librarian does his or her share by encouraging students to read widely, by enticing them to read more and better.

Students learn to read by reading—but reading is not the only way to acquire information. The media center recognizes this more than the classroom, because it has a larger collection of educational materials, both print and non-print. The student who needs information for a project or report but doesn't like to read can still find that information in the media center. When a teacher directs a student to the center or library to look up information on the life cycle of the monarch butterfly, the librarian produces filmstrips, film loops, and study prints, as well as books and pamphlets. The student discovers that he can find what he needs to know without reading. This is not to discount reading. It simply shows that the librarian can help the student gather the information the teacher has asked him to bring back to the classroom. Here the information is the important thing—not the ability to read.

Textbooks and the School Library

Sometimes the school librarian is responsible for textbooks, as only a limited number of textbooks can be kept in the classroom. When a reading group finishes one book, the teacher sends the children to the library for another book. The teacher may know what book the children should read next or may ask the librarian for a recommendation, based on the librarian's knowledge of the textbooks present in the school's collection. Librarians are often not interested in textbooks—they are not literature, and frequently they are uninspiring. But the teacher sees them in a different light. They are essential tools for teaching whatever must be taught. And the librarian who is familiar with textbooks, and who can assist the teacher in selecting the right one for a class, is valued by the teacher.

Extracurricular Services

Most of what the librarian does supports the curriculum, but he or she performs other services that aid the school and its staff. The librarian offers the media center as a meeting place for parents and teachers when this can be done without disrupting the center's regular program. The librarian enjoys having faculty meetings in the library before and/or after school and often puts out new materials for teachers to look at before the meetings begin. This can be a better introduction to the materials than a dittoed list of new acquisitions placed in the teachers' boxes. When the meeting is held in the center, the librarian has a chance to talk to teachers about their class-room needs and to show them materials which could be helpful.

Book Fairs and Special Programs

Many librarians hold book fairs in the library. These encourage students to buy and own books, which in turn stimulates their interest in reading. The book fair can be used to highlight a special occasion, such as National Library Week or American Education Week. If the book fair is open to parents in the evening, it brings them into the school library and demonstrates what the school is doing to make their children better readers.

The librarian frequently organizes special assembly programs for the school. A well-known author may be invited to speak to the entire student body. A book parade in which students appear as characters from their favorite stories might be arranged. Film festivals open to all students who have made home movies and wish to have them shown to an audience have also been initiated by the librarian.

COOPERATION WITH OTHER LIBRARIES

School libraries are inclined to be isolated, and even the libraries within a district may not cooperate with each other to any great extent. This is not because they are opposed to cooperation. Rather, it is the result of their being self-contained to meet the needs of the school of which they are such an intimate part. There are instances of union book catalogs for secondary school libraries in a district, but this is not a common practice. Any cooperation between school libraries in a district is usually confined to personal interchanges among librarians. School librarians like to meet together, to exchange ideas, to discuss common problems, and to share information about new materials.

There may be some exchange of materials between school libraries, but this is not common practice. Since the school library collection is usually small, libraries do not feel free to share materials with other librarians. If something is loaned out, it will not be available when needed by a teacher or student. The school librarian sees meeting the wants of students in the immediate situation as being more important than helping those in another school. Being understaffed is part of the problem. The school librarian must handle interlibrary loans, and this takes time away from service to students and teachers. So, while some borrowing goes on between school libraries, it is not looked on as an important part of their service.

Working with Special Libraries

A number of attempts have been made to establish cooperation between school libraries and special libraries. In most instances, these attempts have not been too successful. There are several reasons why they have failed. When a special library agrees to serve students from a school, the students have to find their own way to get to the special library. Many of them are at a considerable distance from the school, so if the students do not drive or have the use of a car, they must rely on public transportation, which may be inconvenient or time-consuming or both. The hours of the special library may not allow the student to get there from school with time left over to use the collection.

Special libraries, by their very nature, are esoteric and the collections may be too advanced for most students. The simple materials that they usually need can be found in a good public library. Some special libraries are connected with organizations engaged in government research, and a large part of their collections will be classified and not available to students. So even those advanced students who could benefit from the use of the materials are not allowed to have them.

In many cases, these frustrations have discouraged students from using special libraries. However, there have been some successful attempts to bring the two together, and the school librarian should do everything possible to make students aware of the special collections that are open to them.

Working with College and Public Libraries

School librarians frequently make arrangements with nearby college or university libraries for students to use their resources. Such an arrangement is usually limited to the use of the materials in the library, and borrowing privileges are not permitted. The school librarian, after the student has exhausted the resources of the school library, writes a letter of introduction to the college librarian explaining that the student's interest is sincere and legitimate. Such a letter should be written only after the student has failed to find the needed materials in all other cooperating libraries.

Since school library collections are relatively small, students frequently cannot find all the materials they need in them. This has made them steady customers of the public library. Its larger collection provides them with works the school library cannot afford. The longer hours the public library is open also affects student use. The school library may be open from 8 a.m. until 3:30 p.m., but only a few school libraries are open in the evening or on weekends. Students who have a full program have little time to use the school library during the hours it is open, so their only source of materials becomes the public library. Students have always formed a large segment of the public library's clientele.

In the late 1950s and early 1960s, student use of the public library became a serious problem. Students often took over a library in the evening, preferring it, not only because it was open when the school library was closed, but because it was outside of the school setting. It was a way to get away from school while studying. It also served as a dating bureau. Students could meet and talk without being reprimanded by a teacher or a school librarian who insisted that they study or leave.

By the mid-1970s, many of these problems had been solved. School libraries developed better collections. Some tried staying open in the evenings or on weekends; but most of these experiments were abandoned as the crest of the post-war baby boom passed through the schools. Public libraries learned to cope with students. Teachers switched to individualized instruction from mass assignments. And school and public librarians learned to cooperate more effectively. As the tensions eased, the two types of libraries learned to work together harmoniously. Some problems still remain: some teachers still use mass assignments; student discipline can be a problem in the public library; and school library collections are not large enough to meet the needs of all students. But the relationship between the two types of libraries is much better now than it was two decades ago.

COMPARATIVE SCHOOL LIBRARIANSHIP

Since the mid-1960s, considerable work has been done studying school libraries in other countries. Australia and Canada have developed school libraries as good as the best in the United States. But many countries, like Brazil and France, have failed to perfect good school libraries. Unesco has done much to encourage the development of school libraries in many countries, particularly Central and South America. And the International Association of School Librarianship has made school librarians aware of the work of their confrères in other countries.

The kind of education that a country fosters has a great deal to do with the presence or absence of school libraries there. If the system of education emphasizes the memorization of knowledge, if a textbook is all a student has to know to get through school, or if passing an examination based on a syllabus means success—there is little need for a school library. If getting a degree depends on knowing what the professor said in a lecture, the student doesn't need a library but only needs to study notes. A library, no matter how well equipped, will not help a student do that.

When education is limited to the elite, there is little likelihood that school libraries will grow. Elitist education tends to be based on passing examinations. And unless the examinations require a background of wide reading, a library is an un-needed luxury. It is no accident that school libraries have developed in the United States, where compulsory mass education is the rule. To meet the needs of a diverse population of students, a rich curriculum is essential. The belief that different students learn in different ways calls for a wide range of learning materials, and only in a school library or media center can these materials be found. There is a close relation between the American system of education and the growth of school libraries in the United States.

The study of comparative school librarianship has made us aware of these differences between countries. It is foolish to expect school libraries to prosper in a country where education is based on passing examinations. School libraries, as we know them in the United States, cannot be transplanted to Switzerland or Italy or Zambia without first creating an educational system that needs school libraries.

STANDARDS

School Libraries do not lack standards. There is an abundance of them, both national and state. Australia has *Standards for Secondary School Libraries*. Britain has *School Library Resource Centres: Recommended Standards for Policy and Provision*. The United States has *Media Programs: District and School*, prepared by the American Association of School Librarians of the American Library Association, and the Association for Educational Communications and Technology of the National Education Association.

In the United States, many states have their own standards for school library or school media programs. From time to time, the U.S. Department of Health, Education, and Welfare publishes a list of them. The most recent appeared in 1977 with the title *Survey of School Media Standards*. Among the states, California, Illinois, Iowa, New Jersey, New York, and Ohio all have published standards.

Use of School Library Standards

There are more standards for school librarians than for college or public or special libraries. The need for accreditation accounts for many of the standards that have been developed for school libraries. It is customary for secondary schools to be evaluated by an accrediting team from some accrediting association; if the school is accredited, its students have a better chance of entering good colleges and universities. When standards exist for school media centers, the accrediting association makes use of them. They are an already existing yardstick for the measurement of the library, and state standards can be applied objectively to all school libraries in that state. State standards may be developed by the state association of school librarians or by the state department of public instruction. Often the two groups work together to formulate the standards. Since there are up-to-date national standards for school libraries, why are state standards necessary?

National standards are usually much higher than state standards, and they serve a somewhat different purpose. The standards or guidelines published by the American Association of School Librarians set up goals for individual libraries to achieve. If the standards can be met by half the school libraries in the nation, there is no incentive for them to improve. The standards say they are good, so they only need to stay where they are. They have arrived. But if only ten percent of the school libraries in the nation meet the standards, there is much work to be done. And the standards show what is needed to reach a higher level. This goal is not unattainable, or impossible, for ten percent of the school libraries have already reached it or gone beyond. Thus, it is always expected that national standards will be high, as they are the star to which most school libraries hitch their wagons.

State standards are usually lower, and are aimed at the special needs or abilities of the state. It is a common practice to publish state standards in phases. Phase one, for schools that do not have a library or librarian, tells them what they need to begin working toward phase two. Phase two is for schools that have a library but not a librarian or for schools that have a basic media program but want to know what they should do next. Phase three is for schools that have a well developed media program, but one that still falls short of the national standards. The phase approach is used to encourage schools that have just begun to develop a media program. It avoids discouraging them be setting goals that are too high in the beginning. It gives them hope that, after they have reached phase one, they can move on to phase two. The path to excellence is by steps and not by quantum leaps. Colorado, Idaho, Illinois, Iowa, and New York have all adopted school media standards with three phases. Some states, like Nevada, have adopted standards with three steps, which is essentially the same thing. Michigan's *Guidelines for Media Programs in Michigan Schools* call for three levels of resources, facilities, and equipment: basic, better, and advanced. No matter what terminology is used, the purpose is the same—to encourage schools to move to the next higher step, and not to be discouraged because the step is so big.

Need to Revise School Library Standards Frequently

School library or media standards, whether national or state, need to be revised frequently. Standards that are not revised at least every five years quickly become outdated. They must be revised to keep up with changes in the curriculum, with new technological developments, and with the changing philosophy of school librarianship. The

American Association of School Librarians has learned that it must have a committee working on the next set of standards before the latest standards have been published. It takes time to formulate standards, to solicit opinion from the school librarians in the field who will be trying to carry them out, and to prepare the final draft for publication. If work on new standards is not begun until there is an expressed need for them, too much time elapses between publication of the old standards and the new ones. New standards must be ready when there is a need for them, not several years after the need has become a loud demand.

Pattern of School Library Standards

School library or media standards tend to follow a pattern in their development. This can be seen by examining the early standards in Australia or Britain or the United States—or in any of the states within the United States. In the beginning, school library standards are chiefly quantitative. Standards for materials are in terms of numbers of books, films, or recordings per number of students, which is understandable. A school that has no films or videotapes wants to know how many it should have to be up to standard, and quantitative standards are easy to apply. A school library has ten books per student or it doesn't; there is one motion picture projector per classroom or teaching station or there isn't. The result is easy to determine and clear cut. There is no ambiguity.

Quantitative versus Qualitative Standards

But as school media programs become more sophisticated, knowing only the quantities of things leaves a lot unexplained and unaccounted for. Eventually, standards must include qualitative factors, which are more difficult to measure. But the quality of a media program is more important than its quantity: have the right materials and use them well rather than simply to have a lot of materials. Bigger is not always better. The difficulty with qualitative standards is that they are hard to measure. Nevertheless, most standards today recognize the need for quality as well as quantity. The last three standards of the AASL have shown a move in this direction.

BUILDINGS AND EQUIPMENT

The modern school media center requires ample space—for staff personnel, materials, equipment, and students. Few school libraries have as much space as they would like. It is recommended that the school library be the center of the school, both physically and philosophically. In many modern plants, this is the case, but where it is not, the program can still be successful.

Today's secondary school library especially depends on periodical literature for up-to-date information. It is not uncommon for a high school library to subscribe to several hundred periodicals. Individualized instruction fosters the use of magazines as well as of books. So now, a well-equipped high school media center has microfilm and microfiche printers and readers, often as many as three or four. Many high school libraries have stopped binding periodicals, because of the cost and the lack of space for bound volumes. Besides saving space and money, microfilm and microfiche practically eliminate the mutilation of periodicals. The student who wants to include a page from a magazine in a term paper or notebook does not need to cut up the original hard print copy, which the library may no longer have anyway. Instead a copy of the page can be secured from the printer.

High-speed tape duplicators have also been a boon to the school media center. The cost of tape and cassette duplicators is now within the reach of many libraries. It is not unusual for a secondary school library to purchase a high speed duplicator to take care of the home circulation of cassettes. The media center buys a copy of the desired tape, which is kept as a master in a file near the duplicator. The cassettes, of course, are listed in the integrated card catalog, along with books and all other materials. A student wishing to check out a cassette goes to the duplication center, where the master cassettes are kept. The librarian, or a clerk, makes a copy from the original, which is then refiled, and the student takes home the copy. When it is returned, the cassette is put in a box to be recycled. It is re-recorded when the next student makes a request for a recording. In this way, circulation needs are met, and the original tape is preserved in good condition.

Automation of the School Library

A few years ago, there was a great deal of talk about automating the school library or media center. The Systems Development Corporation of Santa Monica, California, for example, announced the ALPS System—Automated Library Processing Services. With the aid of a computer, this system offered a bibliographic data file from MARC and an in-process file for each library in the system, circulation processing computer programs, and book fund accounting reports. The Los Angeles City Schools made use of part of the program with the help of federal funds, but eventually had to abandon the program, as it was too costly. This has been the story with many attempts to automate the school library. The technology is here, and it could be done now—but it would take more money than most schools have. The Beverly Hills Unified School District, also with the help of federal funds, established an information retrieval system that eventually had to be discarded. Automation will work, and there are many uses for it in the school media center. But computers are expensive, and most school libraries would rather spend their money on materials than on electronic gear to keep track of those materials.

However, school media centers have been quick to seize on machines that will help them do their work but that are not so expensive. Security systems, like Tattle Tape, and mechanical or electronic charging systems have been a great help to school libraries. Xerographic duplicating machines and motorized microfilm and microfiche printers and readers have contributed much to the success of the media center.

Production Facilities

A few media centers have added production facilities: a darkroom for processing film, a **Thermofax**® machine for making transparencies, a small soundproof room or booth for making recordings, even a small recording studio for producing videotapes. All of these facilities and/or equipment can be used by teachers or students. English and social studies teachers no longer insist that all student projects be written reports. A book report may be in the form of a tape recording; a social studies "term paper" can be a set of slides accompanied by a sound recording; a science project can be a super 8 motion picture. The media center offers facilities for the students to do part of their work there. Indeed, students are encouraged to experiment with new and different ways of communicating whatever they want to say. Only tradition says that a report must be written. It may be more effective to photograph or record it. Students enjoy these new ways of expressing themselves, and the media center provides some of the equipment and facilities they need to do this.

Teachers also come to the center to produce materials that they need for their classes. They, too, find that some of the visual and aural media are better suited to their needs. If the media center has adequate staff, it may offer to produce some materials for teachers—recordings, overhead transparencies, and filmstrips from a set of slides.

All of this equipment is expensive but not as expensive as a few computer terminals or an on-line service. Even the cost of video tape recorders and cameras is within the reach of many school media centers. Once the equipment has been paid for, the on-going cost is chiefly for tape and maintenance. Junior high schools, which normally have smaller budgets than high schools, are experimenting with half-inch video cassette tape machines. The tapes are relatively inexpensive, and with a simple distribution system, the programs can be broadcast on closed circuit to several classrooms at the same time. The equipment is portable enough so that the teachers can record material at home, then play it back over TV receivers in the classroom from the media center.

Standards for Media Equipment

School media standards include recommendations for amounts of equipment—such as one slide projector for every 100 students in the school, or one microprojector per school and one duplicating machine per media center. The trouble with such recommendations is that they assume that all programs are alike. More super 8 cameras and projectors may be needed in one school than in another, because more teachers encourage students to make their own films. The amount of equipment needed in a center should be determined by the needs of that school and its unique instructional program. However, equipment that is not available obviously will not be used. A center that has no facilities for making filmstrips from slides may argue that it doesn't need these facilities because no one has asked for them. But if such a facility were available it might be used a great deal. Only experience with it would tell. So, a media center has an obligation to make many kinds of equipment available on the chance that teachers and students will use them. With experience, the media specialist can decide whether more of one kind of equipment is needed. Equipment for the sake of equipment is a waste of money, but equipment that is needed and used is a wise investment.

Space Standards

School media standards also recommend certain amounts of space per student, based on a percentage of the total enrollment of the school. The Colorado guidelines for school media programs, for example, recommend seating space for ten percent of the student enrollment at forty square feet per student in phase one, and seating for fifteen percent of the student enrollment at forty square feet per student in phase three. The Michigan guidelines for media programs recommend 3,500 square feet (ten percent of the enrollment at thirty square feet per student) at the basic level and 6,000 square feet at the advanced level. These recommendations usually end up with more space than a school can afford. A city high school with 3,000 students would need seating space for 300 students if space is provided for only ten percent of the student body. Few schools can afford a media center that large.

The main points to keep in mind are these. There should be room for most of the students who will want to use the center at any one time. This will be influenced by the curriculum of the school, by the community it serves, by the number of students who have to be bussed to school, and by the emphasis placed on textbooks. Furniture and equipment should be arranged so they are easy and comfortable to use. It is axiomatic that there must be plenty of electrical outlets. As Marshall McLuhan has said, a lot of wonderful things have happened in the twentieth century, and most of them can be plugged into the wall. The invention of electrical equipment is going to continue. The media center needs to be built for this future.

Study Carrels

Study carrels are desirable, but perhaps their importance in a school library has been overstressed. An elementary school library may find that a few carrels are good. They satisfy the needs of students who want to be alone. However, they can also be a source of trouble, since they make good hiding places and prevent close supervision. This can also be true in the junior high school library. Study carrels are most effective in the senior high school library, where students are mature enough to use them properly.

At one time, it was fashionable to talk of study carrels equipped with everything—TV receivers, cassette tape recorders, super 8 projectors, rear screen filmstrip projectors, and computer terminals. Since then, school librarians have learned that this equipment can be a curse as well as a blessing. It takes continuous maintenance to keep the machines in working order. And unless students are carefully trained and closely supervised, they quickly damage or destroy expensive materials.

KEEPING RECORDS

School libraries, like other libraries, need to keep records—of materials circulated, of expenditures, of the number of new books added to the collection, of materials lost or damaged. The budget of the school library is not based on use as measured by circulation. Yet circulation statistics are important for other reasons. They show what parts of the collection are being used more than others. They are a rough measure of how much use is made of the media center.

Circulation Records

However, in a school library, recorded circulation reveals only a part of the use that is made of materials. Many materials—films, film loops, videotapes—may not be checked out of the library. They have to be used there, because the center has the equipment for projecting or playing them back. Most school libraries do not record the use of materials in the library. It would be nice to have this information, but there is no one to keep track of it.

Students circulate materials among themselves after one of them has checked a book or tape out of the library. The official record shows one use of the item, whereas actually there may have been five times as many as that. Or how can the use of a film in the media center by one student be compared with the circulation of the same film to a teacher who shows it to students in five different classes? A record of the circulation of materials is usually kept, but the librarian recognizes that it is a very imperfect picture of what is happening in the media center.

The school librarian is more interested in the number of new items added to the collection, and in the number of items lost, than in how many times they circulate.

Inventory

An inventory of the materials in the collection falls in the same category. It is a luxury for a school library. If the media center can afford this luxury, with the help of paid clerks or volunteer workers, very well. But without adequate help, it is a kind of record keeping that may have to be omitted in a school library. This is not to underestimate the importance of an inventory. It can be very helpful, but if the library has to be closed to allow time for an inventory, most school librarians will decide that it is more essential to keep the library open. An ideal solution is to pay the librarian extra for taking inventory before school opens in the fall or closes in early summer. But this is costly and may not be possible.

Record of Textbooks

Records do need to be kept of textbooks and of new materials received from publishers and producers. Teachers expect the school librarian to have an accurate record of textbooks—how many copies of a title are in the school, what teacher or classroom has them now, what supplementary materials are available and in what quantities. Librarians often consider keeping track of textbooks a purely clerical task, which it is; but to teachers, it is an important record, one that they expect the librarian to have.

Since the school librarian is shipping and receiving clerk as well as media specialist, that person will need to keep careful count of new materials ordered and received. Often many items are ordered from the same source at one time. But some are out of print, some are back ordered, and some are out of stock. Unless the librarian keeps an accurate record of items still outstanding, the business office may pay for them even though they have not been received.

Keeping account of all these materials is time consuming, but necessary. The school district business office handles thousands of items each month for all schools in the district. The library is only one small division, and it must keep many of its own records if its operation is to run smoothly.

Record of Nonprint Materials

The school library's record keeping is complicated by the presence of large amounts of nonprint materials. Recording the circulation of audiovisual materials is more complex than recording the circulation of books. A circulation card can be kept in the pocket of a book until it is checked out, when the card is transferred to a file of materials on loan. This is not so easy with a cassette recording, with a single captioned filmstrip, or with a plastic model of the human heart. Some school libraries do try to keep the circulation card with the material until it is checked out. Others keep a separate file of cards for all nonprint materials in the collection, cards on which checkouts can be recorded. These cards are never with the materials and never leave the library, but they show who has an item and when it is due back or when it left the media center.

At the district level, it is better to list materials in a book catalog than in a card catalog. The need for multiple copies of the catalog for use in the schools makes a card catalog impractical, except for internal use at the district office. If circulation cards are kept in a separate file rather than with the materials, they can be used in the preparation of a book catalog.

If there is a separate book catalog for each major media, one for films, one for filmstrips, and one for recordings for example, there may be a need for special lists or catalogs that bring materials together by subject. These special lists can also be prepared from circulation cards if they are kept in a separate file and not with the materials.

CENSORSHIP

The school library is subject to peculiar kinds of censorship. It is usually self-imposed—by the librarian or teachers or the principal. In most cases, the school staff censors materials before the parents or community become aware of them. This is because school people have been burned so often in the past. They know the harm that can result from censorship fights in the school, so they are careful to avoid future potential battles. It is not that school librarians are more timid or fearful than other types of librarians. It is only that they have learned that certain lines of action lead to certain defeat.

Special School Library Problems

There is a reason for the uniqueness of censorship problems in the school library. Education is compulsory and parents have to send their children to school and to the school library. They have a right, under these conditions, to ask that their children not be exposed to materials of which they do not approve. If the public library has materials that parents do not want to fall into the hands of their children, they can forbid them to go to the library. If the child disobeys, that is between child and parents. The public library is blameless. This is not the case with the school library. The parent cannot, legally, order a child not to go to school—and the school media center is part of the school.

So the school library has to be much more cautious than the public library about the materials in its collection. Another reason for the uniqueness of censorship in the school library is that the school library's patrons are all young people. Those who favor censorship are usually more concerned with harm that may come to young minds. They fear that young minds are not as able as adult minds to discern the truth when it is mixed in with things that are not true. They fear that more harm will be done to young minds by opposing points of view because young minds are more impressionable.

When censorship problems arise in schools, they have a way of becoming political issues. Freedom of thought is soon forgotten, and the real battle is over who will run the schools—the conservatives or the liberals, the public or the educators. The value or lack of value of the book or film that started the trouble gets lost in the political melee.

How to Handle Censorship Problems

Censorship need not be a serious problem in the school library if a few simple rules are followed. 1) There should be a written policy, adopted by the board of education, for dealing with questionable instructional materials. This policy should outline step by step the procedure to be followed when materials are questioned. The same policy should apply to questions by parents, students, teachers, and administrators. 2) The procedure for handling decisions about questionable materials should be designed to encourage deliberate, rational action. 3) There should be a selection policy for acquiring materials. If a librarian or teacher ignores the policy, that person must be prepared to take the consequences of that action. 4) Selection policies and the procedure for handling questionable materials should be designed to avoid haste. When censorship is the issue, emotions run high. A slow, deliberate process is the best way to achieve justice. 5) When materials are questioned, they should be withdrawn from circulation until a decision can be reached. Keeping them in use while debating their suitability for the school library only invites further trouble.

FEDERAL SUPPORT

With the 1965 Elementary and Secondary Education Act (ESEA), school libraries began to receive federal aid. Title II of ESEA allocated funds for the purchase of library materials but not for personnel or library buildings. Each state submitted a plan for allocating and spending the money provided by Title II. In Texas, the money was used to establish regional instructional materials centers. In California, the money was divided among districts on the basis of enrollment and on local assessed property evaluation. The more affluent a district, the smaller was its share of the state's Title II funds. In the 1970s, Title II funds and the earlier National Defense Education Act Title III funds were grouped together under Title IVB. Under this title, monies could be used for personnel, testing, guidance and counseling, library materials, and equipment. There was more money under Title IVB, but there was also more competition for it, and sometimes libraries lost out to other programs in the struggle.

Value of Federal Aid to School Libraries

How effective is federal aid to school libraries? It has given many school libraries money to purchase materials and equipment that they would have been unable to secure otherwise. However, this gift of funds has had its dark side also. Money has been wasted on materials and equipment of poor quality. Manufacturers have rushed in to produce materials that they hoped would sell, without much concern for their quality and value. Schools have been forced to buy things they did not really want because they were prevented from getting the things that they needed. Federal and state regulations governing the use of funds are often mountainous and not too well thought out. Many school librarians question whether the funds are worth the effort it takes to get them. The real need is for legislation that supports school libraries, not just money.

SCHOOL LIBRARY ASSOCIATIONS

During the past two decades, with the growth of school libraries, there has been a noticeable increase in the number of school library associations. Their importance in the development of school library standards has already been noted, but they have contributed much more than this to the improvement of the profession. The associations have done a great deal for the growth of school librarianship.

State Associations

Many states have associations of school librarians—California, Illinois, Indiana, Ohio, and New York, to name just a few. Beginning in the mid-1970s, there was a movement to combine school library associations and audiovisual associations. This has been an outgrowth of the media center concept. Since the media center uses all kinds of media, both print and nonprint, it was natural to combine the two types of personnel who work with this media. In July 1977, for example, the California Media and Library Educators Association replaced the California Association of School Librarians and the California Association for Educational Media and Technology. The Illinois Association for Media in Education, at about the same time, replaced the Illinois Association of School Librarians. A little earlier, in 1976, the Long Island Education Communications Council and the Nassau-Suffolk School Library Association voted to unite in a common organization. The movement toward unification had been going on for many years before official action was taken to combine the two types of groups. School librarians became media specialists as they worked with more and more kinds of instructional materials. Audiovisual experts found a place in the library. The librarian, working with audiovisual materials and equipment, developed a realization that they had common goals and purposes. In some states, the two groups or associations held joint conferences before they thought of merging into one association. Their work in the media center brought them together, and it was logical that eventually they should become one.

This merging of the two associations often created friction. There were jealousies (who would be in charge of the media center—the librarian or the audiovisual expert?). The struggle for power spilled over into credential and certification requirements (should there be one credential for school librarians and a separate credential for audiovisual specialists? should training for media specialists include both library science and educational technology?). Much of this friction, which characterized the early 1970s, has now disappeared. In most organizations, the two groups work together toward a common goal.

Importance of School Library Associations

The important thing is that these associations, whether they are media associations or still school library associations, have contributed a great deal to the profession. Many of them publish journals with articles and news of significance to school librarians. Many members of the associations are not able to take an active part in the affairs of the organization, but they can keep up with the profession through their journals. The associations hold annual conferences that bring members together. They publish special bibliographies of materials useful to school librarians. They take an active part in developing legislation in support of school libraries and media centers. They offer aid to librarians embroiled in censorship difficulties. And they put on workshops to assist the librarian who wants to know more about media or television or legislation affecting school libraries.

National Associations

Besides the state associations, there is the national organization—the American Association of School Librarians, one of the largest divisions in the American Library Association. For many years, there has been a running debate as to whether school librarians would be better off as a division of the National Education Association. Under NEA, they would be outnumbered by teachers, but under ALA they feel that they are often pushed aside by college and university and public librarians. School librarians have an interest in both librarianship and education, so neither association can meet their needs alone.

To the building librarian, the national association is pretty far removed. It does publish a journal, *The School Media Quarterly*, it does issue the national standards for media programs, and it sponsors legislation that would benefit school librarians. But most school librarians have little contact with AASL and do not feel that it plays an important part in their professional life. Their state association is closer to them and answers more of their needs.

If the national association is distant from most school librarians, the International Association of School Librarianship is even further away. IASL was organized in 1971 at the Jamaica meeting of the World Conference of Organizations of the Teaching Profession. Its aims are to encourage the development of school libraries in all countries, to promote the professional preparation of school librarians, to encourage the development of school library materials, and to bring about collaboration between school librarians in all countries. The Association held its first meeting in London and has published papers and proceedings.

SERVICE TO SPECIAL GROUPS

Besides serving students who can't read and who don't want to read, the school librarian serves students who are visually handicapped, physically handicapped, emotionally disturbed, and to whom English is a second language. Each group presents special problems to the school librarian.

The modern approach to *handicapped students* is to include them in the regular classroom with normal students whenever possible. At one time, it was fashionable to have special schools for the handicapped. There were schools for the blind, for the mentally retarded, and for the physically handicapped. Today's special education teachers believe that handicapped students should spend as much time as possible · with normal students. That will be their fate after they leave school, so their education should prepare them for that life.

Schools that have some *blind* or visually handicapped students need to provide a library experience for them, just as they do for other students. There are books in Braille, talking books, and specially prepared materials (like raised relief maps and globes) for them. The school librarian should provide these materials as a matter of course. In some school libraries, there is a special drawer in the card catalog for Braille materials in the collection. Braille books are usually shelved separately, and the cards in the catalog for them are printed in Braille. Blind students are taught to find their way to these drawers and then to the shelves. They can be given lessons in the use of the card catalog along with sighted students. They come to the library with their class and share in whatever lessons the librarian teaches. They listen to stories, select books, and read them just as do the sighted students. They are made to feel a regular part of the class of which they are members.

If they are visually handicapped, but not blind, the library has a collection of large print books for them. The librarian may choose to have a special drawer in the card catalog for these materials. The information on the cards has been printed with a primary typewriter, in large type, to assist them. The librarian will supplement the regular collection of materials for the visually handicapped by sending to the American Foundation for the Blind for additional materials. If the school has a Braillest, the librarian can Braille special materials for individual students, and these materials can later be added to the library's collection.

The librarian will develop a special collection of captioned films and filmstrips for *deaf students*. Many producers now publish captioned material for use by deaf students. A few film companies produce 16mm motion pictures in sound with captions added. When the media center has some of these films, both deaf and hearing students can view the same material. There is no need to segregate some students simply because they are deaf.

Benefiting from the experience of Patricia Corey at the Lexington School for the Deaf in New York City, school librarians have learned to improve their skills in storytelling for deaf children. They choose books with large pictures and a simple story. They use gestures and facial expression to help them convey the plot and action to their audience. They find that storytelling for deaf children can be as exciting as storytelling for hearing children.

Service to the *physically handicapped* is largely a matter of making things easy for them to reach and to use in the media center. Students with braces or in wheelchairs need to have materials within easy reach. When this is not always possible, library helpers can be trained to assist them.

ESL students, students for whom English is a second language, form another special group using the media center. The majority of ESL students speak Spanish, but by no means all of them. Since the mid-1970s, a large number of Vietnamese students have enrolled in schools in the United States, and from time to time, there are students whose native language is French, German, Italian, or Chinese. All of these students require special help and materials in the school library.

It is often difficult to find suitable materials for these students. A secondary school student whose native language is Chinese and who is just learning to speak English needs content material in the mother tongue. Few media centers have 10th grade biology books in Chinese or 11th grade civics materials covering United States state and local government, but written in Chinese. The library can provide simple materials for students who need to increase their facility in English. But the problem is this: most of these materials have been written for very young children whose native language is English. These materials are too babyish for students ten and eleven years old, who have experiences far beyond those described in books for much younger pupils. There is also the problem of whether these materials should be written in two languages or only in English. If they are produced in two languages, there is the likelihood that students will use only the parts printed in their own language. They will be slower to gain the skill they need in English. The media center's collection of audiovisual materials can help these students. They can gather the information they need from pictures with a simple oral explanation in English. In time, this will lead to a facility in interpreting the written language.

EVALUATION

With the growth and improvement of school libraries, evaluating the media center program has become increasingly important. Evaluation is a vital part of accreditation. The National Study of School Evaluation (NSSE; formerly known as the Comparative Study of Secondary School Standards and later as the National Study of Secondary School Evaluation) publishes *Evaluative Criteria* and *Junior High School/ Middle School Evaluative Criteria*. It also issues *Elementary School Evaluative Criteria*, which does the same thing for grades K-8. All three of these publications contain sections on instructional materials services—library and audiovisual.

Methods of Evaluating the School Library

The sections on the library are basically checklists, which have been widely used to evaluate the media center. The checklist method is simple to apply and provides a quick evaluation of the library's services, staff, collection, and facilities. The NSSE checklists include sections on "numerical adequacy," e.g., number of full-time professional librarians, total number of hours per week provided by volunteer student assistants, full-time equivalence of adult clerical assistants, and full-time equivalence of professional audiovisual personnel. The preparation section covers the professional courses in education, reading instruction, and library science completed by the staff, as well as specialized preparation in the selection of materials and the use of reference tools. Services, such as assisting teachers in the development of reading lists and guiding students in their selection of books and other instructional materials are included, as well as sections on facilities and equipment.

These checklists can be used for self-evaluation as well as accreditation. The librarian does not have to wait for accreditation to measure the effectiveness of the program. The trouble with checklists is that they tend to be quantitative rather than qualitative. However, the trend is toward qualitative measurement, and as school libraries become more sophisticated, this development will gain momentum.

In 1977, Gaylord Professional Publications announced the publication of *School and Public Library Media Programs for Children and Young Adults*, by Philip Baker. This work included a discussion of exemplary media programs in a number of school libraries. Baker raised the question, what makes a media program exemplary? Is it money? Is it staff? Is it a new and shining facility? From his study of fifty model programs, he developed ten criteria for evaluating exemplary media centers. It is encouraging to find that he emphasized the qualitative differences of these programs, for example, the programs "involved staff in ways that heightened their sense of personal and professional value." They offered some kind of reward for a superior program, they devoted considerable attention to learning basic skills, and they could be adapted to other situations and institutions and still be outstanding. They met a need in the school.

New Method of Evaluation

This is the kind of evaluation that school libraries are beginning to adopt. No longer are they judged by the number of books or films in their collection, the number of microfilm readers they possess, or the amount of seating space per student. Books, films, projectors, seating space are only means to an end. They contribute to a good program but by themselves, they do not make a program. And the program of the media center, what the librarian *does* with the books or films or projectors, is the important thing. This is what the librarian and center should be judged by. In the future, evaluation will pay more and more attention to program; and with a concentration on program, we will develop better and more effective school libraries.

BIBLIOGRAPHY

American Association of School Librarians and Association for Educational Communications and Technology. *Media Programs: District and School*. Chicago: American Library Association, 1975.

Blazek, Ron. *Influencing Students toward Media Center Use: An Experimental Investigation in Mathematics*. Chicago: American Library Association, 1975.

Brown, James. *AV Instruction: Technology, Media and Methods*. 5th ed. New York: McGraw-Hill, 1977.

Cabeceinas, James. *The Multimedia Library*. New York: Academic Press, 1978.

California Association of School Librarians. *Guidelines for California Library Media Programs*. Burlingame, CA: California Media and Library Educators Association, 1977.

Chisholm, Margaret. *Media Personnel in Education*. Englewood Cliffs, NJ: Prentice-Hall, 1976.

Cleary, Florence. *Discovering Books and Libraries: A Handbook for Students in the Middle and Upper Grades*. 2nd ed. New York: H. W. Wilson, 1977.

Delaney, Jack. *The Media Program in the Elementary and Middle Schools*. Hamden, CT: Linnet Books, 1976.

Gillespie, John. *A Model School District Media Program: Montgomery County*. Chicago: American Library Association, 1977.

Hicks, Warren. *Managing Multimedia Libraries*. New York: R. R. Bowker, 1977.

Illinois. State. Office of the Superintendent of Public Instruction. *Standards for Educational Media Programs in Illinois*. Springfield, IL, 1973.

Jones, Milbrey. *Survey of School Media Standards*. Washington, DC: U.S. Dept. of Health, Education, and Welfare, 1977.

Liesener, James. *A Systematic Process for Planning Media Programs*. Chicago: American Library Association, 1976.

Marshall, Faye. *Managing the Modern School Library*. West Nyack, NY: Parker Pub. Co., 1976.

Minor, Ed. *Techniques for Producing Visual Instructional Media*. 2nd ed. New York: McGraw-Hill, 1977.

Peterson, Gary. *The Learning Center: A Sphere for Nontraditional Approaches to Education*. Hamden, CT: Linnet Books, 1975.

Prostano, Emanuel. *The School Library Media Center*. 2nd ed. Littleton, CO: Libraries Unlimited, 1977.

Prostano, Emanuel. *School Media Programs: Case Studies in Management*. 2nd ed. Metuchen, NJ: Scarecrow Press, 1974.

Rosenberg, Kenyon. *Media Equipment: A Guide and Dictionary*. Littleton, CO: Libraries Unlimited, 1976.

Rufsvold, Margaret. *Guides to Educational Media: Films, Filmstrips, etc.* 4th ed. Chicago: American Library Association, 1977.

Schuster, Marie. *The Library-Centered Approach to Learning*. Palm Springs, CA: ETC Publications, 1977.

Wehmeyer, Lillian. *The School Librarian as Educator*. Littleton, CO: Libraries Unlimited, 1976.

MANAGING THE TECHNICAL LIBRARY

by Jerry Cao

INTRODUCTION

In this chapter, it is proposed to define and delimit the technical library and its director, to locate that library in its parent organization, and to delineate that library's functions and objectives as administered by the library manager. Budgeting, space requirements, staffing, services, measurement and evaluation, and library cooperation are examined. Definition of and differentiation between the technical library and other types of libraries occupy the major part of the remainder of this section.

The term management, in preference to administration or supervision, is used in most cases throughout the chapter for various reasons. First, in the technical or scientific environment, the designation so often applied to the head of the technical library or information center is that of manager. Also, the term administration is associated with ownership or corporate leadership, while the term management implies direction of activities at the operational level. The terms supervision and supervisor usually represent the concept of directing a small unit performing tasks on a short-range basis. While the size of the unit is not an overriding consideration (the manager of the technical library may direct only one or two people), the manager commonly will be responsible for long-range planning for the library, among other management operations. The technical library manager may be thought of generally as a part of middle management in the corporate environment in which the library is usually found.

The term technical library is one of several that could be used to designate the collections of staff, resources, and services to be examined. In one sense, many special libraries could be considered technical libraries. Philosophy, education, and sociology, as examples, are highly technical disciplines; therefore, a special library supporting research and/or study in one of these areas could be termed a technical library. However, by restricting the concept of the technical library to a more specific purview, it is possible to differentiate between technology/science libraries and libraries supporting disciplines of a technical nature, such as those noted above.

Strauss, Shreve, and Brown, in their work on the organization and management of scientific and technical libraries, list sixteen designations known to be in use in this field, including those of technical information service, information center, research and development library, engineering library, etc.[1] Among other terms not listed by them, and one that has come into common usage, is that of technical information center; in some cases, this designation has been given a more comprehensive meaning than that of technical library and may include the latter as one of its units. For purposes of consistency and brevity, and because it probably is still the most widely recognized, the term technical library is used in most cases throughout this chapter to represent the many agencies performing bibliographic and other support services to science and technology. Use of the term special library (or other variations from the term technical library) herein results from such usage in the literature cited.

The philosophy behind the technical library does not differ noticeably from that of, for example, the tax-supported library. It may be said that the philosophy of any "public" library, which term includes all of the four commonly defined types—public, academic, special, and school—is to provide the user with the best service possible with the means available. In the words of one supporter of information services, the province of the technical library is to make available "a summary of anything that has ever been published in any form anywhere in the world" on the subject interests of the clientele.[2] This may be too idealized a mission, but another writer has proposed a similar philosophy: "The identification, provision and use of the document or piece of information which would best help the user in his study, teaching or research, at the optimal combination of cost and elapsed time."[3] In Strauss, the purpose is expressed as securing, assembling, and making available all information that relates in any way to a specific subject.[4]

As to objectives, those promulgated in 1964 by the Special Libraries Association (SLA) are less idealistic than the above cited purposes, and two of the objectives are more functional than goal setting: to serve as a major source of information in the organization; and generally to perform the functions usual to any type of library, with the proviso that these be germane to the organization's activities. The third objective is to serve "all who have appropriate need of its services."[5] This last is more a statement of an objective than are the first two, but it gives no indication of the quality of service to be provided.

The imperative behind the service differs between the technical library with which this paper is concerned and the general library (i.e., academic, other special, public, school): the technical library with which this chapter is dealing is most commonly part of a for-profit organization and must justify its existence fiscally, the difficulty of which is noted in the section on measurement and evaluation. Bakewell, in his international survey of industrial libraries, justifies the library on the generally accepted principle that time and money are saved by the industrial organization because the research staff will not be duplicating work that has been done somewhere else.[6] Meltzer[7] and Strable[8] buttress this justification by citing examples of egregious waste of company funds because of duplication of research effort.

The technical library differs from other types of libraries in that it deals with a more homogeneous clientele. Probably the most heterogeneous of all library clienteles are those of the public library. School and academic libraries serve generally more compact communities of users than do public libraries, but both academic and school library clienteles are composed basically of faculty and students having fairly diverse needs. The technical library serves a technical and/or scientific clientele, which requires normally a greater depth of coverage in a more restricted number of disciplines.

The third edition of the *Handbook of Special Librarianship* makes another important differentiation between technical and general libraries, one that concerns the unit of information involved. The user of the general library usually must locate the unit of information, e.g., a book or other "gross" item, while the user of the technical library more often requires a specific piece of information found within such a gross item.[9] This concept is expressed differently in the fourth edition of the *Handbook*: the technical librarian must be "proactive, dynamic, participative, involved and interpretative."[10] This description ideally should fit any librarian or type of librarian, but these adjectives help to delimit the unit of information. Ladendorf writes that time is money in the industrial environment and that special library services must be designed to minimize user effort,[11] a restatement of the smaller unit of information concept.

It should be noted that, although the technical library can be differentiated from the other types of libraries, it may be found as a part of large public libraries and academic institutions. Other locations include professional associations, research organizations, government agencies, and service institutions, such as hospitals.[12] For purposes of the present paper, it is the technical library in the industrial or research organization that is under discussion.

The location of the technical library in the industrial organization may differ from one institution to another, but those libraries serving the organization in general (as opposed to specialized libraries supporting a unit of the organization, such as marketing) are most commonly found as a part of administrative operations, administrative services, operation services, or a similarly designated group. In the research organization, the technical library will most likely be responsible to the director of research.[13] The placement of the technical library in the organization can create problems for the professional librarian, and this possibility will be examined later in the paper.

There are no precise statistics on the number of technical libraries in the United States. Figures for 1975-1976, found in *The Bowker Annual* for 1978, indicate more than 12,500 special libraries, without further differentiation.[14] The *Directory of Special Libraries and Information Centers* includes a large number of agencies serving scientific or technical disciplines.[15] A meaningful count of technical libraries probably would involve more effort than scanning the pages of the *Directory* and tallying those institutions fitting the criteria of supporting technological or scientific efforts. Libraries with ambiguous listings and the probability of some unlisted technical libraries would dilute the accuracy of the count.

MANAGEMENT

That forward-looking thinker on management, Peter Drucker, writes that there are five basic operations in the work of the manager, whatever type of organization involved. Drucker is particularly appropriate for librarians to adhere to in matters of management, because he was one of the earliest theoreticians to recognize the transition of the American society and economy from an industrial basis to one of information or knowledge. Unfortunately for the library community, Drucker has never recognized the library as a knowledge organization that should be in the forefront of managing information for the new society. This is one of his few oversights.

Here are Drucker's five basic operations in the manager's work. First, the manager sets objectives or goals. The goals of the technical library may be said to be subsumed as objectives under the overall goals of the corporate organization. Second, the manager organizes. He or she classifies the work and divides it into manageable activities, grouping these units and activities into an organization structure, then selecting people for the supervision of units for activities to be implemented. Third, a manager motivates and communicates. Constant communication is maintained with subordinates, superiors, and colleagues; and communication moves upward, downward, and laterally. Fourth, the manager measures and insures that applicable measurements are available to each person. The manager also analyzes these measurements and communicates their meanings to subordinates, superiors, and colleagues. Fifth, a manager develops people, including himself or herself.[16] The best manager may be the one who assembles the best possible people with the means available, sees that they know their authorities and responsibilities, and allows them to perform their tasks with as little interference as necessary (bearing in mind the need for communication).

To perform the five basic operations, the manager requires certain skills and qualities. Setting objectives needs a sense of balance, e.g., between short-term and future needs, and between desirable ends and available means. Analytical ability is necessary for setting objectives, for organizing, for developing people, and for motivating and communicating. Social skills and integrity are requisite to motivating and communicating and for developing people. Measuring requires analytical skills, but more than that, it requires self-control. The manager must not use this tool to control and dominate subordinates; violation of this principle, says Drucker, makes this area the weakest one in management performance at this time. He goes further to say that whether the manager develops subordinates into bigger and richer persons will determine directly whether the manager will improve personally or deteriorate.[17]

Drucker's five operations summarize more succinctly the responsibilities of management than do the seven elements of the acronym POSDCORB (proposed in the classic work by Gulick four decades ago) representing planning, organizing, staffing, directing, coordinating, reporting, and budgeting.[18] POSDCORB remains, nevertheless, pervasively influential in the literature and study of management, including that of libraries, as Evans indicates in his general work on management techniques for librarians.[19] The influence is strikingly exemplified in the 1977 text on library management by Stueart and Eastlick, which is organized somewhat after the fashion of POSDCORB, with four chapters having headings taken directly from the acronym.[20] Arnold's monograph on the information department is also structured similarly to POSDCORB, and the chapter on management includes most of the elements in the acronym.[21]

So, despite the continuing evolution of management theory and practice, old bases remain upon which it is necessary to build. The question is not whether Taylor or Mayo, Fayol or Simon, or someone else is right: each has been right and wrong about different things. The successful manager draws elements from more than one management school and combines them into a style suitable for that person, based upon personality, objectives of the unit, strengths and weaknesses of different styles of management, and capabilities of staff members. Evans indicates the desirability of a similar process.[22]

Technical Library Management

Evans sees library management as having gone through essentially the same stages as business or industrial management but at later times. Prior to 1937, the traditional ideas of administration suffused what literature there was on the subject of library management (or library economy). Almost without exception, the head of the library made the decisions, which tended to be made on the basis of what had been done in the past. Library administration, including education for it, was concerned mostly with ways of organizing and operating various library units: reference, cataloging, branches, etc.[23] Scientific management had been posited in the last quarter of the nineteenth century, but libraries in general saw no relevance to their situation prior to the 1930s.

A decade after business and industry had moved from the theory of scientific management to the human relations school, librarianship, largely influenced by dissertations coming from the University of Chicago Graduate Library School, entered a period in which Taylor, et al., were considered seriously for possible library applications. According to Evans, libraries moved belatedly into a human-relations period of administration around 1955 and are still making tentative moves toward a synthesis of management theory to be applied to libraries. By contrast, general management theory began a process of synthesizing in about 1950.[24]

Various factors militate against adoption by technical libraries of those manifestations of a unified theory of library management evident at present: democratic administration, participative management, use of committees, and involvement in decision making.[25] These factors include the sometimes anomalous status of the professional librarian in the corporate organization (professional, administrative, clerical?), the possible uncertain future of the technical library in those industries that shrink and expand depending on federal contracts, and the relative smallness and thus condensed structure of many technical libraries. The technical librarian with questionable status, managing a small library for a company engaged in an industry dependent on government contracts (to take the worst case) is not likely to be interested in sharing what status is available by diluting his or her authority. This apprehension may be compounded by the presence in technical libraries of many "librarians" who do not hold a degree in library science, a problem examined in the section on staffing.

The management philosophy followed by the technical librarian will be dictated to some extent, of course, by that of the corporate parent. The extent to which corporate policy is to be modified depends on such factors as the degree of authoritarianism manifested by higher administrative levels and the initiative exhibited by the library manager in departing from company philosophy. The environment in an organization known for allowing no independence or autonomy in its operating units will not be conducive to departures from traditional forms of management. If, on the other hand, the organization emphasizes results more than adherence to formal administrative practices, the librarian might feel freer to experiment with a less structured decision-making apparatus. It should be borne in mind that "management by committee" is normally a slow-moving process when compared with decision making done by one person. The benefits to be accrued from giving the staff a part in decisions that affect them must be weighed against the possibility of a decision delayed or made incorrectly.

The Technical Library Manager

Titles given to heads of technical libraries vary widely: technical librarian, research librarian, director of library, manager of technical information service—in fact, whatever is appropriate to accompany the designation given the technical library. When the head of the technical library is at the same level as managers in other units of the organization, it is desirable that the library head be designated manager. Less common, but suggested in Strauss as an alternative, is the term "supervisor."[26] However, this term usually denotes a lower level in the organizational hierarchy.

Aside from the responsibilities common to administrators of any type of library (facility, budget, personnel, etc.), the manager of the technical library in some cases has additional duties peculiar to that position: executing literature searches, providing current awareness services, translating, contributing to or editing organizational publications, and supervising files of special materials.[27] Some of these responsibilities can be delegated, but in the small technical library, little or no delegating of management duties will be done. The library head in any case is responsible finally for the satisfactory completion of any delegated tasks, and the SLA standards illustrate this delegation by making managerial responsibilities generalized.[28]

Qualifications needed by the manager of the technical library are difficult to specify. As indicated in Strauss, the most effective ones do not fit a pattern and so do not provide data on which to base conclusions.[29] The question of whether technical librarians require a degree in library science has been settled de facto. It is not too uncommon for the manager of the technical library to have no degree or previous experience in librarianship. It is likely that this practice began to flourish during the period up to about ten years ago, when there was an undersupply of degreed librarians. The devaluation of the library science degree as a prerequisite for technical librarianship was no doubt encouraged by statements such as that found in a 1954 study of education for librarianship: "The subject specialist with some natural inclination and ability in librarianship can become, if he wishes, an effective science and technology librarian. . . ."[30]

The SLA standards mandate some specific requirements for the manager, such as a degree from a library school of recognized standing and three years of professional experience in a special library. Alternatively, the standards allow for a combination of subject expertise and professional experience. The intangible qualities required are, as the standard states, important for all librarians, and the combination of all of them certainly indicates a high level of competence: administrative ability, knowledge of an organization's functions and special areas of activity, analytical ability, capacity for investigation, perseverance and thoroughness in searching for information, flexibility, tact, poise, and initiative.[31]

Apart from academic degrees or personal qualities, it is necessary that the technical library manager have sufficient status in the organization to accomplish the objectives of the library. Lines of reporting and levels of authority external to the library should be clearcut, so that there will be no misunderstanding as to whom the librarian is responsible and what the librarian's place is in the organizational structure. This place should be such that the librarian can work with other professional staff outside the library as a colleague. As Campbell points out, some of the technical librarian's best sources of information are the professionals in the organization. The librarian can utilize best the expertise offered by these professionals by being able to solicit their assistance from somewhat the same level of status as their own.[32] In Strauss, this point is expressed more as a matter of maintaining pleasant relations with the clientele: "Ideally the individual should be personable, well-adjusted, poised in manner, and able to deal pleasantly with people."[33] Although this probably does not imply subservience, and these are certainly desirable qualities in anyone, the overall impresssion that it leaves is not one of interaction between equals.

BUDGETING

The budget of the technical library, as with other types of libraries, depends in its structure and administration on the type of budget system employed by the parent organization. The technical library budget may be known only as a lump sum, as part of a larger budgetary unit, without a detailed breakdown. In Strauss, this is considered undesirable, because discrete figures for salaries, acquisitions, etc. may be needed at some point for justifying the library's operations.[34]

In some cases, the technical library may have what is called an open-end budget. Funds for salaries are not included as a part of the budget but are maintained separately by company budgeters. The manager of the library is not given a firm budget figure but is directed simply to spend money for materials, supplies, and equipment until told to stop. Normal expenditures would not be questioned, but capital outlays would have to be approved by the monitoring authority. The disadvantages of this system are obvious: collection building necessarily would be subject to abrupt revision at some point in the budget period; supplies necessary to the operation of the library might be exhausted without funds for replacement; and needed repair or replacement of small pieces of equipment might have to be postponed to the next fiscal year.

Sources of income for the technical library, at least for that type with which this paper is most concerned, are found finally in company sales. Budgets for technical libraries commonly are part of administrative costs, because the library usually is part of administrative operations. Whether this is the case, or the library is part of a research and development unit, library funds are likely to fluctuate as the amount of business and/or research changes. There is some evidence that library budgets as a percentage of sales or of research budgets fall somewhere between 2 percent and 10 percent.[35] Recognizing the existence of fluctuations in the income of companies dependent to some extent on federal contracts, solvent companies usually are increasing sales at least moderately from year to year; library budgets should increase accordingly, assuming that demands on the library increase proportionately. Library budgets in steady-state companies (if there are such) that desire merely to maintain current levels of service should be enhanced by an increase matching that of inflation, so long as that is the trend of the economy.

As an alternative or complementary method to budgeting for the library as a percentage of sales or research, dollars expended per user can be established as a guideline. There are some published data available in a survey of 46 companies, showing ranges of budgets compared to the average number of users served.[36] These would have to be adjusted to reflect current dollars because of the age of the data. Furthermore, a determination must be made of who the users, or potential users, are. They normally will include managers and executives, staff research people, research and development scientists, etc. If appropriate, the number of outside users must be estimated also,[37] although these comprise usually an insignificant number in a technical library.

The standards issued by SLA provide no quantitative guidelines for budgets, but they do suggest bases for control of the budget by the library administrator:

> The budget of a special library should be based on recommendations of the special library administrator. . . .
>
> A special library administrator has the responsibility and authority for expenditure of his budgeted funds.[38]

The standards provide also some documentation to the person initiating a special library, in that they recognize the need for larger expenditures for materials and for capital purchases in setting up a library. New company programs and new subject areas also require more money for publications, and possibly for staff.[39]

Certain items may take disproportionate shares of the technical library budget compared with other types of libraries: salaries, journals, and report literature. The SLA standards recommend 60 to 79 percent of the budget as salaries,[40] and 70 to 80 percent is indicated in Strable.[41] Leonard's special library profiles, covering six examples, found salaries ranging from 67 to 72 percent of the library budgets.[42] These figures reflect another aspect of the smaller unit of information dealt with by the technical librarian. Proportionately, more professional staff are needed to provide this smaller unit.

Most technical libraries will collect several times as many technical reports as books, and some will receive five to twenty times as many.[43] Although books are more expensive to purchase than reports as a rule, and many reports are received free,[44] the sheer number of reports acquired makes this a substantial expense little known to other types of libraries. Reports available from National Technical Information Service (NTIS), the source of a majority of reports purchased by most technical libraries, have increased significantly in price over the past ten years. Microfiche are available and less expensive, of course, but they raise problems such as poor quality, user resistance, etc.

It should be noted that technical reports are not examined as an element of the suggested budget in Strauss;[45] and, while they are mentioned briefly in Strable, they are not assigned a place in a survey of seven sample library budgets.[46] In SLA's checklist for a company library under "Budget," reports are put with pamphlets, reprints, and technical bulletins.[47] However, Meltzer's work on the information center assigns about seven percent, certainly a significant part of the budget, to technical reports.[48]

An additional cost of the technical report is hidden in the frequently difficult task of identifying and acquiring it. In the case of the older report, indexes used for finding are often inadequate or difficult to use. The cost for time spent searching and ordering should be made a part of the cost of the report, but in reality, it cannot be. The price of the report may be charged against a job number, but the time expended by the librarian or other searcher has been lost so far as other projects are concerned.

The larger percentage of the budget required for journals in the technical library may be offset somewhat by the reduced number of books bought proportionately than is the case in the general library, although science and technology books tend to be more expensive than those in other fields. Books in science, medicine, and technology were in the top five in average price in 1977 among the 23 subject fields designated in Bowker's *Weekly Record*.[49]

STAFFING

Two requirements may differentiate staffing in the technical library from that in the general library. With some exceptions, librarians in public and academic libraries require, respectively, a broad educational background and scholarly specialization. The technical librarian is most likely to need a strong subject competence and the ability to provide a more intensive type of information service.[50] Again, to some extent, this reflects the different unit of information involved: the technical librarian most commonly is required to furnish a smaller unit of information, in a narrower field, to a more homogeneous clientele.

The second likely difference is in the use of professionals from outside library science in the technical library. This is not to say that this is not practiced in other types of libraries, but it is found more often in technical libraries. The positions of reference librarian and literature searcher are suggested in Strauss as suitable for people holding bachelor's degrees in the appropriate disciplines, with advanced subject study recommended. Requirements for the positions of translator and systems analyst are given as, respectively, knowledge of English and other languages, plus courses in science and engineering, and a bachelor's degree in systems analysis, supplemented by courses in library or information science.[51]

With the increasing use of automated retrieval systems, people knowledgeable in computer technology and/or having appropriate subject expertise comprise another group of professionals who are not from library science but who may be found in the technical library. This dual-ladder structure, an informal practice for years, coincides nicely with "Categories of Library Personnel—Professional," promulgated by the American Library Association (ALA) in 1970 and revised in 1976.[52]

The relative oversupply of degreed librarians at present may have begun to make technical libraries more selective in hiring for professional staff positions. It may be possible to require both the master's degree in library science and either a bachelor's or master's degree in an appropriate subject field. This has been the trend increasingly in academic libraries, where the double master's is now required in some cases, at least for tenure-track positions, e.g., in the California State University and Colleges system.

The process called career ladders, whereby non-degreed personnel move from subprofessional to professional positions on the basis of experience and/or course work (short of the professional degree) is now operating in some public and federal libraries. It has been present informally in technical libraries for some time. During the time of an undersupply of qualified librarians, i.e., to about 1968, many people with bachelor's degrees (often not even in an appropriate subject area) or lesser preparation were employed to fill professional places in technical libraries. There may still be some argument as to whether experience will substitute for the library degree,[53] but it is probably fortunate that technical libraries at present appear to be moving away from quasi career ladders and toward more stringent qualifications for filling professional positions.

SERVICES

It is posited in Strable that there are three levels of service that may be provided by the special library: minimum, intermediate, and maximum. Although services may vary in their rankings within a library, most special libraries will make the maximum level of service in all activities their final goal.[54] These three levels can be examined in regard to acquiring, organizing, and disseminating information. Because the final text of the library's services is that of the quality of dissemination of information, that service primarily is examined here. A high level of service in dissemination cannot exist, of course, without high levels in the two other areas.

The services provided the user of the technical library will be somewhat different in their emphases and may vary in some elements from those provided by other types of libraries. It has been mentioned previously that the unit of information commonly sought by the user of the technical library is smaller than the unit needed by the patron of the general library. This tends to affect the allocation of library resources, as was noted in the section on budgeting. The technical library usually spends more on salaries, technical reports, and journals, while spending less on books, public relations, and special services (in the sense of special services offered by public libraries, e.g., to special clienteles such as the blind, remote users, etc.).

The percentage of funds expended for salaries must not be so high that funds for resources are inadequate. And, as pointed out in Strable, an important task of the manager of the technical library is to maintain a balance between staff used for acquiring and organizing information and staff used for disseminating information.[55] Both statements are merely an application of one of Drucker's five operations engaged in by the manager: balancing one thing against another.

It is also necessary in any library to keep a balance between unlimited service to certain users and limitations of staff time. There is a point in some cases at which the technical library manager must be responsible for not allowing further time to be devoted to the needs of one user. This curtailment must be used with discretion, however. The manager must depend to some extent on personal knowledge (or staff knowledge) of the value to the company of the special service being requested. The extreme example of misused staff time is found in the client who requests the compilation of a bibliography for his or her child on some topic for use in school.

The scope of services to be provided by the technical library will depend on several factors, but as Meltzer points out, the basic functions of the library "must be the acquisition, organization, and maintenance of primary information pertinent to the company."[56] This mission is taken the next step in Strable: "The major effort of both the special library and the special librarian is devoted 1) to disseminating new information as quickly and efficiently as possible to the staff members of the organization and 2) to answering specific reference questions that arise."[57] It is with the implementation of these two broad elements that the manager of the technical library must be concerned. Both elements suggest the primacy of the smaller unit of information.

The allocation of more money to salaries, journals, and technical reports presumably provides the user of the technical library with that smaller unit of information. This is not to say that the larger unit of information represented by the book is of little or no value in the technical library, for monographs provide scientific information in an advanced state of development and provide maximum knowledge in a minimum package.[58] However, the technical report and journal normally give the user the results of significantly more recent research than is feasible in the book format.[59]

It is the dissemination of the results of current research and of current writing in general that comprises one of the basic service responsibilities of the technical library. These are the services usually gathered under the umbrella term "current awareness services." This designation generally excludes the routing of periodicals to company researchers, because the time factor in routing materials normally precludes those persons at the end of the list from receiving a periodical in a timely manner. An alternative, or adjunct, to routing periodicals in the way just described is to furnish contents pages of journals to those users known to be interested in the subject area covered. Recent copyright law changes may curtail this activity, but the SLA overview on copyright seems to indicate otherwise.[60] In a small company, a library staff member of long standing may be able to implement and maintain this service on an informal basis, and personal knowledge of individual needs is always best; but a large clientele requires a file that records the interests of users receiving this current awareness service. This would be the rudiments of a selective dissemination of information (SDI) service.

More sophisticated SDI services may be implemented. The technical library environment is particularly suited to this type of user accommodation: the clientele are for the most part involved in one or a few disciplines, they are keenly interested in development in their fields, and they usually are collected in a compact physical area served by the technical library. Geographic dispersal of some of the users need not preclude their participation in the service, depending on the mode and speed of communication between the central unit and the outlying users.

It is probably best if access to computers is available for implementing the SDI system, but the process is basically the same, whether manual or automated. Experienced literature analysts interview users in some detail as to their interests, compile profiles of user needs, and match incoming materials of all kinds against these profiles. When a match is made, the user is notified in one of various ways that the library has new material of interest to him or her. Notification may be in the form of citations with an abstract of each document, a list of titles, a list of complete citations, citations with corresponding descriptors, the first page of each document, or some variation or combination of these methods. A final and important step in the system is that of evaluation and feedback. Through a process of feedback from the user to the library staff profiler, the precision and recall capabilities of the profile are measured and the profile is adjusted accordingly on a continuing basis.

As alternatives to maintaining an in-house, manual SDI system, the technical library may buy the services of a commercial indexer (such as the Institute for Scientific Information) or combine its manual system with a commercial service. Advantages of combining the two are found in the higher relevancy of citations found in the manual system and the broader coverage, and sometimes prepublication citations, found in the commercial services.[61]

Other manifestations of disseminating information to clientele include accessions lists, bulletins, and personal notification by mail or telephone. The library may be responsible also for compiling and distributing news summaries in organizations in which this is important. Timing is, of course, of paramount importance in this service, and the compilation must be put into the company's early mail distribution to ensure its reaching its destination the same day.[62]

What may be considered traditional reference services in the general library must be somewhat different in the technical library. Meltzer differentiates between the two as passive reference and active reference services, respectively.[63] Again, this is a manifestation of the smaller unit of information with which the technical library is involved. The active reference service in the technical library requires a member of the library staff to locate the information needed by the user, rather than have the requester find it in the materials available, as with the passive reference service.[64] Parenthetically, it is convenient and useful to maintain a ready-reference file of answers to frequently asked questions, preferably on a rotating card file such as Rolodex.

A relatively recent addition to the literature search function is the commercial service that brokers various data bases. Prominent examples of this are Lockheed's **Dialog**®system and System Development Corporation's **Orbit**®system. For a fee, various services are available: searches of the data base using various access points (including subject access using Boolean logic); online printout of citations and/or abstracts; and offline printout. Because computer time is expensive, it is important that literature searchers become experts in search strategy in using these data bases. If searches are to be made by clientele as well as by library staff, users should be assisted by literature searchers to the extent users require and/or request it. Sometimes in a technical library in which the clientele are searching the data base personally, company policy will provide that search costs be charged to the job number of the user.[65]

Other reference services that may be offered by the technical library, depending on staff levels and competencies, include translations, bibliographies, and report editing. If staff competencies do not include languages and there is need for translations, there are alternatives available: utilizing one of the professional translation services listed by SLA,[66] or consulting the National Translations Center at John Crerar Library.[67] The compilation of bibliographies may have to be done on the basis of available time and the importance of the request. Economic necessity may require that time-consuming projects be charged against the requester's contract number. Staff levels, on the other hand, may allow for a permanent group in the library whose function is compiling bibliographies; there would normally be no charge to job numbers for bibliographies in this case. Editing of company publications is not often a function of the technical library, but it is listed in Strauss as one of the manager's responsibilities.[68] Deserved or not, engineers and scientists have a reputation as poor writers of English, and this editing activity possibly should be more common to technical libraries.

FACILITY AND EQUIPMENT

In contrast to the academic and public library environments, it will seldom be necessary for the manager of the technical library to plan a new building. In most cases, the technical librarian will be concerned with acquiring adequate and suitable space for the library in a building already in existence and probably housing additional activities of the parent company. The literature reflects this reality.

There is a chapter in Strauss on space planning and equipment[69] and a chapter on physical planning in the *Handbook of Special Librarianship*.[70] The *Handbook* devotes about a page to the accessibility of the library, in which the possibility of the library's having a separate building or being housed with other activities is noted.[71] In a section on planning, Bakewell spends one paragraph on siting the library.[72] Campbell merely hints at the possibility of a separate building, in the one page concerning library space and position.[73] In Strable, there is a chapter on space and equipment, with no discussion of siting or building a library.[74] There is a short chapter in Lewis's work on planning and equipping special libraries.[75]

Writers on special and technical libraries are in general agreement that it is necessary to define the scope of services to be offered before planning the utilization of space, and indeed before determining the amount of space necessary. As pointed out by Campbell, the manager of a newly formed library must accept in many cases whatever space has been allocated; the manager should, however, make a case for adequate space and provide evidence to support the case.[76] Such documentation may include standards promulgated by organizations, as well as current practices in the field.

The Organization for Economic Cooperation and Development's pamphlet on setting up a company technical information center suggests a minimum of 250-400 square feet of space for even the smallest library, fifty square feet per user (excluding stack space), and 100 square feet per library employee.[77] Redmond's minimum recommendations for a small industrial library are 600 square feet, which would provide space for about 2,000 volumes, six to eight readers, and fifty to sixty users. He also indicates the need for planning three to five years ahead of expected expansion.[78] The SLA standards recommend space sufficient to allow for five years' growth. The standards also provide guidelines regarding dimensions of shelving, space occupied by stacks and aisles, shelf requirements, and general space requirements.[79] For dealing with larger space requirements, sample libraries ranging in number of users from 120 to 3,100 and in size of collections, from 1,700 to 25,000 bound volumes are found in Strable; library areas ranged from about 2,000 to 10,000 square feet.[80]

Although the SLA standards make no specific mention of separate buildings, they do provide support for inclusion of the library manager in consultations among the company space planners, architects, and engineers in providing adequate and safe physical facilities. The standards also cite the need for the library manager to be involved in the layout of the facility, in consultation with the company's space planners.[81]

The act of arranging the operations of a library should involve more than intuition or tradition. As noted previously, space requirements depend on the scope of services to be offered, as well as the number of users anticipated. Anthony's section on physical planning in the *Handbook of Special Librarianship* provides a systematic approach to the entire process. First, the flow patterns of the library are determined, i.e., the flow of materials, the flow of information, and the flow of users. Once these are determined, the relationships of various activities to each other can be assessed to determine which activities *must* be close to which other activities, which activities it is undesirable to place close to which other activities, etc. Once these rated relationships are established, a preliminary diagram can be prepared showing all the activities of the library in an optimal physical arrangement. It may be necessary to modify the diagram in order to get the best fit for all elements. It is cautioned to be certain that all activities and areas in the library are included in determining the relationships.[82]

Anthony points out that it may be misleading to speak of standards in estimating space requirements for the various materials found in the library. In the established library, he recommends sampling one's own collection to determine averages for the amount of space occupied by different types of materials; these averages can be used to predict future space needs. Space must be left also for flexibility in adding, shifting, etc. Generally speaking, when stacks are at about 66 to 70 percent of capacity, planning for expansion should begin. A library is said to have reached its maximum working capacity when the shelves are at about 86 percent of capacity.[83]

Because space is limited, procedures should be instituted to limit the number of journals necessary for a technical library to give satisfactory service to its users. The logic of the procedure is that a relatively small core of journals contains a high percentage of articles relevant to a discipline or combination of disciplines. If a technical library collects all journals containing papers relevant to its field during one year and counts the number of papers relevant during that year, it can be determined how many journals must be subscribed to on a continuing basis to provide a certain percentage of the relevant articles published each year. It has been estimated that a very high proportion of the world's scientific literature of value may be found in a relatively small number of journals, possibly between 2,300 and 3,000.[84] The number needed by any specific technical library should be much smaller, as indicated in a survey of 21 libraries presented in Strable: the maximum number of periodicals subscriptions reported was 1,100, and the number ranged down to 125.[85] Determination of the composition of the core collection of journals will, of course, be made to some extent by the users of the library, but reliance on this method without selectivity being practiced by the librarian will lead to proliferation of subscriptions, many of a peripheral or irrelevant nature.

There are several guides to furnishing and equipping the technical or special library, and it is outside the scope of this paper to go into detail regarding these matters. The chapter by Anthony in the *Handbook of Special Librarianship* has been mentioned. The checklist compiled by Fisher for SLA includes a section on equipment and furniture, as well as providing suggestions and reminders concerning all other phases of the operation of a company library.[86] Strable provides a general summary of space and equipment needs.[87] Lewis's compilation on planning and equipping special libraries is dated but still valuable as a comprehensive overview of the entire process.[88] Strauss has a chapter on space planning and equipment that is comprehensive, and in some cases detailed, in its coverage.[89] Depending on the age of the guide, it may be more or less obsolete with respect to brand names and commercial firms. However, the annual directory issue of *Library Journal* helps to update commercial sources of library equipment, furniture, and services. The *Library Technology Reports*, issued by ALA, provide information on equipment as well as on aspects of library environment such as heating, lighting, and ventilation. Certain journals outside librarianship, such as *Information and Records Management* and *The Information Manager*, help library managers to keep abreast of developments in furniture and equipment, particularly in new technologies involving microforms. Maintaining a current file of catalogs from library suppliers and service companies provides up-to-date information replacement of or additions to furniture and equipment as planned.

EVALUATION AND MEASUREMENT

Because the expense of the technical library often is charged to overhead, it cannot be allocated to the direct cost of the end product of the company. Nevertheless, there are certain methods for determining to some extent whether the library measures up to other, similar libraries and whether it is doing a satisfactory job. Too, as noted, there is some inherent justification for the library if it is performing its task of preventing duplication of effort by company researchers.

Evaluation and measurement as management responsibilities and tools may comprise several activities: user surveys, comparative studies, statistical reports, annual reports, and the application of standards and formulas. These elements are examined in this section.

Basic to evaluating and measuring is the concept of improving service to the user. Statistics of holdings, number of users, circulation, bibliographies compiled, etc., have little meaning to anyone except the library staff. In a well thought analysis of evaluation, in response to the appearance of the SLA standards, Randall concludes that circulation growth means little in itself.[90] Surace reinforces and amplifies this in her overview of special libraries, deprecating the value of the size of collection, budget, staff, etc.[91] She includes also the quality of cataloging, but this is important, of course, in that good cataloging assists the user in gaining access to materials more quickly; poor cataloging frustrates access. She may be aiming at what may be called pedantic or "picky" cataloging practices. Corporate management may be somewhat impressed by increases in circulation, but normally, the company heads will not reciprocate with a bigger budget solely because of such an increase. If library management can demonstrate the desirability of a new or improved service that will assist the researcher in perfecting a product that will result in more sales (which will mean more profits), then corporate management is likely to be impressed to the point of granting big money.[92]

User surveys are appropriate not only after a technical library has begun operations but prior to establishment of the facility, writes Meltzer. Comparing a preliminary user survey to one conducted within six months after beginning operation will reveal the degree to which users feel they are receiving the services expected. The second survey may indicate also additional services now considered desirable by the users.[93]

Surveys should not be conducted so frequently that users become annoyed at being taken away from their work or begin to suspect that library management is lacking in direction and confidence. Arnold suggests that a reasonable balance in the number of surveys has to be established and that certain indicators available to the library manager may reveal the need for polling the users. These indicators include library control mechanisms that monitor such things as staff productivity, changes in library use, and changes in external services to the library; perceptions of library staff members in close contact with users; and the manager's assessment of library statistics and of contacts with the company library committee (liaison officer).[94]

Comparative studies of other, similar technical libraries can be used to determine whether one's own facility measures up in a quantitative way. Libraries are selected from directories on the basis of industries in the same field and reasonably near the same size as one's own parent company in net worth, investment, or total sales, and preferably in general age and status. Next, a questionnaire is directed to each corporate office, accompanied by a list of other companies receiving the questionnaire and an offer to furnish a copy of the results of the survey. Questions should be framed to show areas in which operations may be comparable, as well as differences that could make other figures not comparable. Questions should provide data on dollar sales per librarian, number of company employees per librarian, number of technical and/or scientific personnel per librarian, library square footage per librarian, library budget per technical and/or scientific personnel, and other data.[95]

This type of study would be particularly useful to support the library manager's recommendations regarding space, staff, and budget in the initiation of a technical library. This is essentially a statistical comparison, and it was indicated at the head of this section that such things normally do not impress corporate management. The difference is that the comparative survey should be used as a baseline, not as justification for increments in budget.

Certain types of statistics can be used in a qualitative way. More useful than bulk statistics showing a comparison of this and last year's circulation would be figures showing the types of materials borrowed, the age of the materials, the identity of the users, the length of time needed, etc. Random sampling can be used to monitor library usage rather than keeping a complete cumulative record of all transactions.

The annual report, in addition to fulfilling a public relations function, can be used as a tool for comparison not only of quantitative changes from year to year but also of accomplishments against goals and objectives. It should include a record of completed special projects that added to or improved services to the users.

There are seven elements subsumed under the section on services in the SLA standards. Basically, these elements are merely a list of the types of services that a special library is expected to provide; they are not quantifiable. The standards do, however, relate the services to the objectives of the library and of its parent organization: "The special library functions as a service unit that provides information to further the objectives of the organization it serves."[96]

A measure of the degree to which a library fulfills the above objective would be reflected in the quality of its services. In relating objectives to evaluation in special libraries, Wasserman asks:

First, is there in writing, in clear and specific terms, a statement of the library's fundamental goals, objectives and philosophy, with respect to its functioning in the organization? ...

And second, is this broad planning implemented in the actual functioning of the library ... ?[97]

If the library can answer these questions truthfully in the affirmative, it may have made a better evaluation than statistics will reveal.

It is doubtful that formulas such as those widely used in public libraries in the past (but now in general disrepute) concerning increments of books per capita, expenditure per capita, etc., are of any great value in measuring the success of a technical library. Comparison studies of similar libraries noted above may have value, in that they provide an external yardstick taken from the real world. Preoccupation with formulas probably does not lead to improved service and may distract the manager from considering innovative activities that *would* better serve the user. Surace comments that the degree to which the library accomplishes the transfer of information to its user group should be the measure of its success.[98] This is true, and it is simply the means of measuring this transfer that must be reexamined repeatedly and, if possible, improved.

LIBRARY COOPERATION AND THE FUTURE

Cooperation among special/technical libraries has not followed the pattern best exemplified by public libraries, e.g., the cooperative cataloging, acquisitions, and storage involved in the larger system of library service. Special libraries, however, have been somewhat active in recent years in networks that meet their needs in cooperation: interlibrary loans, union lists, etc. Two cases are mentioned later in the section. As the possibilities of national networks are examined more fully by the National Commission on Libraries and Information Science (NCLIS), which has included special libraries in its preliminary considerations, the technical library may figure even more prominently in networking. There are potential problems in the participation of technical libraries in networks, as is noted later.

Modes of cooperation among technical libraries have been the same in some cases as for other types of libraries, but they have differed in the degree to which employed. Because of limited collections in many cases, technical libraries tend to use interlibrary loan more heavily than do other types of libraries, and they may depend more on telephonic contacts and on an awareness of outside sources than do staff in general libraries.[99] Technical libraries make heavy use of nearby academic and large public libraries to supplement their own limited collections. The SLA standards make specific mention of dependence on and knowledge of outside sources by special libraries.[100]

Prior to the 1975 NCLIS report on a national program for library and information services, special libraries were relatively neglected in the library literature about cooperation and networking, as exemplified by the October 1975 issue of *Library Trends*. Its state-of-the-art treatment paid little attention to special libraries.[101] However, the importance of special libraries to a national network is recognized in the NCLIS report, which points out that "devising a network mechanism by which selected holdings and services of special libraries can be made available to more people throughout the country would be extremely beneficial to the nation." The Commission concludes that the resources of special libraries *must* be included in a nationwide network if possible.[102]

Company proprietary materials, security precautions, and industry competition may create difficulties for the technical library in networks, as recognized in the NCLIS report, by Bakewell,[103] and by Meltzer.[104] Proprietary material normally will not be circulated outside of the company, and security-classified materials may not be transferred to other holders without proper clearance and need-to-know. Open transmission lines could not be used in any case for sending classified materials. Even a bibliography of unlimited-distribution documents generated by one company in a specialized field could have research meaning for another company in the same field, and, therefore, proprietary value. Other technical libraries presumably would be aware of distribution limitations of the above cited types of materials, but general libraries in an intertype network might not understand such restrictions. However, experiences reported below by technical libraries in intertype networks do not indicate such difficulties.

In areas of cooperation involving physical access to technical libraries, the matter of proprietary and classified materials again presents obstacles. Because of the nature of some of their holdings, among other reasons, technical libraries usually are located in secure buildings, and users from cooperating libraries must be accompanied by company personnel while in the facility. This does not make for convenient and optimal use of cooperating libraries.

There are other problems to be faced by the library manager involved in cooperation/networking. One is the matter of accurate bibliographic description of holdings. Local cataloging conventions and shortcuts practiced for years will not suffice for input to an automated data base. Resistance to upgrading records may be encountered on the basis that no time is available for such activity and that library internal operations do not require such modifications. Resistance may arise also in the parent company because of inability of corporate leadership to see the value of networking, particularly when it is difficult to quantify the supposed added benefits to the company. Staff members may not recognize that it is possible to provide better service to the user through cooperative activities. These problems, and others, were identified by the executive director of the Illinois Regional Library Council in a report of that agency's experience.[105]

SLA has recognized the necessity for special libraries to become more involved in formal networking than has been the case in the past. The theme of the national conference in 1975 was systems and networks, and the Association in the same year established a networking committee, with five subcommittees to address the areas of guidelines, state of the art, barriers to networking, a prototype network, and means of informing members of networking activities. To date, the guidelines subcommittee has submitted a report designed to promote both intratype and intertype networking by special libraries. These guidelines provide assistance for the library manager in implementing the three steps involved in becoming part of a network: exploratory, planning and development, and operational and evaluation phases.[106] A report by the subcommittee on barriers to networking by special libraries would be especially valuable, if it addresses problems cited above and suggests solutions to them.

As to desirable ends to be gained from networking, the experience of the Rochester Regional Research Library Council suggests to the manager of the technical library that those services that have been utilized most by technical libraries in the past are still of most value. Rated most useful was the union list of serials, and the delivery service for photocopying and interlibrary loan was heavily used, with 21,553 requests during one calendar year. The fast patent copying service seems to be used primarily by corporate special libraries and their parent firms; other services little used include a media center/film collection and a teletype service.[107]

It is not certain at this point what part technical libraries will play in the relatively recently conceived idea of a national information policy. The foreword of the report to the president, submitted by the Domestic Council's Committee on the Right of Privacy, indicates the scope of such a policy: "interrelationships which exist between and among information communications, information technology, information economics, information privacy, information systems, information confidentiality, information science, information networks, and information management. . . ."[108] Technical libraries presumably would be part of such a policy, but probably not as much as in the past, when technology and science were the most important foci of government attention in the matter of information transfer.

These earlier federal concerns were manifested by the creation of such bodies as the Committee on Scientific and Technical Information (COSATI), the office of the President's Science Advisor, the Defense Documentation Center (DDC), NTIS, the Science Information Exchange (SIE) in the Smithsonian Institution, and the National Referral Center for Science and Technology at the Library of Congress. Technological developments probably are still of primary importance to the federal government, as evidenced by a chapter on the interaction between technology and government in the cited report on national information policy; however, other disciplines must be considered now as well.

As a case in point, the title of the recent National Forum on Scientific and Technical Communication indicates its primary emphasis but not its entire scope, which was broad enough to include "the generation, utilization, maintenance and dissemination of information of all kinds—that is, scientific and technical information with social and economic information."[109] The Forum report cites such problems as access (including inability to identify the "universe" of scientific and technical information), economic factors interfering with communication, and requirements for centralized planning for communication. The report recommends that a focal point for information policy be established in the federal government,[110] thus fitting into the aforementioned concept of a national information policy.

Another national activity into which the technical library presumably must be fitted is the proposed national periodicals center. It is possible that some libraries with unique or exhaustive collections would come within the scope of the second tier in the proposed structure of the center's operation, that of the referral center. These centers are intended as the sources for "specific periodicals that are seldom used but which are intentionally retained by one library or another because they are pertinent to specific subject fields in which an exhaustive collection is sought and supported."[111] As stated in the technical development plan for the center, many referral centers will be chosen from major academic and research libraries but will not be limited to those categories.[112] The comprehensive journal coverages in some disciplines by some technical libraries may qualify them as referral centers.

Based on the activities of the federal government, library associations, and the information community in general, the technical library of the future may be much more involved in cooperation/networking than has been the case in the past. Whether this emphasis will contribute to maintaining or improving the delivery of the smaller unit of information necessary in the technical library remains to be seen. The well-chronicled information explosion shows no sign of abating and may, in fact, be accelerating. Science and technology become increasingly interdisciplinary; they diversify and subdivide. As stated by a practitioner, even online data bases were not designed to access the multidisciplinary answers often required today. Her conclusion is that new, flexible systems of information access must be developed and that single libraries cannot do it.[113] The answer, or part of it, may lie in cooperation/networking.

SUMMARY

Technical libraries comprise a subset of special libraries, and they support research, study, and teaching in the fields of technology and science. They are found in several environments but most commonly, in the industrial/research sector. Technical libraries differ from other types of libraries in that they are commonly part of a for-profit organization, they serve a more homogeneous clientele, and they deal with the smaller unit of information.

Management is an evolving discipline, but the seven elements defined by Gulick still underlie much of the writing, teaching, and studying of management, including that of libraries. The five managerial operations posited by Drucker are broad, comprehensive guidelines for the manager of any type of activity. There is no final answer to management needs. The successful manager will select an eclectic style from several schools of management, the whole being suited to his or her personality, to the objectives of the organization, and to the capabilities of the staff.

Library management, in both theory and practice, has lagged behind management in general in moving from the classical theorists, through the human relations era, to a period of a synthesized or unified theory of management. The ambiguous status of technical librarians in the organization may restrict any tendency toward innovation, and they may be limited in managerial style by corporate policy.

Managers of technical libraries bear many different designations but should be given titles commensurate with the level of the library in the organization, and this is found commonly at the managerial level. Qualifications needed by the manager of the technical library cannot be precisely identified, but current standards prescribe a master's degree in library science and appropriate experience, or a combination of subject expertise and professional experience. The library manager should have status sufficient for dealing with other professionals in the organization as a colleague.

Budgeting in the technical library generally will be structured like that of the parent company. Lump-sum and open-end budgets are considered unsatisfactory, because they contain no detailed data needed at times of justifying the library to corporate administration. Sources of the library budget in the for-profit organization are found finally in company sales. There is some evidence for basing library budgets on a percentage of sales or of the research budget; alternatively, or additionally, dollars per user may be used as guidelines. Salaries, journals, and technical reports usually require a disproportionate share of the technical library budget in comparison to other types of libraries.

Two differentiations from other types of libraries may characterize staffing in the technical library. First, the technical librarian usually requires a strong subject competence, in contrast to a generalized educational background necessary in the general library. Second, professionals from disciplines outside of library science are more likely to be found on technical library staffs than on those of other types of libraries. A relative oversupply of degreed librarians at the present time makes it more feasible to require higher qualifications in the technical library staff than in the past.

This oversupply should obviate the formerly common practice of filling librarian positions with holders of bachelor's degrees or less, a variation of the concept of career ladders.

The ultimate goal of technical libraries should be the maximum service described in Strable. Based on the concept of the smaller unit of information, services performed by the technical library may have different emphases than those of the general library. The technical library is concerned with rapid dissemination of information to the appropriate user and with answering promptly specific reference questions that arise. SDI and other current awareness services are the primary means of meeting the first obligation, and an interpretive, active reference service, that of the second. Online systems may be almost necessary to fulfill these obligations.

Seldom is the technical library manager required to plan a building to house the facility, but this person should be consulted when such is the case, or when library space, equipment, and environment are being planned. Standards and guidelines are available regarding general space needs, dimensions of library equipment, furniture, and holdings, and arrangement of library operations.

It is difficult to measure technical library operations as part of direct costs, because they are most commonly charged as an expense of overhead. However, such tools as user surveys, comparative studies, statistical reports, annual reports, and standards and formulas may be used to evaluate the library's contribution to company success. Criteria such as increments in circulation, holdings, and budget generally are not effective as units of evaluation unless they reveal in-depth information, such as types of materials borrowed, etc. Evaluation should be related to objectives: if services provided are helping to meet company objectives, then the library is fulfilling its purpose.

Cooperation by technical libraries until recently has been practiced somewhat informally and has been restricted primarily to certain types of activities, such as interlibrary loan and telephonic contacts. The SLA standards recognize a dependence by special libraries on outside sources. Proprietary and security-classified materials could pose problems for technical libraries in networks, although current experience does not indicate this to be the case. Problems that have arisen may be common to all types of libraries: quality of bibliographic records, and resistance to networking by the parent company and by the library staff.

Networking on a national scale, predicated upon reports such as that by NCLIS and by the Council on Library Resources on a national periodicals center, as well as the concept of a national information policy, probably means an increasing role for technical libraries in cooperation. The increasingly complex information requirements of the technical library may require that new means of accessing information be implemented, and the single library may no longer be able to meet the task satisfactorily without substantially increased cooperative activities.

NOTES

[1] Lucille J. Strauss, Irene M. Shreve, and Alberta L. Brown, *Scientific and Technical Libraries*, 2nd ed. (New York: Becker and Hayes, 1972), pp. 6-7.

[2] Julian Blackwell, "Publicizing the Value of Information Work," in *Proceedings of the 1st Conference of the Institute of Information Scientists, Merton College, Oxford, 17-19 July, 1964* (Orpington, Kent: 1965), p. 49, cited in K. G. B. Bakewell, *Industrial Libraries throughout the World* (Oxford: Pergamon Press, 1969), p. 4.

[3] A. G. MacKenzie, "Systems Analysis of a University Library," *Program* 2 (April 1968): 7-14, cited in Denis V. Arnold, *The Management of the Information Department* (Boulder, CO: Westview Press, 1977), pp. 19-20.

[4] Strauss, Shreve, and Brown, p. 3.

[5] "Objectives and Standards for Special Libraries," *Special Libraries* 55 (December 1964), p. 672.

[6] Bakewell, p. 7.

[7] Morton F. Meltzer, *The Information Center* (New York: American Management Association, 1967), p. 12.

[8] Edward G. Strable, ed., *Special Libraries: A Guide for Management* (New York: Special Libraries Association, 1975), p. 8.

[9] B. Kyle, "Administation," in *Handbook of Special Librarianship and Information Work*, W. Ashworth, ed., 3rd ed. (London: Aslib, 1967), p. 14.

[10] M. S. Magson, "Management," in *Handbook of Special Librarianship and Information Work*, W. E. Batten, ed., 4th ed. (London: Aslib, 1975), p. 389.

[11] Janice M. Ladendorf, *The Changing Role of the Special Librarian in Industry, Business, and Government* (New York: Special Libraries Association, 1973), p. 3.

[12] Strauss, Shreve, and Brown, pp. 8-9.

[13] Ibid., pp. 12-24. On p. 57, it is said that technical libraries located in industrial organizations are usually part of a research and development activity, but the organization charts in the work belie this.

[14] *The Bowker Annual of Library and Book Trade Information, 1978*, 23rd ed. (New York: Bowker, 1978), p. 237.

[15] Margaret Labash Young, Harold Chester Young, and Anthony T. Kruzas, *Directory of Special Libraries and Information Centers*, 3rd ed., 2 vols. (Detroit: Gale Research Co., 1974).

[16] Peter Drucker, *Management: Tasks, Responsibilities, Practices* (New York: Harper and Row, 1974), p. 400.

[17] Ibid., p. 401.

[18] Luther Gulick, "Notes on the Theory of Organization," in *Papers on the Science of Administration*, Luther Gulick and L. Urwick, eds. (New York: Augustus M. Kelley, 1969), p. 13.

[19] G. Edward Evans, *Management Techniques for Librarians* (New York: Academic Press, 1976), p. 4.

[20] Robert D. Stueart and John Taylor Eastlick, *Library Management* (Littleton, CO: Libraries Unlimited, 1977).

[21] Arnold, pp. 28-32.

[22] Evans, p. 50.

[23] Ibid., pp. 29-30.

[24] Ibid., pp. 24-32.

[25] Ibid., pp. 31-32.

[26] Strauss, Shreve, and Brown, pp. 41-42.

[27] Ibid., pp. 42-43.

[28] "Objectives and Standards," pp. 672-73.

[29] Strauss, Shreve, and Brown, p. 43.

[30] Melvin J. Voigt, et al., "Education for Special Librarianship," *Library Quarterly* 24 (January 1954), pp. 9-10.

[31] "Objectives and Standards," p. 673.

[32] D. J. Campbell, *Small Technical Libraries* (Paris: Unesco, 1973), pp. 8-9.

[33] Strauss, Shreve, and Brown, p. 44.

[34] Ibid., p. 57.

[35] Ibid.

[36] W. T. Knox, "Administration of Technical Information Groups," *Industrial and Engineering Chemistry* 51 (March 1959), p. 57A.

[37] Strable, p. 58.

[38] "Objectives and Standards," p. 673.

[39] Ibid.

[40] Ibid., p. 679.

[41] Strable, p. 62.

[42] Ruth S. Leonard, ed., *Profiles of Special Libraries* (New York: Special Libraries Association, 1966), pp. 7, 13, 19, 25, 31, 37.

[43] Strable, p. 65.

[44] Ibid.

[45] Strauss, Shreve, and Brown, p. 59.

[46] Strable, p. 61.

[47] Eva Lou Fisher, *A Checklist for the Organization, Operation, and Evaluation of a Company Library*, 2nd rev. ed. (New York: Special Libraries Association, 1966), p. 19.

[48] Meltzer, p. 90.

[49] *Bowker Annual*, p. 320.

[50] Strable, p. 38.

[51] Strauss, Shreve, and Brown, p. 51.

[52] *Library Education and Personnel Utilization* (Chicago: American Library Association, 1976), p. 2.

[53] Strauss, Shreve, and Brown, p. 44.

[54] Strable, pp. 10, 13.

[55] Ibid., p. 28.

[56] Meltzer, p. 66.

[57] Strable, p. 26.

[58] Strauss, Shreve, and Brown, p. 120.

[59] Meltzer, p. 88.

[60] Special Libraries Association, Special Committee on Copyright Law Practice and Implementation, *Library Photocopying and the U.S. Copyright Law of 1976* (New York: 1977), p. v.

[61] Greg Mullen, "Current Awareness Services: SDI," unpublished paper, 1978.

[62] Strable, p. 27.

[63] Meltzer, p. 68.

[64] Ibid.

[65] Cecily J. Surace, "Special Libraries—An Overview," Rand Paper P-6152, June 1978.

[66] Frances E. Kaiser, ed., *Translators and Translations*, 2nd ed. (New York: Special Libraries Association, 1965).

[67] Strable, p. 29.

[68] Strauss, Shreve, and Brown, p. 42.

[69] Ibid., pp. 67-97.

[70] L. J. Anthony, "Planning Library and Information Services," in *Handbook of Special Librarianship and Information Work*, pp. 16-41.

[71] Ibid., pp. 54-55.

[72] Bakewell, p. 144.

[73] Campbell, pp. 15-16.

[74] Strable, pp. 47-55.

[75] Chester M. Lewis, *Special Libraries: How to Plan and Equip Them*, SLA Monograph No. 2 (New York: Special Libraries Association, 1963), pp. 8-11.

[76] Campbell, p. 15.

[77] Organization for Economic Cooperation and Development, *Setting up Your Company's Technical Information Service* (Paris: 1963), p. 30.

[78] D. A. Redmond, "Small Technical Libraries," *Unesco Bulletin for Libraries* 18 (March-April 1964), p. 50.

[79] "Objectives and Standards," pp. 677, 679-80.

[80] Strable, p. 80.

[81] "Objectives and Standards," pp. 677-78.

[82] Anthony, pp. 16-22.

[83] Ibid., pp. 23-24.

[84] Ibid., pp. 27-28.

[85] Strable, p. 50.

[86] Fisher, pp. 25-27.

[87] Strable, pp. 47-55.

[88] The case histories are still worthwhile.

[89] Strauss, Shreve, and Brown, pp. 67-97.

[90] G. E. Randall, "Special Library Standards, Statistics, and Performance Evaluation," *Special Libraries* 56 (July-August 1965), pp. 381-82.

[91] Surace, p. 3.

[92] Herbert White, Lecture, SLA Management Institute, Los Angeles, April 7, 1978.

[93] Meltzer, p. 100.

[94] Arnold, pp. 122, 128.

[95] Fisher, pp. 12-13.

[96] "Objectives and Standards," pp. 676-77.

[97] Paul Wasserman, "Measuring Performance in a Special Library, in *Reader in Library Administration*, Paul Wasserman and Mary Lee Bundy, eds., Reader Series in Library and Information Science (Englewood, CO: Information Handling Services, c1968), p. 178.

[98] Surace, p. 3.

[99] Ibid., pp. 5-6.

[100] "Objectives and Standards," pp. 676-77.

[101] It is an excellent treatment otherwise.

[102] United States, National Commission on Libraries and Information Science, *A National Program for Library and Information Services* (Washington: 1975), p. 27.

[103] Bakewell, pp. 161-62.

[104] Meltzer, p. 126.

[105] Beth A. Hamilton, "Principles, Programs, and Problems of a Metropolitan Multitype Library Cooperative," *Special Libraries* 67 (January 1976), pp. 28-29.

[106] Special Libraries Association, Networking Committee, Guidelines Subcommittee, *Getting into Networking: Guidelines for Special Libraries*, SLA State-of-the-Art Review No. 5 (New York: 1977), p. 1.

[107] Evaline B. Neff, "Contracting in Library Networks," *Special Libraries* 67 (March 1976), p. 129.

[108] United States, Domestic Council Committee on the Right of Privacy, *National Information Policy* (Washington: National Commission on Libraries and Information Science, 1976), p. xii.

[109] National Forum on Scientific and Technical Communication, *Report: Critical Issues in Scientific and Technical Communication* (Washington: Science Communication Division, George Washington University, 1978), p. ix.

[110] Ibid., pp. vii-viii.

[111] Council on Library Resources, *A National Periodicals Center: Technical Development Plan* (Washington: 1978), p. 63.

[112] Ibid., p. 64.

[113] Surace, p. 10.

BIBLIOGRAPHY

Arnold, Denis V. *The Management of the Information Department*. Boulder, CO: Westview Press, 1977.

Bakewell, K. G. B. *Industrial Libraries throughout the World*. Oxford: Pergamon Press, 1969.

Batten, W. E., ed. *Handbook of Special Librarianship and Information Work*. 4th ed. London: Aslib, 1975.

Campbell, D. J. *Small Technical Libraries*. Paris: Unesco, 1973.

Council on Library Resources. *A National Periodicals Center: Technical Development Plan*. Washington: 1978.

Drucker, Peter. *Management: Tasks, Responsibilities, Practices*. New York: Harper and Row, 1974.

Evans, G. Edward. *Management Techniques for Librarians*. New York: Academic Press, 1976.

Fisher, Eva Lou. *A Checklist for the Organization, Operation, and Evaluation of a Company Library*. 2nd rev. ed. New York: Special Libraries Association, 1966.

Gulick, Luther. "Notes on the Theory of Organization." In *Papers on the Science of Administration*. Edited by Luther Gulick and L. Urwick. New York: Augustus M. Kelley, 1969.

Hamilton, Beth A. "Principles, Programs and Problems of a Metropolitan Multitype Library Cooperative." *Special Libraries* 67 (January 1976), 19, 23-29.

Ladendorf, Janice M. *The Changing Role of the Special Librarian in Industry, Business, and Government*. New York: Special Libraries Association, 1973.

Leonard, Ruth S., ed. *Profiles of Special Libraries*. New York: Special Libraries Association, 1966.

Lewis, Chester M. *Special Libraries: How to Plan and Equip Them*. SLA Monograph No. 2. New York: Special Libraries Association, 1963.

Meltzer, Morton F. *The Information Center*. New York: American Management Association, 1967.

Neff, Evaline B. "Contracting in Library Networks." *Special Libraries* 67 (March 1976), 127-30.

"Objectives and Standards for Special Libraries." *Special Libraries* 55 (December 1964), 672-80.

Randall, G. E. "Special Library Standards, Statistics, and Performance Evaluation." *Special Libraries* 56 (July-August 1965), 379-86.

Strable, Edward G., ed. *Special Libraries: A Guide for Management*. New York: Special Libraries Association, 1975.

Strauss, Lucille J.; Shreve, Irene M.; and Brown, Alberta A. *Scientific and Technical Libraries*. 2nd ed. New York: Becker and Hayes, 1972.

U.S. National Commission on Libraries and Information Science. *A National Program for Library and Information Services*. Washington: 1975.

Wasserman, Paul. "Measuring Performance in a Special Library." In *Reader in Library Administration*. Edited by Paul Wasserman and Mary Lee Bundy. Reader Series in Library and Information Science. Englewood, CO: Information Handling Services, c1968.

MANAGING THE LIBRARY SCHOOL

by Martha Boaz

THE LEGAL BASIS OF THE UNIVERSITY
AND THE LIBRARY SCHOOL

To understand the place of the library school within the institution in which it is located, one must know something about the legal and governance base of that institution, usually a university. The legal status of any institution of higher learning is an important factor in the work of that institution. Most universities have charters granted by state legislatures that authorize the establishment of the institution and define its powers and privileges. There is a distinction between publicly and privately controlled colleges and universities. The public institution is controlled by a government agency, and the degree of control depends on its articles of incorporation. The private college or university is usually incorporated as a nonprofit charitable institution, controlled by a private corporation whose structure and authority are specified in the institution's charter.

Most institutions also adopt bylaws to implement the more general grants of authority found in their articles of incorporation. These "spell out" the regulations that govern the trustees and also outline their relations with the institution. Both public and private institutions exercise certain powers and rights, which are generally vested in a board of trustees or board of regents. The trustees are empowered to own property, make contracts, and engage in development plans for the institution. They assume responsibility for the actions of its officers and employees and also approve new programs and certain high level administrative and faculty appointments.

In state institutions, the boards of trustees/regents are usually selected by the governor and confirmed by the state legislature. In some state universities, the board of regents meets monthly. In the private sector, the number of trustees, the method of selection and terms of office are specified in the institution's charter. Usually the board is self-perpetuating, with the members of the board selecting new members as vacancies occur. Members of the boards of both public and private groups are selected from well-known, prominent business and professional people; often, there is also alumni representation.

Governance

The method of operation of a not atypical hypothetical university might be characterized as follows: the members of the self-perpetuating board elect one-third of its members each year for three-year terms. The board also elects a chairperson and one or more vice-chairpersons. At each annual meeting, the board elects certain officers of the corporation; these include the top administrative officials of the university. There are standing committees of the board as well as ad hoc committees.

Consultative Bodies

Within the university structure there are consultative bodies such as the president's academic council, the president's advisory council, the council of deans, the faculty senate, the university associates, the board of councilors, and others. In many universities, the academic senate has been delegated responsibilities and powers in the area of academic programs.

Academic Organizations

Again, using one university as an example, within the academic organization the president of the university appoints certain academic officers who are not corporate officers: academic deans and directors, division and department chairpersons, and such other academic officers as may be designated by the board. All academic officers are subject to the immediate direction of a particular vice-president.

Academic Relationship between the Parent Institution and the Library School

In the administrative organization, there are a number of principal officers with whom the library school dean works. Titles vary from one institution to another, but the following are probably representative: the vice-president of academic affairs, the vice-president of business affairs, the vice-president of student affairs, the vice-president of development, the vice-president of legal affairs, the director of admissions, the registrar, the head of government contracts. Some multi-campus state university and college systems use the titles chancellor and vice chancellor for the head officials. The dean of the library school consults with these and other officials in any matters that relate to the library school and that may fall within the jurisdictional areas of the respective divisions.

Approval must be secured for any new faculty or staff appointments or for budget changes, or for program or curricular changes. The library school cannot singlehandedly change policies that have required approval by other bodies of the university, nor can it violate the equal rights employment practices or change contracts or abridge legal rights. These are some of the restrictive policies that must be observed.

The library and information science education program, like the educational programs of most other professional schools in North America, is now located in the university. The professional program is based on a specialized body of knowledge; it is concerned with specific goals and objectives; and it has a deep-rooted philosophy of service. In order to attain its goals and objectives, a library school needs the support, facilities, and services of a larger institution of higher learning. For this reason, most schools with accredited programs in the United States are now affiliated with universities and have their legal bases in and through the universities in which they are located.

The standard for the administrative relationship of the library school to the parent institution is defined in the *Standards for Accreditation* of the American Library Association (ALA):

The library school should be an integral but distinctive academic unit within the institution, and its autonomy should be sufficient to assure that the content of its program, the selection and promotion of its faculty, and the selection of its students are controlled by the school within the general guidelines of the institution.[1]

Legal Basis

The first library education courses were more or less technical in content and were offered as training classes in libraries. It was therefore a natural sequence for the courses, when they were transferred to the university setting, to be under the direction of the librarian and for the librarian to be both the head of the library and of the library school. This pattern had changed in most schools by 1950, and the library school had become an autonomous unit with its own dean or director and was no longer an appendage of the library.

Authority of the School

From studies that have been made and from the official listing of library schools with programs accredited by the American Library Association (and this chapter deals only with this group), it is readily apparent that most accredited programs are offered by independent schools, with their dean or director reporting sometimes to the president or provost, but more often to an academic vice-president. In some cases, the library school may be a department within another school—the graduate school, the school of education, or some other school—but the majority of the 64 accredited schools are autonomous units within the university. The library school can and is expected to exercise the rights, privileges, and responsibilities within its academic jurisdiction. At the same time, the school should be integrated with and supportive of the goals, policies, and activities of the university of which it is a part, and it should maintain a good relationship with the other administrative officers and department heads. This type of relationship is a professional responsibility in any professional situation, but it is a particularly helpful practice in advancing the goals and objectives of a professional school within a university complex.

The Position of the Dean in the University Structure

The dean, by delegation from the president, is responsible for the content and direction of the curriculum; for recruitment of faculty; for curriculum planning; for maintenance of student, faculty, and school records; for high standards in teaching, conduct of courses, and research; and for communication to faculty, students, and staff as to their responsibilities in the total program of the school.

Administrative and Faculty Participation in Governance

The dean and faculty of the library school usually have the same opportunities as do people in other professional schools to serve on university councils and committees. The dean and elected representatives of the faculty serve on such bodies as the council of deans, the president's advisory council, the faculty senate, the resource management committee, the affirmative action committee, and others.

Responsibilities and Rights of the Faculty

Members of the faculty are responsible for teaching and the conduct of courses. They are responsible for a high quality educational program, for counseling and guidance of students, for evaluation of students' academic work, and for general departmental and university service. They are also expected to do research and to publish scholarly works that will advance the profession and increase knowledge.

ADMINISTRATION OF THE LIBRARY SCHOOL

Today, as stated earlier, the majority of the 64 library schools with ALA accredited programs are autonomous units within their universities, with the dean or director reporting to an academic vice-president or provost. In some schools, there are departmental divisions; the department is a unit within the school, headed by a chairperson.

The names of the schools vary. A school may go under the heading of the school of library science, the graduate school of library science, the school of library and information science, the department of library science, or other titles. The names differ, but all of the schools offer a master's degree program. As of the summer of 1978, these were the types of degrees offered by the 64 schools: 24 offer the master's degree; thirteen schools offer the master's as well as a post-master's specialist or certificate program; fifteen offer the master's, post-master's, and a doctoral program; ten offer the master's and doctoral; and one offers a single specialization in school library media. One school, because it is being discontinued, was not included in this count.[2]

The titles of the administrative officers also vary. In 39 schools, the title of the head administrator is dean; in twenty schools it is director; and in four schools, it is chairman. (Again, the one school being discontinued was not included in the count.)

The Dean—Appointment

The dean is usually appointed by the president of the university. This is now done with advice and recommendations from a selection committee composed of representatives from the library school faculty, the student body, the alumni, and several other divisions of the university. The president has the final authority in making the appointment. Throughout the process, affirmative action policies are strictly observed.

The period of tenure in the position of dean may be indefinite or it may be for a fixed period, such as five to seven years, with other persons in the department being selected for succeeding periods in this rotation pattern. Appointments can be renewed following a favorable performance evaluation. There are advantages and disadvantages to each system. One problem with the shorter fixed term is the lack of time available to the dean to carry out a program of any magnitude.

The Dean—Qualifications

The dean of the library school is expected to have administrative qualifications similar to those expected of the deans of other professional schools. Generally, the dean is expected to have a degree in library science and a doctorate, either in library science or another field, as well as practical experience in professional library work.

The dean should also have had research experience and a record of publications. Obviously, it is preferable, if the dean is to carry out the goals and objectives of the school (which include research and publication), that he or she should have had personal experience in these areas; also, if the dean expects the faculty to do research and to publish, he or she should fulfill the same requirements. As a matter of fact, the dean is also a faculty member, and, as such, must have academic as well as administrative qualifications.

In addition, the dean of the library school should have the intellectual and professional qualifications to direct the school and must have an interest in higher education in general and a special interest in librarianship. Moreover, this person must feel a loyalty to the university and to its programs. Today, deans are increasingly concerned with the goals and objectives of higher education in the institution as well as in the school; and they are striving to find the means for achieving these goals and objectives through academic budgets, facilities, and resources.

The Dean—Responsibilities

The dean's first responsibility, according to Earl J. McGrath, the former United States Commissioner of Education, is "to consider the ends and means of education and to arouse the faculty to similar activity."[3] To carry out this responsibility, the dean must understand and appreciate scholarship and be knowledgeable in educational theory. The second most important responsibility of the dean, says McGrath, is the selection of faculty members. The quality of the program will depend on the excellence of the faculty and on the dean's leadership. The dean's third most important responsibility, notes McGrath, is the preparation of the budget. To a large extent, the educational program depends on fiscal planning and the availability of resources.

The dean has a responsibility to plan the general program of the school, to involve the faculty in the planning, and to set standards for the curriculum as well as for student admissions and graduation requirements. The dean should also plan for the future of the school and work for the advancement of the profession. In order to be fully informed and involved in the latter area, the dean should be active in the work of professional library associations.

The dean, working with the higher administration of the university, speaks for the school and requests support and assistance for its work; the dean works with other schools and departments within the university in interdisciplinary planning, with faculty and students in the school, and with alumni. The dean also works with accrediting agencies and professional associations, with outside organizations, with foundations, and with government agencies in securing "extra-institutional" funding. Another liaison responsibility for the dean has developed, in recent years, with the consortia of independent universities.

In working with students, the dean has the over-all responsibility for recruitment, admissions, advisement, registration, class schedules, and guidance. Some regular activities involving faculty include the assignment of classes, supervision of the curriculum and changes in this area, the supervision of faculty and development of faculty talents and abilities, and the encouragement and support of research. Also included are participation in faculty meetings, committee meetings, and conferences with individual teachers. The dean should be aware of and concerned about the personal and professional needs of faculty, students, and staff, On the other hand, the dean must have the strength to say no to unreasonable or unprofessional demands from any group.

The responsibilities of a dean are often burdensome and unpleasant, but with the position goes responsibility, and one of the administrator's responsibilities is "the enforcement of rules and regulations and the maintenance of standards. Enforcement of standards is not a simple problem. Standards are only in a very formal way prescribed—for example in the form of requirements for graduation."[4] There are problems about grades and grading and pressures from students for high grades. Students hold a weapon over the faculty now in their evaluations of each faculty member and each course, for these student evaluations may be used for review for faculty promotion and tenure. The result sometimes is an exchange of favors: high grades from faculty members in exchange for high ratings from students in their evaluations. The dean has a responsibility to try to maintain high standards and quality education despite these opposing forces.

Another problem area for the dean involves appointments, promotions, and salary increases. In these days of participatory management, a faculty group is usually assigned or elected to a committee, which works with these matters in consultation with the dean. There are problems with this process. When a decision has to be made that may not be pleasing to certain persons, especially peers, the committee members are not always willing and eager to be involved or to incur the resentment of their colleagues. The unpleasant job is usually left to the dean, who then may be perceived as a "henchman" of university officials.

The dean has to be concerned about the development of the school and the whole institution, whereas faculty members seem to be more interested in their own personal development, which in fact the "system" encourages through its criteria for retention and promotion. For this reason, there is sometimes a consequent tension between the faculty and the administration. The dean's position is often a lonely one, but anyone who goes into administration must realize that this is a part of the job and, if it is too unpleasant, one should leave it and find other work.

The dean, in addition to business details, housekeeping chores, and working with faculty and students, is responsible for leadership in educational and professional development and for intellectual leadership.

Delegation of Authority

Because of the current proliferation of administrative details and routine responsibilities, the dean should organize and delegate many of the practical affairs of the school to other faculty and staff. Associate and assistant deans and administrative assistants can carry many daily routine responsibilities, thus freeing the dean for innovative educational programs through study and research, through conferences with internal and external faculty members and with other deans, and through general planning and development activities. Unless there is some relief from some of the aforementioned administrative chores, qualified people will no longer be interested in being deans because they are virtually prohibited from functioning effectively.

Other Administrative Officers of the Library School

The positions and number of persons in other offices of the library school depend somewhat on the size of the school and its program. An associate or assistant dean is usually needed, and there may be more than one. The associate dean should be selected by the dean, since the two have to work together in a cooperative alliance; there must be confidence and trust between them. The dean customarily would have other members of the faculty meet the candidates for the associate dean's position and would ask either an ad hoc committee or the personnel committee of the faculty for advice about the candidates. The final approval of the appointment of the associate dean candidate would be made by the appropriate vice president, i.e., the one to whom the dean reports.

Associate Dean and Other Administrative Officers of the Library School

The associate dean should have authority, delegated by the dean, to work in whatever assignments the position entails. This varies according to the abilities and specializations of the person and the needs of the job. In the absence of the dean, the associate dean may serve as the acting dean. In addition to the associate or assistant dean(s), there are other staff positions in a library school that have responsibility for the admission of students and placement of graduates, for preparing class schedules, for counseling, alumni relations, and other matters. The duties of the associate dean(s) and of other staff are assigned by the dean.

In summary, the administration, faculty, and staff of a library school need a clear vision of their goals and objectives, and the chief administrator needs strength, courage, and skill in directing the program to achieve these goals and objectives. To be successful, a dean must work closely with the faculty, students and staff in the school and also with other deans and departmental chairmen in the university. For the administrative organization of any school must be seen in relation to the structure of the entire university, and the university is a part of the total picture of higher educational institutions, with their shared objectives of "excellence."

PROGRAM GOALS AND OBJECTIVES

The University Professional School and the Library School

One of the major functions of the professional school is to transmit to students the general and systematic knowledge that will serve as the foundation of their particular professional performance. Also, information about how to keep abreast of advances in the field should be conveyed. This involves research and the continuing creation of new knowledge.

A library school, like any other professional school, seeks to educate students to become future practitioners; and, like any other profession, the library profession delivers services to individuals, groups, government, or the public at large. Professionals profess. They profess to know more than others about certain specialized matters or esoteric services in their field. A philosophy of library education is based on a feeling of mission and of meaning about the importance of delivering and disseminating knowledge and information to society.

Clearly defined goals and objectives for the educational program are essential for any university or professional school. The Committee on Accreditation of the American Library Association spells out as a standard: "The library school should have clearly defined, publicly stated goals. It should also define explicit objectives for its specific educational programs, stated in terms of the educational result to be achieved."[5] The general goals of the library school are consistent with the goals of the university of which the school is a part; these goals are instruction, research, and community service.

In addition to being consistent with the goals of the university, the program goals of the library school in the specialized profession of librarianship should reflect, according to COA:

1) Consistency with the general principles of librarianship and library education as these are identified by common agreement through the major documents and policy statements of relevant professional organizations.
2) Responsiveness to the needs of the constituency which the school seeks to serve.
3) Sensitivity to emerging concepts of the role of the librarian in the library and the library in a multicultural society.
4) Awareness of the contributions of other disciplines to librarianship.[6]

After the general overall library education goals have been determined, specific objectives should be set up for the master's degree as well as for any other programs that the school offers.

Most schools offer more than the traditional master's degree program. Some of these are the formal degree structures—i.e., the doctor of philosophy (Ph.D.) and the doctor of library science (D.L.S.). Other types of programs and instructional components should be clearly defined and objectives set up for each. These other components may include: 1) a school-library media program, which usually has state certification requirements; 2) an undergraduate component; 3) a research program; 4) a colloquium program; 5) an interdisciplinary program; 6) an inter-institutional program; and 7) a continuing education program, among others.

The overall objectives of the library school should be to provide a program of academic excellence, one that will accomplish the goals and objectives of the school and will instill in the graduates of the program concepts of competence, responsibility, and service. These include general, specialized, and research competencies, and they emphasize individual, institutional, and societal responsibilities.

THE CURRICULUM

The Academic Program

Although new programs and courses in a library school usually require approval by an all-university committee such as a curriculum committee or graduate studies committee, the library school has the responsibility for the planning and direction of its own curriculum. It is responsible for initiating new courses and programs, for changing and revising existing courses, for innovations in teaching methods, and for the general quality of the total program of the school.

Criticism of modern education seems to be growing. One critic, Myron J. Lunine (Dean, the Western College of Miami University), gives suggestions for curriculum reform. He says, "I have been arguing that the proper education of human beings is not occurring because the curricula are . . . imbedded in vested interests, are captive within intentionally disintegrated and sometimes disorganized large institutions, and are not creating persons with the necessary and appropriate values and skills. To accomplish this we need radical curricular change."[7] Lunine continues: "To have radical curricular change we need radical reorganization of our colleges and universities with respect to their departmental and divisional composition. To have this kind of radical reorganization, we need a transformation of values about what constitutes professionalism, professional identity, and professional mobility."[8]

What is needed in the library/information science field is a consensus within the profession as to its mission. In simple terms, this may be expressed as a realization of the basic value of knowledge and information and an attempt to provide this knowledge and information to the people who need it, quickly, efficiently, and on an international scale. In a practical way, the curriculum of the library school should include study of principles, practices, and services common to all types of libraries and information centers. The curriculum should be based on the school's statement of goals and objectives and should be a composite, integrated program rather than a series of independent courses. Emphasis should be placed on principles and understanding rather than on memorization of facts. In the learning environment, students should have the advice and counsel of qualified faculty members in a setting that provides adequate supportive materials for the program. The curriculum should be under continuous review and revision, which can be done by several methods: through formal faculty and committee meetings, through student participation in their own committees and in collaboration with faculty groups, through advisory boards, through alumni, and through advice and suggestions from practitioners.

The degree most commonly granted by the accredited library schools in North America is the master of science in library science (M.S.L.S.). It usually requires one academic year and a summer session to complete the requirements for this degree. Some schools now have a two-year master's degree program, and a number of schools offer doctoral programs as well as the one on the master's level. A few schools offer both the doctor of philosophy (Ph.D.) and the doctor of library science (D.L.S.) degrees. The latter is more professionally oriented, whereas the Ph.D. has a research and academic slant, with a librarianship specialization.

Master's Programs

There is concern among educators about both master's and doctoral programs in colleges and universities, as the quality of these scholarly degrees declined in the early part of this century. However, as Laurine Fitzgerald has noted, "current societal factors and institutional responsiveness in the provision of innovative and specifically targeted programs strongly point to a resurgence of popularity of the master's degree and to the extension of graduate study at the master's level"[9] In many master's programs, attention is given to individual needs, and innovative interdisciplinary programs are receiving more attention than they formerly did. "These reasons, combined with economic factors and the relatively inexpensive degree, will influence continued institutional support for master's programs."[10]

Doctoral Programs

Due to a decline in the academic market, recommendations have been made that the leading universities could easily produce all of the Ph.Ds needed and that lesser programs should be closed down.[11] An alternate recommendation is that there be greater diversification among graduate programs. The latter suggestion does not downgrade the traditional Ph.D. degree, but it advocates that this degree does not meet needs such as the training of practitioners for nonacademic careers. The impact of the increase in library doctorates, and the potential fragmentation and compartmentalization, was the subject of a recent article[12] which, along with other studies, rather confirms the feeling of a number of people that new models or alternates for library/information science doctoral education should be tried with a possible redirection of effort.

Curriculum Details

In the traditional program of many schools, a student takes a certain number of required basic courses and then elects a specialization by type of library service or function, such as technical processes, reference and bibliography, children's services, administration, and others. The basic course concept referred to above, and usually called the "core" curriculum, has been in effect since the 1930s. The theory on which this is based is that a certain basic core content exists that every librarian should know regardless of the type of work or type of library in which he or she works. Core courses usually include foundations of librarianship, reference, technical services, selection of materials, and administration. Newer subject areas—such as computer science library systems, communications, educational media, and research methods— are also included as important components in the official announcements of schools today. Although complete agreement as to what the "core" should be is not possible, the areas mentioned are usually viewed as essential for complete preparation.

"Block" Courses

Certain schools have revised their curricula, replacing core courses with an introductory block course. This term-long, twelve-unit (units may vary in different schools) course is considered to be an integrated, coordinated learning experience and is team-taught by various members of the faculty. Among the schools that have tried this approach (with variations in their programs) have been Drexel, North Carolina, Illinois, and South Carolina. As an example of the block course, the Drexel Library School has a course called Fundamentals of Library and Information Science, which a student is required to take during the first quarter. The typical program of study, according to the 1977-1979 Graduate Bulletin of Drexel University, consists largely of courses chosen from five functional groupings of courses: 1) organization and retrieval of information; 2) information technology; 3) resources and their use; 4) information services, and 5) management and evaluation. Presumably, while enrolled in this "block" course, each student will decide on an area of concentration and will work with a faculty adviser in pursuing a course of study in line with that student's own background and career goals.

The "block" type of course offering does enable a student on a full time study program to get most of the basic principles of librarianship through one introductory course; however, it practically excludes the student who works and attends school only on a part-time schedule. If the block course is not offered in every academic term (including summer school), this will prevent students from entering the program except at a specific time or two during the year.

There are administrative problems in scheduling and in faculty and resource allocations for block courses that do not exist in single-teacher classes, but there are advantages and enrichment in the team teaching. After sufficient time has passed, the schools offering the block course should be able to evaluate their programs and decide what direction to take.

Alternatively, as a variation of the regular curriculum and to allow for innovation, it has been recommended that schools might have an experimental and/or contingency curriculum within the total curriculum. Students in the courses would be graded, not on memorization of facts, but on their competencies and capabilities in solving real, practical problems and also on how well they succeeded in meeting the behavioral objectives of each course. Along this line, some of the newer courses that have been added to library school curricula in recent years include one dealing with library user needs, such as "The Library's Community"; others deal with media design and production; in the technology area, there are courses in library networks, programming languages, and information retrieval.

Generally, the policy of having students take certain basic *required* courses varies from one school to another. Regardless of curriculum structure and format (required courses vs. non-required courses, block courses, or single courses—whatever the plan may be), it is important that there be some basic content in all programs so that the graduate is prepared to take a place as a professional in the library/information science profession. There will be much discussion, dissension, and experimentation before the "perfect" curriculum is discovered.

THE FACULTY

The faculty of any school is its most important asset. The ALA *Standards for Accreditation* of library school programs declare that "the success of the instructional and research programs of the school is dependent upon the ability of its faculty to teach, stimulate independent thinking, and provide stability and continuity"; the importance of faculty research is noted in the statement that "research enriches both teaching and learning and provides means for adding to a body of professional knowledge."[13] These two statements stress the importance of faculty teaching and research, and a third comments on the importance of professional experience and participation in professional organizations.

Selection of Faculty

In the selection of faculty, the dean is concerned with finding persons who meet the above criteria and have whatever specializations are needed for the curriculum. Before making any selection, the dean usually gets recommendations from experts in the field of the particular specialization. The dean also works with an ad hoc or regular committee of the school in making decisions on appointments. Each position is advertised in national journals, in letters sent to other library schools, and in correspondence with other people who may know of potential candidates. The dean or a designated replacement interviews candidates at professional meetings where placement services are provided. References are obtained from names of persons given by the candidate and from employers under whom they have worked. In all of these processes, affirmative action and equal employment regulations are followed, and, when the final selection of the successful candidate has been made, the dean forwards the recommendation for appointment to the vice-president (or immediate superior), along with documentation showing that affirmative action and equal opportunity policies have been observed.

Contractual letters are issued to all personnel, part-time or full-time, by the appropriate university officer. These letters specify rank and title, salary, tenure, or duration of appointment for all academic persons.

Criteria for Faculty

The selection of qualified faculty and the maintenance of excellence in teaching and research is one of the major responsibilities of the dean. Members of the faculty should, as a group, have the following qualifications, abilities and characteristics: 1) advanced degrees in both library and information science and other fields; 2) library experience in different types of libraries; 3) specialization in the subject areas taught in the school; 4) interest in research and evidence of publications; 5) effective teaching ability; 6) interest in students and concern for their progress; 7) participation in the work of appropriate professional associations; and 8) interest in the total program of the school, including a willingness to work cooperatively with other faculty and with the administration.

Faculty Responsibilities

When possible, within the limitations of a small faculty, teaching assignments and other work are related to the special interests and competencies of the faculty, and work loads are as equitable as possible. In addition to teaching and research, faculty members are expected to advise students, serve on appropriate committees in the library school and in the university, and participate in professional and association work. Each school's faculty handbook lists the rights and responsibilities of faculty members, usually in accord with those outlined by the American Association of University Professors (AAUP). Such things as the use of academic freedom (and allowing it to others) are covered in these statements, as are the more practical matters such as course assignments, record keeping (grading), performance evaluation, etc.

Promotion and Tenure

A faculty member may be promoted in rank upon the recommendation of his or her dean, in consultation with and with the advice of appropriate committees of the school (which may include faculty and students). After this comes the approval of a university promotions committee, followed by the final approval of the president of the university. Tenure is the right of a faculty member to hold his or her position until retirement. In conformity with the American Association of University Professors' policies, tenure is held by persons holding the rank of associate professor and professor. From the time one is appointed at the rank of full-time instructor or higher rank to consideration for tenure, the probationary period should not exceed seven years, including all full-time service in other institutions of higher education. After two or more years of non-tenured service, notice of non-reappointment must be given in writing at least twelve months before the expiration of the appointment if the faculty member is not to be continued in service.

STUDENTS

A school exists for students. The faculty, the administration, the whole structure—all are there for the benefit of students. Each school, working within the framework of its university, establishes its own criteria for admission and for graduation. Usually considered in the admission requirements for an individual are academic qualifications (e.g., grade point average), intellectual qualifications (e.g., the Graduate Record Examination), and personal qualifications (e.g., information obtained from reference letters and personal interviews are used here).

Flexibility and Variety in Programs

In general, graduate training in librarianship is directed toward career objectives and the specialized interests of students. Now, though, more variable entry patterns are open to students than were available only a few years ago. There are full semester courses, short term classes, intensive study programs, and other variations in schedules. Another current practice is that of awareness of and response to the special needs of different groups of students: minority populations; women who are entering new careers or entering professional work after rearing children; mid-career people who are updating their knowledge or making changes in their career objectives; and the elderly. All of these may increase institutional costs or, depending on the management of the programs, may bring in additional revenue.

Student Evaluation of Faculty and Courses

Today in many library schools, there is an on-going evaluation of the faculty, done by students in their courses, usually at the end of the term. The aim is to get an evaluation both of the course and of the teacher by way of both short-answer and discussion responses. After grades have been turned in, the evaluations are turned over to the individual faculty members. Prior to this, the dean or an evaluation committee will have recorded a consensus of each faculty member's evaluations for his or her file. These evaluations may be used when a faculty member is being recommended for promotion.

Placement

Keeping of student records, providing recommendations, and giving or providing placement service is a service that a library school handles for students. The placement service may be within the library school or the educational placement office of the university, or it may be shared between the library school and the placement office.

Alumni, Support Groups and Honor Societies

Library schools try to keep in touch with their graduates through alumni associations, library honor societies, advisory councils, and support groups. Each of these is usually organized, with officers and boards to direct their interest and support, and deans often find the groups to be valuable allies.

FINANCIAL RESOURCES AND BUSINESS AFFAIRS

Because higher education has enjoyed years of plenty and luxury up to the mid-70s, it is now difficult to adjust to lean years, shrinking budgets, and a depressed future. The various authorities on budgets list these rules for school or institutional success: 1) the need for long range planning, 2) fiscal flexibility, 3) dollar budgeting, 4) broad participation in governance, 5) fixed priorities, and 6) a feeling of administrative responsibility. Confronted with possible zero increases or even decreases in funding, the university administrator may have to set up contingency plans to carry on the work of the organization, for the problems of increasing costs, declining enrollments, and limited resources are a matter of concern not to one but to all educational institutions today. How do a university and a professional school cope with recession?

Several measures for dealing with institutional decline are suggested by Randolph W. Bromery (Chancellor, University of Massachusetts at Amherst). Dr. Bromery concludes that 1) flexibility must be built into the planning and budgeting system so that major budgetary units can affect dollar budgeting with dwindling resources at their own levels and with their own internal expertise; and 2) everyone involved in either seeking or spending funds should think in terms of steady-state systems, plus or minus specific increments, and individual faculty members should have a greater level of departmental concern for budget problems. Along with this, Bromery says, goes the participation of students and faculty in governance and decision making in general and in program and fiscal matters in particular. Sometimes faculty and students do not fully realize that dropping a program can save money or that adding a new program requires additional money.

There are some differences between budgeting in public versus private institutions. For example, in the public, the argument is largely about workload (i.e., FTE). In the private, workload is argued to some extent, but more importantly, the school or department must earn the revenue along with a reasonable return to the university for its indirect cost. However, in the final analysis, admonishes Bromery, the administration is obligated to retain the final authority and responsibility for the budget.[14]

The *standard* for support of a professional library education program, according to the Committee on Accreditation of the American Library Association, is that "the institution should provide continuing financial support sufficient to develop and maintain professional library education in accordance with the general principles set forth in these standards. Support should be related to the size of the faculty required to carry out the school's program of education and research, the financial status and salary schedule of the institution, and necessary instructional facilities and equipment."[15] Other sections of this standard specify that funds for salaries, research projects, travel, sabbatical leaves, student financial aid, and other necessary items should be available on a basis comparable to that of other departments and schools.

Usually the largest item in a library school budget is the one dealing with salaries and wages. Sometimes, but not always, summer session and extension budgets are separate from the regular library school budget and may be provided by the other two departmental budgets. Some secretarial and student work funds may be from government sources and thus issued by a general business office. Special activity areas (non-regular tuition, sales, and services) should be budgeted with information as to their costs and/or contributions to the total program.

THE BUDGET

The budget should represent the goals of the school. This so-called "program budgeting" outlines a plan for the use of the budget, assigns priorities to its various parts and estimates the staff, equipment, and other elements required to carry out the budget and the program for which it was set up. This planning takes into account any anticipated changes or needs. Flexibility should be an important factor in planning the use of the budget.

Preparation of the Budget

The dean of the library school usually works with several business office persons as well as the vice-president of academic affairs in the preparation of the budget. Procedures differ among universities in the mechanical details, but a fairly general pattern is presented here. Preliminary plans for a budget begin in the fall of the preceding year and go through several stages before the final document is issued. The dean or the dean's designated representative and sometimes a committee of the school prepares an over-all general budget. On a scheduled date, the dean (and perhaps a committee) presents the budget to the budget review committee. The budget review committee may include representatives from several groups as well as other administrators who are directly involved.

A sample chronology of the budget formulation process used by one university is as follows: 1) in early October, budget workpackages are distributed to academic and non-academic units; 2) budget procedures, financial performance, and a five-year forecast are reviewed by budget staff and relevant vice-president(s) with individual deans during the third week in October; 3) all budget workpackages are completed and returned to the Budget Office by mid-November; 4) intensive budget hearings are held for units over a two-day period, with the budget review group, in early December; 5) tentative budget allocations are reviewed with each dean by the budget staff, the relevant vice-president, and the executive vice president in early January; 6) tuition and salary increases are announced and salary pools and guidelines are distributed to academic units in late January; 7) budget allocations are presented to vice-presidents, deans, and directors in early March; and 8) detailed departmental budgets are prepared and salary increases awarded after mid-March.

The budget package will probably contain information in support of the budget request and may include such items as 1) a synopsis of the recent history of the school from both a financial and a programmatic standpoint and the anticipated trends in the immediate future and the next five years; 2) a summary of the school's regular program expenditure request in priority sequence (this is supported by a rationale for each item in the budget request); 3) a rationale for the enrollment forecast and expected tuition income; 4) an explanation of the nature of any non-regular tuition income or restricted funds that the school has or expects to have and the plans for using these funds. Specific guidelines and forms are supplied to each dean for the preparation of the budget.

Forecast of Fiscal Performance

Important guidelines for budgeting may be established by trying to prepare a three- to five-year forecast of fiscal performance. Some universities require this type of budget forecasting. One university's directive to persons setting up a budget requested that the budget: 1) describe the consequences of receiving a level of funding from the university that was consistant with the trend of the past three years (to be included here were any significant changes in other forms of funding—gifts, federal capitation program funds, etc.—which would have to be replaced by university funding to maintain the program at the same level); 2) describe the opportunities that could be fulfilled if a significant increase in funding were provided to the school (include an assessment of additional revenues which would result from the increased funding); 3) assume that the school's budget base were to be cut on the order of 5 percent

per year, or if a significant portion of salary increase funds had to be generated from
the school's internal resources, then describe the strategy in imposing these cuts so
as to have minimum negative impact on the school's programs.

Indirect Costs

In total budget planning, both direct and indirect costs must be considered.
(This is particularly true in private institutions. In many publicly supported universities, schools are not called upon to budget for, or even to estimate indirect costs.)
Indirect costs include employee fringe benefits, building and equipment use and
depreciation, campus operations and maintenance, library operations and acquisitions,
student services, admissions and registration offices, school and departmental administration, research administration, and central university administration. Both direct
and indirect costs are real costs. However, indirect costs usually are more difficult
to identify, measure, and allocate equitably (as distinct from the direct costs of instructional programs). Still, indirect costs must be shared, in proportion to use, by each
unit within the university.

When there are government grants and sponsored research activities, the government reimburses universities for direct and indirect costs incurred in performing
sponsored research. Indirect costs are reimbursed through an "indirect cost rate,"
which is negotiated annually by each university with its cognizant audit agency for
the government. Private foundations vary in their support of indirect costs. Usually
indirect cost reimbursements are treated as a portion of the university's general
operating budget.

Funds other than the salaries and wages required for the regular courses in the
curriculum may be used for special programs. Sometimes special budgets are set up,
usually on a one-time basis and as needed. These have to be approved by the official
to whom the library school dean reports, and there is accounting afterwards, on all
financial transactions.

The final budget proposal in a library school must take into account a number
of uncertain factors. These include final enrollments and enrollment projections and
estimates of the effect of indirect cost recovery rate levels. The total university budget
must take into account increases in cost due to assumed levels of inflation, foreseeable
changes such as in minimum wage, health insurance, Social Security, and cost of
building maintenance. Anticipated increases in tuition are also estimated.

Budget Questions

If there is to be quality enhancement in programs, what will the added cost be?
What changes outside of the university may affect the university: regulatory changes,
legislation, etc.? If costs must be cut, what programs or services will be phased out?
(It is easy to add programs, but difficult to delete them.) Are there changes in course
requirements, changes in majors, shifts in demands for services? What are the changes
in priorities and goals? Will there be shifts in research funding? These questions are
a part of the budget process.

Budget deficits may require a budget adjustment program. Stanford University
has undertaken such a program, which aims to reduce costs and to develop new sources
of revenue while still generating selective increases in quality. It is hoped that improved
budget processes will provide some alternatives in the future.

Overview of the Budget Process

In estimating income and costs in a university budget, one should look at economic parameters such as the rate of growth of the national Consumer Price Index and the rate of growth and disposable personal income per capita. Some of the factors affecting *revenues* are: 1) enrollment, 2) tuition rates, 3) unrestricted endowment income, 4) unrestricted gifts, 5) income derived from investment of current funds, 6) recovery of indirect costs, and other income such as sports events. Do each or all of these increase or decrease? Factors affecting *expenditures* include 1) salaries, 2) the national minimum wage, 3) fringe benefits, 4) instructional and non-instructional supply bases (these include book acquisitions, binding, and equipment bases), 5) student aid, 6) travel expenses, 7) costs of utilities, 8) insurance, 9) taxes, 10) building and grounds maintenance, 11) remodeling and new buildings, and, 12) security costs. It is likely that the costs on all of these areas will continue to rise, as will the need for funds for quality enhancement of programs. Achieving a balanced budget is the objective and, in the process, one must be watchful for careful management of resources, for unproductive effort, for improved management, and finally, for accountability.

Sources of Income

The main source of funds for a library school is the current institutional operating budget. There are some funds from endowment sources. Other sources are gifts and grants from individuals and foundations and government grants. Institutions are becoming increasingly concerned about the effective management of their institutions on limited resources. Consequently, they are looking more and more for outside "extra" funding. Thus, large universities with development offices plan fund-raising campaigns and approach the matter with considerable sophistication. One trend in fund-raising is toward projects that have great advantage to one institution but at the same time are relevant to more than one school or group. This trend may increase, as funding agencies seem to favor such concepts. (Suggestions for obtaining "extra-institutional" funding are given in the chapter in this book, "Extra-Institutional Funding: Strategy for Survival."

The management of a professional school provides paradoxes, one of the most striking being the emphasis on long-range planning for the institution with the contradictory habit of planning its budgets one year at a time. As a matter of fact, management itself has been neither a science nor an art in the educational tradition but usually an inept effort on the part of intellectuals to cope with business processes. Today, there is definite emphasis on recruiting persons who have business backgrounds, qualifications, and experience.

Library School Business Records

The monthly summary of budget expenditures provides both a record of the transactions for the month and a total of the expenditures for the year to that month. Library school records provide up-to-the minute information that is sometimes needed, compared to the monthly business office record, which has a greater time lag. The library school and the business office records can be checked against each other, one of the objectives being that the library school will guard against excess or over-draft expenditures. The dean works through the office of the director of financial services in the placement of purchase orders, payment of bills, and the checking of monthly business office statements against the library school's records.

Cost Analysis

Cost analysis, formerly almost ignored by academic leaders and left to business managers for accountability, is now, of necessity, having to be given serious attention by top leadership in both academic and business staffs in educational institutions. As most universities and professional schools are examining and modernizing their administrative and business systems, cost analysis is important in identifying cost reductions or efficiency improvements. Some new systems such as computerized accounting require cost analysis to show their feasibility. Such systems do not necessarily reduce cost but do increase speed and efficiency in supplying needed information for administrative and academic use. Cost analysis, when costs are rising, provides facts and figures that justify raising student tuition and fees.

In making budget decisions, depending on availability or non-availability of funds, the university and the school have to consider costs of making improvements, expanding or changing programs and, if cost reductions must be made, what programs to drop. Total cost estimates of a school are based on the financial commitment to it; the size of the program, the methods of instruction; the scholarship, research, and quality of the faculty; and plans for improvement and excellence. These items combined with efficiency in the use of resources bear heavily on financial allocations and use.

EVALUATION

The purposes of evaluation are to make a critical study and analysis of the program and operations of a library school and to follow up with whatever improvements are appropriate. Several basic principles should be observed. First, evaluation should begin with an examination of the goals and objectives of the program (long-range, general goals as well as short-term, immediate, and specific objectives). Second, evaluation should be a continuous and continuing process that examines all parts of a program—administration, faculty, students, budget, facilities of all kinds, and any other components that are involved in the total program of the school—and these should be measured against the desired results. Finally, the evaluation process should involve the administration, faculty, students, and graduates of the school and should request the commitment of all to achieving the goals and objectives of the school.

Objectives by Which the Program Is Evaluated

Four objectives by which the professional program of study may be judged are succinctly summarized by Jesse Shera in the following list: "(1) it (the program) must represent a well-developed theory of the social function of the library; (2) it must extract from the totality of the librarian's knowledge and skills those which are professional; (3) it must present librarianship as a unified cluster of specializations as opposed to the earlier concept of a 'universal' librarian; and (4) it must be directed toward the training of the intellect. Only to the degree to which the professional program of study can meet these criteria can it maintain its position as a graduate program in an academic setting or be anything other than vocational training in manipulative skills."[16] Keeping these objectives in mind, it is suggested that each library school should periodically review its program and make whatever changes may be required to meet the objectives.

Frederick Balderston, speaking about this concept, but in relation to the larger university, says "the assessment of how well a university is doing in these obligations is complicated by philosophical difficulties and by problems of evaluating the significance of lives and ideas over very long horizons—working lives of thirty to fifty years, and idea-life times that are sometimes as long or longer."[17] He continues: "Neither the data to trace what happens over these long periods nor the techniques of disentangling the specific impact of one university from the numerous other forces at work in intellectual life and in society are well developed."[18] Lacking the perfect solution for long-term evaluation techniques, institutions must focus on more immediate results and short-term indicators. A practical operational approach in a library school may be to try to get a consensus of the current views of the school, its reputation, academic quality, strengths, and weaknesses.

Some of the indicators used in the evaluation of a school are: admission requirements for students; grading standards; graduation requirements; the strength and quality of the curriculum; the market rating of students and of the image of the school at time of graduation; and the competency, qualifications, and reputations of the faculty. These latter qualities are usually shown by the faculty members' teaching reputations and/or by their ability to get research funding and to put out quality publications. Other faculty indicators are honors they receive, service on scholarly editorial boards, and recognition in professional associations; still other indicators of a school's quality are the interest and leadership of its administration in the excellence of the program and in expanding and improving it. In the evaluation of a school's achievement or lack thereof, one must also examine some factors other than students, faculty, administrators and curriculum. Namely one also looks at supportive resources such as the building space and physical resources, laboratory and library facilities, teaching aids, and the total budget.

A more valid system for evaluation should be set up by schools and by their accrediting agencies so that schools might compare their progress over a period of time and could also compare their programs with those of other schools. An effort has been made in this direction by the ALA Committee on Accreditation, which now requires an annual report for "Continuing Review" from each ALA-accredited school. This report compels each school to assemble facts and figures that are valuable in a continuing evaluation and annual self-study. The form that is returned to the ALA headquarters office in October of each year is in three parts: statistical data; specific actions taken; and, program review. The "statistical data" include information about faculty, students, and financial data. The "specific actions taken" refers to actions taken in response to any recommendations the Committee on Accreditation may have made at the time accreditation was granted. The "program review" requests information on changes or anticipated changes in the school's program goals and objectives, curriculum, faculty, students, governance, administration and financial support, physical resources and facilities, and any other developments in process or planned for the next year or two.

Continuing inquiry into the nature of and reason for library and information science education is essential to a library school's educational program in a university.

It follows that continual change and up-dating of the curriculum is mandatory to a vital program and that new methods of instruction should be used on a continuing basis.

In the final analysis, the objectives of a library school must be evaluated in terms of the final products (the graduates) who go out from the school. If the librarian is to be more than a keeper of books or an organizer of materials, there must be a recognition of the social goals of the library and of the social utilization of graphic records. In these concepts, the needs and interests of the individual and of society are inherent and the intellectual challenge of the library and of information is emphasized.

DIFFERENT PROFESSIONAL LEVELS

In the opinion of this writer, much of the work done in all types of libraries is not professional, nor does it require a college degree; much of it is paraprofessional in nature and could be learned on-the-job. This is not to say that the work is not important; it is, but a distinction between this type of work and that of a highly intellectual or professional service is important if the library profession is ever to attain recognition and status and respect as a real profession. Efforts are being made in a few states to determine what constitutes professional library work. This should be pursued by the entire profession. We must ask: what are the competencies, skills, and attitudes that characterize professional work in librarianship and information science?

Library schools have a responsibility to consider educational programs on several levels (although this does not imply that all schools would include all of the programs in their curricula). The paraprofessional, bachelor's, master's and doctoral levels all have a place, and libraries have a responsibility to assign jobs on appropriate levels, in accordance with the educational levels and qualifications of the individual staff members. If this were done, many jobs now performed by professionals would be done by paraprofessionals, thus "freeing up" the professionals for higher level services. There would be many more paraprofessional positions, fewer professional ones, and presumably better services on the part of all, coupled with higher job satisfaction and superior services to the clients using library/information services.

ACADEMIC DEGREE PROGRAMS

With strong evidence of a decline in the academic market, and a somewhat stagnant situation in graduate education, educators and library school deans and faculty should take a look at a renovation of or a new direction for higher education, particularly the Ph.D. programs. David W. Breneman says that "the overwhelming majority of doctoral programs in the country appear to identify the preparation of researchers and/or scholars as their primary goals."[19] The implication is that there should be a quality assessment of this goal to see whether it is still valid. Some educators are proposing a re-direction of effort and alternative models for doctoral education.

Along with the critical look at the Ph.D. degree, there is a call for reassessing graduate education in general and for a renewed emphasis on the master's degree, in particular. Whereas, at one time, the master's degree was highly respected, it has lately lost prestige as a scholarly and research achievement. But, according to Laurine E. Fitzgerald, "current societal factors and institutional responsiveness in the provision of innovative and specifically targeted programs strongly point to a resurgence of popularity of the Master's degree and to the expansion of graduate study at the Master's level."[20] Practical economic considerations may give new strength to master's programs because they are inexpensive, compared to the doctoral degrees, and they could be more flexible, more adaptable to innovation and change, and more suited to individual needs.

Library education is pursuing several different courses in some of the schools. Most schools are continuing as they have for some years, with the master's degree program, which requires one calendar year of graduate professional study. This gives an introduction to the fundamentals of the profession and some exposure to a speciality and is adequate for a beginning professional position. However, it is not adequate for in-depth study of a speciality, and there is now pressure from employers for more extensive specialization. This can be attained through a second year; or a two-year master's program in a library school, with some electives in other schools; or through interdisciplinary courses developed between two or more schools or through a second master's in another field of study. Still another and, in the opinion of this author (and contrary to David Breneman's theory about the doctoral degree), a better direction is that of the Doctor of Library Science (D.L.S.), which provides more in-depth study as well as more research orientation in the profession. In the long run, the degree is a doctorate instead of a second master's, which is still, however you describe it, a master's. The doctorate provides more job opportunities; with it in hand, the graduate may elect to go into specialized library work, administration, or teaching. This seems to be more applicable to the library profession than to others, at this time, probably because librarianship is a young profession and must try to establish itself through advanced degrees and research.

PARTICIPATORY MANAGEMENT AND THE POLITICAL PROCESS

Because of changes in administrative patterns, it is likely that the library education administration courses of the future will give more attention to participatory management. And, because government is expected to be more financially involved in supporting library services, there will probably be more course content dealing with the political process. In general, there will probably be more emphasis on developing administrative rather than bibliothecal knowledge and skills for future librarians.

SUMMARY

Institutions of higher education and library schools have and will continue to have problems. They will face changes and will make changes but they will survive. Teaching and research will continue to be important, as will the commitment to learning, knowledge, and humane ideals. And, in a practical sense, knowledge may become the most valuable commodity in the world. To end on a note of optimism, we anticipate not only the survival of the library school and the university, but a future in which they will advance toward higher ranges of excellence and toward greater service to society.

NOTES

[1] American Library Association, Committee on Accreditation. *Standards for Accreditation, 1972* (Chicago, American Library Association, 1972), p. 9.

[2] American Library Association, "Graduate Library Programs Accredited by the American Library Association," March 1978 (leaflet).

[3] Earl J. McGrath, "The Office of the Academic Dean" in *The Administration of Higher Institutions under Changing Conditions*, by Norman Burns. Proceedings of the Institute for Administrative Officers of Higher Institutions, Vol. XIX (Chicago: The University of Chicago Press, 1947), pp. 40-49.

[4] Marten ten Hoor, "Personnel Problems in Academic Administration," in *The Academic Deanship in American Colleges and Universities*, ed. by Arthur J. Dibden (Carbondale: Southern Illinois University Press, c1968), p. 157.

[5] *Standards for Accreditation, 1972*, p. 4.

[6] Ibid.

[7] Myron J. Lunine, "Outward Forms of Inward Values," in *Leadership for Higher Education*, ed. by Roger W. Heyns (Washington, DC: American Council on Education, c1977), p. 125.

[8] Ibid.

[9] Laurine E. Fitzgerald, "Reassessing Graduate Education," in *Leadership for Higher Education*, ed. by Roger W. Heyns (Washington, DC: American Council on Education, c1977), p. 140.

[10] Ibid.

[11] David W. Breneman, "New Quality Ratings: A Force for Reform" in *Leadership for Higher Education*, ed. by Roger W. Heyns (Washington, DC: American Council on Higher Education, c1977), p. 136.

[12] Herbert S. White and Karen Momenee, "Impact of the Increase in Library Doctorates," *College and Research Libraries* 39 (May 1978), pp. 207-214.

[13] *Standards for Accreditation, 1972*, p. 6.

[14] Ralph W. Bromery, "Doing Well with Less," in *Leadership for Higher Education*, ed. by Roger W. Heyns (Washington, DC: American Council on Education, c1977), pp. 149-55.

[15] Ibid., p. 11.

[16] Jesse H. Shera, *The Foundations of Education for Librarianship* (New York: Becker and Hayes, Inc., c1972), p. 362.

[17] Frederick E. Balderston, *Managing Today's University* (San Francisco: Jossey-Bass, 1975), p. 119.

[18] Ibid.

[19] Breneman, p. 136.

[20] Fitzgerald, p. 140.

MANAGING THE PLANNING OF LIBRARY BUILDINGS*

by Ellsworth Mason

In the planning of library buildings, the librarian has a double problem. He must make sure that the entire planning process is managed, and he must also make sure that he is on top of the management. At every point he must either be in control or have a large voice in the control of what is being done. The planning of a library involves library technicalities and a sophisticated knowledge of library processes at all the times. His knowledge makes the difference between designing a "reference room," and designing a building area that responds sensitively to the movements that reference librarians make in their work and to the proper presentation of the materials they work with. Non-librarians generally are not even aware of this fact. It therefore is crucially important for the librarian (the only one with this knowledge) to be at the center of the process.

It takes a strong librarian to move into the prime position of managing the planning, especially in a large university, and if the librarian is weak, it will be impossible to achieve a totally successful building. He is in a good position from the beginning, because no one else will know the steps required to move into the planning process, which at first seems vague and indefinable. At this point, the librarian can focus on what must be done and in what order. Planning will proceed through four distinct stages:

I. The Local Decision and Learning Phase.
II. The Programming Phase.
III. The Design Development Phase.
IV. The Construction Phase.

STAGE I, THE LOCAL DECISION AND LEARNING PHASE

The very first action in Stage I should be the formation of the local planning committee, in which the librarian should be chairman or have a very strong voice, endorsed by the authority that appoints the committee. The members of this committee should NOT be political representatives of interest groups. They rather should contribute the specialized knowledge of such groups, act as communicators of their needs and preferences, and report back to them the progress of the planning as it unfolds. It is far more important for the committee to be effective than for it to be representative. If it is not possible to form an effective committee that is representative, representation should give way. It is of great importance that members of this committee should be decisive people, deeply interested in the library, and willing to work hard in its interests, since that is what they must do.

Each member must be told what his specific function will be on the committee (functions will vary slightly) in writing that goes to the entire committee. A clear

---

*Copyright © 1979 Ellsworth Mason.

schedule of reporting to the person responsible for the committee's action on the progress of planning should be set forth. Then this committee should be empowered as the ONLY body to negotiate with the architects. All local differences must be represented to this committee and resolved within it. No matter how logical the arguments that may be carried to the higher authority by a local interest or the architect (as both have been known to do), they must always be referred back to this committee for resolution, since no one outside the committee can possibly be informed of all the detailed alternatives that have been sifted to arrive at any given point in planning. The formation of this committee and the centering of authority to negotiate with the architects in it are among the most important decisions to be made in the entire range of planning.[1]

The next step is to hire a good library building consultant who is a librarian. He can be identified like any other person hired, by asking people whose judgment is respected for recommendations, then following up at libraries he has served to find out: 1) how well he worked with the client, 2) how well he worked with the architect, 3) the range of his expertise (just library layout, or other things like mechanical, lighting, interior design concerns, media, computerization, etc.?), 4) his availability (can he easily arrange at short notice to get free for a day or two?), and 5) the success of the buildings on which he has consulted.

The consultant should be involved immediately. His advice makes the greatest impact at the very initial planning stage, where he will 1) discuss comparative advantages of different sites, 2) propose the sequence of steps to follow in planning, 3) pinpoint sources of information (readings, libraries to look at, etc.), 4) raise the sights of local people from what they have to what their future library should be, 5) suggest possible architects and explain what is involved in working with them, 6) describe pitfalls in planning and how to avoid them. In sum, he will focus a vague situation, instill it with confidence based on his experienced presence, and set procedures on the steps they must ascend to achieve a building. He is a critically important bridge between architects and client, since he knows the different way that each side views the same matter and can translate between them. It is impossible to control development of floor plans without his expertise, since usually there is no one on the client's team who can read floor plans, and if there is, almost certainly he does not understand library functions and movements.

The architect should then be hired for the project, from among firms with a proven record of having built successful library buildings. At least two of their library buildings should be examined by the planning committee to gather information about them before final selection. It should be clear that one does not just hire an architectural firm, which is composed of a vast range of talents and knowledge; a specific architectural team from the firm must be hired. If it has built good libraries, the team responsible for the successful planning, or the core of it, must be hired to be assured of the same level of skills and knowledge represented by those libraries. These architects must be designated in the contract; otherwise a team not experienced in library design may be assigned to the job and have to suffer the extensive process of learning about the nature of libraries and their parts, what they do, and similar facts that are unusually demanding on the architect in the case of libraries, which are second only to hospitals in their complexity.[2]

If you now have a strong librarian substantially at the center of control of planning, an able and motivated local planning team, a good, broadly experienced library building consultant, and an architectural team that has designed good libraries, you are in fine managerial shape. I have seen a planning group brought together at this level only eight times in the hundred and twenty library buildings I have participated in over the past twenty years.

However, you have not finished; you are just prepared to begin. Accumulating new knowledge now becomes the focus of the management process. There should be joint exploration of the sources of information, to provide everyone involved in the planning with a common core of information, as the knowledge of the local planners becomes more sophisticated. Everyone possible should participate in developing this knowledge. For academic planning, there is a clear and simple book by Ralph Ellsworth, *Planning the College and University Library Building* (Boulder, Colo.: Pruett Press, 1968). Keyes Metcalf's *Planning Academic and Research Library Buildings* (New York: McGraw-Hill, 1965) is still the monumental work in this field. There is a good book on planning small public libraries by Rolf Myller, *The Design of the Small Public Library* (New York/London: R. R. Bowker, 1966). There is no similarly important book on school libraries, large public libraries, or special libraries. An extremely useful collection of articles on library building planning is by Hal B. Schell (editor), *Reader on the Library Building* (Englewood, Colo.: Microcard Editions Books, 1975).[3]

The Library Administration Division of the American Library Association in Chicago maintains a collection of library building programs, floor plans, and a list of library building consultants (including a record of buildings they have consulted on). The Educational Facilities Laboratories in New York can advise on consultants in a variety of specialties.

After acquiring a basic knowledge by reading, at least three library buildings that are similar to yours in size and nature and are known to be successful should be visited for study. If possible, the architects should join members of the planning team and the librarian on such visits. At least one full day is needed for the discussion with librarians and observations of details that is required. My published reviews of library buildings indicate the kind of information to be gained by such a study.[4]

STAGE II, THE PROGRAMMING PHASE

Though ideas will have been accumulating already, with the assembling of the specialists and accumulation of basic knowledge, the writing of the library building program should begin in earnest. The fact must be emphasized that the architect should not be involved in writing the program, which is a definition of the library's needs, complete with the area requirements and relationships of each, divided into separate components that the architect can comprehend and manipulate in massing the building. The architect should be involved in selection of the site, which will probably be going on collaterally if more than one location is possible; but if he is involved in the writing of the program he is likely to urge requirements desirable to the architect, whereas this document must present what is desirable to the library and its constituency.

This phase depends largely on the librarian and his staff, with the advice and consent of the planning team. It involves heavy interaction with the consultant. The librarian's function is to elevate the vision of his staff above what they have now and to convince them they can plan physical areas that will reach out a helping hand to what they are doing. The importance of the program is indicated in the fact that its emergence as a fixed element in library building planning in the United States by 1960 established the clear supremacy of American library buildings in the world, although we by no means have a monopoly on fine architects.

Ideally, the program sheets should be written locally, because they force local librarians to examine carefully what they are trying to do in each department, whether they want to change what they are doing, and precisely what their physical needs are. The consultant should be used in continuing dialogue with the entire library staff, posing questions that they have to answer, delineating alternatives that can be considered, and informing them fully about areas in which they have had no experience. He must be used to review the program sheets after they are written. The additions and alterations that he proposes for each should be enough to make the second draft of the sheets close to definitive. The consultant can then assign area requirements to each area, based on the furniture and equipment that are required in them. It is important to have the contents of each area listed, along with the area required, so the architect can understand why that much space is requested.

The program should go through at least two versions, the first of which should be distributed widely to the informed constituency of the library in order to keep them informed and to solicit reactions. Many reactions will be worthless, but the few that improve the building are worth the time required.

STAGE III, THE DESIGN DEVELOPMENT PHASE

This is a process of attrition in which the different expertise of the client and of the architects works on each other's product to refine the plans into a final form that is as totally good functionally as possible while at the same time being as totally good architecturally as is possible. Since compromises must be made at this stage, and choices made between alternatives all of which are not realizable, they should not be made in the library program. After careful study of the program, the architects will return graphic plans that represent their understanding of what the program asked for, in as fine an architectural form as they can achieve. These plans must be reviewed in the most minute detail, compared with the program to see where they deviate, measured and counted in their internal properties to detect errors, and a critique prepared listing all the ways in which they fall short of what is needed. These comments must be given in writing to the architects at each meeting for discussion with the entire planning committee. The committee must be prepared to stay throughout each meeting, even if this means missing academic assignments, such as other committee meetings, and even classes. Popping in and out of meetings like this, which are cumulative in providing understanding, is a sure way to get muddled ignorance of what is going on; and anyone who pursues such a course is doomed to be cut off from the planning early in the game.

These meetings will discuss each point made by the client, explore the advantages of what is presented in the plans and alternatives that might be developed to meet the library's needs. The next set of plans should include improved alternative solutions. It is important to have the consultant at these meetings, since the client often does not understand precisely what he needs and insists on solutions that are not the only ones available and would seriously impair the feeling of the building. On the other hand, architects sometimes insist on their solution because it is good esthetically. The answer to this contention is that beauty is achievable in an infinite number of forms, and that indeed the client is interested in esthetics, but he wants better solutions from the architects, which he expects to be good esthetically.

The consultant will act as ambassador-on-the-spot, to avoid a condition in which the client minimizes esthetics and the architect minimizes function. A successful library must fuse both qualities, and if the architects dictate to the client and refuse to suggest reasonable alternatives to problems, a situation not unknown in history, they must be hit over the head at once and told that they must respond to the client's reasonable requirements or be terminated. Before such radical surgery, which is necessary once in a while, it must be clear that the client is not taking unreasonable positions about what he wants.

Client-architect friction is rare these days, since building activity has shrunk. However, I find that two assumptions that clients make in these negotiation meetings are not invariably true. They tend to assume that details in floor plans agreed upon as satisfactory will be retained in all future plans. Because of changes in the architect's staff that works on the drawings, and the eternal difficulties of controlling the 300,000 details incorporated in the plans, desirable details are frequently changed from plan to plan, and sometimes details that have been constant for five months will change, just when librarians have stopped checking them and are taking them for granted.

The magnitude of such changes, from actual experience, are—the change of a single wall line that eliminated 32 group study rooms; the disappearance, after four months of constant capacity as programmed, of 20 percent of the book stack; the change in drawings, very nearly final, of lines on the library's facade that radically diminished its appearance. These traumas were produced in fine architects' offices. When first encountered, they tend to terrify the client, but until you let bids, the plans are merely marks on paper, which can be converted to satisfactory solutions *if errors are detected*. Management of the drawing stage therefore depends on one single librarian-planner, who reviews meticulously every detail in every drawing as though he had never seen the plans before, who makes sure that they retain everything accepted in former plans, and that they improve everything that was posed as a problem at the last meeting with the architects.

The second mis-assumption made by clients is that alternatives discussed clearly at meetings with the architects, and accepted by both parties without any reservations, will appear in the next set of drawings. Again, through the multiplicity in plans and work patterns in the architect's office, it is unusual in my experience for any sequential set of plans to incorporate all changes agreed on at the last meeting. It therefore is imperative for the chairman of the planning committee to make meticulous notes on changes discussed at each meeting and send a written list of them to everyone involved in the planning. The following meeting must begin with a review of this list against the plans, asking the architects what their response to each has been. Those that have not been met should begin the list to be discussed at the following meeting. The librarian must make sure that such constant and meticulous follow-up is maintained, or else much that is desirable and well-thought will be lost in the planning process.

Throughout the process of reviewing sequential plans, a sophisticated learning process will have to take place between the consultant and the librarian-planner, who must develop some ability to read plans, to judge the size of spaces, and to ask intelligent questions. The consultant must review each set of floor plans and write comments and questions about them. But to hire him to count, check each detail formerly accepted, measure details, and do the other infinitely detailed checking that is necessary on each set of plans would be extremely expensive. It should be done by a local librarian, both for economy and because the librarian's heart is in the building, motivating him to unusual thoroughness. Management of the entire development phase hinges on the librarian-planner and the consultant, who will identify what needs to be negotiated, and on the planning committee for negotiating with the architects.

The development phase will go through two stages—the development of floor plans, and the development of working drawings. There are two essential points in the development of floor plans that require special attention. Very early, generally in connection with the first presentation of floor plans, the shape of the building is fixed. The architects, after study of the program, will define the minimum space required on the main floor, the most demanding floor since it contains the card catalog, and around this basic requirement will decide how it can be shaped in the form of (usually) a multi-story building. They will usually present two or three general shapes that the building could take. Careful consideration of the potential of each to meet the requirements of library spaces and relationships is critically important before approval is given to one direction for the building's mass. If it is not clear how the building will look in the different forms, then drawings or models should be requested from the architects. Anything other than simple drawings or small simple models are expensive to make and should be requested (at extra cost, of course) only if really necessary to firm the client's mind about which massing is preferred.[5]

The second essential point requires the architect to lay out all furniture and equipment detailed in each unit of the program, after the massing of the building and the general development of the layout are accepted. This assumes that the program must detail in each of its units the furniture and equipment it must contain.[6] Nothing except a furniture layout shows what human movements are possible within a given space, and whether they can be arranged for efficient library movements. In addition, the furniture layout is the basis to which must be related a range of mechanical and electrical services, as discussed below. In the early stages of floor plans, furniture layouts are critical in showing not only whether enough space has been provided for the library function that it contains, but whether its shape will accommodate the work that it must perform.

The dynamics of refining floor plans to final acceptance have already been discussed. When they are completed, there will be a large, general meeting of everyone concerned for a formal acceptance of final floor plans, lest some power hidden in the woodpile might dash out later and reverse work already completed.[7] To complete floor plans will take six or seven months.

On the basis of these plans, working drawings will then be developed, which contain the layout and details of the engineering elements that produce the working building. There are four different kinds of working-drawings, produced by four different engineering specialists, who are located in at least two different engineering firms. The space requirements of each must be related to and reconciled with those of all the others. A dropped ceiling contains plumbing pipes, electrical lines and fixtures, and ducts and control boxes for the air-handling system. This already accident-prone multiplicity is made even more difficult to control by the fact that the engineers are set to developing plans before floor plans are final, a necessary process to get early confirmation that the floor plan arrangement will reasonably accommodate the requirements of the mechanical systems, and to get an early indication that the costs of the building will fall within the budget. But if adjustments are not made precisely to the final floor plans developed, strange things will appear in the course of construction, such as a sink on one wall whose water taps are on another (an actual case).

Each engineering specialty involves the client in a different way. Structural engineering firms tend to be very good throughout the land. Praise heaven, because the client is almost totally in their hands, not even able to ask intelligent questions about their product. There are complications of material choices these days (1978) involving differences in building costs. Steel frame library buildings are occasionally cheaper than poured concrete, something that was never true ten years ago. The possibility of using preformed concrete elements instead of poured-in-place buildings, or a combination of both, usually must be considered in the course of planning the structure.

The client must depend entirely on the judgment of architects and structural engineers in these matters, which are especially critical in a building that must support a live load of 150 pounds per square foot all over and even more in compact storage or map storage areas. However, the client can make a major contribution to the building by encouraging the development of the widest spans possible (within the budget) for the structural bays, planned in dimensions that accommodate multiples of the three-foot width of stack sections.

Mechanical elements in the building are referred to as "HVAC"—heating, ventilation, and air conditioning. In the development of these systems, clients must be involved in some important considerations. First, they must review the size, location, and interrelation of the HVAC control zones, which are areas of the building (usually indicated by different color shading) that respond to a single temperature control (or humidity control, if used). Zones must not be too large and must not combine small occupancy rooms with large occupancy open areas. The small expense involved in multiplying temperature controls pays large dividends in the comfort of buildings, and therefore in their use.

If mechanical air-tempering units, such as fan-coil systems or air induction systems, are used on the periphery of the building, the client must be sure they do not generate noise. The solution to this problem is to have them oversized enough so that they produce the required air tempering capacity at medium velocity or medium speed, rather than at high velocity. Fan-coil units can be brought in and run so that everyone can listen to the noise level of their fans.

If the HVAC system is dispersed on different floors instead of centralized, which is at present a tendency in order to reduce the cost of ducts, the client must be sure that sound attenuators are used in the duct system, and that the walls and doors of these mechanical rooms are heavily insulated to prevent passage of noise.

Finally, when plans are completed (and before they are accepted), the client must request a review of the HVAC plans with the mechanical engineer, to pinpoint the location of each temperature control. Make sure it is not in a location influenced by any other temperature factor (such as sun or a hot-duct wall) other than ambient air. Have the engineer show the location and extent of the zone that will be controlled by each thermostat. Don't be surprised to find the control on a different floor from the zone, and in each case, ask the engineer whether this is a satisfactory arrangement for comfort or whether it should be upgraded. I find that this simple review of the zone and control plans is almost never requested.[8]

The electrical drawings are divided into separate sheets for each floor for power and for lighting fixture layouts. The client must supply engineers with separate schedules for locations of the following utilities, which can be done only after a furniture layout is accepted:

telephones
clocks (avoid centrally controlled systems)
electric outlets
computer conduits
TV cable conduits

electronic security systems
inter-building communication systems

A new device commonly owned by students, the electronic computer, requires
more sophisticated thinking about where to locate outlets than we are accustomed to.
I keep seeing their extension cords strung across walkways throughout the land. Locations for these utilities should be marked by symbols on furniture layout drawings
for the engineers, and exact copies of them should be kept for follow-up in subsequent
electrical drawings to make sure that they are supplied and keep appearing in the same
location each time. In addition, provision for changing the location of electrical elements in the future must be provided (to the extent it can be afforded) in technical
services areas, media areas, and circulation and reference areas in order to convert
uses to future needs without blowing up the building.

Selecting lighting fixtures that provide good quality illumination with adequate
intensity, and arranging their layout to provide maximum convertibility of the areas
they light, may be the most difficult task in the entire range of planning. Most architects and electrical engineers, illogical as it is, do not know how to choose good quality
lighting fixtures. The fixtures proposed for the building should be defined early in the
working drawings and must be examined as early as possible in a mock-up of at least
four fixtures, each containing exactly the same number of tubes, the same color-tone,
and the same wattage that will be specified. They must be hung in two rows, at the
exact height and on the exact spacing to be specified. Then they must be examined
from all angles to determine if they produce uncomfortable glare. If they do not, you
are the fortunate one out of five in my experience.

If there is high glare, they must be rejected, and it may be necessary in such
cases for the client to propose the fixture to be used in his building, by identifying
the model number and manufacturer of one that supplies good quality illumination,
by observing it in an electrical supply shop or in another building, or by inquiring
of other libraries known for good lighting what they have used.

If freestanding stacks are used, lighting troffers should run at right angles to the
stacks to allow for changes in range spacing. If fixed stacks are used, such as tier-built
stacks (once again returning in different form for economy), much cheaper lighting
can be supplied in single-tube fixtures with a diffusing lens hung above aisles parallel
to the stacks.

It is extremely important to require a transparent overlay of the lighting layout
(called the "reflected ceiling plan") that can be laid over the furniture and equipment
layout to make sure light is supplied where it is needed. It is commonplace to find
that lighting at the walls of rooms, where single carrels (the most intensive use furniture) are located, have scanty light because lighting troffers that run at right angles
stop two feet short of the walls. In this case, a three-foot wide carrel on the wall
would be quite inadequately lit, and supplementary lighting is required.[9]

In all matters relating to managing the adequacy of the lighting system, the
central burden is likely to fall on the librarian-planner and the library building consultant. Needless to say, this places a premium on obtaining a consultant with lighting
expertise.

Plumbing drawings are comparatively easy on librarians. It is necessary to oppose
to the last ditch the installation of sprinkler systems in libraries, since water can do
far more damage to books than fire. If driven by local ordinances to install fire sprink-
lers, make sure the system is of the type that provides dry sprinkler heads, with no
water supplied to any of them until called for by an activated sprinkler head, and that

they are divided into zones as small as possible that work independently of each other. It is also useful to have water taps *above* sinks, and if overflow pipes from water-discharging machines, such as air conditioners, empty into custodial sinks, the pipes must extend below the rim of the sink. It is important to make sure that no water pipes are in the ceilings of rare book areas and workrooms.

Developments in the mechanical plans will cause changes in the floor layouts that seemed fixed forever when they were finally accepted. Some walls will have to be moved to accommodate structural elements or to enable the passage of pipes or ducts from floor to floor, or for other reasons. In each case, the client should make sure that the changes accepted provide as much as possible of whatever was intended in the original layout. To do so may, in some cases, require switches in the location of rooms from the originally accepted plan.

Bid drawings, which control what the contractor builds, and written specifications, which control the quality of building elements and machinery, are the final documents produced in the design development phase. It must not be assumed that they contain accurately everything that has been developed in previous plans. They must be examined in critically minute detail, as though no previous plans for the building have ever been seen. If the planner remembers a telephone location that was right in the next to last plans, he may miss the fact that it is wrong in the bid drawings. This is not the place to relax vigilance, but to intensify it. The consultant should be requested to examine these drawings in great detail. Every other set of drawings can be changed by asking the architect to do so. To change drawings after bids have been accepted requires a change order, and change orders are time consuming to process and very expensive to obtain.

This review consequently will take time and great concentration. Getting completely away from ordinary work locations is highly advisable. Meanwhile, the authorities are probably itchy to go out for bid right away (they don't know anything about the plans), and the planner will be under pressure for approval. The pressure must be resisted long enough to spend a reasonable amount of time for an exacting review. It is then important to write down a list of the changes that must be made, upon agreement by the architect, and make sure that his supplementary plan correction sheets contain all these changes, because very often they do not.

The specifications are highly technical, but it is possible by surveying them closely to detect things in certain parts of them (especially if they specify the stacks) in which changes must be made. It is worth both the librarian-planner and the consultant going through them, reading them where they yield to logic and common sense, and asking questions about anything that seems open to question.

STAGE IV, THE CONSTRUCTION PHASE

This phase involves the client only in examining the building physically as it progresses (get a hard hat) to make sure that telephone outlets, walls, and the like are where they are supposed to be. The best possible manager for this stage is a superlative clerk of the works, hired by the library to make sure that the construction conforms meticulously to both drawings and specifications.[10] The best money spent on the entire building is on his salary, if he has a record of superior performance, because in the sequence of developments in construction, highly unsatisfactory work can be irretrievably covered up by subsequent construction. In one building I was involved with, a telephone conduit that had been planned to run twenty feet on an angle from one wall to another actually ran 75 feet straight down, when probed by the installer.

Job meetings are held at frequent intervals by those involved in the construction phase, often involving the architects and always the clerk of the works, to resolve difficulties in interpreting what the plans and specifications intended to call for, and to make changes required by the realities of metal and concrete as the building progresses. ["The manufacturer has discontinued that model," or, "We can't run that two-inch conduit directly through that four-inch plumbing drain."] Sooner or later, the decisions made at these job meetings will make changes in the building as planned, in the floor plans (generally wall changes), or in the comfort level or appearance of rooms. They also provide opportunities, by change orders, for the client to correct undetected esthetic horrors, such as a drain pipe like a crooked elephant's leg visible in a rare books reading room that I once saw.

It is therefore important for the librarian-planner to be present at all these meetings to control any changes in the building that affect the library as originally projected. Much of the procedure will be far over his head, but much of it will be understandable, especially when it involves changes in the layout, and all of it is extremely interesting anthropologically as a study of the construction genus, its language, habits, and mores.

If carried through these four stages, the management of the building planning has been as complete as possible, and the contribution to its success that is possible through managing has been made. This fact alone should make the new library a better building than it otherwise would be. The rest of its success depends on the intelligence and talent that have been brought together in the planning group.[11]

NOTES

[1] One university library was planned under almost ideally bad conditions. The librarian was better than reasonably competent, but his personality had not convinced his faculty of this fact, and his judgments were distrusted by the rest of the committee. The committee chairman was using this position to run for an administrative office and, in addition, was unusually blockheaded. Only a few members of the committee were really interested in the library, and the procedure was rather free-form brainstorming, with each person allowed to get into the library some architectural feature he preferred. Nothing like the responsible "back and forth" that must occur between client and architect could possibly have occurred with such a committee. And if it could have, the architect-designer of the building was related to a high member of the university administration. Need I say that the building is highly unsatisfactory?

[2] There have been two exceptions to this rule in my experience, but every other architect's first experience at a library I have seen has been far short of satisfactory.

[3] My book, *Mason on Library Buildings*, to be published by the Scarecrow Press in the near future, will add depth to the materials useful to beginning planners.

[4] "The Beinecke Siamese Twins: an Objective Review of Yale's New Rare Book Library Building," *College and Research Libraries*, May 1965, pp. 199-212. "The Rock; A Critical Analysis of the John D. Rockefeller, Jr., Library at Brown University," *Library Journal*, December 1, 1968, pp. 4487-92. "Underneath the Oak Trees; The Sedgewick Undergraduate Library at U.B.C.," *Journal of Academic Librarianship*, January 1977, pp. 286-92.

[5] I have seen two building models that cost more than $20,000 each.

[6] As indicated above, furniture and equipment details in the program units are required in order to make an accurate space requirement estimate. Still, I see building programs without this detail.

[7] A weeping architect once described to me his experience in planning a building for one governmental agency. He had probed carefully to determine that final authority for the building was located in the agency, and he was assured in every way that this was so. After he had put more than $150,000 in labor costs into the plans, a superior authority that did have final control entered the picture and threw out everything done up to that point.

[8] My forthcoming book on library buildings contains a chapter on air-handling systems in libraries.

[9] My forthcoming book contains a chapter on library lighting.

[10] The use of a construction management firm throughout the planning process, with consequent radical changes in planning and construction strategy, is a highly controversial practice too complicated for presentation in a general article like this one. The field of construction management is still in the process of formulating its procedures and defining what it can do, for what specific aims, and with what spread of expertise for the client to select from. Right now, it is difficult to determine from clients why they hire construction management, what they expect from them, and whether they have received from them what they wanted. But the emphasis in the process seems to be coming down hard on management, and in five years, this field will probably be significant in construction practice.

[11] I have found no literature on the management on library building planning.

BIBLIOGRAPHY

Ellsworth, Ralph. *Planning the College and University Library Building*. Boulder, CO: Pruett Press, 1968.

Metcalf, Keyes. *Planning Academic and Research Library Buildings*. New York: McGraw-Hill, 1965.

Myller, Rolf. *The Design of the Small Public Library*. New York: R. R. Bowker, 1966.

Schell, Hal B., ed. *Reader on the Library Building*. Englewood, CO: Microcard Editions Books, 1975.

MANAGING THE PLANNING OF FACILITIES FOR LIBRARY AND INFORMATION SCIENCE EDUCATION PROGRAMS

by Martha Boaz

GENERAL PRINCIPLES FOR PLANNING A BUILDING

People are probably more affected by a learning-study environment than they realize. For this reason, it is important that space, facilities, lighting, temperature, comfort, and many other factors be planned for the most effective, efficient, and comfortable use by students, faculty, staff, administrators, and all who use a building designed for an educational program. In light of this, the physical resources and facilities of a library/information science school should be planned to carry out the general objectives of the program and the unique requirements of the particular school.

The over-all plan for a library school building should include administrative quarters, faculty offices, classrooms, and laboratory facilities and a library school library. Variety in the types, sizes, and furnishings of classrooms makes them both more interesting and more satisfactory for long-range use. Laboratories should be planned for the types of activities that will be carried on in them; these may be labs for technical processes, instructional technology/media, automation/computer, and other functions. Each needs its own type of space and supportive equipment.

The customary location for a library school has been within the university library. Part of the rationale for this location in the past was that frequently the director of the library was also director of the library school, and it also seemed reasonable that access to a university library's collections was a vital factor in placing these schools in this setting. Now each ALA-accredited school, for the most part, has its own dean or director who is not the librarian, and there has been a move toward separate physical facilities for the school, although the latter has not been achieved in many schools. In many universities, the library school's library is still under the jurisdiction of the university librarian, as are the libraries of most of the other professional schools.

Location of the library school in its own building is highly desirable, for the school can then focus more directly on its own program and can maintain greater independence in pursuing its objectives. Having the library school library in this building (regardless of whether it is autonomous or under the jurisdiction of the university library) is essential to the educational welfare of the students and faculty of the school. The library school library may, in addition to its usual function of housing books and other educational materials, serve as a laboratory and demonstration center for activities and projects that are being carried out in the classes. It may also serve as an internship center for students to get practical experience, somewhat as hospitals are used by medical students for their internships. The library and laboratories should, therefore, be planned as settings for research studies or other work that will be done there. When possible, the building should be planned with an eye to change and modification as the program of the school changes. This is especially pertinent in the spaces that house automation equipment and media facilities, for rapid changes will take place in these areas.

Buildings exist in both space and time. Ada Louise Huxtable, architecture critic, notes that the promise of the art of building is very much alive. She says, "It is not in the individual structure as traditionally designed, but in the relationships of people, land and buildings for life and use—it is in the esthetic and human ferment that is currently called architecture."[1]

The questions to be considered in planning a library school building are many. Stephen Longmead and Margaret Beckman list some of the problems involved in planning libraries in their book, *New Library Design*.[2] Several of these apply equally to a building for a library school and include:

> Are the buildings flexible enough to meet demands created by modern communication and automation technology? Have librarians defined a philosophy of librarianship which meets the needs of today's spiralling enrollments and rapidly increasing book collections, and does the library building reflect that philosophy? . . . Have librarians or architects given adequate consideration to the library as a social organism in which specific needs of individual users can and should be met?[3]

A beautiful, functional, well-planned building should be satisfying to its users, and it may eventually be the inspiration for additional funding from donors who may be interested in expanding and developing the program of the school.

As in the design of any other facility, the planning for each library school should be an individual matter and should reflect the program and objectives of the school. Building planners generally point out the need for space for the current needs, but also stress that plans be included for future expansion when necessary. Advice is also given about buildings designed with generalized space, movable partitions, and other possibilities for adjustment, but as Margaret Rufsvold notes,

> space which is so generalized as to be adaptable to any future use, may not satisfactorily meet the specialized needs of the current program. Therefore, in providing library education facilities, our problem, like that of other educators, becomes one of designing quarters which will be functional in the immediate future and flexible enough to be adapted to educational activities, teaching methods, and various types of equipment unknown or unused today.[4]

Location

Opinions about the location of the library school usually fall into two areas: one recommends that the library school should be in the main library building on the campus, and this has been the usual spot where the school has been traditionally housed; the other recommendation favors a separate building close to the main library. The separate building has the advantages of being planned and built for the particular needs of the school and of having all of its space allocated to the school. The school also has its own separate identity, which it could not have if housed in the library or in another building.

The separate library school building ideally situated would be close to and within easy walking distance of the research library of the university.

Financial Matters

Fund raising for a building may be considered as a thankless yet "continually thanking" job. But, there are satisfactions, too, and interesting, rewarding contacts. The development office of the university and the top administration are often if not usually involved in fund raising efforts and the development office is usually staffed by knowledgeable, capable, and well-trained people.

Items that should be included in a budget for a new building include—in addition to the architect's fees—actual construction costs, engineering fees, clearing the site, the soil engineer's fee, building permit and inspection fees, legal and administrative expense, landscaping, furnishings and movable equipment, extension of utilities, and other expenses.

In addition to money for the actual construction totals for a new building, the budget should include an endowment for the maintenance of the building over a period of 25 years. If trends of recent years continue, operating costs of heat, air conditioning, electricity and janitorial services will increase. Building costs continue to rise and have skyrocketed since the early 1970s. Inflationary costs, of necessity, have to be taken into consideration in all of the services and functions carried on in the building, and they will include all salaries, book collections, and services. The money for the library science building may be from the university's budget or it may be raised from outside sources: foundations or from private donors. The building may well be named for the major donor.

Planning the Building Program

Prior to the development of actual plans, the person responsible for writing the program for a library school building should review the *Standards for Accreditation* of the American Library Association. The section labeled "Physical Resources and Facilities" is brief and very general in nature, but the standard says:

> Instructional resources, services and facilities should be provided and organized to meet the needs of the specific programs. . . . Facilities should be adequate in number, size, and arrangement to carry out the functions and instructional experiences implied in the preceding standard.[5]

A written program is essential. The purpose of this is to outline for the architect the purpose of the building, the functions and services to be performed in it, and how the various parts are to interrelate. In the preliminary study leading to the written program, certain points should be noted. Wheeler and Goldhor, listing pointers for planners of public library buildings, give suggestions that also apply to planners of library school buildings. They say that clear statements should be made about the following points: "the general functional objective of the building . . . the list by priority of major public service facilities . . . a schedule of estimated spaces for all facilities, arranged by floors."[6] They add:

A preliminary schedule of equipment and furnishings, especially those influencing ducts, conduits and other service lines. A statement as to heating, ventilating, washrooms, maintenance points, lighting, services access, etc. A statement as to ceiling and cross section heights, and modular or "bay" dimensions suggested, as affecting costs. A summary as to square and cubic areas and estimated costs.[7]

A typical program, according to Rutherford D. Rogers and David C. Weber, includes the following points:

A typical program will cover the following points in detail, although some may be generalized and detailed only in later memoranda:

Title page
Table of contents
Program justification (often in the form of a separate document written by the director and approved by the provost and the trustees)
Academic plan or function of the building (an articulate exposition)
Location of site and orientation (usually determined by the director, the provost, and the trustees)
Architectural compatibility (usually determined by the planning office, the president, and the trustees)
General building configuration and access (determined by the director)
Functional relationships (includes the juxtaposition of major bibliographic instruments and primary departments—as illustrated on p. 334—a description of processing work flow and book circulation flow, a detailed statement or chart of typical reader traffic, and any special implications of developments such as microphotography or remote storage or computers)
General restraints on spaces and mechanical equipment (includes ceiling heights, fenestration, module determination, wall insulation and mobility, electric power, lighting, sound control, and ventilation and air conditioning)
Memorial name requirements (specified by the director)
Architect's scope of work (usually specified by the planning or business office)
Code references and procedures during design and construction (written by the business office)
Synopsis of space requirements
Detail of space requirements (each administrative unit to be described in terms of individual spaces and each space to have a statement of (1) desired net assignable square footage; (2) location in relation to other spaces, when important, and special character; (3) built-in or attached equipment, e.g., shelving, counter, book conveyor, or washbowl; (4) movable furnishings).[8]

The person responsible for the written program and for the general plan will ask for and hope for suggestions from the faculty and staff of the library school. This person will also comb the literature on buildings, will go to visit other similar structures, and will contact other building planners and consultants.

It is the particular responsibility of the faculty—by getting suggestions from each other, students, and other disciplines—to determine the general goals and objectives of the curriculum and educational program of the school, both for the present and for the predictable future. These plans would include the space needs of the various programs, master's and doctoral degree levels, plans for teaching and research, for book and non-book materials, and for classrooms, laboratories, seminar rooms, conference and lecture rooms, and display areas. Plans for the future must include estimates and projections about enrollment increases, curriculum changes, faculty and staff size, administrative organization, communication and traffic patterns, inter-relationships, and service needs.

Classrooms and seminar rooms for various sizes and types of classes are needed (seating from fifteen to 150) and should be adapted to various types of teaching and equipment needs. Each room should be wired for the particular purposes that it will serve—some rooms will require plans for closed circuit television or radio or public address systems, for video tape recorders and television monitors. Carrels and seminar rooms for small group or individual work should be provided.

Environment for Learning

Planning a building to be used for educational purposes will take into account various methods of teaching as well as sizes and types of classes. Functional, esthetic, and economic criteria must be considered. Certainly, effective use of media will depend on the type of classroom in which it is housed. Design of facilities will include the traditional type of classroom, seminar rooms and independent study facilities.

The selection of furniture, audio-visual equipment, and hardware items are often left until late in the planning process. Furniture and equipment should be considered as an integral part of the plans for a building when its functional requirements are being outlined; esthetic and economic considerations must be combined with the functional and based upon careful planning. It is suggested that professional advice be sought in the early stages.

The furniture and equipment should be selected to suit the size and space of the floor plans and coordinated for service in the building. Both decorative and utilitarian principles should be bases for selection of these items. Built-in furniture should be kept to a minimum. The furniture and equipment should be of the highest quality and purchased from reputable dealers. The dean and architect or decorator—whoever is selecting the furniture—should write quality specifications for the required items, and dealers should furnish samples and demonstrations of performance. When possible, the library school dean should visit the showrooms of furniture and equipment dealers and should ask dealers to submit bids.

Decisions will have to be made about space requirements and standards for seating a percentage of the students, for staff work space, and for the square footage requirements for book and non-book materials. Information about these and about sizes and types of tables and chairs, bookshelving of various kinds, charging desks, atlas stands, periodical shelving, card catalogs, and other standards for furniture and equipment can be found in books by authorities in the library profession. (Several of these are listed at the end of this chapter.)

The use of color furnishes a cheerful atmosphere and adds interest to the building. Used in a planned design, color can serve as a unifying theme throughout a building. A general background of white walls and white draperies allows great variation in the colors used; warm or cool colors set the tone for different floor levels. In general, reds, yellows, greens, and oranges used in carpeting and furniture provide a cheerful as well as a practical color scheme. However, the choice of color, furniture, and other items are matters of individual preference.

Preliminary to the actual writing of the building program, consideration must be given to these questions: what will be the approximate size and type of building for present needs and for future expansion? how will it be funded? and if funds are to be raised, how long will it take to raise the money? when should the actual planning for the physical structure begin? and, how long will it take to finish the building? After consulting all possible sources, the person responsible for the written program (usually the dean of a library school) will then prepare a written program.

The Planning Team

The dean should work closely with the architect; usually two members of the architectural firm are heavily involved—the design architect and the project architect. The dean will also work closely with the university director of planning, the director of the physical plant, the business manager, and the construction manager. The architect and the building construction contractor are usually selected by the board of trustees of the university from among several competitive bidders. One person, who may be the director of facilities planning, serves as director of the project and works with the different people who are involved. He checks to see that each person does his job, according to scheduled time, and within the budget limitations. He sometimes has to act as an intermediary in resolving differences of opinion.

The dean may work with a building consultant and will probably involve one or more faculty members of the school; the entire faculty will probably be asked for suggestions, especially in specialized areas such as automation and instructional technology and members of the faculty should be able to see the building plans and asked to give their reactions to them. From the time that a fund raising drive is initiated, through the planning and blueprint stages to actual occupancy and until four to six months after moving into the building, the dean may spend a third—maybe half—of his or her time on the building.

Great care should be used in planning the building, but speed is a practical consideration, too, particularly if it is a time when the inflationary rise in construction costs may add greatly to the cost of a building, if delayed over a period of years. Attention also should be given in every building plan for potential expansion needs. Frequently the original blueprints can include items that will facilitate expansion if it becomes necessary. Often, this can be done more economically if certain items are incorporated in the original plan.

Progressive Stages in Building Planning

After the program has been written and revised and approved, the architect begins. He submits preliminary drawings and then working drawings which are reviewed by the library school dean and the buildings committee. After the drawings have been revised and final approval is given, the construction begins.

At least six months before the projected moving date, the furniture and equipment should be selected and purchased and installed well in advance of the actual move.

The moving process should also be carefully planned, if a move from one building to another is involved. Boxes and other items should be clearly labeled for their destination in the new building.

It is suggested that the date of dedication be scheduled several months later than would seem necessary, for everything is always slower than scheduled. Thus, in order to have everything in and in working order and to have landscaping completed, it is wise to plan a dedication ceremony four to six months after the first occupancy. It is also wise to allow a period of a year for a settling-in and settling-up process, for there will be problems—perhaps with construction errors, or air conditioning, or overlooked necessities. Anyway, there will be complaints—some justified.

After the Move into the Building

Problems seem to be "par for the course" in any new building, and for six months to a year after occupancy, these problems arise and most be reported and corrected. Irritating matters such as drooping covers on ceiling lights, doors that stick, door stops that become uprooted, the lack of a telephone in an elevator, no public telephone, folding doors that will not fold, storage closets without locks, air conditioning that is either too hot or too cold—these and many other things are a part of the settling-in process in a new building.

The dean should plan to save time to show visitors through the building. (They may really want to see it, or the dean may just hope that they want to see it.) At any rate, visitors will probably have a grand tour in spite of themselves. Eventually, though, everything settles down to routine, and the building is no longer new or the subject of conversation.

THE USE OF SPACE

A library school building is conceived as a progression of functional and hierarchal spaces, with these spaces molded to function and form. Several generalizations about the use of space are given below.

Varied Sizes of Study and Classroom Areas Desirable

Small-group study areas and seminar rooms, for fifteen to twenty people, promote discussion and group interaction. Rooms for 25 to forty people continue to be practical and in constant use. Furniture and equipment pose no particular problems, as a wide variety of furniture and equipment is available, and the person or persons selecting these items may exercise great imagination in the decisions.

Large-group facilities are very effective in the use of learning media, but the planning for the large-group area must be given careful attention. It must ensure an optimum viewing area. Sloped floors and raised seating introduce intimacy, and if the seats are fixed they can be "staggered" so that nobody is sitting directly behind anyone else. In recent years, there have been no windows (by design); hence air conditioning and humidity control are important aspects. (This may change with the problems now experienced in energy shortages.) Also, lighting is very important; usually three levels of illumination are necessary. Proper acoustical design is very important, too.

In addition, there should be plans for adjunct storage and projection areas. Due to the fact that lighting, acoustics, and climate conditions are so important, the planning for them should be done in the early stages of the blueprints.

Media that is used in teaching will require storage room, preferably in the room or rooms where the media will be used. An overhead projector can be located on a table when in use; there should be a rear projection screen for films and slides and chalk board and tackboard surfaces.

Lighting in a classroom may be either fluorescent or incandescent; two levels of illumination are desirable, with a lower level for use during projection.

Lighting

Concepts about lighting have varied from time to time. It is suggested that the planner and architect consult the literature on this subject and that they consult electrical engineers who are specialists in this field.

Fenestration

The matter of windows and glass walls has been the subject of much study and debate. Ralph Ellsworth points out that "windows no longer are relied upon to supply the air and light needed by the inhabitants of the building. They are, on the other hand, needed because people like to know what the weather is like outside and because readers like to raise their eyes from the book occasionally and stretch their eyes. It is pleasant to be able to see a tree, or a mountain, or the sky or a pretty girl."[9] Ellsworth notes a paradoxical fact that has been commented on for some years. This is that architects use glass walls to enable people inside a building to see a beautiful view outside; then, in order to keep the books from a bright glaring sun, they install floor-to-ceiling draperies so that the view is concealed except in the early mornings. Faintly tinted, smoke-tone glass and draperies throughout a building add to its aesthetic appearance.

Air Conditioning

Depending on the climate, air conditioning may or may not be needed, but it is a reasonable bet that air conditioning will be welcome in most places and will be worth the cost. However, if an energy crisis should happen again, as it did in the winter of 1974, or if the threat of an energy shortage is serious, architects and planners will need to consider variations in planning. For in a building that is sealed, with no windows that will open, it can be very uncomfortable if air conditioning is not available or if the air conditioning machinery gets out of order.

Carpeting

The colors and materials of carpeting should be selected with attention to their suitability for particular areas, durability, and noise control.

Elevator

The elevator should be large enough to accommodate eight to ten people or several people and a book truck. It is suggested that any elevator purchase be made with great care and only from a well-known, well-established, reputable company.

Custodial Work Space

Custodial work space should be planned with the advice of the buildings and grounds department.

Provision for Disabled Individuals

A ramp must be provided at one side or at the front entrance of the building for wheel chair patients. In addition, provision must be made in the toilets for them, and the public telephone on the first floor should be placed so that wheel chair patients can reach it. (A telephone also must be in the elevator. Federal regulations now require these installations.)

CONCLUSION

Each library school building should be planned and designed to carry out the goals and objectives of the program of the school. The persons working on the plans should read widely about the building process and should visit already-constructed buildings to learn what to do and not to do in the design of a building. The model following the bibliography to this chapter is the library school building at the University of Southern California. It provides a concrete look at an actual building in order to complement the previous theoretical discussion.

NOTES

[1] Ada Louise Huxtable, *Will They Ever Finish Bruckner Boulevard?* (New York: The Macmillan Company, c1970), p. 147.

[2] Stephen Longmead and Margaret Beckman, *New Library Design: Guidelines to Planning Academic Library Buildings* (Toronto: John Wiley and Sons, c1970), p. 2.

[3] Ibid.

[4] Margaret I. Rufsvold, "Designing Facilities for Library Education," *Journal of Education for Librarianship* V (Summer 1964), pp. 10-11.

[5] American Library Association, *Standards for Accreditation* (Chicago: ALA, 1972), p. 12.

[6] Joseph Wheeler and Herbert Goldhor, *Practical Administration of Public Libraries* (New York: Harper and Row, c1962), p. 558.

[7] Ibid.

[8]Rutherford D. Rogers and David C. Weber, *University Library Administration* (New York: The H. W. Wilson Co., 1971), pp. 333-35.

[9]Ralph E. Ellsworth, *Planning the College and University Library Building* (Boulder, Colorado: Pruett Press, Inc., c1968), p. 108.

BIBLIOGRAPHY

American Library Association. Association of College and Reference [later: Research] Libraries. *Building Plans Institutes.* Proceedings. Chicago, American Library Association, 1952.
See especially Robert H. Muller, "Evaluation of Compact Book Storage Systems," in Third Library Building Plans Institute (ACRL Monographs, No. 1), 1954. pp. 77-93.

Educational Facilities Laboratories. *The Impact of Technology on the Library Building.* New York: Educational Facilities Laboratories, 1967.

Ellsworth, Ralph E. *Academic Library Buildings.* Boulder, Colorado: The Colorado Associated University Press, c1973.

Ellsworth, Ralph E. *Planning the College and University Library Building.* Boulder, Colorado: Pruett Press, Inc., c1968.

Galvin, Hoyt R., ed. *Planning a Library Building.* Chicago: American Library Association, 1955.

Green, Alan C., et al. *Educational Facilities with New Media.* Washington, DC: National Education Association, c1966.

Harlow, Neal. "Planner to Architect." *Journal of Education for Librarianship* IX (Summer 1968), 5-12.

Langmead, Stephen, and Beckman, Margaret. *New Library Design: Guidelines to Planning Academic Library Buildings.* Toronto: John Wiley and Sons Canada, c1970.

Library Administration Division, American Library Association. *Problems in Planning Library Facilities.* Chicago: American Library Association, 1964.

Library Administration Division, American Library Association. *Libraries, Building for the Future.* Chicago: ALA, 1967.

Library Administration Division, American Library Association. *Library Buildings: Innovation for Changing Needs* Chicago: ALA, 1972.

Metcalf, Keyes D. *Planning Academic and Research Library Buildings.* New York: McGraw-Hill, 1965.

Rogers, Rutherford D., and Weber, David C. *University Library Administration.* New York: The H. W. Wilson Company, 1971.

Rufsvold, Margaret I. "Designing Facilities for Library Education." *Journal of Education for Librarianship* V (Summer 1964), 10-15.

Weber, David C., ed. "University Library Buildings." *Library Trends* XVIII (October 1969), 107-270.

Wheeler, Joseph L., and Githens, Alfred Morton. *The American Public Library Building*. New York: Charles Scribner's Sons, 1941.

Wheeler, Joseph L., and Goldhor, Herbert. *Practical Administration of Public Libraries*. New York: Harper and Row, c1962.

MODEL:*

SPECIFIC AREAS IN THE ONE LIBRARY SCHOOL BUILDING AT THE UNIVERSITY OF SOUTHERN CALIFORNIA

First Floor

The library user's first impression of the library's interior is made in the lobby, which in this building is both practical and decorative. The lobby channels people into the building and to their destinations. The lobby offers a psychological transition from the outside of the building to the indoors. A floor-to-ceiling built-in display case, which serves as a transparent glass wall, also serves as a sound barrier to the library, allows conversation and a see-through view into the library, and has generous space for displays and exhibits. The lobby provides access to the stairway and elevator, to a public telephone, a directory, and to restrooms.

Directly beyond the lobby, one sees the charging desk, catalog cases, and other service furnishings. One also sees the open reading areas, the lounge areas, the open stacks, and the individual study cubicles. The bright, cheerful colors of carpeting, the pleasing furniture, and the quiet richness of the full-length draperies over wide spans of glassed walls give a feeling of openness and simplicity and of restrained elegance.

The Library

The library occupies the entire first floor of the USC building. There is a feeling here of spaciousness and of warm and cheerful color combined with a clear view through the building. A counter controls access to the librarian's office, the work room, and the reserve book area. The large room has an open center with tables and chairs in the middle and lounge areas at each end. Open book stacks are at each side of the room; beyond these, along side the glass walls, on two sides, are individual study carrels.

Reserve books are kept behind the circulation desk next to the librarian's office and are checked out at the circulation desk. Several compact storage stacks are located behind the circulation desk for the reserve collections.

The charging desk area has an acoustical cloud above the desk, which serves as a sound barrier from the nearby library area where readers are studying. The card catalog is near the charging desk, as are dictionary and atlas stands and several vertical files.

Group Study Rooms

Several group study rooms are provided adjacent to the library. These may be used for reading and study but may also be used for purposes of discussion or

---

*There are many limitations in this building, due in large part to the amount of funding for it. A larger budget would have allowed for more space and more luxuries.

committee meetings; or they could be used for a small seminar. These rooms are equipped with sufficient electrical outlets for various types of microforms and are adaptable for use as listening rooms. One was especially planned for "wet carrel" use.

Photocopy Room

A copying machine is located in a photocopy room at one end of the library. In this, copies can be made quietly and without disturbing persons studying in the library.

Typing Facilities

One small room at one side of the library was planned for the use of persons who wish to use a typewriter and wish to have space for spreading out materials. The typing room will contain the noise and on the main floor, can accommodate one person. A typing room on the third floor can accommodate six to ten people.

Second Floor

In the original plan, administrative offices were placed on the first floor, the theory being that persons coming to the school for the first time would be seeking admission or coming on business or for other information; but, the plan was changed and the library was placed on the first level. This was done for three reasons. First, it gives primary attention to the library, especially noted in this case because the major business of the library school is librarianship. Second, the library is usually open at night and weekends and for longer hours than are the administrative offices; as an economy measure, the other floors of the building (second and third floors) can be closed for use, even when the library is open. This proved to be a useful plan, particularly during the energy crisis in the early months of 1974. And third, the library, on the first floor, is isolated from the noises and activities on the other floors of the building.

Administrative Offices

The dean's office in the school is cheerful, colorful and equipped with a large desk, a credenza, bookshelves, and lounge furniture in one section of the room (for informal committee meetings). Adjacent to the office is a conference room for larger and more formal meetings.

The administrative suite includes a large reception and secretarial office, the dean's office, a coat closet and lavatory, a conference room, and has kitchen accommodations and an administrative assistant's office. Other administrative offices on this floor are the associate and assistant deans' offices, the admissions director's office and the office of the director of research. There are also an interview office and three storage rooms. The three latter rooms are "inside" rooms, as is the large audio-visual classroom with a drop screen and a large storage area. Across the corridor from this room is the *information science classroom*, which has a lecture area with armchairs and a work area with tables and chairs. Adjacent to this room are two office areas, one to house the computer equipment, the other for the faculty member supervising the laboratory work of this specialty.

A small seminar room, which seats twenty people, is at one end of the second floor. Just beyond this, at the corner of the building, are fifty student lockers. A second seminar set-up includes a large area that has a folding partition that allows the room to be used for a group of 75 people or to be divided into two separate seminar rooms, each equipped with tables, chairs, blackboards, and tackboards.

Third Floor

A cataloging and classification classroom-laboratory that seats 55 persons is located on the third floor. This is equipped with tables and chairs and has book shelves on two sides of the room for the practice collection and cataloging tools. It also has a drop screen for audio-visual use and blackboard and tackboard facilities. Immediately adjoining it is a typing room for those who wish to use typewriters. Two seminar rooms, seating twenty to 25 persons each, are on this floor, and a lecture hall-auditorium that seats 155 persons can be used for public lectures, conferences, and for large classes.

Auditorium

The auditorium has a sloping floor and a small stage. The carpeting and seats upholstered in color harmonizing with the carpeting make a pleasing setting for formal lecture programs or for classroom purposes. The seats have adjustable arms for taking lecture notes when the room is used for a classroom. A large drop screen at the front of the room and numerous electrical outlets provide for audio-visual presentations, and the storage closets at the back of the room have space for storing a-v equipment.

Lounge

A lounge with a sofa, armchairs, coffee tables, and smoking stands can be used for informal meetings or for a lounging area.

Faculty Offices

Faculty offices are located on the third floor, away from heavy traffic routes, with a private office for each person, furnished with a desk, armchair, several guest chairs, vertical files and book shelves.

Seminar Rooms

The seminar concept of a small group of students engaged in advanced study and original research under a member of the faculty has affected architecture at USC and has resulted in small rooms being included in university buildings. Several seminar rooms are located in the second and third floors of the library school building. One of these rooms has been designated as the Bertha Mohony Miller Seminar Room, in honor of the founder and first editor of the *Horn Book* magazine in the field of children's literature.

THE APPLICATION OF COMPUTERS TO LIBRARY TASKS

by Hillis L. Griffin

One of the vexing problems faced by library administrators is that of finding ways to maximize the proportion of the budget expended for direct service to users, and to minimize the amount devoted to the supporting services of the library. The supporting services (e.g., circulation, cataloging, catalog maintenance, serials, acquisitions) are labor-guzzlers, and labor (in one form or another) is usually the largest item in the library budget. There are always competing demands for more materials, more space, and for more staff both to provide more and better services for users and to make the collection more usable by the staff. Budget reductions may require that ways be found to reduce operating costs with minimal reductions in user services. More efficient operation could provide additional funds for books, periodicals, and whatever else makes up the stock of the library (including pencils and p-slips), as well as for the staff to provide service. The library administrator must keep everyone happy by allocating the funds to achieve the right objectives.

WHAT ARE THE "RIGHT" OBJECTIVES?

Every library should know what its objectives are and what priority is attached to each of them. This should help the library to relate its resources to its goals, keep it from trying to accomplish the impossible, and identify non-productive areas that require redirection. One way to define objectives is to assess the current program, see what is good about it, and see how it might be improved and extended. Such an analysis takes time, hard work, insight, and creativity. It may reveal certain programs that are superfluous. It should certainly reveal the strengths of the library, but it may reveal how inefficient some present methods really are and how poorly certain parts of the present system are performing. The application of common sense and the most primitive techniques of work simplification may be especially productive. Outdated procedures and work patterns may be discovered and dealt with. Reasons for low productivity need to be questioned and justified in relation to the real objectives of the library, not in relation to irrelevant criteria. Such a course may be entirely successful, and the library may thus find itself able to attain its defined objectives simply by restructuring its present procedures.

Sometimes things are not that simple. We may redefine our objectives or seek other ways to accomplish them. These may include increased budget, more employees, additions to the buildings, or other items—depending upon the problem. People and space are often limiting factors, and there are various ways around these limitations. One solution might be to find an outside vendor to provide services, such as obtaining catalog cards from the book vendor. Another would be to see whether certain processing operations might be shifted out of the library building into other quarters. One might also investigate whether computerized services of one kind or another would free staff and space for more appropriate work. On-line data base searching, for example, has certain costs associated with it; but it also makes staff more productive, searches more relevant, and may reduce the need for hard copy indexes, their massive cumulations, and the space to house them.

LET'S JUST HIRE MORE PEOPLE!

While the computer does very poorly at shelving books in the stacks, it excels at maintaining files of information, manipulating the information in these files, and producing reports based upon this information. Banks, department stores, airlines— all depend upon up-to-date files of information, and all use computers to maintain them. They really have little choice in the matter, for they simply could not function without using the computer for file maintenance and for the production of products (bills, inventory reports, tickets, etc.) based upon the information in the files. These jobs usually can no longer be done (in the above cases, at least) by people, but it is also the kind of work that people will no longer do.

Libraries are in much the same situation. Files of information that support the library are used and maintained by people who must be hired, trained, and supervised. Many libraries have difficulty attracting and retaining good clerical employees who will file catalog cards or type overdue notices day after day. Even an auspicious job title (such as Bibliographic Technology Assistant) cannot hide the fact that most library clerical jobs are tedious, dull, and dead-end—the kind of jobs that people least like to do. Many businesses have difficulty recruiting competent clerical employees, as the number of young people coming into the labor market is decreasing, and they do not have to settle for dull jobs. Older people returning to the labor market often have minimal skills, and want part-time work adapted to THEIR schedule, not to that of the library. The computer provides an alternative to these problems. It is a fast and accurate typist, processes information quickly and always according to directions, works night and day, and never takes a vacation. It is only one of many alternatives that must be considered.

THE COMPUTER SYSTEM

A computer can perform many tasks for the library, and there are many ways to make use of it. Computers are available in sizes large and small; some will do our jobs very well, while others are totally inappropriate. Some have desirable options (such as the capability to print in upper and lower case), and others are very utilitarian. The computer capabilities needed for a given task depend upon the requirements of that job, and libraries always hope to find a flexible, well-equipped, computer facility.

A good way to start is to survey the computers available and record their vital statistics, e.g.:

- memory size (in thousands of characters, NOT "words")

- availability of disc storage; amount available for temporary and permanent files (are setups of private discs allowed?)

- availability of magnetic tape drives; recording density (800, 1600, or 6200 characters/inch, nine-track recording mode)

- what kind of line printer is available? how fast does it print? can it print in upper and lower case? and what is the quality of the printing (get a sample)?

- what programming languages are available, and which is in most common use? is PL-1 available? COBOL?

- is time available on the system or is it saturated? what is the average [turn-around] time for jobs submitted for processing? how many hours/day is the system available? is it available evenings, nights, weekends?

- what is the pricing structure? does it encourage use during nights and weekends by offering reduced rates for jobs run during that period?

- does the management seem friendly and interested, or is it hostile, super-cilious, and too busy to care?

- is the computer room clean and tidy, accessible only to staff and computer operators?

The list could continue for many pages, but these basic questions will provide the answers needed to see whether the computer center can handle the work, or whether it will only provide an exercise in frustration.

OBTAINING THE USE OF A COMPUTER

There are several different sources of computer time. Most libraries use the computer available in their school, municipal, university, or company computer center. Others may rent time on a computer at a nearby commercial computer service bureau or utilize a remote computer time-sharing service. Some might have a small computer in the library for certain tasks and utilize another computer outside the library for other work. It is important to note that most work is done on shared, general-purpose, medium- to large-scale machines; and there are great advantages to letting someone else be its nursemaid.

Most medium- to large-scale computer systems are leased from the computer manufacturer on a month-to-month or annual basis. While this is usually less economical in the long run than purchase, it offers more flexibility to change the system to respond to rapid growth, new equipment developments, or fiscal requirements. Because the cost of the equipment is known (either as a function of the monthly rental cost or as a proportion of the purchase price), it is not difficult to distribute these and related costs among those who use the equipment in proportion to their utilization of it. It is important to realize that 1) every job done in the library has a cost attached to it—nothing is free; and 2) the largest item in the library budget is labor—not books. The computer is a labor-saving device, in spite of the fact that the price schedule for work done at the computer center may make it seem exorbitant. Computers perform work so rapidly that the job is soon completed—this is the way in which they achieve their economies. Although computer time may cost $500 per hour, some of the products cost less than $5 simply because of that electronic speed.

KINDS OF COMPUTERS

Main-frame Computer

If looking for a generalized computer system that would handle a broad range of applications, one would look for a medium- to large-scale system with an IBM System 360, 370, or similar central processing unit (CPU), a punched-card reader for input, a line printer that can print 1,100 lines per minute in an upper case font, and magnetic tape and disc drive devices that, like magnetic audio or video tape, store information in coded magnetic form. IBM line printers usually have the option of an easily interchangeable type unit to enable the line printer to print in upper/lower case at about 700 lines per minute, and some other line printers may offer a similar capability. Two upper/lower case fonts are available for the IBM line printer: 1) the "TN" font has all normal upper and lower case characters and the appearance of pica typewriter type, and 2) the "ALA" font has a distinctive appearance because the type is "squooshed" from top to bottom to allow room for diacriticals to be printed over and under the letters on the print line. The "ALA" font is meant to be used at a printer setting of eight lines per inch, while the "TN" font may be used at either six or eight lines per inch. The "TN" font is frequently used in direct mail advertising to print upper/lower case "personalized" letters or additions to pre-printed letters.

Mini-Computers

Mini-computers come in a great range of speeds, sizes, and prices. The larger mini-computers are extremely sophisticated machines, with sophisticated programs to make them work. Some of these rival the medium-sized main-frame machines in capability, and they are priced remarkably low in relation to those Goliaths. It would seem that there must be a catch; it is simply that it takes much more work to write the programs, keep the equipment in repair, find and correct the problems in programs furnished by the manufacturer, and become skilled in knowing in detail how the entire system works, rather than knowing only the particular part that affects one's product, as in using a main-frame machine.

Although the supporting software furnished by the manufacturers is marvelously sophisticated, they simply do not have the resources to refine, text, document, and support their products in the same manner as the main-frame supplier. In time, these machines will become the link between the library and a network of computers, both large and small. They will perform certain local tasks independently and act as an interface to the network. They handle communications tasks better than the main-frame machines, and they certainly handle them more economically. The lack of suitable programming languages is probably their greatest drawback from the library point of view, since large capacity data storage devices are now becoming available for them at very reasonable cost.

Micro-Computers

A great deal is said these days about micro- and mini-computers. Micro-computers are useful for certain limited applications, such as supporting a simple book ordering system. Their memory capacity is so limited that they can support only very simple programs, and there is insufficient space for required data manipulation. The programming languages presently available to utilize these machines are primitive and difficult to use for library tasks. The devices for magnetic storage of information are slow, of very limited capacity, and incompatible with those found on larger computers. Their printers are slow with poor output quality. In their present state of availability, micro-computers usually offer no facilities to communicate with other systems over communications lines according to normal practice. These conditions will pass, however, and within the next few years, we will see micro-computers playing a very important role in library data processing applications.

Software

In addition to the "hardware" described above, the manufacturer will provide certain "software" with the computer. This consists of programs that make the computer do certain tasks of rather general utility in every computing facility. Such programs copy data from magnetic tape onto a magnetic disc, print the data from a disc on the line printer, or read punched cards through the card reader, and write the information that they contain onto magnetic tape.

Another program will be a generalized sorting (or alphabetizing) program, which will enable users to alphabetize catalog cards or book orders or other items according to rather simple conventions. There are ways to make the computer sort data so that "U.S." sorts as if spelled "United States" and to prevent sorting on initial articles of titles. Still other programs will be the language translator programs, which enable the easy production and testing of programs to do the specific application programs that users of the computer will write to do *their* work. The main program will be the "operating system" program, which manages the flow of jobs through the computer, keeps track of the availability of hardware resources (such as tape drives, disc space, etc.), and allocates them to jobs as required.

METHODS OF DOING THE JOB

Batch Processing

Probably the most efficient method is to process information in batches rather than processing one individual item at a time. Under such a system, the machine-readable data would be prepared for ordering the new books for a given period (e.g., daily, weekly, etc.), and it would be taken to the computer center at the end of each day, week, etc. A book order writing program would be loaded into the computer to process the data and write the orders sometime during the night, and the output would be picked up next morning. Hundreds of batch jobs might run, each occupying the machine for only the amount of time required to process the job. In this way, one pays only for the time actually used to process the job, not for any dead time (i.e., when the machine is not being used for productive work).

On-line Processing

Another alternative would be an "on-line" system in which a typewriter-like terminal would be connected to the computer via a communications or telephone line. The orders could be entered into the system one by one as they were received, the system would save the information and, on command, arrange it and send it back to a typewriter (via communications lines) to print the orders to be sent to the vendor. The "on-line" system provides prompt interaction, but the system resources are also being used all day, rather than for just a few seconds as in the batch system. Because these resources are being used all day, a larger bill may result from using the on-line system than would result from batch processing. The benefit, of course, is the immediate interaction that the "on-line" system provides, and it may be worth the cost if it improves the efficiency of the ordering process.

Dedicated System

Another method would be to have in the library a book ordering system that used a small, self-contained micro- or mini-computer designed and programmed to do this task, supplied complete and ready to go by a commercial supplier of such systems. This might be regarded more as a book ordering machine than as a computer, just as we might view an electric typewriter as a book ordering machine. In this case, the capabilities of the computer would be very limited and inflexible, although it would handle book ordering very well within defined limits.

MAKING THE COMPUTER DO THE JOB

Like any clerk, the computer requires specific, detailed directions in order to do the job correctly. These directions comprise the computer "program" for that task (or sub-task), and some jobs require a series of programs. The program is quite analogous to a recipe; it defines what the ingredients (i.e., circulation records, catalog information, etc.) are to be and how they are to be processed by the computer to obtain the desired results or output.

Programs are designed and written by programmers using a somewhat artificial language. This description of the processing steps to be done by the computer is translated by a language translator program into a syntax utilized by the machine to accomplish the task described. Typical languages used for library programs are PL/1 (Programming Language One), COBOL (COmmon Business Oriented Language), and the more primitive Assembly language. Although programs may be written in FORTRAN (FORmula TRANslator) or BASIC (Beginner's All-purpose Symbolic Instruction Code), these languages are not easily utilized for handling the non-numeric and variable length information that characterizes library data.

CREATING PROGRAMS FOR OUR SYSTEM

Most programmers find it difficult to deal with the variability of library information, since most non-library applications deal with information that occurs regularly in each transaction. Library information features authors with short names and authors with long names, and sometimes no author at all (the title main entry!). Many programmers cannot understand why the library does things in such "strange" ways, is so insistant upon using upper and lower case printing, or has such senseless requirements. Good programmers are generally creative and can be challenged to devise techniques to deal with the needs of the library, much as a good reference librarian perseveres to find an answer while others may throw in the towel rather early in the search because they cannot devise alternative strategies to uncover the answer. Unfortunately, poor programmers often deal with new challenges in only one way—by constraining the problem to fit the same design that they used for their last program.

In developing programs for library tasks, it is important that the library insist that it obtain what it reasonably needs, and that it not compromise to a level of what it "thinks" the computer can do. People usually underestimate the computer; it is a remarkably versatile device in the hands of a skilled and creative programmer. Many people don't realize that the computer CAN print subject headings in red on catalog cards, and that it CAN print on the front and the back of catalog cards as well! It may cost more to do it that way, but it's not impossible.

The systems analyst is another member of the cast who may be involved in the library task analysis. This person must understand the problem, define a solution, and relate it to the capabilities of the computer. Obviously, the best person for this purpose is a logical person who is familiar with libraries and library procedures and who is also familiar with the computer and (one hopes) has had some solid programming experience. A creative programmer-analyst can relate both disciplines to library needs by combining systems analysis and programming skills in the solution to a problem. This person serves as the intermediary between the library and the computer.

Programming assistance may be obtained in various ways. If the library is to undertake some substantial amount of computerization, then it would be quite appropriate to have programmers on the library staff. It is especially advantageous that they work IN the library, and WITH the people who will use the systems that they develop. Assistance in programming might also be obtained from the computer center or under contract with a consultant or a commercial software company. These latter alternatives will place a great responsibility upon the library to thoroughly define its requirements for each task, since the programmer will probably know nothing about libraries or their strange kind of data processing. The library, alas, may not know enough about what it wants to do or how to communicate it to the programmer-analyst.

It is important to look at what others have done before one begins. Programs written by others may be located and, if they fit the individual library's needs and are compatible with its computer, this library can probably adapt them fairly quickly on its computer with some assistance from a programmer. However, beware of transferring the super-program to the computer without considering how it fits the individual library's needs, and whether it does the job which is desired. Every time that program runs, it will cost money; and it might just as well do things right as do them only half-right or worse. The library might be able to use programs written by others for use on its computer, as exemplified by BALLOTS and OCLC. Thus a lot of work might be avoided, and the library can get into production more rapidly than if it developed a whole system as an individual project.

Some programs are available for no charge, or simply for the cost of duplicating the program and related descriptive documentation. A system comprising several programs and reams of documentation, represents a substantial investment on the part of the originating institution. Such systems have a higher price-tag on them; some are

available only on a license or lease basis. Several questions need to be answered in
regard to software products obtained elsewhere:

1.   will only the machine-language version of the program be received, or will
a "source" code be received, which can be read and modified if necessary?
2.   what language is it written in, and does the library have anyone who can
work with that language?
3.   how complete and understandable is the descriptive material (documentation) describing the program and its use?
4.   how efficient is the implementation of that language on the library's
machine, and will its language translator accept the program? There are
many dialects of FORTRAN, for example, and it is quite possible that a
program written in FORTRAN for a Control Data 7600 computer will not
translate properly with the FORTRAN for the Interdata 7/32 computer.
Sometimes, although a particular language translator is available on the
host computer, it may not be available on our machine of the same make.
Languages such as ALGOL, PASCAL, and SNOBOL, for example, are not
common outside the university community.
5.   will this library be allowed to modify the programs under the terms of the
lease or license?
6.   what provision is made for correcting errors in the programs, and for passing such corrections on to users?
7.   how long does it take to correct reported errors—one day or six months?
8.   what would be the effect of loss of program support by the originators
after one had been using the program for some time and had become
dependent on it? One should make thorough inspection of a house before
buying it, and one probably should check around to see whether any auto
wrecking yards were scheduled for construction next door. The same
concerns also apply here so that there will be confidence in the programs
that represent an investment in time AND money.

THE "READY-MADE" SUIT: THE TURN-KEY SYSTEM

Another way to solve a problem is to adopt a total ready-made approach. This
involves leasing (or purchasing) a computer and the related software, all ready-to-go,
from a commercial concern. It might be a circulation system, or a "catalog" system,
or a book-ordering system, or it may incorporate shades of all of these and others
perhaps. The vendor will demonstrate it, show how it fits requirements, and give a
price for the system. After it is delivered, the vendor will help the purchaser learn to
run it, train the staff, and convert the library's data for the new system. There is a
price attached to all of this and one must deal with sales people anxious to sell their
merchandise. Obviously, there will be prices attached to services, equipment, training,
and the like, for the buyer is dealing with a commercial enterprise. While most systems
allow some "tailoring" to special requirements, the library usually finds that it must
sustain the greatest adaptive trauma. Using a simplistic parallel, if a man has all of his
bulges in the right places, both arms the same length, and shoulders with the right
slope, then a suit "off-the-rack" may provide a satisfactory (but not ideal) fit; the
tailor-made one will always be more satisfactory but more expensive. So it is with
turn-key systems; the vendor can really do only a limited amount of personalizing

the system to make it "yours." Many libraries should welcome an opportunity to scrap the old system and start over again under new rules. The library must be careful that the new system that is a time and labor saver isn't so slick and simplistic that it doesn't provide the services that the library needs (or finds highly desirable) in the pattern of service it wishes to provide. Turn-key systems are not inexpensive and may not be the "magic" solution they're cracked up to be, but they have a definite place for those who are willing to adapt to them.

DEVELOPING THE PROCESSING SYSTEM

There are many ways to approach the job of developing a processing system and computer programs that will make it work. Each library is different, and each situation presents different problems and requirements. The ideal solution in one library might be a disaster in another. Stereotyped solutions are dangerous and are acceptable only if they are demonstrated to be entirely responsive to needs.

The classical way to approach the task often tends to emphasize intensive analysis of current operations and their ultimate computerization. While it is a good thing to know what one is presently doing, and to use this as a device to discover the present requirements for this procedure, there is the risk of accomplishing the same old problem at electronic speed if it is simply duplicated on the computer. It is important to realize that the computer-based system can provide a whole new outlook, with products and schedules impossible with manual systems. It can, for example, do away with maintaining the files of 3x5 slips about which every library revolves, but it can also print these slips at 1,100 lines per minute and deliver them to be alphabetized and filed, thus providing the library with more work than it had before! It is important to keep those objectives clearly in mind and not settle for the easy way or for second best.

Analyzing and Defining Requirements

The first step is to analyze the problem, define requirements, and come up with some suggested solutions. While a systems analyst may be involved in the study to contribute insights and a logical approach, it is the task of the library participants to be quite firm about their needs and requirements. Here is a typical meeting between the librarian and the systems analyst. Let's listen:

Librarian: (shows catalog cards to systems analyst) We'd like to make catalog cards on the computer. It surely can't do that, can it?

Systems Analyst: You want to print these funny little cards with the hole in them?

L: Well, they've always been that way, but I suppose we could change if we had to.

SA: I've never seen computer paper like this. Can we print them in big sheets on computer paper and let you cut them out with scissors?

L: Well . . .

SA: If you don't need that funny hole we can get more information on each card.

L: But . . .

SA: Here, see how this grabs you. The name of the person who wrote the book can be up to 40 characters long . . .

L: But what about the American Society for Testing and Materials. Subcommittee E-33 on the Size of Concrete Aggregates in Unrelenting Structures?

SA: Can't you abbreviate that? . . . This thing called the title can be 20 characters long and we'll have lots of room for the abstract.

L: The what?

SA: The abstract—all that stuff in the middle. It'll be all capital letters, of course.

L: But we've seen cards like these printed in upper and lower case that were done on a computer.

SA: Impossible! Can't be done! I've never seen it. Now, when shall we get started?

(Lights dim. Music rises and fades.)

The analysis step is a major undertaking in education and communication. In the example above, it hardly seemed that the librarian had read even an elementary book on computers or data processing, and was barely aware of the state of the art in catalog card preparation for libraries. The analyst, on the other hand, was never able to understand that the library job was not in any way similar to writing accounting reports, but seemed quite willing to try to force the task into that mould rather than do what was required by the ultimate user of the system.

In this step, one should expect to identify what is needed and some ways to provide it. If a good job has been done in defining needs and objectives, it will be easier to relate them to possible solutions.

Many libraries have monumental problems handling circulation control, while others may view catalog production as their local mill-stone. Thus each library will have a different set of problems with which to work, and different solutions will be appropriate. Each prospective solution must be evaluated in relation to the library and its objectives. The adoption of a solution should be based on value received, not upon what other libraries may do or say. After all, the problems of the individual library are (unfortunately) uniquely its own, and those of other libraries (for better or worse) are theirs. It is not difficult, however, to arrive at a demonstrably right solution for a situation if one has done the homework, analyzed the problem, and properly evaluated the available solutions.

If the problem is catalog production, there is a broad range of possible solutions. They may range from obtaining an electric typewriter (*with* the correcting feature), to finding a good photocopy machine, to using a word-processing sytem, to producing cards on a computer, to using BALLOTS or OCLC for card production, to producing a micro-form catalog, to a printed catalog, to an on-line catalog. How to choose? Unfortunately, some libraries just follow the crowd (it is easier and less controversial, you know!) and never know that some other way might have been better. In this case, the librarian needs to know:

1. what is the problem? Is it locating the cataloging, doing the original cataloging, typing the unit card for photocopying, typing the whole set, typing the tracings on the cards, alphabetizing the cards, filing them, expanding the catalogs?

2. is there a manual solution available? Is Cataloging in Publication information being used? Is the cataloger competent in the area of activity? Is the typewriter in poor repair, or the typist incompetent?
3. what is the unit cost of this system, and can it be installed? Sometimes, for reasons known only to those who make the rules, one may find that he cannot buy typewriters but can lease a word processing system. And although it would have been less expensive to do it the typewriter way, the other system has to be used.
4. what are the alternative solutions, the unit cost of each, and can they be installed? One way to compare several systems is to define the requirements which the system must meet, those features that would be desirable, and those attributes that are not desired.

Assign each a value or weight to each and, on a chart, range these values across one axis (across the top, let's say) and the name of each system from top to bottom on the left margin. This will do two things: a) it will force the planner to evaluate and re-evaluate requirements, and b) it will produce a rather unemotional ranked list of possible solutions.

Methods of Input and Output

There are various ways to provide information to the system and receive information from it:

a. dedicated terminal (video display and/or hard copy printer) connected via dedicated communications line.
b. dial-up terminal (video display and/or hard copy printer) connected via dial-up telephone line when required.
c. library key-punch operators prepare input on punched cards or other machine-readable medium (tape cassette or "floppy" disc), which is then:
    1. carried or transported to computer center.
    2. sent via remote job entry station over communication lines.
d. library personnel complete work-sheets, which are sent to computer facility for key-punching or transcription.
e. library personnel prepare work-sheets for Optical Character Recognition (OCR) scanner at computer center by using a special type ball in the typewriter.

Output may be received:

a. displayed on screen of video display terminal connected to computer system via communication line.
b. printed on hard-copy printer connected to computer system via communication. Hard copy printer may have limitations of:
    1. non-impact printer that requires special paper—unable to print catalog cards, labels, and other items.
    2. impact printer that may form characters with dots (matrix printer), and characters may be difficult to read.

3.   character set that may be limited (upper case only, no diacriticals, no overprinting for underscore, etc.).

c.   output that is returned via remote job entry station printer connected to computer via communication line (usually all upper case).

d.   output that is printed at host computer, returned by mail, UPS, courier, or picked up by library staff.

While it may look very complicated, few systems would offer all of the above options. There are only two ways to provide input to OCLC (dedicated or dial-up terminal) and one way to get printed cards back (from the OCLC printer). The system often places limitations upon the use of certain methods. That is why it is so important to know what is wanted from the system before becoming too involved with it.

CONVERSION OF FILES

One should consider the problems of conversion of manual files and methods for doing this. In some cases, there is no retrospective conversion of data files because it is not required. An acquisitions system, for example, could simply begin processing orders on the first day of operation and ultimately, after some time, the only orders remaining in the manual open orders file would be those items that had not been received in a timely manner and required expediting activity. Perhaps the old acquisitions file would never have to be converted. At most, one might convert only that portion of it that represented standing orders. If the objective was a book-form catalog, however, some or all of the catalog data would have to be converted to machine-readable form simply to provide a usable product.

CONVERSION OF PEOPLE

There also has to be "people conversion," with a training and instruction program for those who will have to use the system and for those who will be served by it. Methods of data input will have to be taught, and the keyboard operators will have to learn how to use the appropriate equipment and related programs. Those who prepare the initial order data may have to fill out different forms or provide additional information, so they must be trained. Users must be trained to interpret the new products from the system in order to be able to take advantage of them. Manuals and other written reference materials must be produced, tested, revised, and distributed, together with appropriate introductory work with those who will be expected to use them. Everyone must appreciate the reason for the new system—that it is to help them to do a better job and to provide better service to the library users. People must understand that there will inevitably be problems and that the only way that they can be corrected is for them to be reported in some defined way to some person who can deal with them. Problems often indicate that a user has not learned how to use the product properly (or does not want to learn to use it properly) or they may indicate oversights in the system that need to be reviewed and corrected. The commitment of management to make the system work, and the message conveyed that there will be no return to the old system in any event, often need to be made strongly apparent to discourage foot-draggers and those who were more comfortable with the old system because they could do things the old way almost (?) without thinking.

ESTIMATING COSTS

Even at this early planning stage, costs of alternative solutions should be considered. There are probably as many ways of charging for computer time as there are computer centers, and the rates charged are different in each one. When someone says they can produce catalog cards for their library on the computer for ten cents a set, there is no reason for optimism that this feat can be duplicated. Another library probably has a different computer, a different volume of work, different labor costs, different prices for computer time, and harder books to catalog. It is difficult to equate costs from one system to another, but if the volume of work is known in the one library (the number of lines printed, number of cards used, and other facts), then this can be related to the volume and costs of another situation.

Some installations may simply charge for the use of the system in increments of one minute, or tenths of an hour. Larger installations have pricing systems of remarkable complexity, which sometimes seem to change with the slightest change in the weather. These schemes charge for the actual use of each part of the computer system involved in executing the job at a rate that reflects the cost of each of these resources. In addition, there may also be priority multipliers. In the example shown (Figure 1, page 218), there are four priority levels: Top, High, Normal, and Low. Jobs submitted to be run at Top Priority go immediately to the front of the queue of jobs waiting to be executed: these also cost three times the normal rate. Jobs run at High Priority cost only 1.5 times the normal rate. Jobs run at Low Priority are run when all higher priority jobs have been run, and cost only 80 percent of the normal rate. Depending upon the requirements of the job, a low priority job might be run almost immediately when submitted if it required a minimum amount of computer memory, no changes of disc packs or mounting magnetic tapes, and if most other jobs were waiting for availability of such resources. It would be certain of completion overnight, or over a weekend. If the computer is saturated (i.e., has insufficient capacity to meet the demand), a priority scheme is of little value. Everyone will run their jobs at a higher priority in an attempt to force their work through the system early.

The cost to run any program is obviously a function of the resources that it uses and the amount that must be paid for these resources. If we want to estimate the cost for one run of a projected program, we might best compare it to other programs that we run in terms of print lines, special set-up charges, and actual processing time. The most difficult thing to estimate is processing time, since this can vary greatly for one program from one run to another. This is because of the influence of other programs being run in the machine at the same time, their demands for resource useage, and the interference of these demands with those of our program. Many library programs generate a great deal of printed output with a relatively modest amount of central processor time. Printing the serials list, printing catalog cards, and printing book orders are examples of this type of program. If some estimate of the number of output lines for a typical run can be made, then previous experience with similar programs will provide a starting point for estimating the cost to run the program. The program that has little printed output but that does a great deal of processing presents a different situation. Typical of such a program would be one that generates the sorting records for the production of catalog cards or a file maintenance program. In this case, print lines are not a good measure and are an insignificant part of the cost. The type of processing is important, because if the program is manipulating information character-by-character, this will obviously require more machine cycles than for processing fields of information. Another factor is the efficiency of the program itself, which is often a

Figure 1. Job cost reports.

RESOURCE	QUANTITY	UNITS	CURRENT RATE/UNIT	PRIORITY N MULTIPLIER	APPROX. COST
CPU-TIME	9	SEC	$ 0.0381	1.00	$ 0.34
WAIT-TIME	56	SEC	$ 0.0381	1.00	$ 2.13
CPU*CORE	14	100KBSEC	$ 0.00430	1.00	$ 0.06
WAIT*CORE	84	100KBSEC	$ 0.00430	1.00	$ 0.36
PRINTING	31791	LINES	$ 0.00013	1.00	$ 4.13
PUNCHING	0	CARDS	$ 0.00127	1.00	$ 0.00
LIB. TAPE SETUP	0	TAPES	$ 0.3175	1.00	$ 0.00
USER TAPE SETUP	0	TAPES	$ 0.635	1.00	$ 0.00
DISK SETUP	0	DISKS	$ 1.27	1.00	$ 0.00
SPEC PRINTER SETUP	1	JOB	$ 6.35	1.00	$ 6.35
CARD INPUT	1350	CARDS	$ 0.00127	1.00	$ 1.71
			APPROX. TOTAL COST AT CURRENT RATES:		$ 15.08
			APPROXIMATE RATION USED:		$ 2.89

RESOURCE	QUANTITY	UNITS	CURRENT RATE/UNIT	PRIORITY H MULTIPLIER	APPROX. COST
CPU-TIME	28	SEC	$ 0.0381	1.50	$ 1.60
WAIT-TIME	110	SEC	$ 0.0381	1.50	$ 6.29
CPU*CORE	41	100KBSEC	$ 0.00430	1.50	$ 0.26
WAIT*CORE	165	100KBSEC	$ 0.00430	1.50	$ 1.06
PRINTING	5642	LINES	$ 0.00013	1.50	$ 1.10
PUNCHING	0	CARDS	$ 0.00127	1.50	$ 0.00
LIB. TAPE SETUP	0	TAPES	$ 0.3175	1.00	$ 0.00
USER TAPE SETUP	2	TAPES	$ 0.635	1.00	$ 1.27
DISK SETUP	0	DISKS	$ 1.27	1.00	$ 0.00
SPEC PRINTER SETUP	0	JOB	$ 6.35	1.00	$ 0.00
CARD INPUT	3100	CARDS	$ 0.00127	1.00	$ 3.94
			APPROX. TOTAL COST AT CURRENT RATES:		$ 15.52
			APPROXIMATE RATION USED:		$ 9.21

[The upper report is typical of catalog card production and was run at Normal (N) priority. The other report is typical of a file maintenance job and was run at High (H) priority.]

function of the language in which it is written. Experience with similar applications will furnish a useful basis for estimation—but only that!

It is especially important to be aware that costs differ greatly from one installation to another. They will never be comparable, so each library must use its own costs in its estimates. The costs of program development are a function of the charges for programmer effort and computer time for program development and testing. The costs of conversion are usually one-time costs. It is important to consider equipment, building modifications, communication charges, furniture, training, supervision, and all related costs, just as was done for the production system.

If the task is comparable to some present manual system, the costs of the manual system can be compared to the proposed automated system. When the costs of the manual system are gathered it is important to reflect the REAL costs—labor and fringe (vacation, social security contribution, employee benefits, supervision, training, equipment, and maintenance). If the manual system can be revised to be more efficient or more productive, this should enter into the calculations.

FEASIBILITY ASSESSMENT

Proposed solutions must be evaluated for responsiveness to the problem, cost versus benefit, and the probability that the best (from the standpoint of all these factors) can be successfully implemented by the people available, within the limitations of time, space, people, and equipment. Alternatives may have to be devised and objectives modified if the problem is to be solved.

Questions arise about the systems proposed as solutions to the problem. Will they meet the needs of the library and its users? Are they affordable, and which are most satisfactory and most economical? What about people, equipment, and space to deal with the new procedure? This step requires some hard evaluation of alternatives and of the present operation. The requirements of the proposed solution may be useable on the machine in the local computer center, or elsewhere. If the costs are based on units of work identifiable in the old system (e.g., card sets produced), then the history of the card production activity in the past will provide a basis for estimation. One must not overlook the costs of equipment (purchase or lease), communications costs, space and remodeling, training (on a continuing basis for new employees), supervision, and other costs. If the process is a new one, consisting of printed output, the rate schedule of the computer center will be useful. Many library tasks are heavily dependent on printed output, and the cost of printing the number of lines of output that are anticipated (from knowledge of the probable size of the file and items to be printed) will be the major portion of the cost of processing in many situations of this type.

IMPLEMENTATION

Implementation and detailed system design follow next. Most systems require a series of related programs to accomplish the job. A catalog card production system might include: a data-input program, a proofreading program, a file correction program, a formatting program, a sorting (alphabetizing) program, a card formatting/printing program, and a master-file maintenance program—seven programs in all. Some of these may already be available, especially the sorting program. If the input is structured in a "free-form" format, without rigid positional constraints for the data elements, an existing on-line text editing program could be used for data input and revision. If this course is to be satisfactory, the edit program must be flexible, easy to learn, easy to use, and reliably available on the system when it is needed.

That still leaves four programs, of varying degrees of complexity, to write. The proofreading program will have some elements in common with the formatting program, and some work on these programs may be combined. Many factors will influence the cost of the programs and the speed with which they are implemented. There is an obvious advantage if the programmer-analyst has done other library jobs and is familiar with the programming techniques for this type of application. The use of an appropriate programming language can also speed the task.

If the library chose to modify programs in a catalog card production system obtained elsewhere, time might be saved, but there is no guarantee that this would really happen. The programs might be hard to follow, extensively patched and modified, or poorly documented. Sometimes it is easier to start over rather than do extensive modification, especially if the proposed system is straightforward and uncomplicated.

Program writing is a creative process, just as is writing a book, designing a house, or composing your "Second Symphony." Thus, two programs to do the same task will be quite different, just as two reports of the same event from two eyewitnesses would be different, but accurate. The process involves preliminary planning of the internal inter-relationships of the programs, the structure of the various files of information, and the characteristics of the input. Flow charts may be prepared for the system as a whole and for each program as a tool to assist the programmer in the design of the program, and as a reference document for all involved. Each programmer has a different approach to designing. Some may develop extensive flow charts before they begin writing program statements, while others may begin immediately to write the program, using flow charts only to solve logical problems as they arise.

One of the operations proceeding concurrently with programming may be conversion of the file and preparation of a file of test data to be used in testing the program. As programs are written, they are checked, keyed into machine-readable form, and then translated by the compiler (language translator) program into a form that can be used by the computer to execute the instructions contained in the program to perform the desired task. Testing, correction, recompilation—this cycle will be repeated until the program appears to perform satisfactorily. Finally, when the programs have been tested individually, they will be run and tested in the same sequence as required by the system, using the test data. This will disclose any problems of transition and will also disclose any problems resulting from unanticipated differences in the file or the information resulting from the operation of one of the programs. Too, it tends to assure that subtle changes have not crept in during program development to redefine the file content or change the rules informally.

If the system is poorly designed or poorly conceived, then it is the fault of management and the systems/programmers for ever letting it emerge from the cocoon in that condition. It is also up to them to make it work and work well. Change is difficult, and it often seems to come too rapidly, so administrators need to help employees to deal with it by stressing their enlightened self-interest in the new system. If the system is well conceived and well designed, it should be better than whatever it replaced. It should make people's jobs easier and more interesting and should also provide them with the satisfactions that they need to feel good about what they are doing.

PUTTING IT ALL TOGETHER

When the programs have been written and debugged, when the files of data have been entered into machine readable form and validated, and when the people have been trained to use the new system and whatever phsycial and logistical arrangements have been made for the transition, then the new system is ready to be implemented. Active involvement of the library staff along the way will help to assure that most of the bugs have been worked out. The system should then be installed with confidence in its success, and the former procedures discontinued at that time. Much is made in other applications of running parallel systems for several months until the new system is operating reliably. Such a course in the library would introduce a parallel circulation activity, or acquisition activity; and most libraries have neither the space nor the staff to cope with such a situation. It is, therefore, more necessary that the system be well conceived and well tested so that it will work without major problems.

It is important to have reaction promptly and continuously from those who are using the system, so that problems can be repaired promptly. It is important that the systems people and programmers be visible and a part of the library team, so that they cannot file requests for changes in the wastebasket and go on with whatever is of interest to them now that the library job (in their mind, at least!) is all finished. As changes are made, the documentation and procedure manuals need to be changed, too, and personnel responsible for operating and using the systems need to be kept informed. It is easy to let the computer print new documentation and manuals through the use of text-processing systems. Last of all, it is important to be sure that the objectives have been attained, that the programs are all documented properly, and that all is going well.

Documenting programs is always a difficult task. Most programmers don't like to write, or write poorly at best, and would rather be challenging the computer than invoking the muse. By the time the job is done, they are embarked on a different project and now know any number of different (and better) ways that they should have done the job. These ways will probably be more elegant, but no more effective, so it is important to document the programs, and get this documentation together with the source programs, procedure manuals, and all other information concerning the individual programs and the system of programs that accomplishes the task. Then, when something happens, one will be better able to cope with the problem of finding out what has happened and how it can be fixed. If the programmer departs for brighter opportunities, this collection is the only foundation for extending or repairing the system. Program documentation is expensive in both time and frustration, but the more complex the system, the more important the documentation becomes, primarily as a device to link the parts of the system together in some logical way when someone is trying to determine why a job will not run.

There will be problems—there is no way to dispose of them entirely. Many of them are communication problems, so effective communication is essential in every aspect of the project. There are people who are afraid that the whole system will collapse and crumble if they enter a wrong character or push the wrong key on the terminal. If it does, then it indicates poor design and implementation on the part of the system designer. Some people like to "play" with the system, perhaps to satisfy themselves that it has weak spots. Such actions are a waste of time and have little positive value in relation to the system. Others may be put off by having to use a terminal in the job, since it smacks of clerical work. Some people are never able to visualize what is happening or their part in the program. Others may have some vested interest in the old system (perhaps a security blanket or a featherbed is in jeopardy) and will attempt to sabotage the new system in one way or another. There are inevitably problems associated with change, but they must be anticipated and dealt with. One of the problems that librarians have is that they love rules but they love exceptions more. The system will constrain people to some reasonable rules, and some sacred cows will vanish. If these had been valid, they should have been included in the system design; and if they have no validity, there will not be problems, if the planner has communicated properly and done the design work well.

OBSOLESCENCE

One needs to consider the various guises of obsolescence at some point. People become obsolete when they do not keep up with what is going on in the world—such as MARC, ISBD, AACR2, and all of the other intrusions that conspire to keep people from knowing everything after all. Machines become obsolete (cars, especially).

Procedures become obsolete, especially as they deal with new technology and its effects. Computer equipment will become obsolete, no longer repairable, and will have to be replaced (just like the Woodstock typewriter that was formerly used in the catalog department). The computer programs will probably have to be rewritten for the new computer. All of this will occur within five to ten years because new, faster, less expensive computer hardware continues to be developed and sold. What are the implications for the library?

If the use of a computer is shared with others, one can be sure that the others will face the same problem and that they will give it major attention when they acquire their next machine. If they have any way to do it, they will probably stay with equipment that will require the least possible disruption in their routines. Computer manufacturers realize that such conversion costs can be staggering. However, there is a great deal to be gained by bringing the library programs up to date as the result of operational experience gained with them. It would be a shame if they were static, doing the same things in the same way in which they were done when the programs were first (without benefit of hindsight) devised.

If one owns or leases a computer for the library, the same problems arise, except that he will have to contend with the aspects of computer selection, facilities conversions, and the problems of operator training to operate the new system. If one is upgrading a turn-key system, the vendor must accommodate and accomplish any reformatting of files and retraining that is necessary; and if one is changing turn-key vendors, then they will also be responsible for the conversion. While some kinds of change are enjoyable, changes of computers are among the *least* enjoyable. Even the things that cannot go wrong will not go right and, in spite of the best planning, any change or transition has many of the characteristics of disaster about it. But ultimately, it all gets put back together, things get started again, and the old patterns of reliability return. Because, after all, that is the problem. The old system has become reliable and predictable, and people know how to interact with it to obtain the results they want. When starting all over with a new system, nursing it along through the problems associated with new equipment, one encounters the whole spectrum of implementation problems compressed into the conversion process.

One aspect of concern is the data base. If it is accurate, comprehensive, and up to date, with each data element identified as to its function, then the job of converting that data base from one system to another will be much easier. A data base of abbreviated authors, truncated titles, and no subject headings, without identificational elements, entered in upper case, will always be just that. It can be revised and changed, but such activities are more expensive later than if they are done in the beginning. Programs and machines may change, and they will inevitably offer greater capabilities for less cost. A high quality data base will enable people to exploit the capabilities of a new system to the greatest possible extent, while a data base of low quality will always reflect its antecedents by the limitations it imposes on improved software.

KEEPING UP

The world of computers and data processing moves very rapidly. New hardware, new communications techniques, new network plans, and the opportunity for extensions of systems in the library demand an awareness of what is happening. The news of what is happening in libraries is communicated in various ways but probably travels most rapidly at conferences and conventions of one kind or another. It is important to read the literature—not only library literature but computer literature—to be aware of new equipment, new trends, and how they affect a situation. There are a number of library magazines to read, and they should be quite obvious: *Journal of Library Automation, Special Libraries*, and *Library Journal* are probably the leaders, although almost any library magazine has automation articles or a special issue now and then. The computer newspaper is *Computerworld* (published weekly); a section of *Electronic News* (also a trade weekly) is devoted to computer hardware. *Datamation* is the computer monthly magazine, with topical issues. All of these have advertisements and classified ads—good sources of information on terminals, prices, and services. *Data Communications* is a magazine covering that topic at a fairly technical level. Two excellent and very readable foreign journals are the Australian *LASIE* and the British *Program*.

An excellent source of reference information for computers and related equipment (including terminals and related communications devices) and software is a series of loose-leaf publications from Datapro Research Corporation. The series of volumes provides facts, details, comparisons, evaluations, and listings for main-frame and mini-computers, software for various business applications, and data communications specifications and equipment. These are published as *Datapro-70, Datapro Directory of Software, Datapro Reports on Data Communications*, and *Datapro Reports on Minicomputers*. In addition to individual product reports, numerous survey reports include detailed comparison charts that are extremely useful. A monthly newsletter highlights significant equipment announcements and industry trends.

A similar service is *Auerbach Computer Technology Reports*, a nineteen-volume loose-leaf service (available also as separate subject-oriented volumes) covering the same material in a similar way, and including some other materials as well. These services are both invaluable in equipment selection. Both provide telephone reference service and are extremely helpful in this regard.

Library Technology Reports, published by the American Library Association, reports on library-related computer problems such as catalog conversion, COM (Computer Output Microfiche) catalogs, turn-key circulation systems, and other topics of interest.

A large number of books are concerned with explaining computers to the neophyte. The publications slanted at the business administration or MBA curriculum are generally useful, because they don't assume that the reader is a mathematical wizard or that his/her interest is in mathematical processing. Two books by Gordon B. Davis (*Computer Data Processing* and *Introduction to Computers*) are similar, the first being more comprehensive but somewhat more dated. Junior colleges offer excellent courses in data processing (usually labeled 101) and instruction in programming languages. The course in PL-1 taught with a business (not a scientific) slant would be the best choice for those with access to equipment with a PL-1 compiler. While PL-1 was formerly available only on IBM equipment, compilers are available on several main-frame machines and at least one large mini-computer.

One learns how to write library programs by writing them, beginning with simple ones and proceeding from there. Two very simple books on writing library programs, one featuring PL-1 (*Illustrative Computer Programming for Libraries*, by Charles H. Davis) and the other featuring COBOL (*COBOL Programming: An Introduction for Librarians*, by Peter Brown) are available. Neither is comprehensive, but they serve as an introduction to the application of the language to certain simple library tasks. The author admits to being a PL-1 partisan, as it is an especially good language for library applications. (This tends to be confirmed by the literature.) COBOL is a poor second choice, since it tends to handle variable-length data, translation from one character set to another, and other string processing requirements with great difficulty, if at all. It is a good (but wordy) learning medium, however. FORTRAN is for everyone except text processors, which is what library data processors are.

Ultimately, the choice is made by the individual library or the library system. The easiest way is to follow the status quo and not get involved, or (at best) be second or fifteenth but never first to do something different with the computer in the library. Some people exist from year to year talking a good game and studying the situation "exhaustively" or "thoroughly." Some wait for the "right" system to appear; but it never will. Others dig in, do their homework, evaluate the options, and make progress. They are the ones who help to bring the real benefits of computers and automation to the library, to relieve staff members of the burden of "donkey work," extend their capabilities, and provide better, more responsive service to the users of the library.

SUGGESTED INFORMATION SOURCES

Books:

Brophy, Peter. *COBOL Programming; an Introduction for Librarians*. London, Bingley; Hamden, CT, Linnet, 1976.

Davis, Charles H. *Illustrative Computer Programming for Libraries*. Westport, CT: Greenwood Press, 1974.

Davis, Gordon B. *Computer Data Processing*. 2nd ed. New York: McGraw-Hill, 1973.

Davis, Gordon B. *Introduction to Computers*. 3rd ed. New York: McGraw-Hill, 1977.

Loose-leaf services:

Auerbach Publishers, Inc., 6560 North Park Drive, Pennsauken, NJ 08109. (*Auerbach Computer Technology Reports, DataWorld*).

Datapro Research Corporation, 1805 Underwood Blvd., Delran, NJ 08075. (*Datapro-70, Datapro Directory of Software, Datapro Reports on Data Communications, Datapro Reports on Minicomputers*).

Newspapers:

Computerworld. 797 Washington Street, Newton, MA 02160.

Electronic News. Fairchild Publications, 7 E. 12th Street, New York, NY 10003.

Non-library periodicals:

Data Communications. McGraw-Hill, 1221 Avenue of the Americas, New York, NY 10020.

Datamation. Technical Publishing Co., 1301 S. Grove Street, Barrington, IL 60010.

Library periodicals:

Journal of Library Automation. American Library Association, 50 E. Huron Street, Chicago, IL 60611.

LASIE: Information Bulletin of the Library Automated Systems Information Exchange. P.O. Box 581, Brookvale, N.S.W. 2100, Australia.

Library Journal. R. R. Bowker Co., 1180 Avenue of the Americas, New York, NY 10036.

Library Technology Reports. American Library Association, 50 E. Huron Street, Chicago, IL 60611.

PROGRAM: News of Computers in Libraries. Aslib, 3 Belgrave Square, London SW1X 8PL, England.

Special Libraries. Special Libraries Association, 235 Park Avenue South, New York, NY 10003.

(This list is obviously very brief. It is intended only as a starting point to describe literature about computers and programming that would be useful to a library engaged in developing systems to support its own services.)

EXTRA-INSTITUTIONAL FUNDING:
Management and Strategy for Survival

by Martha Boaz

As society enters a post-industrial age, the most crucial challenge facing libraries, information centers, and universities is that of coping with economic problems and managing change. Business men and economists predict continued inflation and declining revenues in many institutions. Educational institutions and libraries, faced with no growth or decline in enrollment, may be forced to find financial resources above and beyond their "regular" budgets. The problem thus becomes almost a matter of survival, and funding from outside the normal channels is a matter of life or near death—or a great decline in the institution's program. Thirty years ago, only a few institutions had fund-raising or development offices. Today, nearly all institutions of higher education have a person or staff whose major responsibility is fund-raising for academic programs.

Many public as well as college and university libraries have a publicity staff and fund raising committees. Sometimes the "Friends-of-the-Library" group takes on this job on a volunteer basis. In other instances, there is a formal budgeted staff for such work. The availability of skilled, experienced personnel in developing a fund raising campaign is, of course, a crucial factor in the success of intensive fund-raising programs. Because development and public relations departments in educational institutions and libraries are highly competitive with each other in their drives for funding, the leaders of fund-raising campaigns need to use sensitivity and tact in their approach, and they should prepare carefully for their work, regardless of the scope of the campaign.

An institution that has a professional fund-raising development and research staff will know how to identify various kinds of prospects: individual, business, foundation, and government. One of the basic principles in fund raising is that the fund-raising staff must be thoroughly knowledgeable about the institution, its programs, its resources, and its objectives.

Fund-raising may be focused in several directions and toward certain types of prospective donors. These include: 1) foundations, 2) government agencies, and 3) private donors. The number of foundations varies from one year to another, but in an average year, some 25,000 foundations dispense over 400,000 grants that total several billion dollars. Grantmaking has become BIG BUSINESS! The material that follows describes general guidelines for fundraising for educational institutions, libraries, and library education. The first section deals with suggestions about procedures to follow in seeking funding from private foundations and government agencies. The latter section deals more with approaches to the private sector; however, in many instances, areas overlap.

The assumption in fundraising is that ideas and plans need financial resources for their implementation and realization. Frequently, one person is responsible for an original concept that grows into a large program. It is important to remember, however, that other people in an institution will usually be affected by the plan and should be informed about it. Communication is therefore necessary and, when possible, the support of one's colleagues and the assistance of interested individuals, groups, or a staff will add to the strength of a project.

The originator of the plan is obligated to share the idea and request permission to pursue it with the chairperson of the department and/or the dean. This is required of any proposal that might affect staff or facility commitments, departmental adminis-tration, or the duties of the chief investigator. (Funding can chart the course of a department or school. At times, money determines policy, which is why departments carefully review proposals to see if what others want them to be is what *they* want to become.) In a library, the person to be consulted would be the department head and the librarian. (In the material that follows, the titles and designations will be those used in a professional school in a typical university and it is assumed that the reader concerned with a particular library will find parallel titles in that library's personnel staff listing or in consultation with other officials who have authority over the library.) Those officers likely to be involved in academic planning within the university include the vice-president for academic affairs, the grants officer, and the president. The presi-dent, who speaks officially for the institution and bears the final responsibility for its programs, may and often does deputize a vice-president or some other individual to sign a proposal requesting funding. In some institutions, before a proposal is sent out, a proposal coordination form must be processed through the following channels: the principal investigator, department chairman, dean, personnel office, director of facili-ties planning, director of department of contracts and grants, appropriate vice-president (or president).

GUIDELINES FOR GRANTS-SEEKERS

Before deciding on sources and amounts of funding, certain key elements in an effective planning program and in the documents are used. Various agencies issue their own guidelines as well as their own restrictions. Information about preparing proposals is available from individuals, agencies, professional schools, and others who have had experience in seeking financial support for projects and programs. In addition, there is an ever-growing literature of grantsmanship.

Plans for a project usually begin with an outline, followed by a plan of attack, later by a rough draft of the plan, and finally, by a sound, well-developed proposal. Preparation of a formal statement is an important process regardless of where the pro-posal is to be submitted—whether to an outside funding agency, a government depart-ment, or to a private business or individual. This document helps to clarify ideas, disclose strengths and weaknesses, and convey information to colleagues. The project should be consistent with departmental and institutional goals and objectives, not solely in compliance with the restrictions of the funding agency. After the proposal has been prepared, the next step is to find a funding source that has an interest in the type of program described in the proposal. After an appropriate agency has been iden-tified, the proposal may need to be re-drafted to fit into this agency's guidelines.

Letter of Interest or Informal Contact

Preliminary to a formal proposal, in some instances, a letter of intent (brief, usually not more than two pages) will be helpful. This letter, outlining the proposal project, permits the investigator to approach several foundations at the same time to determine their interest in receiving an expanded proposal. This letter is very important. It outlines the scope and nature of the work to be done. The letter should be concise, to the point, and should highlight the significance of the project, the need for it, its timeliness, objectives, the methodology, and the benefits that will result. It should clearly indicate the connection between the planned work and the stated purpose of the particular foundation. An over-all cost estimate should be included in the letter. Only essentials should be included, however; if all goes well, there will be time and space later to present a full proposal.

A letter of intent allows the agency to eliminate proposals that do not conform to its stated objectives, thus saving its time and that of the inquiring institution. If the funding agency is interested, it may provide oral or written guidance that will be of great assistance to the proposal writer. Information about foundations and their areas of interest may be obtained from composite foundation directories, from annual reports of foundations, and from personal contacts.

Government Agencies

In dealing with government agencies, it is especially important that one obtain copies of their guidelines and follow all directions pertaining to content and format. Different government programs have different specialized interests, responsibilities, and proposal formats. Thus, the National Science Foundation may sponsor a proposal sharply different from one sponsored by the U.S. Office of Education. Each government agency is limited and controlled by its own legal restrictions, financial capabilities, and board of governing officials.

In approaching a government agency, one usually follows the guidelines, directives, and forms issued by the particular agency. Or, one may seek advice and help from a congressman or government official. The latter technique should be used with caution, however, if at all, for such an attempt might antagonize the governmental agency.

Different Categories of Proposals

Proposals fall into different categories, depending on the type of research or project envisioned. These include survey studies, experimental studies, historical studies, pilot studies, methodological studies, predictive studies, longitudinal studies, and others.

The most funded fields, according to a recent issue of *Foundation Grants Index*, are education, health and science, and technology. Others receiving money in lesser amounts are welfare, international activities, humanities, and religion.

STEPS FOLLOWED BY GRANTS-SEEKERS

The steps generally followed by grants-seekers include:[1] 1) define the goal(s); 2) assess your chances; 3) organize your resources; 4) identify your prospects; 5) research your prospects in depth; 6) make your initial contact; 7) meet with the foundation; 8) write your formal proposal; 9) submit your formal proposal; and, 10) have a follow-up.

A goals statement should be clearly defined, then pretested on other persons in the department to see whether or not it is well defined. Clarity and specificity are vital in this step. In the matter of assessing chances for success, the applicant's objectivity combined with an awareness of the foundation's guidelines, regulations, and grant-making policies are crucial factors. The grant-seeking chairman should organize staff members, proceed with the proposal, and make contacts or ask an influential person to gain an entree to a trustee or influential board member of the foundation.

After making a list of promising prospects, the next step is to make a careful study of the foundation most likely to fund the proposed project. This involves checking the agency's grant patterns, including its purpose, size, annual grants, grant policies and patterns. Another factor is its location; the distance may be a deterrent if travel is required and if substantial travel expenses are involved. Still another factor is the matter of contacts; for example, does one of the officials of the requesting institution know a trustee of the funding agency?

Equipped with background knowledge of the prospective donor, the chief investigator of the proposal contacts the foundation and tries to arrange an exploratory meeting between appropriate representatives of the institution and the foundation. A person-to-person contact is highly desirable. If an exploratory meeting is arranged, the person who attends it should be well prepared to present the plan of action with confidence and enthusiasm while remaining professional in attitude. He or she should have well in mind the significant facts and details of the plan and be ready to answer probing questions. If it is not possible to arrange a meeting, a telephone call or a preliminary letter of inquiry may elicit information and pave the way for the presentation of a formal proposal.

The formal proposal is a very important document. Most foundations do not have a required format for proposals. Government agencies vary somewhat from one department to another, but their forms are more standardized than are those of the foundations. For example, there is rather general consistency, from year to year, in the U.S. Office of Education in those forms used for research-project support or for fellowships for students. The guidelines and format furnished by the government agency are clear and explicit in their instructions.

After the proposal has been completed, the applicant institution prepares the required number of copies, checks the deadline for submitting the proposal, and either delivers it personally to the foundation executive or sends it by way of registered or certified mail, with a return receipt requested. The U.S. Post Office now guarantees one-day delivery from any place in the United States to Washington, DC. Specific and more detailed suggestions for preparing proposals are given below.

Components of a Formal Proposal

The contents of a proposal generally are presented in the format below.

Title Page

Table of Contents

Abstract

Problem Statement (including the needs statement, questions to be addressed, and significance of the project)

Goals and Objectives

Methods and Procedures (method of approach, activities and operating plan)

Evaluation

Organization's Qualifications and Resources:
personnel (capabilities and special competencies of key staff)
facilities (space and equipment)

Dissemination

Budget

The Program's Future

Appendices

All of the above topics may not be included in every proposal. Each proposal should be "geared toward" any special circumstances that may exist. Also, other material will accompany the actual proposal. The following explication of the various parts of a proposal will include these items as well.

Proposal Style and Language

It is important to write clearly, precisely and to the specific audience being addressed. Avoid jargon, grandiose ideas, esoteric terms, unnecessary technical language, and flowery writing. Use the active voice in presenting the plan. Use simple words. Be specific, be objective, and come to the point. Be enthusiastic yet realistic. Explain why the project is important and what effect it will have.

The Title Page

The title should be a clear, comprehensive one-sentence (or phrase) description of the proposed work, preferably containing words likely to be selected by a computer preparing bibliographies. Other items on the title page will be the name and address of the principal investigator, the organization submitting the proposal, and the date of submission.

Table of Contents

This should include all section headings and subheadings, with the page on which each begins.

The Abstract

Although the abstract usually appears first in a proposal, it should be written last, only after the proposal has been completely developed. It should be concise (no more than two pages) and should contain a summary of the project, the need for and timeliness of it, its relation to the funding agency's grant policies, how the work will be done, how it will be evaluated, who will benefit from it, and its cost. The quality of the abstract may determine whether or not the reader looks at the rest of the proposal.

The Problem Statement

The beginning sentence(s) should state the problem clearly and simply. Begin by explaining the need for the project and whom it will benefit. Undertake only a manageable problem and describe it in realistic terms; undertake only what the institution can solve with available resources. A realistic agenda and time table should be presented. Tell what is original or unique about the topic. Explain what additional long-range goals have been achieved. Link the proposal to the foundation's area of interest and indicate that this is an opportunity for the foundation to achieve some of its stated goals.

Goals and Objectives

List specific, concrete objectives that seem to be achievable. In planning a formal project, one generally lists certain goals and objectives. In distinguishing between goals and objectives, a "goal" is usually more general, more qualitative, and more inclusive, while an "objective" is more specific, quantitative, and measurable. (For example, *goal*: "to improve the competency of doctoral candidates in writing proposals for dissertation studies"; *objective*: "to enroll 12 doctoral candidates in a class and teach them how to design a research proposal, the specific components to include, and how to evaluate the final product; this objective to be accomplished in a three-weeks portion of a semester's course in research methods."). Each goal and objective should be attainable and stated in clear, concise language.

The relation of this section to the problem statement should be made clear, for the remainder of the proposal may be judged in relation to this section. A general guideline to remember is that hypotheses should be related to a theoretical base and that hypotheses and objectives should be testable.

Methods and Procedures

Special attention should be given to procedures. This section is the heart of the proposal, because it explains how the researcher plans to meet the stated objectives and serves as the main basis for judging the proposal. Here the actual operational procedures are described, and the foundation executive can readily detect whether or not the researcher knows how to go about achieving the objectives.

This section may begin with a short (one-paragraph) summary of the overall design, followed by specific procedures that will be used. Describing the procedural steps in detail, with a time-table schedule for accomplishing each phase of the work, will help the foundation understand the priorities and the planned chronological developments. After the schedule of activities has been set up, each activity should be described in detail with appropriate charts or tables. Where appropriate, provide specific information on: 1) the research design, 2) population and sample, 3) data and instrumentation, 4) analysis, 5) end product, and 6) schedule.

Evaluation

An essential part of the proposal is a plan for objective (versus subjective) evaluation, which should include: 1) a monitoring of the project as it progresses (with possible changes, if advisable); 2) methods and procedures, described in detail—for example, how the researcher plans to meet the objectives and measure the results of the study. This will include specifying the evaluation techniques to be used, who will be involved in the process, the qualifications of the evaluators, how the results will be disseminated, and the cost of the project.

Organization's Qualifications and Resources

This section informs the reader about the requesting organization's qualifications for undertaking the project. It also gives supporting evidence about resources, such as available personnel and facilities.

Personnel. This section is usually given in two parts: 1) an explanation of the proposed personnel arrangements; 2) the *curriculum vitae* of each person involved in the project, especially those with key roles. These biographical data sheets should be in common format. The first part deals with the number and catetories of staff and the criteria for their selection. The aim is to establish the competence of personnel involved in the project. Such a list would include the project director or the principal investigator and other persons who will be on the staff. If a certain required specialization or competency is not available on the institution's staff, it will be necessary to plan for additional staff to be brought in, and this will be reflected in the budget request. Usually, the biographical data sheets follow the introductory statement about "personnel," but if the staff is large, the data sheets may be placed in an appendix.

Facilities. This section is not necessary in all proposals, but it is very important in others and should include information about the availability of needed facilities. It is important to analyze and anticipate needs; if special technical equipment and audio-visual facilities are necessary, provision should be made for these in the "facilities" section and also in the budget section.

Dissemination

Funding agencies are concerned about results and benefits of projects that they have funded; for this reason, it is important to specify in a proposal how the results will be disseminated to potential recipients or users. Frequently, a proposal will state that the study will be beneficial to other institutions. Dissemination can be done through a publication, through reports, through newspaper and periodical articles, through films and workshops, and through many other channels.

Budget

Usually the budget is divided into different categories such as: personnel, communications, equipment, materials and supplies, travel, and indirect cost. Each cost should be listed and adjusted to projected inflation trends. Often, initiating agencies are asked to share part of the cost of the project; for this reason, the amount to be supplied by the institution and the amount from the funding agency must be clearly delineated. Cost sharing can be shown in separate columns (for example, one column might carry the heading "University Portion" and the other, "Sponsor Portion"). Budget lines should give clear explanations about how each total has been reached. For example, a salary item might record: principal investigator (½ time for 3 months on a $24,000–9-month appointment basis) $4,000.

Indirect costs are shown in a separate budget category. Indirect costs, in federal agencies, are figured as a fixed percentage of the total of salaries and wages. These costs are subject to negotiation between the institution and the sponsoring agency.

The business officer or director of the research office in the initiating institution should be consulted if help is needed in compiling the budget figures. This person can also check to see that costs in all categories have been realistically estimated and that all items have been included, such as Social Security, withholdings figures, and others that are not familiar to many proposal writers. The authorized business officer in any organization will have to approve the budget and sign financial reports.

Program's Future

This section is needed only if the requestor is seeking funding beyond the initial grant period. If future funding will be needed, or if the institution must ensure the continuance of the program on normal funds after the "soft" money is exhausted, this should be indicated, and plans for obtaining the money should be outlined. Otherwise, the funding agency may not wish to support a partially completed program. Various methods for future financial support might include: 1) a request to the funding agency to renew the grant, 2) a plan for local support—public and/or private, 3) a request for funds from other funding agencies, 4) a plan to sell services or products that have developed from the initial project.

Appendices

The appendices should contain relevant documentary materials that may be informative, but perhaps are too long or not particularly appropriate to the continuity of the general body of the proposal. Appendices may be used for biographical data sheets; or for letters of endorsement from cooperating agencies, authorities, or community leaders; or for supplementary information about the proposal. Other documents might include the names of board members or officials, newspaper clippings or publicity about the requesting organization, a list of previous projects and funding sources, and other related items.

Evaluation of the Proposal

Individuals or a group of persons representing different disciplines or points of view may be asked to review and to criticize a proposal before it is sent to the prospective donor or funding agency. Elicit direct, honest, constructive criticism. If the criteria or standards of the government or the particular agency are available, these may be used by the internal review group in judging the proposal. It is likely that flaws and weaknesses will be found and can be corrected before the final document is prepared. This internal review process is valuable and worth the time spent in improving the proposal.

Final Steps in Processing the Proposal

It is assumed that the director of the project consulted with the institution's grants officer about the plan prior to developing a fully fleshed-out proposal. Clearance from the grants officer or another authorized official is important; this is especially necessary in a large institution in which more than one individual or department may be approaching the same funding agency. An independent approach might prevent either individual or department from obtaining funding and would place the institution in a dubious light. Coordination and information are needed in these operations.

The originator of the proposal and the grants officer working together can identify potential sources of funds and a list of prospects. The grants officer's experience and his knowledge as to prospective sources of funds and the current interests of the funding agents will guide the director of the project to those sources that seem most compatible with the project and whose history of giving may be a guide to the director of the proposal.

An experienced grants officer often knows how to approach private agencies and government departments. Various techniques may be used in approaching a private source. One may go directly to the source or one may seek help through a member of the institution's board of trustees or some other influential person. This may be done by a personal telephone call, through an appointment, or by a letter, but it is recommended that the requesting agency make a preliminary telephone call or send a letter of inquiry before submitting a formal proposal. In this way, one can get guidance and clarification about procedures and perhaps save much time and energy in the long run.

In addition to the contents of the proposal that have been described earlier, each proposal should also have a *cover letter*, a *cover sheet*, and a *letter of endorsement*.

The *cover letter* should be short, no more than one page in length. It should be on the letterhead stationery of the organization or institution and should include: the statement of request, the relationship of the proposal to the field of interest of the foundation, the director of the project and this person's qualifications for carrying out the work, and the keen interest and enthusiasm of the director or the institution for the proposed project. A concluding statement should offer to provide any additional information that the funding agency may request. Sometimes this letter is signed by the president or chief executive officer of the institution.

The *cover sheet* usually contains the following items: 1) the title of the project; 2) the name and address of the institution; 3) the project director's name, address, and telephone; 4) the amount of funding requested; 5) dates covered for carrying out the project, 6) date when proposal is submitted, 7) the chief fiscal officer's name, title, address, and telephone number; and, 8) the signature of the official authorized to speak for the institution, usually the president.

The *letter of endorsement* may or may not be required, but it is a desirable document to include, as it indicates the institution's approval of and commitment to the project.

Practical Final Check Points

After all materials have been prepared, check the following points for accuracy and for completion: 1) required assurances: Civil Rights Act, treatment of human and animal subjects; 2) Internal Revenue item on tax-exempt status; 3) budget review (be sure that everything is clearly itemized and accountable—check with the business office on this); 4) prepare proposal in attractive professional form, but avoid fancy, expensive covers; 5) correct number of copies; 6) required signatures of officials of the institution; 7) and dates for mailing and receipt of the proposal (send by registered mail to have evidence of date of mailing). It is suggested that the proposal be sent several weeks before the required deadline, if to a government agency, and at least a month before the board convenes, if to a foundation or private agency. A more effective method than the postal service, if it is possible, is personal delivery of the proposal directly to an official at the agency's headquarters. Ask the grants office if your institution has a Washington-based lobbyist who can hand-deliver your proposal.

The format of the proposal will depend on the requirements of the agency being solicited. Most federal agencies have very specific guidelines for proposals, whereas foundations seldom have a format for requests; but in each case, both need specific information, which usually includes the following points: title, table of contents, abstract, a statement of the problem, the objectives, procedures that will be followed, evaluation, dissemination, facilities, personnel, and budget. If agencies want additional information, they will request it.

Grant Administration and Follow-up

After word has been received from the outside agency, if it has been favorable, the recipient writes a "thank you" letter to the grantor and he/she, if the information has not already been received, requests instructions about accounting and reporting procedures. The grantee provides reports in the number and the form specified. If none is required, it is suggested that both periodic progress and final reports be forwarded anyway. If an agency has been generous in funding a project, the least that the recipient can do is to report on its progress. It is also courteous to invite foundation officials for an on-site visit to see the work in progress. Involving the sponsoring institution may lead to further grants in the future.

If the answer to the proposal is negative, it is still important to write a letter to the foundation. In this case, there would be an expression of disappointment but at the same time, a hope that the contact with the donor could be maintained for a possible future project. Experience shows that many organizations are successful in their efforts after a long "courting" period.

Still another follow-up step is that of an "in-house" evaluation of the proposal. If it was funded, why was this so? What were its strong points? If it failed, why did this happen? Sometimes it is helpful to write directly to the foundation asking what criteria were used and why a proposal was rejected. Ask for reviewer's comments and ask the agency about possible resubmission of a revised proposal, or rewrite it and send to other funding sources. Some foundations and government agencies respond to such inquiries and provide information that is helpful in the preparation of future proposals.

Check-list for Handling Administrative Details

After the award has been acknowledged, the project director meets with the appropriate fiscal officer about the accounting procedures to be followed. An institution with a large government grants staff is usually well-informed about all legal requirements and is organized to handle fiscal details smoothly and efficiently. The project director: 1) discusses the work and budget with the staff persons who will be working in the project; 2) tells the staff to review any expenditures and to secure his approval for all expected costs before spending money; 3) signs all approved expenditures and forwards them to the fiscal officer for payment; 4) keeps file copies of all vouchers requesting payment; 5) requires receipts for hotel bills, air tickets, and other reimbursement items (as required by the institution's policies); 6) prepares reports for the funding agency with copies for the institution's files.

Publicity about Grants

Remember that the proposal specified that information about the grant would be disseminated. Copies of all news releases and other materials should be kept. These can be used in later grant applications to demonstrate already achieved objectives of the institution.

FUND-RAISING IN THE PRIVATE SECTOR

A trend in fund-raising in the private area is toward long-range planning. This is necessary in order to assure the prospects that the current objectives take into account the institution's future needs. The plan will also indicate priorities and immediate objectives.

There are many causes that may serve as launching pads for fund raising campaigns. In a university and in a library school (or in any other professional school), fund-raising programs are designed to further the over-all objectives of the university, and/or the school. Often a university works toward large increments to its endowment and uses interest from the endowment for improving the program and the image of the university. Important items include the creation of innovative new programs of research and teaching that are of national and international importance, the encouragement of excellence in both these fields through endowed chairs and professorships, the establishment of multidisciplinary centers, and the continuous search for responsible leadership in all fields.

Frank Robeson[2] lists key elements that should be in an effective fund-raising statement: 1) a worthy cause; 2) a genuine need; 3) a proven record of capability; 4) a practical solution for meeting the need; and 5) a plan for participation that can be offered to the prospects. The logical approach begins with an effort to motivate the prospective donor and goes next to a description of the achievements and progress of the institution. An explanation is then given as to the immediate need, the proposed solution, and the ways in which the prospective donor(s) can help. The written document should be straightforward, brief, and presented in a dignified manner.

To ensure good business practices and legal protection in its fund raising, the development staff of the institution will include persons qualified in business, in publicity and public relations, and in the practice of law. One university has established a donor financial planning committee composed of certified public accountants, certified life underwriters, attorneys, and other professional planners. These professional people assist donors in planning the ways and means most convenient for each donor (according to personal preference) for distributing gifts through wills, life insurance, trusts, and other methods.

Trustee Involvement

Trustee involvement in development is very important in an institution that has such a group. The president or chief development officer should be the leader in assembling a good board of trustees. The trustee involvement begins with the invitation to this person to serve on the board; this is followed by orientation and information sessions and a little later with the trustee's participation in the fund-raising program. The wealthiest and most important members of the board should be asked to serve on the fund-raising and development committee, as this increases the importance and the visibility of the development functions to the other trustees and officers of the institution, to alumni, to friends, and to volunteers.

The development staff of the institution prepares materials and compiles lists of individuals, corporations, and foundations to be approached. Trustees are asked to contact directors whom they know in the funding agencies, and either a trustee or the president of the institution calls on large donor prospects.

Trustees usually help with a development program by 1) giving themselves to the cause, according to their ability to give, 2) making contacts with other possible donors, and 3) calling on a few selected potential donors.

Identification of Donors

One of the early steps in a funding campaign in the private sector is the identification of special individuals or audiences as prospective donors. What appeals to one person may have no appeal to another. There are those who are wealthy and those who are in average income brackets. With the right motivation, both may give. Alumni groups, support groups, professional associations, and other civic or social organizations may be invited to participate. Different presentations may be used to appeal to local groups, corporations, and foundations.

In identifying prospects, certain information is definitely necessary and other information is helpful. The information should include: 1) name, address, and telephone number (both business and home); 2) business or profession; 3) source of wealth; 4) connections with the "applicant" institution; 5) membership in social and/or professional organizations; 6) other business, social, and family connections; 7) principal interests or hobbies; 8) possible gift range: $1,000,000 or more; $500,000 to $1,000,000; $200,000 to $500,000, etc; 9) other pertinent information. The person who provides this information should give his/her name and place of contact, also.

Volunteer Leadership

Volunteer leadership is available through community leaders under groupings such as advisory councils, annual giving programs, and alumni funds. Local, state, and national chairmen and co-chairmen may include well-known persons who hold high offices in corporations or business or who are recognized leaders whose names lend importance to whatever they do.

TYPES OF GIFTS

With the increasing income tax burden, people are looking for tax relief through charitable deductions. Federal income tax laws allow a charitable deduction of up to 50 percent of a donor's adjusted gross income for any gift made from income or principal. Cash, securities, personal property, and real estate all qualify as eligible deductions. In a given year, if more than the legally deductible amount is given to a university, the charitable deduction not used that year may be carried forward for as many as five years. Capital gains taxes are not usually incurred in gifts to a university, and outright gifts to an institution do not incur gift taxes. (Because tax laws are subject to change, it is wise for a donor and an institution to check periodically to be sure that their actions are in conformity with current laws.)

Several plans for giving that are beneficial to the donor as well as to the recipient institution follow:

Life Income Trusts

These may consist of money, securities, or other property and may be set up by the donor during his/her lifetime or by will. These are done under trust agreements that allow the university (or other institution) to manage the investment of the assets of these funds. Income is paid to the donor or to someone of the donor's choice for his or her lifetime, and in some cases, this extends to a surviving beneficiary. The tax advantage from such a gift may result in the donor's spendable income being increased rather than decreased. After the lifetime income provisions have ended, the trust principal goes to the university. This may be used as the donor has specified, in the donor's name, for a named professorship, for research, scholarships, unrestricted endowments, or other purposes. Generally speaking, the unrestricted gift is the most useful to a university.

Several basic life income plans qualify for charitable deductions. The *annuity trust*, the *unitrust*, and the *pooled income fund* are programs that provide donors with flexibility in giving. These are described briefly below.

The *annuity trust* allows a fixed dollar return to the donor; this amount must be at least 5 percent of the initial fair market value of the property, which has been transferred to the trust. The stated dollar amount is paid each year, regardless of the income earned by the trust and may continue for the lifetime of one or more beneficiaries who are living when the trust is established.

A *unitrust* is an arrangement whereby the donor, in return for an irrevocable gift, is guaranteed a life income. The amount of the payment is based upon a fixed percentage of the value of the trust assets, as valued annually, but no less than 5 percent. An advantage of the unitrust is that the trustee can invest against inflation, and the payment to the beneficiaries may increase over the years, as this is not fixed to any specific dollar amount.

In both the unitrust and the annuity trust, the recipient institution is listed as trustee of part of the donor's assets. These trust funds cannot be added to other institutional funds but must be invested and re-invested, each as a separate fund with the income paid to the donor and spouse or some other designated beneficiary.

A *pooled life income fund* is a trust established at an institution by a donor who transfers cash, securities or other property to the institution but keeps an income interest for himself/herself and spouse and/or other beneficiary. In this case, the assets are put into a common pool along with those of other donors. Then, the donor, according to his proportionate share of the income earned by the total investment fund, is paid a variable amount.

Gifts by Will

Gifts by will to an institution are exempt from federal estate taxes and from inheritance taxes in a number of states. These gifts may be in the form of cash, securities, or real or personal property. They also may be either "unrestricted" or designated for a particular purpose or for a particular school or department.

Gifts of Life Insurance

Some donors use a life insurance bequest to make a large contribution to an institution at a comparatively small annual cost. The annual premium is not large and these may have beneficial tax advantages. When the institution is listed as the owner and beneficiary of the policy, the premium cost is allowed as a yearly income tax deduction.

Gifts by Short-Term Charitable Trust

Through the short-term charitable trust, a donor may transfer assets to an institution on a temporary basis. While the institution may receive the income from these assets, the donor does not report the earnings as taxable income. By this method, a donor can decrease his annual taxable income, but still bequeath the entire assets to his or her heirs.

The plan which is most practical for a donor can be determined by the donor in consultation with professional business advice and an attorney's guidance.

Foundations As Affiliates of Non-Profit Institutions

Because of the change in tax laws and the restrictions placed on private foundations, non-profit institutions might try to persuade "likely" foundations to become affiliates of an institution such as a university. Benefits for the private foundation would be that they would avoid current expensive legal restrictions, they could pass on many of the detailed administrative duties to the affiliate organization and, at the same time, they could support worthwhile, beneficial programs.

FUNDS FOR CAPITAL IMPROVEMENTS

Because few foundations or funding agencies will furnish money for buildings and other capital improvements, institutions often have to resort to intensive local and personal drives to achieve goals in this area. A university, or professional school, or a library may seek help from business, from the professions, and from individual citizens. In the case of a professional school such as a library school, the major ultimate goal is, of course, to provide an educational program of excellence. In order to carry out this purpose, physical facilities, equipment, staff, and other requisites must be provided wherein the promise of faculty, students, and programs can be fulfilled.

In order to stimulate interest, the person who is spearheading the drive has to prepare a plan showing how the facility will be used, outlining specific space areas that will be included. Cost estimates are also prepared and a set of materials developed to present to prospective donors. These materials may be leaflets, booklets, articles—anything that is direct, demonstrates the need, and is well presented will be useful. The prospective donors will first have to be convinced of the need and then that the planners and developers of the project know what they are doing. An ill-conceived, scatter-brained plan will not do. Good will is important and to be cultivated, but more than this is needed in an effective fund drive.

SPECIFIC GIFT OPPORTUNITIES IN A BUILDING

The brochure or booklet that describes the building can outline specific gift opportunities. The building itself can be named for a major donor, as can the library in a building. Halls and wings, laboratories, lounges, auditoriums, classrooms, offices, seminar rooms, and carrels may bear the names of donors. The prices for the memorial names may vary greatly. A donor might give several million dollars to have a building named for himself or for someone whom he wishes to honor. A library in a building might carry a price tag of $500,000, a research laboratory might be $150,000, an office $10,000, and a carrel as little as $2,000. Thus the range is extensive enough to match almost any donor's capacity for giving. A paragraph inserted in the booklet can carry a message, such as:

> Your assistance in this project is earnestly solicited. Why not honor your family name or pay tribute to someone you love by having a room in the building named for a person or persons of your choice? By so doing, you not only perpetuate the name of the individual(s) or the name of a firm but you will also help develop and strengthen or contribute to a great educational enterprise. Hundreds of students, faculty, and visitors, through the years, will see the name which is being honored and hundreds of students will be provided the educational opportunity which they might otherwise miss.

Thus the prospective donor sees that appropriate recognition will be made to any donor who will help support the drive. An attractive booklet can present the entire plan in a few pages.

THE CAMPAIGN

A chairman of the project, preferably drawn from outside the institution, should assist the institutional representative(s). It is also wise to invite a well-known and highly respected community leader, such as a member of the institution's board of trustees or a wealthy/influential person who has contacts with many other people of wealth and/or influence. These contacts are very important to the success of the campaign. The person who will work directly with the project and who is fully informed about it should present the content of the proposal to the funding agency.

The institutional representative(s) working with the fundraising chairman should develop a time schedule and plan certain activities and functions to reach specific audiences. Part of this is a matter of making contacts and getting acquainted with prospective donors. This procedure will vary in accordance with the nature of the prospect. One prospect may like attending luncheons, dinners, football games, lectures, or other events—public or private—while others may not be interested in such affairs and will say so. One may work with groups such as alumni associations or civic and social clubs. Often there may be little monetary return from such groups, especially if the persons involved are not in high income brackets. One should remember that a gift of a hundred dollars from one person may mean as much to that person, in proportion, as a million dollars to someone else. But, again the interest and support are valuable, and sometimes other "contact opportunities" come about through a small donor.

After enough money has been collected and blueprints for the building are in process, plans can proceed for a site dedication. News of this event may "trigger" more donations, and such an event brings interested people together and spreads enthusiasm for the project. When the building has finally been completed, dedication ceremonies are in order. These can be elaborate and impressive and can provide an occasion for the usual formal dedicatory speeches as well as a chance to have an internationally known speaker or public figure. The exercises may be an hour in length or be spread over several days. Interested people and supporters assemble and feel a participatory pride in the building, which stands as solid evidence of what has been done.

After the building is occupied, there may still be opportunities to get funding; if rooms or other spaces have not been named, prospective donors may be invited to see the building and invited to memorialize their own or someone else's name. Combining a visit with a program, luncheon, or dinner attracts some people. Others may become interested in funding certain projects that could be carried out in the building; a research center is one that should be of interest, and such a center could carry the name of a donor. Many other opportunities may be available and should be pursued.

ENDOWED CHAIRS AND PROFESSORSHIPS

In the academic world, an endowed chair is regarded as one of the most honored positions in a university. The first endowed chair in America was established at Harvard University in the eighteenth century. Harvard now has more than 200 professorships supported by separate endowments. Other universities and professional schools have followed Harvard's example and established endowed chairs and professorships. They offer many advantages: they provide good salaries and research funds for their distinguished holders; they enable a university to attract and retain scholars of international reputation; they add incentive and stimulus to teaching and research and, in general, exert great influence on the quality of higher education.

Incentives for a Donor

An endowed chair or professorship reflects most favorably on the donor in the following ways: 1) important achievements by the professor in the chair reflect on the name of the donor who has funded the chair; 2) this type of contribution named for the donor is connected with the strength of the university; 3) the chair named for the donor contributes to the intellectual and social development of the community; 4) a professorship supported by a donor is one of the most prestigious forms of philanthropy and has far-reaching effects on higher education.

The major strength of an endowed chair or professorship is that only the interest from the endowment can be used, thus preserving the principal of the fund.

Ways of Establishing an Endowed Chair or Professorship

There are several ways of establishing an endowed chair or professorship. The difference between a chair and a professorship is usually indicated by the level of funding. Approximately a million dollars is required for a chair, while a professorship may range from a smaller amount up to a million. If the endowment is small and will not bring in enough interest for an annual salary, a "visiting distinguished professorship" can be set up and can be used to bring in a visiting person for part of a year or of a semester.

An endowment can be set up as an outright gift of cash or other assets in the total amount of the endowment, or the donor may prefer to give a certain amount at the beginning and pledge a certain amount each year thereafter over a period of from two to ten years. If the latter method is chosen, part of the annual payment is used each year, and part is put into the permanent endowment.

A chair or professorship may be funded through life insurance, through trusts, through bequests, and through other methods. These gifts are usually exempt from both federal and state estate taxes.

In the matter of endowed chairs and professorships, as with other donations, a university official or legal advisor is available to work with the donor and his/her financial advisors on each individual case.

Preparation of a Proposal for a Chair or Professorship

In preparing a proposal to present to a donor or to a foundation, the author of the proposal outlines these parts of the presentation: 1) the statement of request, which specifies whether it is a chair or a professorship and the amount of money being requested; 2) the need for the position; 3) the responsibilities of the chair or professorship; 4) the qualifications required of the holder of the position; 5) the effect on the current faculty pattern; and 6) a brief statement about the school/university and its reputation.

Non-Academic Funding Requests

A school or a library or any other non-profit institution or organization may be interested in different versions and variations of themes, similar to but different from the above. For example, a library might wish to have a funded lecture series or some educational or service programs. Some of the same techniques described in the preceding plans might well be successfully applied to other projects.

Other Requests for Funding

Numerous projects are interesting and valuable and hold potential possibilities for funding. In library work and in educational institutions, these include research centers, conference centers, laboratories, special studies, and experimental projects, to name a few. These hold possibilities for donor identification or for foundation or government funding. The opportunities are practically unlimited and very rewarding when successfully pursued.

BASIC INFORMATION SOURCES

Persons seeking funding need information and acquaintance with basic information sources. These include: 1) basic library or reference sources; 2) publications from agencies and foundations; 3) publications from private and professional sources; and 4) information sources that provide basic information packets, along with possible periodic update services. A staff that plans to do its own research work has access to many grant-seeking research tools. There are also professional agencies which will do this research for an institution. In either case, many publications are available and give information about foundations and other funding sources. Information about these sources is vital to any sophisticated level of fundraising. For a person who is inexperienced in the field, a useful guide is Virginia White's *Grants, How to Find Out about Them and What to Do Next* (Plenum Press, 1975).

One of the most important tools of the trade is *The Foundation Directory*. This much-used directory gives vital information about several thousand of the largest foundations in this country. It gives state-by-state information about these foundations. The information about each foundation usually includes the following facts: 1) the name and address of the foundation; 2) type of foundation; 3) year and state of incorporation; 4) donor(s); 5) financial data, including: fiscal year of record, total assets, total gifts received, total expenditures, total dollar amounts, and number of grants awarded; 6) personnel, including: officers, trustees, directors, managers, distribution committee, trustee bank(s), and names of person(s) to whom a letter of inquiry should be sent.

A selected list of research tools are listed in the bibliography that follows. There are many other sources, but only a few are included here. (The availability and prices of these publications are subject to change, hence prices and dates are not listed.)

NOTES

[1] Howard Hillman and Karin Abarbanel, *The Art of Winning Foundation Grants* (New York: The Vanguard Press, c1975), p. 16.

[2] Frank H. Robeson, "Writing to Motivate the Heart and the Head," *Case Currents* III (June 1977), pp. 8-10.

SELECTED BASIC INFORMATION SOURCES

ALA Washington Newsletter
American Library Association
110 Maryland Avenue, N.E.
Washington, DC 20002

Annual Register of Grant Support
Marquis Academic Media
Marquis Who's Who Inc.
200 East Ohio Street
Chicago, IL 60611

Catalog of Federal Domestic Assistance
Superintendent of Documents
U.S. Government Printing Office
Washington, DC 20402

Catalog of Federal Education Assistance Programs
Superintendent of Documents
U.S. Government Printing Office
Washington, DC 20402

The CFAE Casebook
Council for Financial Aid to Education
650 Fifth Avenue
New York, NY 10019

Directory of Research Grants
The Oryx Press
7632 East Edgemont Avenue
Scottsdale, AZ 85257

*Directory of the Education Division of the United States
 Department of Health Education and Welfare*
Capitol Publications, Inc.
Suite G-12
2430 Pennsylvania Avenue, N.W.
Washington, DC 20037

Federal Register
Superintendent of Documents
U.S. Government Printing Office
Washington, DC 20402

The Foundation Center
88 Seventh Avenue
New York, NY 10019
(Free upon request: "What Makes a Good Proposal?" "How to Find Information on the Foundations")

Foundation Center Source Book
Columbia University Press
136 South Broadway
Irvington, NY 10533

Foundation Directory
Columbia University Press
136 South Broadway
Irvington, NY 10533

The Foundation Grants Index
Columbia University Press
136 South Broadway
Irvington-on-Hudson, NY 10533

Grant Administration Manual
National Science Foundation Publications
1800 G Street, N.W.
Washington, DC 10550

Grant Information System
The Oryx Press
7632 East Edgemont Avenue
Scottsdale, AZ 85257

Humanities
National Endowment for the Humanities
Public Information Office
806 15th Street, N.W.
Washington, DC 10506

NIH Guide—Grants and Contracts
National Institute of Health
Division of Research Grants
Room 2A - 14
Westwood Building
Bethesda, MD 20014

NSF Bulletin
National Science Foundation
Publications Resource Office
Washington, DC 20550

Taft Information System: Foundation Reporter
Taft Products, Inc.
1000 Vernon Avenue, N.W.
Washington, DC 20005

APPENDIX I:

The Need for Research in a Young Profession

by Martha Boaz

INTRODUCTION

Research is vital and essential both in the growth and development and in the recognition and status of a profession. It is difficult for a young profession to produce extensive research in the early years of its history, but the importance of research activity in the growth and potential recognition of a profession cannot be over-emphasized. The term "research" as used in the paper is defined as careful, systematic study and investigation in some field of knowledge, undertaken to establish facts or principles. This usually involves critical and exhaustive investigation or experimentation, having as its aim the revision of accepted conclusions in the light of newly discovered facts.

Some Historical Highlights on Research

In checking the history of research, it is evident that much of the research activity and graduate school education in the United States had its basis in German models. The research institutes that were started in German universities in the 1880s have been described as "scientifically the most exciting places at the university, but organizationally they never became a part of it. The university was a teaching institution. Professors were appointed on the basis of their attainments in research, were supposed to continue with their research after their appointment, and to publish and lecture about the results of their research."[1] In spite of these expectations, the university did not assume responsibility for research and institutionally, research was not considered to be a career. It was assumed that honors or a named chair would be awarded for unusual research accomplishments. In the United States, on the other hand, at a later date, research was regarded as a career, and a professional researcher was educated in sophisticated research methods and techniques. One of the functions of the American graduate school is to train professional researchers.

The *raison d'etre* or the major objective of a research degree as noted by W. L. Saunders, Director of the University of Sheffield Postgraduate School of Librarianship, Sheffield, England, is "to provide research training and to develop *critical* and *analytical* thinking; it is the business of a university to satisfy itself that the holder of such a degree has acquired and demonstrated research competence at the appropriate level."[2]

Before the nineteenth century, a major reason for research was its effect on teaching. In earlier educational developments, concern for education was predominant; professors were intellectuals and tutors of the "social elite." Today, especially in the large universities, says Alain Touraine, "the links with the elite are established and preserved through research rather than through teaching."[3] This bears out the concept held by many academic people that the "publish or perish" theory prevails and that a professor's career depends more on research than on the quality of teaching. Touraine declares that "the research orientation is predominant in the best universities and especially in the most scientific fields, and professors would like it to be developed still further. When asked about their conception of the doctoral program, professors in all disciplines acknowledged that it is oriented mainly toward research."[4]

Theory in a profession and in the education for a profession is generally considered as groundwork for practice, and theory (other than mere opinion) is based on scientific systematic research. "To generate valid theory that will provide a solid base for professional techniques requires the application of the scientific method to the service-related problems of the profession," says Ernest Greenwood. He comments on developing professions: "In the evolution of every profession there emerges the researcher-theoretician whose role is that of scientific investigation and theoretical systematization. In technological professions a division of labor thereby evolves, that between the theory-oriented and the practice-oriented person."[5]

The Status and Prestige of Research

Everett C. Hughes expresses somewhat the same philosophy in an article on "The Social Significance of Professionalization." He says, "Not the least important of the symbolic steps in raising an occupation to more fully professional standing is to go in for research. The object of research may be the occupation itself, or it may be study of the phenomena with which the occupation is concerned. . . ."[6]

Expanding on this theory, Martin Trow and Oliver Fulton develop an academic essay concerned with the research activities of men and women. The authors begin with the premise that research is one of the core functions of American higher education and that "its influence is felt in every academic institution, both through its effects on the growth of knowledge (and thus on the content of higher education everywhere) and through its role in providing the basis of institutional prestige."[7] Trow and Fulton also comment on the widespread belief that research is done at the expense of teaching and that this is a fallacious theory. They base their statement on a questionnaire survey of 23 institutions of higher learning in the United States, conducted by the staff of the Carnegie Commission Survey in the fall of 1969. The authors point out that four-year colleges may have a primary commitment to teaching, but that the really high quality colleges have approximately as many research persons on their faculties as do the weaker universities. Further, "the high quality universities contain about twice as many men and women devoted to research (that is, whose interests lie 'very heavily' in research) as does the system as a whole."[8]

"It is research that confers elite status on an institution and a discipline; and the fields where research is done dominate the universities . . . intellectually and politically (though not always numerically)."[9]

The recognition and respect accorded research is expressed widely, but some disciplines and subject areas have achieved much more in research results than others have. From a general observation as well as from surveys such as the one edited by Martin Trow and the one sponsored by the Carnegie Commission, it is evident that academics in the biological, physical, and social sciences publish a great deal more than those in the humanities. And, "the professional schools of law, medicine, and engineering, show rates of publication that are always higher than the mean for their quality stratum."[10]

It appears that in the schools of the new semiprofessional fields, a sizable proportion of the teaching faculty are also practitioners, and research either is not of prime importance or there does not seem to be as much emphasis on it as in the older, more established professions.

RESEARCH IN LIBRARY AND INFORMATION SCIENCE

As compared with most well-established disciplines, the library profession has done little actual research. One of the reasons is that it is still a very young profession, and the establishment of research as an important part of a library school curriculum has also been slow in developing. Library school faculties are usually small, and their teaching loads are often heavy. Even the few schools that have research institutes usually begin with the time of only one faculty member being given wholly to the institute. This situation seems to be improving and it is likely to become more favorable with the interdisciplinary trends that bring together faculty members from various fields. As noted, the history and patterns of library schools do not indicate much progress in research to date, but if librarianship is to attain noteworthy recognition and status as a profession, it will have to rectify the above conditions and engage in research which will be of value to society.

Criticism has been directed at that library research which has been done. Jesse Shera says, "Because of the empirical character of library research and its excessive dependence upon local observations and limited data, more frequently than not it is provincial and parochial rather than general in its applicability. Such investigations tend to be 'service studies' rather than true research."[11] Paul Janaske agrees with this statement when he says, "Librarianship as a service-centered discipline tends to produce studies and investigations rather than highly structured research projects."[12]

Although research activity in the field of librarianship has been minimal, forces are bringing about change. Speaking of these forces, W. L. Saunders says that "technological and social changes are presenting librarians and information workers both challenges and opportunities which not only justify but demand the investment of resources in research and development. We are seeing the emergence in our profession of research attitudes; we are beginning to realize the importance of research skills."[13]

That research is becoming increasingly important in the field of librarianship and information science is evidenced by the fact that 22 library schools now have doctoral programs and research methods courses are listed in the curricula of many of these schools. A stimulus for the increase of research has been the fact that foundation grants have supported several major studies and funding is available for these studies. Saunders, discussing the need for interaction of research and teaching in a library school, stresses the importance of research when he says, "It is involvement in research which above all sets a university apart from other institutions of higher education, and a department which is not involved in research activity might just as well—possibly better—be attached to a different sort of institution."[14] He gives reasons for the library school to be engaged in research, saying, "If a school of librarianship is to be on the same footing and enjoy the same respect as any other department in a university, it must be known to be and be seen to be active in research—real research."[15]

The Research Institute—Setting for Research Activities

The research institute in a university setting seems to be taken for granted as the natural environment for research work. There are several reasons for this. One is that of the interdisciplinary opportunities open through cooperation with other university departments; thus, there is the advantage of the proximity and of the expertise of the various faculties and experts. Another advantage, in the opinion of Saunders, is that raising research money is a less difficult operation in a university than it would be elsewhere, because, "funds, foundations, government departments, are used to dealing with universities, understand and respect their standards, and have learned that well-conceived university research projects can be supported with confidence. This is as true of librarianship as any other subject. . . ."[16] Saunders notes the prime advantage of a library school being in a university setting as being "the opportunity it presents for associating with, contributing to, and drawing on a whole range of scholarly disciplines."[17]

Some of the same principles that apply to the management of industrial laboratories could be applied, with good results, in research institutes in library schools. Thomas S. McLeod notes wide differences in the organization and management of industrial laboratories: "Many of these are due to the fact that, unlike the majority of human activities in which it is desirable that the participants should concentrate on their work without excessive discussion, it is crucial to a research and development program that there should be continual discussion and mutual criticism among the participants."[18] McLeod says that the appropriate people should be kept in close contact, by the organization, but he adds: "At the same time, the chain of command must be such that decisions are made promptly and implemented without confusion or misunderstanding."[19]

Developing Appropriate Attitudes for Research

Abraham Bookstein points out that education in the use of quantitative methods may very likely receive increasing attention as part of a librarian's education. Bookstein is more concerned with developing appropriate attitudes as an intellectual framework than as a kit of techniques. He says:

> If the library school is responsible for introducing its students to the techniques of O.R. (Operations Research), it has the more subtle but equally important task of developing their powers of judgment and critical thinking. A student must be able to . . . make judgments of validity. Though much of this maturity will develop only after he gains experience in the field, the process should begin at school, which is, in a sense, an institution for providing guided and accelerated experience. This experience could prove crucial in determining his ultimate success.[20]

The Need for More Research in Library and Information Science

A number of people have expressed the need for more research in librarianship and information science. Haynes McMullen says in discussing the place of research in library schools, "As the art or science of librarianship becomes more complex in the future, it will become increasingly clear that society's needs for faster and more complete information services can be met only through research. This method of solving our problems will be expensive, but less expensive than the waste and inefficiency which will result if research is not employed."[21] McMullen comments further on the "increasing recognition of the need for research about libraries," saying that this will "cause a sharp increase in the number of advanced students engaging in research in order to prepare themselves for the larger number of positions which will be open to well-trained investigators."[22]

In an analysis of the subjects covered in 224 dissertations relating to librarianship, written at 33 American universities, McMullen[23] noted that 42 percent of the studies were historical in nature or about "background" materials. The question arises as to what can be done to stimulate interest in the investigation of current problems. How can persons with technical backgrounds and research abilities be intellectually attracted to what has been traditionally regarded as a humanistic discipline? Certainly there are challenges connected with large libraries, with information transfer, and with the influence of information in the decision-making process.

In relation to research methods and basic statistical techniques, Abraham Bookstein speaks of the amount of mathematics required and says that "algebra and elementary statistics will be important, with the emphasis being put on math as a form of communication, supplementing speech in much the same way as diagrams do."[24] He asks the question, "Will the introduction of quantitative methods increase the time required for a library education? On this little can be said at this stage. We merely note that the time required for obtaining a degree in sister disciplines, such as business administration, has had a tendency to increase as these fields become more quantitative."[25]

It seems both likely and desirable that library research will be concerned not only with traditional and specific library science and mechanistic problems, but with research in related fields. This may be more appropriate in this profession than in most, because librarianship extends into all areas of knowledge. McMullen expands on this when he says, "It is quite possible that advances in the ability to understand the human mind and spirit will enable librarians to become far more successful at matching library materials to the needs of users. If so, proponents of a new 'science,' perhaps to be called psycho-bibliomics will be worried about the amount of time being wasted on what they see as unduly mechanistic and rather simplistic study of information science. The automation people will defend, with vigor, their old fashioned approach to library problems, and will see little good in the expensive and unproven methods of the new field; they will not welcome psychiatrists to the library school faculties."[26]

Funding for Research

A lack of financial support is one of the problems associated with a paucity of research production. Paul C. Janaske (Program Manager, Library Research and Demonstration Program, U.S. Office of Education) points out that "many sources of funding within the federal government—the National Science Foundation, the Department of Defense, the Department of Health, Education, and Welfare (National Library of Medicine, Office of Education, and National Institute of Education), etc., are available to support research for library-related activities."[27] Janaske notes that several research and development activities have been funded with federal monies. These include the MARC project (machine readable cataloging), the MEDLARS project (medical literature analysis and retrieval service), the TISA project (technical information support activities), and others. According to Janaske, "government sponsorship of research is generally mission oriented."[28] In addition to federal agencies, other possible sources of funds, outside of the university, are state and local government agencies, private foundations, and private industry.

National Assistance for Research

National impetus was added to library and information science research when a national plan for library and information services was authorized by Congress in Public Law 91-345. This law established the National Commission on Libraries and Information Science. As part of its directive, the law "authorized the National Commission to 'promote research and development activities which will extend and improve the nation's library and information-handling capability as essential links in the national communication networks.' "[29] In supporting research and development, the Commission proposes a stronger federal program, through contracts and grants, with the idea of providing "an overall framework within which common investigations can be carried out. By concentrating specialized skills on crucial common problems, the Federal Government helps reduce duplicate and costly piecemeal research that would otherwise be performed by the states, provides for research and demonstration across jurisdictional boundaries and, at the same time, greatly accelerates the rate at which new methods and equipment can be transformed into operating systems."[30] The National Commission expressed the opinion that a vigorous federal research and development effort is essential and would foster state, regional and national networks.

Some research projects that could be shared responsibilities include studies and experiments with technological developments and communication systems that would promote greater interlibrary communication services. The National Commission thinks that new developments in relevant computer software, prepared at government expense, should be shared.

An operative plan for one country, Australia, is described by Doris B. Marshall:

> In Australia the largest government body conducting scientific research is served by a network of sixty-five libraries, widely spaced geographically, and holding unique collections, but linked through a central library. The central library performs many translation, "house-keeping," and information retrieval functions for the cluster. The research body itself publishes extensively in fields related to agriculture and associated research, while the central library publishes extensively with respect to indexing, abstracting and documentation of research.[31]

Marshall says that studies and evaluations are being made of government research services in relation to the information needs of the whole country.

A Listing of Research in Progress

One of the problems relating to research in the library field has been the lack of information about what research has been done and what is in progress. One of the first efforts to compile a list of what had been done in the library field in the United

States was made in 1959 by the Research Committee of the Association of American Library Schools, under the chairmanship of Martha Boaz (then Dean of the Library School, University of Southern California). A bibliography of dissertations completed at the University of Chicago was assembled. (Chicago, for many years, had been the only school offering a doctoral program.) In addition, a group of abstracts of dissertations was collected from all library schools accredited by the American Library Association. These abstracts covered the years 1951-1959. This list was used as the basis of the bulletin, *Library Science Dissertations, 1925-60*, published by the Office of Education, U.S. Department of Health, Education and Welfare.[32]

An important reporting medium was established in 1959 by the Library Service Branch of the Office of Education, under the title *Library Research in Progress*; it listed current studies, including theses and dissertations, but this publication "folded" in 1965. Although several other agencies collect information about research, there is not now a comprehensive, authoritative, or complete list describing research in progress. Such a list would be an important source of information. It would also perhaps serve as a coordination record, it might prevent duplication of effort, and it might identify topics that need research attention.

An example of an attempt to identify research topics was made in a study relating to what research is needed to improve library education, done by Harold Borko, a professor in the Graduate School of Library and Information Science, University of California at Los Angeles. Using the Delphi method to determine the priority needs for research in library science education, Borko established five statistically determined priority groupings of topics (selected from 36 items). These are the following:

Priority Group I—Projects of very great importance:
Improving and updating the skills of professional librarians.

Priority Group II—Projects of great importance:
Library school educational planning and relevance.

Priority Group III—Projects of moderate importance:
Administration of the library school and library with regard to specific courses, skills, and programs.

Priority Group IV—Projects of lesser importance:
Forms of instruction and supportive facilities for maintaining instruction.

Priority Group V—Projects of least importance:
The role of professional associations and communication among librarians.[33]

The Future of Research in Library and Information Science

In spite of librarians' seeming lack of interest and lack of involvement (participation) in research, the future may hold promise for more research activity and production. One favorable condition is the interest on the part of some of the people who are discussing this matter for more cooperation among scholars and researchers in attacking problems. Along with individual studies, team studies and interdisciplinary projects may become more important. Interdisciplinary research is especially appropriate in the field of library and information science, because this field is involved in all disciplines and in the whole circle of knowledge.

It is difficult to predict what may happen to research in library schools, but the indications are, if current trends continue, that more schools will have courses in research methods and statistics, and there will be more research centers or research institutes officially connected or integrally involved in the schools.

As faculty members become better informed and more sophisticated in research, without doubt they will transfer some of this knowledge to their students and will require more research papers in their classes. If practitioners have any effect on the curricula of the schools, they will insist on research that is more useful to the needs of libraries and perhaps fewer historical studies.

It stands to reason, with more library schools offering doctoral programs and with the increasing number of doctoral graduates, that more people will become involved and interested in being actively engaged in research.

Summary

Discussing research and the need for it, identifying topics and projects needing research attention, and making plans are all important, but without implementation, action, and active research production, the prior activities are a waste of time and exercises in futility. The library and information science profession has an obligation and a responsibility for research in both pure and practical areas, with almost unlimited subjects requiring research attention and action.

The ultimate goal of the library and information science profession should be the pursuit of knowledge, which has been traditionally the theme of a university community of scholars. This involves study, investigation, teaching, learning, and research.

NOTES

[1] Joseph Ben-David, *American Higher Education—Directions Old and New; Essays Sponsored by the Carnegie Commission on Higher Education* (New York: McGraw-Hill, 1972), p. 89.

[2] W. L. Saunders, "Identifying Viable Research Topics," in Patricia Layzell Ward, ed., *Introductory Guide to Research in Library and Information Studies* (London: The Library Association, 1975), p. 9.

[3] Alain Touraine, "The Academic System in American Society," *A Report for the Carnegie Commission on Higher Education* (New York: McGraw-Hill, 1974), p. 160.

[4] Ibid., p. 159

[5] Ernest Greenwood, "The Elements of Professionalization," in Howard M. Vollmer and Donald L. Mills, eds., *Professionalization* (Englewood Cliffs, New Jersey: Prentice-Hall, c1966), p. 12.

[6] Everett C. Hughes, "The Social Significance of Professionalization," in Howard M. Vollmer and Donald L. Mills, eds., *Professionalization* (Englewood Cliffs, New Jersey: Prentice-Hall, c1966), p. 67

[7] Martin Trow and Oliver Fulton, "Research Activity in American Higher Education," in Martin Trow, ed., *Teachers and Students* (Berkeley: McGraw-Hill, 1975), p. 40.

[8] Ibid., pp. 42-43.

[9] Ibid., p. 57.

[10] Ibid., p. 56.

[11] Jesse Shera, *Foundations of Education for Librarianship* (New York: Becker and Hayes, c1972), p. 418.

[12] Paul C. Janaske, "Federally Funded Research in Librarianship," *Library Trends*, XXIV (July 1975), p. 102.

[13] W. L. Saunders, "Identifying Viable Research Topics," in Larry Earl Bone, ed., *Library Education: An International Survey* (Champaign, Illinois: University of Illinois, c1968), p. 7.

[14] W. L. Saunders, "The Library School in the University Setting," in Larry Earl Bone, ed., *Library Education: An International Survey* (Champaign, Illinois: University of Illinois, c1968), p. 97.

[15] Ibid.

[16] Ibid.

[17] Ibid., p. 99.

[18] Thomas S. McLeod, "Research and Development, Industrial," *The New Encyclopaedia Britannica, Macropaedia*, Vol. 15 (Chicago: Encyclopaedia Britannica, Inc., 1974), p. 742.

[19] Ibid.

[20] Abraham Bookstein, "Implications for Library Education," *The Library Quarterly* XL (January 1972), p. 145.

[21] Haynes McMullen, "The Place of Research in Library Schools," in Larry Earl Bone, ed., *Library Education: An International Survey* (Champaign, Illinois: University of Illinois, c1968), p. 368.

[22] Ibid., pp. 368-69.

[23] Ibid., p. 353.

[24] Bookstein, p. 150.

[25] Ibid.

[26] McMullen, p. 369.

[27] Janaske, p. 101.

[28] Ibid.

[29] The National Commission on Libraries and Information Science, *Towards a National Program for Library and Information Services: Goals for Action* (Washington, D.C.: Govt. Printing Office, 1975), p. 1.

[30] Ibid., p. 58.

[31] Doris B. Marshall, "The Commonwealth Scientific and Industrial Research Organization in Australia," *Special Libraries* LXVI (April 1975), p. 223.

[32] Cohen, Nathan M., et al., *Library Science Dissertations: 1925-60; an Annotated Bibliography of Doctoral Studies* (Washington, D.C.: U.S. Govt. Printing Office, 1963).

[33] Harold Borko, "Predicting Research Needs in Library Science Education," in Harold Borko, ed., *Targets for Research in Library Education* (Chicago: American Library Association, c1973), pp. 216-220.

BIBLIOGRAPHY

Ben-David, Joseph. *American Higher Education—Directions Old and New; Essays Sponsored by the Carnegie Commission on Higher Education*, 1972.

The Carnegie Commission on Higher Education. *Report*. New York: McGraw-Hill, 1973.

Newman, Frank. "The Professionalization of Learning" in *Report on Higher Education*, prepared for the U.S. Department of Health, Education and Welfare, March 1971.

Saunders, W. L. "Identifying Viable Research Topics" in *Introductory Guide to Research in Library and Information Studies*, ed. by Patricia L. Ward. London: The Library Association, 1975.

Touraine, Alain. "The Academic System in Higher Education," in *A Report for the Carnegie Commission on Higher Education*. New York: McGraw-Hill, 1974.

Trow, Martin. *Teachers and Students*. Berkeley: McGraw-Hill, 1975.

Vollmer, Howard M., and Donald L. Mills, eds. *Professionalization*. Englewood Cliffs, NJ: Prentice Hall, c1966.

APPENDIX II:

Research as a Basis for the Recognition of Librarianship as a Profession

by Martha Boaz

This paper attempts to ascertain the attitudes, opinions, and beliefs of several hundred university faculty members about the status of research in selected professional fields. Professors were asked to respond to several questions related to the status of research, the value of research institutes, and the rather general "state of the art" of research. Faculty members were asked to tell about the amount of time they spent on research, on teaching, how many publications they had produced, and their opinion about other relevant or related topics.

Research on this topic began as a result of an invitation to the author to serve as a panelist on the Research Interest Group program at the meeting of the Association of American Library Schools in Chicago, in January 1976. The author prepared a questionnaire that was sent to faculty members of the 22 accredited library schools offering doctoral programs, and to faculty members in a selected group of professional schools at the University of Southern California (USC). The latter group included the schools of architecture, education, law, public administration, and social work. A total of 264 questionnaires were sent to library school faculty members and 142 persons answered; 106 questionnaires were sent to the other selected professional schools at USC, and 61 persons answered, with the respective percentages of response being 53.7 percent for the library schools and 57.9 percent for the other professional schools at the University of Southern California.

IS RESEARCH A PRIMARY BASIS FOR THE RECOGNITION OF A PROFESSION?

The first question asked was "Do you agree that research is a primary basis for the recognition of your field as a profession?" The answers from the library schools and from the other professional schools were almost equal in the number of those who "*heartily* agreed" with this statement. Some 35 percent of the library schools and 36 percent of the other schools checked this answer, while 37 percent of both groups answered in the next question that they "agreed," thus making a total of 72 percent who either "agreed" or "heartily agreed." Some 21 percent "disagreed," and 4 percent "disagreed strongly." The few remaining persons either had no opinion or did not answer the question.

One library school faculty member agreed with the premise, but explained that it was so "because societies value research orientation not because the research necessarily benefits the profession."

One library school respondent pointed out that research has much greater importance in library education than in the practicing section of the profession.

One professor in the USC School of Education "agreed that research is a "primary basis for recognition," but said it is not *the* primary base. Another education professor thinks this "varies somewhat in specific areas of the profession." Still another education representative said, "Research is one of many primary bases." A professor in architecture said, "Research and practice are totally inter-dependent."

DOES RESEARCH CONFER ELITE STATUS
ON A SCHOOL OR DEPARTMENT?

In response to the question, "Do you agree that research confers elite status on a school or department?" 35 percent of the library educators responded by "heartily agreeing," and 54 percent "agreed"; from the other professional schools, the response was 43 percent on each of the two lines, with a combined total percentage for these two groups of respondents being 85 percent in either agreement or strong agreement. Some 10 percent disagreed, and the remaining 5 percent had no opinion or no answer.

One library school faculty member disagreed with the "elite status" designation saying, "It may cause envy or objection but usually the result is apathy on the part of the professional. '

One School of Education instructor agreed with the "elite" characterization of research but said that "this should apply only to published research." Another professor said, "The research must be good." A professor in the School of Public Administration said that he "agreed heartily" with elite status conferred by research and commented, "Top universities are judged by their research contributions, not teaching quality or public service or sports ability.

DO THOSE FIELDS IN WHICH RESEARCH IS DONE DOMINATE
A SCHOOL INTELLECTUALLY AND POLITICALLY?

The next two questions asked whether or not the persons answering agreed or disagreed with the sometimes stated opinions that those fields in which research is done dominate the school or university intellectually and politically. Of the Library School people, 30 percent "heartily agreed" and 45 percent "agreed," with a total of 75 percent indicating their belief in the concept that fields in which research is done dominate a school intellectually. Some 60 percent of the responses from the other schools agreed with this philosophy. A total of 20 percent of the combined percentage for both groups of schools disagreed with the concept. In the political area, the figure was lower, with 53 percent either "heartily agreeing" or "agreeing" that there was political domination, while 25 percent "disagreed," and the remaining group did not express an opinion. The consensus was that fields in which research is done do dominate a school or the university both intellectually and politically. In the matter of research "dominating intellectually," one library school faculty member said, "I do not feel that this should necessarily be so. ' Another library school spokesman said, "It depends on the individual institution." A USC School of Education professor said, "This tends to be true; there are exceptions." A USC School of Social Work professor said he "heartily agreed" that research confers "elite" status "to the extent that the university views research in this light and journals give preference to research reports for publication."

One library school faculty member pointed out that he thought research dominated the university politically because of the funding and PR possibilities. "This is especially so in the case of sponsored research," said another person. Still another said that he "heartily agreed" and commented, "Money speaks! Administration loves it."

DOES A RESEARCH INSTITUTE PROVIDE AN ATMOSPHERE IN WHICH THE CONDUCT OF RESEARCH IS A PRIMARY OBJECTIVE?

The fourth question was "Do you agree that the establishment of a research institute in connection with a professional school provides an atmosphere in which the conduct of research is a primary objective?" Some 62 percent of the library school responses were either in agreement or hearty agreement, and in the other schools, 73 percent of the responses fall into these same catagories. The combined total percentage for both groups was 66 percent. In the combined total, 14 percent disagreed and 2 percent strongly disagreed with the idea that a research institute provides an atmosphere in which the conduct of research is a primary objective.

On the negative side, one person expressed strong feelings about the effect of establishing research centers in library schools, saying, "I expect the effect would be disastrous as far as any last remaining concerns for humanity in the library school. . . ." Several others thought that such a center would have little effect on curriculum, research, or publications.

One library school dean commenting on publications expressed the need for more "but better quality publications . . . too much junk appearing as 'research.' " He went on to say that he thought an "identification of problems to be very important at this time," and he reiterated his position that "too much time is spent on trivial research, we must have quality."

Several people commented on the need for secretarial assistance, computer line and photocopying facilities as essential "back up" for research activities.

Another library school dean, speaking for the present research centers in library schools said, "they do not seem to have lived up to their promise."

One piece of advice could be taken from another person's statement that the research center would be beneficial "only if planned cooperatively and clearly funded."

A positive, affirmative attitude toward the value of a research center, depending on relative conditions, was expressed by a library educator who said, "If the Center takes a systematic view of the professional area, it can greatly benefit the school's curriculum, instructional approaches, etc., . . . if the Center does relevant quality work, it will affect positively the research environment." Another library school teacher thought that a research institute would be beneficial for the school's curriculum by making "theoretical study more visible as part of the educational process," it would have a "positive" effect on publications and would "provide continual, visible stimulus and opportunity" to research activities.

In agreement with these concepts, another library school professor said a research center would "hopefully permeate the contextual structure of every course." A library school dean commented that such a center "would provide significant input to improve the quality of instruction and increase intellectual challenge in the curriculum." He noted that "too much time and energy of faculty is currently wasted in sterile, unproductive curriculum revision which results in 'new courses' that turn out simply to be the old courses with new names." He affirmed his belief that a research center "would provide focus, status and continuity for investigations presently fragmented, poorly organized and unsustained."

One library school respondent said that he agreed with the concept that a research institute in a library school would provide an atmosphere in which the conduct of research is a primary objective; but he added, "I wish there was more of a causal connection between having a research institute in-house and a faculty that is more research oriented." Another library school dean said about the research institute, "I suspect such a unit tends to lend status to research and to provide a focus for organized effort."

One library school faculty member agreed on the desirability of a research institute, but felt that it might drain faculty from the equally important task of teaching. Another said he agreed with the concept, but he added a condition, "if the institute does research. Quite a few, I know of, only talk *about* research."

In agreement with these general ideas, another library educator said that if a library school had a research center, "new ideas would be incorporated in teaching more quickly, faculty publications would increase and faculty interest in research would be substantially increased." Another opinion was that a research center would "bring the case study and new theories into the classroom, attract better faculty, attract money to support students, attract better students, stimulate demand for research methods courses, and increase emphasis on the interdisciplinary nature of the profession."

Still another library school professor said he thought that a research center would have an enriching effect on classroom teaching because of the extra depth gained by teachers who were involved in research. He also thought there would be increased research and more publications. A library school dean thought that a research institute "could be of major import" in a school, "depending on circumstances."

One library educator favoring the research center said that it would upgrade the curriculum, and would give faculty and students "a visible example of applied research in action and a chance to work with this; it would provide funding for research leading to publication; it could 'break down' major research projects into manageable pieces and make relevant approaches"; "it would provide credibility for attracting funds and focusing interest."

One professor summed up the advantages of a research center in his general statement that the research activities in such a center "would enhance library science's contribution to the expansion of human knowledge and, conceivably, the improvement of human existence."

ACADEMIC AND BIOGRAPHICAL DATA OF RESPONDENTS

Academic and biographical data indicated that the persons answering the questionnaire fell into various academic ranks in both the library schools and the other professional schools. The rank of the largest number was that of assistant professor, this category making up 33 percent of the total; the next largest group fell into the professor rank, or 25 percent of the total (and with 41 percent of these being in other schools while only 18 percent were in library schools); 19 percent of the total were associate professors; 4 percent were deans; and other ranks were in the smaller figures. Some 20 percent of the respondents had served as a department chairman for over one year, while 74 percent had never served in this capacity. Most of the persons

answering, who hold research degrees (the Ph.D.), had earned these in recent years—
36 percent of the respondents had earned the doctorate between 1970-75, 15 percent between 1960-69, 8 percent between 1950-59; and only 5 percent of the remaining persons hold the doctorate and these degrees had been earned between 1930-50.
These figures demonstrate that the doctoral or research degree is more common now
than in former years. This may indicate more interest in research, or it may mean that
the advanced degree is now needed somewhat as a "union card" in a profession.

HOW FACULTY MEMBERS SPEND THEIR TIME: ACTUAL AND IDEAL DIVISIONS OF TIME ON PROFESSIONAL ACTIVITIES

In order to ascertain the *actual* division of time spent by the faculty members on
professional activities during the academic year and what they considered to be the
ideal division of time in their capacity as university professors, each was asked to fill
in the two categories of "actual" and "ideal" in relation to the following types of
activity: 1) graduate instruction and preparation (including directing research of
advanced degree students); 2) research and writing; 3) academic administration; 4)
professional activities outside the university (i.e., attending conferences, speaking,
consulting, etc.), and 5) other.

Some 31 percent of the faculty members actually spend 50 percent of their time
on graduate instruction and preparation; however, 63 percent of them think it would
be ideal to spend 50 percent of their time in this area. The remaining percentages
were scattered between 5-90 percent of actual and ideal time. Going on to research
and writing, it was revealed that 50 percent of the faculty members responding actually
spend 10 percent of their time on research and writing, while 31 percent of them
specified an ideal time for this would be 30 percent. The remaining percentages ranged
from 5-90 percent time "actually" spent and ideal time.

As for academic administration, 60 percent of the faculty actually spend 5 to
10 percent of their time on academic administration; and 81 percent consider this
5 to 10 percent to be ideal.

On professional activities outside the university, 90 percent of the professors
actually spend 5 to 10 percent of their time in this way, and 95 percent of them think
this is an ideal amount of time for these activities. Only 17 percent of the faculties
actually spend 5 to 10 percent of their time on *other* activities.

Overall, most of the faculty members prefer 50 percent of their time for graduate
instruction and preparation, 30 percent for research and writing, 10 percent for academic administration, and 10 percent for professional activities.

TEACHING AND RESEARCH INTERESTS

As already indicated, the respondents expressed more interest in teaching than in
research. Combined totals showed that only 1 percent were heavily interested in research, 21 percent were interested more in research than in teaching, 31 percent were
interested equally in research and teaching, while 12 percent were "more" interested
in teaching and 13 percent "heavily" interested in teaching.

FINANCIAL SUPPORT FOR FACULTY MEMBERS' RESEARCH ACTIVITIES

Asked whether or not they had received financial support for research in the last two years, 17 percent of the library school faculty members said that they had received support from federal agencies, while 30 percent of the faculty members of other professional schools said they had received support from the same sources. Both groups received much less from state or local government agencies, with their combined total percentage being 11 percent. From private foundations, only 11 percent of library school people received money, while again, 25 percent of the other professional school people were financially assisted. But 25 percent of library school personnel received institutional or departmental support, as compared with 18 percent of the staff members supported in other schools. On the whole, other professional schools received more financial support from outside agencies than did the library schools; but the combined percentage of all the schools from all sources was not impressive, as 46 percent of the total received no support for research.

NUMBER OF FACULTY ARTICLES IN PROFESSIONAL JOURNALS

"How many articles have you published in professional journals?" To this question, 25 percent of the two groups had published more than fifteen articles, and 29 percent had published between five and ten. The other professional schools made a better showing than the library schools, with 44 percent of them having five to ten publications, as compared to 23 percent of the library schools in this category.

The library schools and other professional schools were much closer together in their answers to "How many of your professional writings have been published or accepted for publication in the last two years?" A combined total for both showed that only 4 percent had more than ten publications in the two year period; 16 percent had between five and ten; 27 percent had three to four; 35 percent had one to two; and 17 percent had none. The largest cluster, 39 percent, fell into the one to four group.

CURRENT RESEARCH ACTIVITY OF FACULTY MEMBERS

The amount of current research activity of all the respondents was limited, with combined totals of only 17 percent from all schools saying that they had "many current publications"; 15 percent had "no recent publications," and 19 percent had "no publications yet."

Several deans said that they have no time to do research. One acting library school dean said that "zero hours" had been spent on research during the deanship, although the same person had been engaged full-time in research at an earlier date. (Maybe this says something about deans or about their jobs. Who would be a dean!)

TYPE OF RESEARCH INTEREST—
PURE, PRACTICAL, BOTH?

The question was asked as to the respondents' types of research interest—pure (basic) or practical (applied)—and these were defined as follows. In *pure* research, the investigator may attack any problem anywhere that appeals to him. After he has selected a problem, he need only apply scholarly methods to the solution and publish the results, with no concern about any practical, social use of the findings. In *practical* research the problem is localized within practice, and the results are applied to the improvement of practice.

Only 2 percent of all the respondents were interested exclusively in pure research, while 19 percent were more interested in pure than in practical, 26 percent were interested equally in both, 39 percent were more interested in practical than pure, 5 percent were exclusively interested in the practical, and there was no answer from the remaining people on this question. Thus, this survey shows that almost twice as many people had more interest in practical than in pure research.

In commenting on a choice between basic and applied research, one library school faculty member said, "You can't have one without the other. Uses of results may differ, but research as reflective inquiry is what it is in any purposive context."

Another library educator said, "A good researcher in any field should, in my opinion, spend some time involved in both basic and applied research." This professor added another important statement that may shock librarians, information scientists, and library educators into action. This statement was, "There is very, very little pure research done in library and information science . . . people in our profession are just not used to doing research for the sake of research with no practical application in mind. This attitude must change if we are to become a profession noted for research."

IS "DEMONSTRATED RESEARCH ABILITY" AN
IMPORTANT REQUIREMENT FOR A
FACULTY CANDIDATE?

The faculty members of both the library schools and of the other professional schools considered "demonstrated research ability" to be one of the first requirements of the faculty candidate; 36 percent of them felt that this research ability was of "heavy importance," and 51 percent thought it to be "of importance." One library school dean marked "heavy importance" as his answer, but qualified it by saying, "For junior rank appointments 'research potential' is more often the basis for evaluation."

In the "comment" section of the part of the questionnaire, several library school faculty members spoke of the importance of teaching. One said "Our primary business is still the training of practitioners, with various levels of expertise, and research ideally should be directed towards ends that can help these practitioners and students or improve our abilities to train them." Another library school teacher commented: "We need some researchers as well as other competencies, a balanced faculty." Somewhat the same philosophy was expressed by a faculty member from the USC School of Social Work.

One library school professor who considered demonstrated research ability to be of great importance for a faculty candidate noted that "Research ability demonstrates intellectual curiosity, self-activation and self-discipline of a personal commitment rather than group activity."

One library school teacher said that he would have marked "demonstrated research ability" as of heavy importance "except that in library education, such people are as rare as hen's teeth. Ideally, however, new faculty should be excellent researchers."

A library school dean described the position of his institution in relation to demonstrated research ability: "If a candidate for a position indicates no research interest, he will be informed that this university demands some evidence of scholarly output in short order, and on a continuing basis."

IS RESEARCH IN OTHER DISCIPLINES APPLICABLE TO RESEARCH IN LIBRARIANSHIP?

Three questions were directed to library schools only. The first of these was, "Do you agree that librarianship does not stand alone, that it is derivative and should be vitally concerned with research in other disciplines that holds promise of being applicable to research in librarianship?" Some 53 percent of the library school people "strongly agreed" with this statement, and 25 percent "agreed" with it. Only 4 percent disagreed, and the remaining respondents did not answer.

One library school teacher felt it was important to find out what people in other fields think of research in library science, saying, "my own guess is that some of what we call research is simply not recognized in other fields. . . ." and "I am personally dismayed that librarianship largely ignores research techniques from other fields that would be valid and applicable. . . ." One teacher stressed the need for research studies that would identify and "provide better services for user communities hitherto unknown, unappreciated, or unaware of us."

The second question directed specifically to library school faculty members asked whether they agreed "that the research papers done by graduates of doctoral programs have had little influence on librarianship." Some 13 percent "strongly agreed," 37 percent "agreed," while 20 percent disagreed and 5 percent "strongly disagreed," but the conclusion was that twice as many agreed as disagreed with the statement. One faculty member added an encouraging note: "Very few of them have much influence, but those few seem to exert a great deal of influence."

Asked what areas in librarianship should be of first importance for research study, the answers selected from a list on the questionnaire fell into the following order, with the first in importance being listed first here and the others following in respective order of importance (according to the respondents' ratings): knowledge and social organization, communication, library administration, man-machine relationships, political environment of the library, and education of librarians. It should be noted that the author is well aware of the limitations of this list. It is hoped, however, that the responses may serve as a general guide to research topics that should or could be explored.

One library education leader, Kenneth Shaffer, concluded his comments with an important statement for the entire profession when he said, "Both the professor of library science and the professional practitioner should show something of promise. Furthermore, both need input to teaching or to their library work through research, writing, speaking, activities in professional organizations of significance, consultant work, etc. While this provides input and authority to the individual, it also establishes both his reputation and that of the school of library science or library."

A comment that, in the opinion of the author, seems important and should be quoted precisely, was made by C. H. Rawski, of the Case Western Reserve Library School faculty:

> Permit me to offer these general remarks on the central issues of research as they relate to the problem area of a service profession and the educational requirements in support of such a profession. If we accept for research serving a profession (as I think we must) C. S. Peirce's position that our science is determined by the problem area and its problems, it follows that the issue is not what, at one time or another, *might* come in handy for the professional librarian to know. The issue is what he *must* know in *order to* function effectively in his profession and to continue to do so when faced with change and a rapidly increasing speed of change. Thus, when it comes to research, he must first of all be able to (a) grasp what is the case or problem in order to (b) ascertain what is needed in terms of (a) and (c) know how to find what is needed (and, in certain instances, but not necessarily, know how to use that which is needed). Problem analysis and grasp of relevant facts alone permit the development of the right strategy—from which follow by entailment the various tactics and techniques we need. This sequence is not reversible. It may be nice if the librarian researcher faced, e.g., with a problem requiring non-parametric statistics in the course of inquiry, can expertly handle these techniques. But it is disastrous if he is unable to analyze his problem and ascertain the terms which require the use of these or any other techniques (which vary from problem to problem and often are supplied more effectively by experts). What counts is the ability of the librarian researcher to ascertain the need for these techniques in terms of his problem, which requires analysis and analytic skills common sense CANNOT be relied upon to supply. These skills of scientific inquiry are of central importance and they are the ones that must be developed in order to assure research which will meaningfully support professional action. If this is accomplished we may be able to stop guessing about what research should be done and have a clear grasp of the topics which *need* to be made subject to reflective inquiry.

SUMMARY

The over-all general response to the questions relating to research as a basis for the recognition of librarianship as a profession were: 1) yes, research is a primary basis for the recognition of a profession; 2) research confers elite status on a school or department; 3) fields in which research is done dominate the school or university both intellectually and politically; 4) a research institute does provide an atmosphere in which the conduct of research is a primary objective.

The academic and biographic data of the respondents indicated that the rank of the largest number of them was that of assistant professor and the next largest group in academic rank was that of professor. Most of the persons answering who hold doctoral degrees had earned these in recent years, 36 percent of them between 1970-75.

Faculty members spend more time on teaching than on research and are more interested in the teaching area. If they could have an "ideal" distribution of time, they
would prefer to spend 50 percent of it on graduate instruction and preparation, 30
percent on research and writing, 10 percent on academic administration and 10 percent on professional activities.

Approximately 25 percent of the faculty members in library schools have had
more than fifteen articles published, and 29 percent have published between five
to ten. Other professional schools had a better score on this item than did the library
schools. The current research activity of all respondents was not impressive.

In answer to the question as whether they were more interested in basic (pure)
or practical (applied) research, almost twice as many people were more interested in
practical than in pure research.

Faculty members in the library schools as well as those in the other professional
schools considered "demonstrated research ability" to be one of the first requirements
of a faculty candidate. Library school faculty members agreed that librarianship is
derivative and should be vitally concerned with research in other disciplines that
holds promise of being applicable to research in librarianship. A majority of the library
school faculty members agreed that research papers by graduates of doctoral programs
had had little influence on librarianship. Answers to what areas of librarianship are
of most importance indicated these areas as most significant: knowledge and social
organization, communication, and administration.

The foregoing points do not provide solutions to problems or earth-shaking
suggestions for any program, but they do point out that research is a basis for the
recognition of a profession, that the library profession has done little in the area of
research, and that there is great need for more research activity in this field.

APPENDIX III:

The Role of Library Education for National and International Needs

by Martha Boaz

The role of library education for national and international needs is a subject that could be discussed at length, but only a few of the most important topics will be covered in this paper. The introductory material will deal with a "selected" list of general trends in the library and information science field. These will, in the opinion of the author, be important to the future of library education, along with the impact of technology, which is already having great influence on the library profession. Following this will be some suggestions for change in library education, the need for research in the field, and the need for greater international development for libraries and library education.

In providing for the information needs of society, the library and information science profession must know about various elements and forces that may now seem remote and very general but that will affect library services. These include: population trends, the environment, physical geography, climate, transportation, and education; other elements involve social conditions, political trends, international affairs, the economy, technology, and the communications industry. Long-range planning should be based on trends in the above areas.

Owing to the highly competitive nature of the business world, access to information is a vital necessity to survival. Information is one of the most important commodities in business. As society changes and as civilization becomes more complex, it is becoming urgently necessary for information to be available in a wider variety of forms and for a wider audience than ever before.

THE ROLE OF LIBRARIES AND INFORMATION CENTERS BACKGROUND STATEMENTS

The information industry will become increasingly important in our post-industrial society, where it has been predicted by several authorities that there will be changes in the professions and occupations. There will be demands for more kinds of specialized knowledge, and the library and information science profession will be heavily involved with the creation, organization, handling, and dissemination of this specialized knowledge. Therefore, it behooves the profession to become more knowledgeable about information and the use of information as well as in the ways of handling it—that is, technology. Knowledge will be a powerful force in decisions and actions in politics and government, in business and industry, in education and international relations, in public and private affairs.

As this author has stated in another paper written recently, "the communications industry may revolutionize society. It has been predicted that a communications revolution will have a greater influence on society than did the industrial revolution."[1]

International, Transnational Trends

The world is going toward an international and transnational society. Many factors contribute to this trend, but the most practical and most mundane is the interdependence of nations in the areas of industry and technology. No country is self-sufficient, and survival may depend upon cooperation and sharing. This is true in the sharing and uses of information.

Libraries are social service institutions and have many audiences, many clients. While, the major purpose of the library is to fulfill user needs, at the same time, the library is an institution and must operate in conjunction with other institutions. The library within the institution has both a social and a cultural responsibility, and as society and culture change, so does the role of the librarian. This role is centered on information and communication, and, increasingly, interpretation may be a part of the librarian's responsibility. And, having the information is not enough. Getting it to users at the right time is a major library responsibility.

Library schools should ensure that graduates will recognize that their role is more than that of custodians—they have a responsibility for the dissemination of information. In doing this, they work with individuals, with groups and with other communication agencies: radio, television, cinema, the press, newspapers, and periodicals. The main business of the latter agencies is that of communication, but they often first obtain information from libraries. They do this through various methods and channels, and technology plays a large part in the delivery of these information services.

THE IMPACT OF TECHNOLOGY

Technological change has a comparatively rapid impact on peoples' habits and customs, but its influence on cultural and intellectual development is much slower. Librarians who are concerned with the dissemination of ideas have a vital interest in the development of technology, especially when it involves the communication media and network centers. These networks serve not only as centers of information but, as stated earlier, as sources of interpretation. They are important social forces.

Networks Develop a Nationwide Library Community

As has been noted in *The Changing Challenge*, the network/consortium system is not just computer communicating with computer, but also institutions and people working with each other.[2] Technology is becoming more and more sophisticated, faster, more expert, and is bringing more leisure to people. It is also providing materials, methods, and programs for filling leisure time. In view of this, shouldn't the library profession "gear up" for the changes in user behavior that are portended by technology? For example, what should libraries do to get ready for the digitization of information? One of the advances predicted in technology includes this digitization of information. John Creps (President, Engineering Index, Inc.) says that by 1983, "all chemical information will be digitized providing full text search and document delivery capabilities through a variety of small remote terminals."[3]

Another advance in technology seems slated for the early future, according to Eugene Garfield (President, Institute for Scientific Information, and recipient of the 1977 Hall of Fame award from the Information Industry Association). He thinks that two-way, on-line communication between citizens and computerized data banks is imminent. He says: "The technology already exists to convert your home television set into a computer terminal operated over your regular telephone line. In less than ten years, more than one million private homes in Britain will have access to information banks that would boggle the imagination of H. G. Wells."[4] Garfield continues: "Through the British Post Office system called Viewdata, there will be in-the-home access to potentially billions of pages of stored data. That is more than enough capacity to store a whole library, including encyclopedias, books, and journals."[5]

Plans are currently underway to supply the occupants of 700 British homes and 300 offices with a market trial of the "Viewdata" system, which allow the viewers to get 100,000 pages of information, by telephone, on a modified type of television set.[6]

Developments of this sort will have great social influence. People will be able to control and be much more selective in the information presented to them on television as well as through other media. How will the library and information science industry benefit from and use these developments?

Intensive Use of Communications and Systems Technology

Another piece of news, according to a one-page National Foundation flyer (dated February 10, 1978), federal agencies are making more intensive use of communications and systems technology for specialized scientific and technical information needs. This announcement was the forerunner of a federal report that lists the highlights of more than 64 scientific and technical information programs in sixteen federal executive departments and independent agencies, the Library of Congress, the Smithsonian Institution, and the Government Printing Office. Two main trends are noted: 1) the continuing growth of the information services provided by federal agencies to other constituencies, and, 2) an increased interest at high policy levels in the roles of information systems in both national and international affairs. Such news items as these indicate the extravagantly rapid growth of technology and the growing interest of government departments in the use of communications and systems technology.

Computer-based data storage and data processing have added a new dimension to modern cost-efficient information management. The smallest computer today, occupying only a few feet of space, is faster, more powerful, and more versatile than those of several years ago. It has been said that even the slowest model measures its internal processing speed in microseconds (millionths of a second) and some measure in nanoseconds (billionths of a second), one thousand to one million times faster than the millisecond (thousandths of a second) speed of the first generation computer. One minute of computer computation equals at least fifty years of manual work, and the achievement of one million additions in less than one second is not uncommon.

By use of interactive devices, which will become more economically feasible within the near future, information can be obtained from across the world in a matter of minutes. Human operators can have two-way communication directly with computer-stored data from remote locations. The new equipment enables a user in

New York to "access" (gain access to the information in) a computer in Los Angeles or Paris or London or other remote areas in a matter of minutes.

Because computers are inoperable and useless without adequate programs, and because information that is only stored is useless unless used, people must be educated and trained in the planning, programming, and delivery of information. The locating of information and the transmission of it to the people who need it—*before* they request it, and when they need it, in forms that are most usable at the time—these are very important services.

Future librarians working as information managers will have to be familiar with all phases of automated data processing; library schools are changing their curricula to meet these demands. It is in the interest of business and industry to support the most modern and future-oriented training of librarians as information managers. The library and information specialists of the future will be a world ahead of the librarian of today. They will be consultants and participants in management decisions and will supply the best available information in the shortest time, at the lowest unit cost.

So, perhaps one of the greatest needs of the library profession today is leadership in the application of technology to the library and information needs of society.

Funding

Assuming that people are literate, informed, and interested in a continuous flow of information, a few issues that should be addressed in planning for national information delivery services to these people are:

1) how to finance the development, implementation and delivery of information services?
2) how to fund research (should every taxpayer be required to pay for this research)?

Questions like these become business and management decisions for the rapidly growing information industry.

Due to technological, social and educational changes, libraries will have to cope with the following problems: 1) establishing new objectives for changing needs, 2) finding new or increased funding sources, 3) meeting changing user demands, 4) coping with the flood of published materials, 5) giving more efficient and speedy services, and 6) evaluating library programs and revising services on a regular and continuing basis.

LIBRARY EDUCATION

Some of the social, education, and technological forces that have implications for the library profession and which ultimately library schools will have to take into account when designing and revising library education programs have been noted. This author is concerned that library schools are not as progressive or as daring as they might be. Are the schools still too involved with techniques of library services to the detriment of philosophy of librarianship and the purpose of libraries? What is the relationship of libraries to social trends, to information needs, and to advanced technology? There is daily evidence that the current educational programs of the library schools are not adequately preparing young men and women to meet the demands of modern, very complex library and information needs.

Evaluation

What factors influence whether or not a user coming to a library for a particular purpose leaves that library with that need satisfied? What measurement and evaluation techniques are applied by library managers to determine effectiveness or improve services and achieve cost effectiveness? How do library schools measure and evaluate their educational programs? Do they go to consumers (employers as well as library users) for feedback about their graduates and about their curricula? These and many other questions are as yet unanswered.

We have in our library education curricula required a broad liberal arts background. This has been a fine cultural asset to the individual, but it has not provided the specific information that more specialized professions have required. We need disciplined study in depth. We also need more acquaintance with subjects related to our particular profession and specialization. Library schools, like the universities in which they are housed, have always been conservative. They should be willing—eager— for change, leaders of change.

Library school curricula should be more flexible; courses should be re-structured frequently. In planning for program changes, the objectives of the program should be planned in relation to the needs and interests of information seekers and library users. This would include new objectives as required by new technology and by changing economic, social, educational, and governmental trends. The ultimate thrust of the program should be on service to library users.

CHANGES IN LIBRARY EDUCATION PROGRAMS

Curriculum

It is suggested that the so-called basic library education program be placed in the junior and senior years of an undergraduate degree program. The present one-year master's degree program could be spread over two years, along with the other undergraduate courses. A paraprofessional program could easily be a part of an undergraduate study program. The legal and medical professions have had great success with their paraprofessional curricula. Why is the library profession afraid of this approach? Most of what we currently teach in our master's programs could easily be taught in an undergraduate curriculum. The student with such a background could then go on to truly advanced graduate work in the professional courses and to study in related fields.

The master's program could be less elementary and introductory, more professional and intellectual. The doctoral degree should be designed more for the specialists and the research-oriented. Continuing education courses should provide more self-direction for students, more incentives for and satisfaction in continuing education for practitioners.

There might be advantages in several approaches to curriculum planning. Instead of a permanent new curriculum, why not design a set of temporary curricula with plans for evaluating and changing them. Include "contingency" curricula for handling problems that do not now and may never exist. Provide for a "Council of the Future" as part of a research institute. These are only a few of the many approaches that could be taken.

Time and Schedule Formats

Experiments have been and are being tried with time and schedule formats. These include, in addition to the regular courses that meet two or three times a week over a quarter of semester, 1) intensive short term courses from one to three weeks in duration; 2) mini-courses, which have one three-hour meeting over a period of five weeks (one unit credit); 3) one- or two-day workshops, with "recognition" certificates instead of course credit; 4) off-campus courses; 5) self-paced courses and many other types of educational offerings. Schools may have to go to more and more ways of attracting students and ensuring enrollment, as a matter of survival. Universities will have a hard time maintaining schools that do not pay their own way. There is evidence of a few schools who already face this dilemma; for this reason, it is a practical reality to consider a large variety of time and schedule formats to accommodate students.

Cooperation among Library Schools

Library schools could plan more cooperative and interdisciplinary programs. Library schools that are willing to work together in cooperative programs might gain in the following ways: enriched programs, fewer faculty, with a resulting saving in budget and more convenience to students. Library schools, especially those that are geographically close enough to do so, could have certain special courses that would not have to be offered on each of the campuses. A student might be enrolled in one school and take several courses in the other school, with credit going back to the "home" school; the "home" school would not have to offer that course. There is such an arrangement between the University of Southern California and the University of California at Los Angeles.

Faculty

The faculty of any school *make* the school. For this reason, the best qualified and most dedicated people in the profession should be urged to go into teaching. Types of persons to recruit are those who have the credentials, the educational background, the practical experience, and the willingness to work hard. The latter is probably the most needed of all the traits. Faculty members are needed who are really interested, who are attuned to modern educational requirements and to change, who are innovative in their teaching methods, who are demanding in their requirements of themselves and of students, and who are concerned about students. It may be advisable, also, that faculty members be required to go back periodically to some practical work experience in a library. This has not been done in our field, but it seems feasible that it could be arranged. Leaves could be planned for such renewal of practical work in a real library environment. It would follow that theoretical courses and practical experience would then be closely correlated. Otherwise, library school courses are too abstract and irrelevant. The main point for emphasis here is that the key to success in any library school program is its faculty.

NEED FOR RESEARCH IN LIBRARIES AND IN LIBRARY EDUCATION

Need for Research

The enormous educational and information requirements of present day society have created an extraordinary need for research that would contribute to library and information science; and this, in turn, would contribute to the information needs of users of library services. As has been noted in another paper by this author, compared with most well established disciplines, the library profession has done little research. One of the reasons is that it is still a very young profession, and the establishment of research as an important part of a library school curriculum has been slow in developing.

Planning for research and experimentation is an important national priority in the information science profession. (The author has made suggestions for a national research and development center in another article, and so will not repeat here.) After national plans have be n formulated—or during the formative stage—efforts could be made to involve other countries of the world in library research activities. This could be pursued through various channels, perhaps beginning in national and international professional associations and in appropriate government agencies. This leads to the next topic, international library education.

INTERNATIONAL LIBRARY EDUCATION

Library education differs widely in the different countries of the world. There is considerable conformity in the North American schools that are accredited by the American Library Association, but this is due largely to the standards and requirements of the ALA Committee on Accreditation. And, many people in North America feel that libraries and library education are more advanced, more progressive here than in other countries. However, this could be hotly debated by countries in Western Europe and Russia. The point is that the countries should work together for progress for all. There are many ways to do this, but in this paper, only one major development is suggested and that is an international library school.

International Library School

If we are to have international understanding and an exchange of library benefits across the world, it seems that an international library school would be a logical step towards achieving these goals. The idea of an international library school is not new. Guido Biagi, an Italian, suggested in 1904 that an international library school be established in Florence "for the study of ancient culture and of American improvements in a friendly exchange of mutual aids."[7] Similar suggestions have been made from time to time, but there is still no international library school. Hopefully, sooner or later, the various national and international library associations will work together to found an international library school. Another proposal might again be channelled through the International Federation of Library Associations (IFLA). (Guy Marco made a proposal at the 1969 IFLA meeting, but it was not followed up.)

Such a school might serve the following purposes: 1) provide a highly sophisticated, scholarly, worldly approach to library and information science education; 2) bring together library education faculty members of international renown; 3) encourage the best and most "select" students to enter the program; 4) develop these students into international scholars; 5) serve as an information and advisory center for library schools around the world; 6) provide leadership in experimenting with new and innovative ideas for disseminating and communicating information; 7) serve as a research center for the development of both practical and theoretical research in national and international library and information science fields.

Establishing an international school will not be simple. Complex issues such as common goals and a basic curriculum, exchange of professors and students, international laws governing educational institutions, equivalency exchange of academic credits, funding, staffing, housing, and many other factors have to be settled.

In spite of the complexities that will be involved in setting up an international school, there are possibilities for some fairly easy answers. For example, in the matter of staffing, there might be a relatively small permanent faculty who would provide continuity and stability to the school. Other visiting faculty might be brought in from many schools. They could be granted sabbatical or special leaves from their home institutions and have this opportunity to engage in a new and exciting environment. The "home" library school might donate the services of a faculty member (pay his or her salary) for a year, and count this as a contribution to the international school. Thus, the salary budget for the international school's regular faculty would be a modest one. With the number of schools that now exist, the matter of supplying faculty should be easy.

Such a school should probably have only an advanced professional curriculum, with one of the requirements for admission being a basic library education background and a master's degree in library science or its equivalent. Thus, only "proven" and advanced students and scholars would be in the international school. Those people could engage in really intellectual and scholarly studies, not introductory and technical courses. They could go forward with research. It might be wise to have the previously mentioned National Research and Development Center located in or adjacent to the International Library School. The ideas that might ferment in such an environment would hopefully arouse, stimulate, and incite to action the library and information science profession.

Other International Channels

Some international channels do exist for people in library education to meet and talk together, but these are few and limited in what they can do. IFLA now has a section of library schools (established in 1972), and some library education news is carried in journals such as *International Library Review*, *Libri*, and the *Unesco Bulletin for Libraries*. Unesco is participating in national conferences that are concerned with library problems, and it is assisting developing countries by providing them with consultant services in their planning for library development. Much needs to be done, however, in the promotion of international cooperation and development of librarianship.

Another international project was suggested in 1963 by Harold Lancour—an International Association of Schools of Librarianship. Like the international school, this idea has never been carried out, but it is an interesting one and might have beneficial results. Such an association could schedule its meetings to coincide with or precede the annual IFLA meetings. By using the same hotel, conference, and travel accommodations, there would presumably be better service and more economical rates. This might be a very effective channel for handling many of the business details of the proposed international library school. The ideas presented in the foregoing notes represent only a few of the opportunities that are open to libraries and library education.

SUMMARY

The increasing importance of information and the rapid advances in technology place great responsibility on libraries and library schools to keep up with these advances, to go forward, and to supply the information needs of society. Libraries should not only keep up but be ahead of and ready to supply these needs before they are requested. As a matter of business and of continued existence, they should stimulate demand for their products and services. Library schools should "revolutionize" their programs and prepare graduates to be leaders ("activists") in the dissemination of information. Library schools and libraries should engage in research. Research can be pursued in various environments—one place that has been suggested is a national research institute. Another would be in an international library school. In the latter, truly international objectives could be pursued. In all of these efforts, direction, support, and assistance could be requested of professional associations, government agencies, publishers, the media, and consumers.

NOTES

[1] Martha Boaz, "Looking Ahead; Managing the Future" (see Appendix IV, following), p. 11.

[2] Nettie H. Seabrooks, "The Computer among the Books," in *The Changing Challenge* (General Motors, vol. 4, no. 3, 1977), p. 20.

[3] *Information Times* [a monthly newspaper], February 1978. Information Times, 4720 Montgomery Lane, Bethesda, MD 20014, p. 26.

[4] *Los Angeles Times*, Wednesday, March 1, 1978, Part I-A, p. 6.

[5] Ibid.

[6] Ibid.

[7] Guido Biagi, "A Note on Italian Library Affairs," *Library Journal* XXIX (December 1904), p. 59.

APPENDIX IV:

Looking Ahead—Managing the Future:
Choices and Alternate Choices for Educational Professions
(for Library and Information Science Services in Particular)

by Martha Boaz

ABSTRACT

The following material is concerned with the critical issues and challenges that the library and information science profession will have to handle in the future. The main thrust of the chapter is the need to plan for change and to prepare to manage the future, not to be managed by it. The topics covered include: reasons for planning ahead, forecasting patterns, some predicted developments, and recommendations for planning for change. The emphasis is on the technological society and some of the anticipated social changes that are especially "information sensitive." The limitations of the article are that no specific examples, methods, or outlines for action are given. Such recommendations would be left to the discretion of the national committee, which is proposed as a planning and action group to set up the proposed program. The central emphasis is the concept that planning and forecasting the future should be an urgent and conspicuous part of the activity of information science.

INTRODUCTION

In a world that is becoming increasingly complicated and complex, the need for anticipating the future and for planning ahead becomes urgent. As social and technological change accelerate, it becomes more difficult to plan, but it also becomes more essential to do so. The hypothesis of this paper is that the critical challenge of this age for libraries and for the information science profession is to develop new and effective plans for strategies for future change. It is important that the profession should manage the future, not be managed by it. (This applies to all other professions with equal force). Unless we are content to look back or stand still, we have to plan ahead. And, as Charles Kettering said: "My interest is in the future because I am going to spend the rest of my life there."

Information is important. It affects individuals, groups—all of society—and has far-reaching influence on civilization. The library profession should plan to make available for universal use the information materials that can now be readily obtained through scientific and technical expertise. For this reason, the library and information science profession should consider and reflect on the types of information services that will be needed twenty years from now and be ready to provide these services.

In the following pages these topics will be discussed: 1) background and reasons for planning, 2) forecasting patterns, 3) some predicted developments, and 4) recommendations for planning for change.

BACKGROUND AND REASONS FOR PLANNING

There have been several major changes through history that have shaken and shaped the world as it now is. One of these was the agricultural revolution that took place about 10,000 years ago and ushered in the first significant foundations of civilization. A second dramatic change was the industrial revolution of some 200 years ago, which began in England. We have lived in a postagricultural state and are now in an industrial and technological stage; from this, we are rapidly proceeding to a post-industrial and a post-technological age. General trends in the latter are from the economic to the social and from the national to international.

As society moves toward the post-industrial age, industrial production is likely to become less important and service activities more important. Along with a much higher standard of living, there will be greater concern with values. Persons who have been doing research and have studied future trends predict that there will be a revolutionary social change within the next twenty years. Paradoxically, many of our current problems have been brought about by our industrial and technological progress. Technology must solve the problems that technology creates. As it follows that technological innovation is one of the major stimulants of economic growth, so it also follows that the economic benefits that require more and better services should create more jobs. Because the forecast for the next decade seems to be basically optimistic, lethargy and complacency may be roadblocks to progress and to a better future society. For this reason, we should be doubly energetic in planning to cope with those forces that may overwhelm us if we are not ready for them.

Certain problems exist and have become worse in recent years. Anyone who reads newspapers or hears news reports by radio or television is aware of these problems: inflation, unemployment, inadequate housing, obsolete transportation systems, increase in violent crime and social disruption, use of drugs, less sense of community, failing cities, more mental illness, more feelings of alienation, purposelessness, consumer dissatisfaction, and environmental deterioration.

In planning, decisions are affected in various ways by these external developments over which there may be little control, such as in: the state of the physical environment, economic conditions, political controls, technological inventions, and social development. Any one or all of these can influence the cost, effectiveness, and desirability of any plans. Some of the particular forces that require planning and changes in libraries are the information explosion, rapid technological change, accelerating inflation, declining financial resources, and changing educational and social forces.

Human Needs

In considering and trying to anticipate future conditions, human needs are of primary importance; otherwise personal life will be very threatened by an intensive, very technical world. Human needs may be divided in two types: individual and social. Man lives as an individual and as a member of a group; he should be able to function alone or in a group with pleasure and satisfaction in both relationships. It may be difficult for many people to determine "human" values, both because they cannot distinguish between beliefs and objectives and because they do not know what they want. Yet the future will be largely determined by our current choice of values.

Transnational Society

We continue to advance and accelerate toward a transnational society. Evidence of this is readily seen in our speedy global transportation system, which moves people, products, and culture from one nation to another. World tourism brings people together from opposite ends of the earth, and international conferences link participants together to work for common goals. There are multinational corporations and international regulatory agencies. These groups have international funding, international staff, and international communications networks. Due to these facts and industrial and technological dependence, there is increasing interdependency among the nations of the world. No longer can any country be self-sufficient and the matter of survival may depend on cooperation, sharing, and assisting each other.

FORECASTING PATTERNS

Given the genius of today's scientists and technologists, one may rather confidently expect that they can look ahead and assemble the proper resources to build a chosen future. Forecasting studies may take different approaches and techniques.[1] They may 1) follow conventional disciplinary patterns; 2) use one of more specific techniques; 3) or, focus on policies and problems. The traditional mold is likely to remain just that—"traditional," with each discipline giving first priority to its own concerns. Specific techniques provide useful and interesting methods for forecasting. Among some of the techniques employed are: systems analysis, scenarios, the Delphi technique, brainstorming, role playing, and others. Systems analysis is a comprehensive and flexible method; scenarios are general descriptions of future conditions and events; they are widely used as planning tools in large organizations and attempt to anticipate and connect social, economic, and political events that may occur. They often use data that are not actually available and they may use several alternate or contrasting sets of conditions to describe "best" or "worst" possible alternative futures. The Delphi technique is based on the theory that objective methods for exploring the future may come up with valid conclusions. The method is based on the simple premise that in making a forecast, "X" number of heads are better than one. The usual procedure followed is to ask a group of twenty to sixty experts to make a forecast, anonymously, in response to specific questions. The questions are usually presented in large batches, in order to force experts to think about both near- and far-term events at the same time. The key to the technique is that all the panelists remain anonymous throughout the several rounds of polling, which are usually done through the mail. There are many other techniques that may be used, such as brainstorming, cross input studies and others that are described in the literature.

Some of the experts who work full-time at future-gazing, such as the scientists in the Stanford Research Institute and those in the Center for Futures Research at the University of Southern California, write scenarios that are narrative descriptions of future states. The explanation of how a particular state came about—in effect, a snapshot—is given in a scenario. A part of the "futures" planning may include a set of discreet alternate futures. These scenarios force planners to think of issues that might not be anticipated in today's world, and they provide opportunity to look at possible future trends and forces, to make decisions in terms of contingencies and to work with alternate options. If plan one fails or turns out to be impossible, plan two and other plans may be in reserve and ready to put into effect. Flexibility and sequential routes are mandatory in such plans. The method that focuses on policies and problems suggests the organization of research teams among groups of disciplines or organizations. Research teams or research groups work together in an interdisciplinary effort. Through one or a variety of approaches, the matter of forecasting is pursued.

Whatever method is chosen should involve these steps: diagnosis, followed by research, followed by plans for the management and direction of change.

Steps in Planning

Before action begins, the goals and objectives that are envisioned in the whole plan should be clearly stated. This will include an estimate of potential developments in relation to their possible importance in the achievement of these goals, or in how goals are affected. The planners will try to:

- determine the probability of an occurrence and evaluate the influence that the development would have on goals, if it happened
- identify and define current and future problem(s)
- try to identify issues and variant or alternate issues
- set up committees or teams to prepare position papers
- develop studies—perhaps scenarios, Delphi studies, etc. [In these studies, estimate the probability of occurrence of the projected development; estimate the impact that the development(s) would have if the goal(s) were achieved, and prepare alternate projections.]
- interpret and evaluate the findings of the studies
- develop plans for action—try to determine the effects on society (This may involve research and development, different use of current materials and technologies, finding new resources, inventing new products, etc.).

SOME PREDICTIONS ABOUT THE FUTURE

Some of the predictions that may affect the information industry (within the next 25 years), as indicated by studies conducted by researchers working in the area of futures research,[2, 3, 4] are:

Population: There will be a reduced rate of growth and smaller families in developed countries. Young adults will be highly mobile. Women will be more involved in the work force, to the point that the female's career may be equal to or dominant over that of the male. However, employee discontent may cause the breadwinner with the less important career to return to the role of homemaker. The number of retired and older people will increase and, with better health, the senior citizens will want to be involved in second careers and satisfying life styles. Life expectancy may be prolonged 20 to 40 percent longer than the current average age, with life expectancy to the age of 100. There will be rapid increase in total world population, with this population becoming stable a hundred years from now. There were four billion people in the world in 1977, and it is likely that there will be eight billion by the year 2010.

Environment: People will continue to demand a less polluted environment. Social priorities will be high.

Social conditions: Rates of unemployment will drop. Social programs will be tied in with a guaranteed annual income. There will be more leisure time and more low cost transportation to more easily accessible work, recreation, education, and shopping facilities. Cars and homes will be smaller. The young adults and the senior citizens will both be aggressively concerned with quality of life. Education will proba- bly be less formal, more geared to individual convenience and preferences; there will be more emphasis on "relevant" education.

International affairs: Nations will become more economically and technologi- cally *interdependent*.

Economy: The economy will be dominated by energy. Energy research and expenditures for this research will increase, with a resulting decrease in other types of research. Inflation with recurring cycles of prosperity and depression will occur.

Technology: Energy and technology will become increasingly important, both economically and politically, and there will be the threatening prospect of war. Excit- ing progress and developments in communications will take place. There will be heavy reliance on research and development. New energy sources and improved portable devices such as batteries and fuel cells will be available. Better engine design may result in cars getting more than fifty miles per gallon in fuel use. Pollution from gasoline engines may become a thing of the past, for two engineers at the University of Miami have modified engines to operate on hydrogen instead of gasoline and produce almost no pollution.

Other science and technology developments that may affect future planning and life styles are noted by Stephen Rosen:[5]

- a Johns Hopkins engineer has designed a stove that is powered by solar energy and costs nothing to operate.

- at the Rand Corporation in Santa Monica, researchers conceptualize a very high speed transit, a "tubecraft" system, which will be able to carry passengers from New York to Los Angeles in 21 minutes, at a probable cost of $50.

- a flying train has been successfully tested at the Stanford Research Insti- tute. By a magnetic process, trains will travel up to 300 miles per hour, moving several inches above their aluminum guiderails.

- touch-tone shopping, debates on issues aired on television, voting by push- button telephones, sorting airport baggage by voice command—all of these will be likely developments in the near future.

- library books for the deaf and blind are being prepared for computeriza- tion. Rosen has noted that books will be able to read themselves aloud and that a synthetic speech will be beneficial to both the deaf and blind. Soon speech will be converted to text while you are talking.

The mundane problems of cost of publishing books and storage space for these books may no longer be such big problems. According to Rosen, an entire book can now be microfilmed on a sheet of paper or film no larger than a single page of a book.

The cost of manufacturing each film copy will be only about $0.25. It has been suggested that libraries could issue such a microfilm for $0.25 and not require that it be returned. New, large costly library buildings could be decreased in size because a thousand books could be accommodated on a single shelf of average size.

Rosen also notes that talking lights experiments are being conducted by Bell Laboratories and by other research labs on a system of communications involving laser light beams. It has already been proved that over one billion bits of information can be transferred over the laser beam in one second. This is the equivalent of transferring the contents of 200 books of average size in a second. The system allows thousands of people to talk simultaneously over a beam of light.

Hear the light—communications may be at the threshold of another revolutionary discovery in technology. Bell Laboratories, Western Electric, and Bell Telephone are testing an experimental system of lightwave communications that has the potential for carrying a large volume of information, ranging from telephone calls, to business data, to television programs. This will be at low cost and in small space. It will be done through pulses of light over a hair-thin glass fiber. To put information onto the light beam, the researchers have designed equipment that turns the tiny laser on and off millions of times a second. In one of their series of messages informing the public of how telecommunications technology is changing the world, Bell Labs, Western Electric, and the Bell Telephone company prophesy that lightwave communication may someday carry business data, visual communication services, and facsimile transmission into our houses and offices.

The Communications Industry Will Revolutionize Society

The impact of technology on the communications industry has already had great influence on the field of library and information science. It is predicted that the information industry will become increasingly important in a post-industrial society and will have profound effect on society. This influence will be felt in business and industry, in education, in politics and government, in international services, and in public and private affairs. The communications industry may revolutionize society. It has been predicted that a communications revolution will have a greater influence on society than did the industrial revolution.

There is no doubt that better, more efficient, and more speedy handling of information would have great benefits for everyone, but the work and materials required to exploit the new information technology will require enormous financial expenditures. The question is: what is the source of the money?

More Predictions

Olaf Helmer[6] is optimistic about funding and progress. He predicts that people will probably have computerized television terminals in their homes before the end of this century and will carry portable telephones. Many activities now being performed in offices will be done at home by electronic television. Helmer thinks that the work week may be reduced to 32 hours, with increasing amounts of time for leisure activities. In the fringe benefits area, there may be a guaranteed minimum income as well as cradle-to-grave medical service. Helmer also predicts that foreign aid directed toward the development of the Third World may come about through the equivalent of an income tax levied and distributed by the United Nations.

These are only a few of the developments and trends that will influence the library, information, and communications industries. Many unbelievable forecasts have been made. We are encouraged and reminded of what might be called miraculous accomplishments having come to pass in the past by the statement: "If God had intended that man should fly he would have given him wings," said a naval officer some years ago. Had the Wright brothers listened to this admonishment, there would be no airplanes today. As has been demonstrated, through the many spectacular and fantastic inventions that have benefitted the world, dreams do come true. In the field of library and information science, there is much to do, much to look forward to.

RECOMMENDATIONS

In preparation for planning the future of the library and information science profession, the two following recommendations are made: 1) that a national research and development center be established, with the primary charge to this center being to study, anticipate, and be ready to deliver the information services that will be needed by the future society; 2) that libraries and library schools become heavily involved in plans and activities for the delivery of information services to this future society. Suggestions for the implementation of these recommendations follow:

NATIONAL RESEARCH AND DEVELOPMENT CENTER

It is suggested a national research and development center, which will be an independent nonprofit center, be established by the President of the United States and financed by three partners: 1) private enterprise, 2) foundations, and 3) the federal government. The objectives of the center should be national-international in scope. A national commission or a committee on organization should be appointed by the President to organize this center. The formal recommendation for the establishment of this commission/committee might come as a recommendation from the present National Commission on Libraries and Information Science, or from the American Library Association, or from some other responsible group.

One person, committee, or group (one force) has to get the program started. The committee might be composed of scientists, technologists, educators, and citizens. Experts in business, government, and education should be consulted for advice and assistance. There should be a distinguished board of trustees and a staff of outstanding, highly qualified persons selected to carry out the work of the center. Flexibility and open-mindedness on the part of the researchers will be of vital importance. The reputation of the center, as that of Brookings Institution, will depend heavily on its reputation for independence and objectivity.

After setting objectives, and determining the course of action and the program to be undertaken, the committee on organization should be disbanded. However, in beginning its work, this committee would have several major tasks:

- study the type of society that will exist in the year 2000
- estimate the information needs of this society
- project the technological changes and progress that will take place in the delivery of information services

- estimate the cost of changes and programs in the area of information delivery services for the next twenty years
- outline a series of steps for developing these programs, with a set of priorities and of alternate routes
- shape a specific program
- disseminate information to the general public about the proposed program (this would furnish a basis for enlightened public discussion and decisions).

Librarians, educators, businessmen, scientists, engineers, and other representatives from various fields should be included in the planning. Groups could meet and be involved on local, regional, and national levels. Before beginning, it should be pointed out that experimentation with new technology is expensive, but past efforts have often resulted in great profit for the sponsors and in great good to society. Increased productivity will more than compensate for the cost. A key factor in the technology and planning for the future of information services will be the response of industrial, business, and governmental leaders to the future problems and prospects. A systems approach will be needed, with interaction among the specialists and non-specialists, the technologists and non-technologists and in the various social-economic elements.

Evaluation

Assessment of the work of the center should be done on an annual basis, with a decision after five or seven years to go forward or phase out, depending on performance and accomplishments. Plans for this should be set up by the committee on organization working with the board of trustees.

LIBRARY AND LIBRARY SCHOOL PLANNING FOR THE FUTURE DELIVERY OF INFORMATION SERVICES

The second recommendation, that libraries and library schools become heavily involved in planning for the future of information services, should probably be directed and coordinated by the American Library Association. The president of ALA, working with other organizations such as Special Libraries Association, American Society for Information Science, the National Commission on Libraries, and similar organizations, could establish a national committee and request it to draw up a blue print for action. All of this might be handled by the current National Commission on Libraries, but it seems that a strong new group with very specific objectives for "futures" planning might be more effective. This is assuming, of course, that the persons involved are well-informed leaders, thinkers, and doers. There could be panels of specialists in different disciplines and in different social and technological fields. These people could collect pertinent statistical trend projections from selected experts. This data could be disseminated to library and information science planners to use in planning models for future library and information science services.

The actual follow-up and implementation of this concept might be handled in several ways: each division and each type of library could have committees appointed to help with the plans. The Association of American Library Schools might take this on as a year-after-year continuing project. They might be the initiators of the project.

Each state library or each state library association might have responsibilities for the plan. Local, state and regional "retreats" or workshops might be held for brainstorming and planning. This might culminate in a national meeting. There could be many ways to go about this. The main thing is that plans get underway, for the future can be what we plan it to be—one of abundance or scarcity; one of problems or one of satisfactions; one of forced, limited existence; or one of satisfying interesting exciting lives. The choices of the future are being made now or will be made soon. What do we choose for library and information science services? One of Murphy's laws is: "Left to themselves, things always go from bad to worse." Long-range planning should provide data bases for future building and, supposedly, any plan is better than no plan—assuming, of course, that the intent of the plan will be for the good of the people.

Conclusions

In any program that is undertaken, there will be chances for success or for failure. Why not risk either or both? There have been many failures preceding successes in most of the great undertakings of history. Why not have the guts to risk failure! We might end up with the concept implied by the title of a recent play, "The Square Root of Wonderful."

NOTES

[1] C. Freeman, Marie Jahodar, and I. Miles, eds., *Progress and Problems in Social Forecasting* (London: Social Science Research Council, 1976).

[2] Raul de Brigard and Olaf Helmer, *Some Potential Societal Developments—1970-2000* (Middleton, Connecticut: Institute for the Future, 1979).

[3] John McHale, *World Facts and Trends*, 2nd ed. (New York: Collier Books, c1972).

[4] James O'Toole, *Energy and Social Change* (Cambridge: The MIT Press, c1976).

[5] Stephen Rosen, *Future Facts* (New York: Simon Schuster, c1976).

[6] Olaf Helmer, "The Future State of the Union" (pph., University of Southern California, Center for Futures Research, 1974).

INDEX

Academic libraries:
  bibliographic structure, 85
  collections, 84-85
  managers, 89
  pressures for change, 83-85
  See also specific topics
Administrator:
  essential traits of, 16
  as innovator, 36-37
  in public library, 62-63, 64, 65, 76-77
  requirements for, 134
  responsibilities, 16
  role of, 16-18
  in school library, 99-102
  in technical library, 135-136
Alonso, William, 20
American Library Association, 23
  accomplishments of, 24
  divisions of, 23-24
  goal of public library service, 20
  standards, 158-159, 164, 171, 193
Anthony, L. J., 143, 144
Anthony, William P., 18-19
Arnold, Denis V., 134, 145
Associations, professional library, 21-24,
  125-126
Authority:
  delegation of, in library school, 162-163
  organizational, 48-49
Automation:
  in academic library, 92-93
  ALPS system, 119
  in school library, 119
  See also Computers; Computer systems

Baker, Philip, 129
Bakewell, K. G. B., 132, 142, 147
Balderston, Frederick, 176
Banfield, Edward C., 27
Barnard, Chester, 44
Basil, Douglas, 18
Beckman, Margaret, 192
Bennis, Warren G., 34
Biagi, Guido, 273
Bookstein, Abraham, 250, 251
Borko, Harold, 253
Breneman, David W., 177
Bromery, Randolph W., 171
Brown, Alberta L., 131
Brown, Peter, 223

Budgetary control, 46
  in library school, 170-175
  in technical library, 136-138
Building program, library school, 191-199
  funding of, 193
  furniture and equipment, 195-196
  location planning, 191-193
  planning team, 196
  provision for disabled, 199
  space requirements, 197-198
  stages of planning, 196-197
Burns, Tom, 42

Campbell, D. J., 136, 142
Carr-Saunders, A., 21
Cataloging systems, shared, 92-93
Censorship:
  in public libraries, 32
  in school libraries, 123-124
Clientele:
  determining needs of, 35
  evaluation, 57
  in technical library, 132
Committees, public library, 66
Communication:
  in participative management, 66
  in public library, 70-75
Computer systems:
  assessing capabilities of, 206-207
  estimating costs of, 217-218
  feasibility assessment of, 219
  implementation of, 219-221
  obsolescence of, 221-222
  sample job cost reports, 218
Computers:
  conversion of files, 216
  determining requirements for, 213-215
  developing processing system, 213-216
  developing programs, 210-212
  methods of input and output, 215-216
  methods of processing information,
    209-210
  obtaining use of, 207
  program documentation, 221
  reference information sources, 222-223
  software, 209, 212
  in technical library, 141
  training users, 216
  turn-key system, 212-213
  types of, 208-209
  writing programs for, 220